National Rhetorics
in the
Syrian Immigration Crisis

RHETORIC AND PUBLIC AFFAIRS SERIES

National Rhetorics
in the
Syrian Immigration Crisis

Victims, Frauds, and Floods

Edited by
Clarke Rountree and Jouni Tilli

Michigan State University Press | *East Lansing*

♾ The paper used in this publication meets the minimum requirements
of ANSI/NISO Z39.48-1992 (R 1997) (Permanence of Paper).

Michigan State University Press
East Lansing, Michigan 48823-5245

Printed and bound in the United States of America.

28 27 26 25 24 23 22 21 20 19   1 2 3 4 5 6 7 8 9 10

LIBRARY OF CONGRESS CATALOGING-IN-PUBLICATION DATA
Names: Rountree, Clarke, 1958– editor. | Tilli, Jouni, 1979– editor.
Title: National rhetorics in the Syrian immigration crisis : victims, frauds, and floods /
edited by Clarke Rountree and Jouni Tilli.
Description: East Lansing : Michigan State University Press, [2019] | Series: Rhetoric and
public affairs series | Includes bibliographical references and index.
Identifiers: LCCN 2018050620| ISBN 9781611863284 (pbk. : alk. paper)
| ISBN 9781609176075 (pdf) | ISBN 9781628953701 (epub) | ISBN 9781628963717 (kindle)
Subjects: LCSH: Refugees—Syria—Case studies. | Political oratory—Case studies.
| Rhetoric—Political aspects—Case studies. | Syria—History—Civil War, 2011–
Classification: LCC HV640.5.S97 N38 2019 | DDC 956.9104/231—dc23
LC record available at https://lccn.loc.gov/2018050620

Book design by Charlie Sharp, Sharp Designs, East Lansing, MI
Cover design by Erin Kirk New
Cover photo: Adobe Stock | Matteo

Michigan State University Press is a member of the Green Press Initiative and is
committed to developing and encouraging ecologically responsible publishing
practices. For more information about the Green Press Initiative and the use
of recycled paper in book publishing, please visit *www.greenpressinitiative.org*.

Visit Michigan State University Press at *www.msupress.org*

Contents

————◆————

Acknowledgments

——— ·◆· ———

Both editors would like to acknowledge the contributions of almost two dozen people who helped bring this complex, international project to fruition. We would like, first and foremost, to thank the chapter authors, whose diligence, scholarly efforts, and patience over this long project have made this volume what it is. We also would like to thank the editors at Michigan State University Press, including Marty Medhurst, Julie Loehr, Catherine Cocks, and the copyediting staff for their support. Each editor has his own individual acknowledgments to make as well.

CLARKE ROUNTREE

I would like to thank Katie Kirkland, who helped with copyediting the final drafts. As always, I want to acknowledge the continued support of my wife, Jennie Rountree. My late, great friend, Lelon Oliver, listened to me discussing this project over many lunches. Finally, this project grew out of discussions with Jouni during his postdoctoral work at my university; it is a monument to our intellectual kinship and personal friendship.

JOUNI TILLI

First of all, I would like to thank my wife Milla and our daughter Sofia. Milla, without your love and wisdom I would not have been able to complete this project. Sofia, when things got stressful, your smile showed me again and again what is truly important. Also, I would like to thank Clarke for inspiration and fruitful cooperation. And finally, the Helsinki Collegium for Advanced Studies has provided a unique interdisciplinary environment to work in.

Introduction

————— ◆ —————

A historic refugee crisis is challenging countries in the Middle East, Europe, the United States, and elsewhere in the world. It has provoked concern and consternation, humanitarian generosity, and fears of security threats from asylum seekers. It highlights social, economic, ethnic, religious, and cultural factors that have fed into xenophobic discourses as well as the voices of our better angels. It contributed to the United Kingdom's "Brexit" from the European Union and the election of Donald Trump as president of the United States.

This book analyzes rhetorical responses to this refugee crisis through a comparative approach that looks to the discourse of leading political figures in select countries across the globe, with particular attention to Europe, Turkey, and tertiary countries of destination for refugees.[1] We look at how refugees are characterized and how national policies and proposals to address this crisis are justified. We situate this rhetorical discourse in its variegated national settings, with their character as

Muslim, Christian, or secular; rich or poor; culturally homogenous or heterogeneous; on the gateway of the refugee exodus or far removed; members or nonmembers of the EU. We consider how arguments for welcoming or shunning refugees are shaped by domestic politics, legal and political frameworks, and historical and cultural factors.

While each chapter looks at a different country, the conclusion highlights the similarities and differences in the refugee rhetorics of these countries. The goal is to understand how national discourses address this common challenge, what that says about the discourse of asylum and of refugees generally and in this historical period in particular, and how such rhetorics represent nations and their place in the international community.

This introduction first examines the origins of the refugee crisis. We then consider the legal and political framework of immigration policy responding to this crisis. Finally, we explain the rhetorical form and function of the discourse of national leaders in this crisis. This introduction will be followed by chapters on immigration rhetoric in various countries and a conclusion with an overall assessment of the comparative findings of this project.

This book is addressed to an international audience, so we include basic information about each national government and its history of immigration policy to prepare readers to understand the political and rhetorical dynamics of the situations faced by the rhetors studied here. To support comparisons among the countries, all chapters consider how rhetors construct the refugee crisis and the refugees themselves. Rhetorical concepts are applied to examinations of particular cases as the authors find them useful; some of the common strategies found in all cases are summarized in this introduction.

Origins of the Refugee Crisis

The refugee crisis facing Europe and the neighbors of Syria, Iraq, and Afghanistan has been building for more than a decade. Following the attacks of September 11, 2001, on the United States, the Bush administration overthrew the Taliban government in Afghanistan, which had provided a safe haven for the terrorist attack planners, Osama bin Laden and his al-Qaeda organization. That war added to the exodus of Afghans fleeing the Taliban that has not abated since this longest war in American history began. President George W. Bush's surprising turn toward Iraq in the midst of this campaign in Afghanistan deposed its military dictator, Saddam Hussein, but failed to find alleged weapons of mass destruction that were used to justify the preemptive attack. Shortsighted American administrators in Iraq dissolved the country's Baathist army only to see it return in a more virulent form as the Islamic State in Iraq, a group of Sunnis resisting majority-Shiite control of the country.[2]

This turmoil in the Middle East gave rise to a democratic movement, the Arab Spring, in late 2010 in Tunisia, aided by the spread of the new communication technology supporting social media. The movement spread to Egypt, Libya, Syria, Yemen, Bahrain, Saudi Arabia, and Jordan. Syria's president, Bashar al-Assad, violently put down the movement in his country, leading to a civil war that has devastated Syria. The Islamic State in Iraq took advantage of the turmoil to extend its control over territory from northwestern Iraq to northeastern Syria and to declare an Islamic caliphate ruled by strict sharia law. In the name of its religious beliefs and territorial conquests, ISIS committed murder, genocide, torture, and kidnapping, and engaged in a war against the governments of Iraq and Syria, as well as many countries trying to end its brutal reign.

The wars in Afghanistan, Iraq, and Syria, as well as the growth of ISIS, led to a spike of over a million migrants and refugees pouring into Europe in 2015—almost four times the total in 2014—with 80 percent coming from these three war-torn countries.[3] Neighboring countries had long felt the brunt of the conflicts, with refugees spilling over borders into Turkey, Pakistan, Lebanon, Jordan, Iran, Iraq, and Egypt.[4] By 2015 Turkey and Lebanon together hosted over 3 million Syrians, and Pakistan had 1.5 million Afghans.[5]

The difficult conditions in the overwhelmed border countries have

driven more than a million refugees to make the longer, more treacher-
ous journey to Europe, where thousands drowned in the Mediterranean
in overloaded and makeshift boats.[6] Others were victims of a growing
market in refugee trafficking, with shocking cases of shiploads of people
left adrift on the sea or suffocating in locked and unventilated trucks.[7]

The Political and Legal Framework for Immigration Policy

During World War II, tens of millions were victims of war or genocide
and forty million people were displaced in Europe. In addition, after
Germany's defeat, millions were forced out of their homelands in the
process of forging the peace settlement. The victims included members
of most ethnic and national groups on the continent, particularly in
Central and Eastern Europe. These forced migrations entailed innumer-
able crossings of national boundaries at a time when many of those
boundaries were in flux.[8]

In response to the war and its aftermath, the newly created United
Nations passed the Universal Declaration of Human Rights in 1948 to establish a floor for individual rights across the globe. Three years later the
UN approved the Convention Relating to the Status of Refugees "both
to protect refugees from persecution and to ensure their widest possible
exercise of fundamental rights and freedoms without discrimination."[9]
Especially important is Article 33, which "committed states not to return
a refugee who reasonably feared serious harm in her state of nationality
or residence," a principle known as nonrefoulement.[10] The UN univer-
salized the definition of refugees and their rights in the Convention in
adopting the Protocol Relating to the Status of Refugees in 1967.[11] The
Convention and the Protocol have created a framework through which
most of the world's countries approach refugee issues.

The first notable Convention refugees fleeing to the West were those
escaping Communist countries during the Cold War, especially two
hundred thousand Hungarians fleeing the 1956 uprising against Soviet
repression.[12] Beginning in the 1970s and 1980s, the refugee populations

seeking asylum in the West shifted from Communist countries to developing nations. In the United States, for example, with the economic downturn in the 1970s, Haitians began landing in Florida, claiming asylum based on persecution from the repressive government of Jean-Claude "Baby Doc" Duvalier. In a policy subject to charges of racism, the United States labeled most Haitian refugees as economic migrants and turned them away.[13] Near the end of his administration, President Jimmy Carter tried to make amends with the Refugee Act of 1980, which allowed a huge number of Cuban and Haitian immigrants in the large Mariel boatlift to receive "temporary legal status," but not permanent asylum.[14] When Ronald Reagan became president the next year, he read the negative public reaction to opening America's doors and proceeded to shut them, notably by intercepting Haitians at sea so they would not make it to US soil, where they could claim asylum.[15] From 1981 to 1991, of twenty-three thousand intercepted Haitians, only twenty-eight were given asylum to protect them from a dictator Reagan considered a Cold War ally.[16] While George H. W. Bush largely continued Reagan's policies, he and President Clinton sought to make the island nation more democratic so Haitians would have less reason to leave.[17] Clinton took additional steps to open US doors to asylum seekers, but he faced resistance from states footing the bill for Haitian refugees and health concerns in light of the AIDS epidemic raging in Haiti.[18]

In Western Europe, the developing countries of origin for the five million refugees who applied for asylum between 1985 and 1995 were primarily in Africa and Asia.[19] Because these refugees typically came from poor countries, European governments have often denied them asylum by categorizing them—as the United States did with Haitians—as economic migrants. Changes in policies and laws gave governments enough wiggle room for the rate of recognition for refugees in Western Europe to fall from 42 percent in 1983 to 16 percent in 1996.[20] Thus, for example, even though many of these developing countries were repressive or engaged in violent civil wars, "Western governments started to deny asylum claims where persecution was not countrywide (invoking so-called 'internal flight alternatives')."[21]

Since the 1980s, concerns over immigration—illegal and legal, for asylum and other reasons—have been shaped by the growth of foreign nationals in the West. In the United States, that population included over eleven million illegal immigrants by 2016. Republicans today proclaim President Reagan's support of the Immigration Reform and Control Act of 1986, which gave amnesty to three million illegal immigrants living in the United States and tightened controls on the hiring of illegal aliens, one of the biggest mistakes of the his presidency.[22] The increasing polarization of American politics since Reagan's presidency has made immigration a wedge issue.[23] Thus, while President Obama sought to increase the number of Syrian refugees accepted into the United States, leading Republicans have called for a "timeout" on Syrian migration, with one even calling for a ban on all Muslims entering the country.[24]

The refugee crisis contributed to the election of Donald Trump, who ran the most xenophobic campaign by a major party candidate in decades. He had recently led the "Birther" movement, questioning whether President Barack Obama was born in the United States. In the announcement of his candidacy, he railed against illegal immigrants in the country, calling Mexicans illegally crossing the border "rapists" who were "bringing crime" and "bringing drugs" to the United States. He claimed Judge Gonzalo Curiel, who was presiding over a lawsuit involving Trump University, could not be fair to him because of his Mexican heritage.[25] He proposed a ban on all Muslims coming into the United States, which became an executive order suspending all immigrants from seven Muslim-majority countries—initially even those holding visas and green cards—from entering the United States for 120 days while his new administration prepared a policy for "extreme vetting." That temporary measure included a permanent ban on refugees from war-torn Syria coming to the United States.[26]

In Western Europe legal immigrants, more than illegal immigrants, have shaped public attitudes toward foreign nationals. Liav Orgad argues that there is moral panic in Europe over the clashing values between the liberal Europeans and conservative foreign transplants.[27] He notes:

There have been wake-up calls across Europe, as immigrant and native Europeans clash on a number of fronts. To begin with, illiberal practices adhered to by immigrant and minority groups have emerged over the Continent. Examples include female genital mutilation (FGM), honor killings, and forced marriages. Furthermore, opinion polls have revealed that native Europeans and immigrants, especially of Muslim origin, often espouse different values and lifestyles. Finally, immigrants and minorities are increasingly challenging the authority of European Constitutions. For instance, 46.7% of German Muslims stated that the Koran's commandments are more important than democratic principles. In the Netherlands, a majority of Muslim students declared that in case of an irreconcilable conflict, they would choose loyalty to Allah over the Dutch Constitution. Among British Muslims, 32% claimed that Western values are "immoral" and should be prohibited, and 61% wished "to be governed by Sharia law." These findings have come to the forefront in part due to demographics as the non-native population in EU Member States has been consistently increasing. Demographic forecasts indicate that foreign-born population, especially of Muslim origin, will become the majority in main European cities before 2050.[28]

As in the United States, such cultural differences have encouraged right-wing parties to fan the flames of "racist and xenophobic resentment."[29] This, in turn, is shaping the response to the current refugee crisis. In the United Kingdom that response helped drive the surprising "Brexit" vote, initiating a process by which the United Kingdom will leave the European Union. The new government installed after the Brexit vote, led by Prime Minister Theresa May, is responding to voters' concerns over border controls.[30]

Another influence on attitudes toward foreign travelers to the West is the terrorist attacks of September 11, 2001, on the United States and, more recently, an attack against the satirical magazine *Charlie Hebdo* on January 7, 2015; attacks on a concert hall, a stadium, and bars and restaurants in Paris on November 13, 2015; attacks against a center for people with developmental disabilities in San Bernardino, California, on December 3, 2015; and three coordinated nail bombings against the Brussels Airport and the Brussels metro on March 22, 2016.[31] These attacks against civilians by Islamic terrorists, starting with the 9/11 tragedy, have led to restrictions on the travel of foreigners to the United States and other Western destinations, especially for travelers from Muslim countries. Such security concerns have had a direct impact on asylum for refugees, notably, "the decline in refugee admittance figures around the world, but especially in the United States—where in 2002 and 2003, [the United States ruled] against the authorized admission of 70,000 refugees, [and] only 27,029 (2002) and 28,422 (2003) were admitted."[32] Coming in the midst of the 2016 US presidential election, the most recent attacks were used to support the extreme policies on Syrian immigration noted earlier.

The current refugee crisis has led to serious divisions in the EU, particularly between the frontline states where refugees enter the EU and the destination states where refugees most frequently seek to settle. Many refugees have attempted to make it to EU countries in the Schengen area, where they are free to travel throughout the EU and avoid border controls. Greece, already suffering from a severe economic downturn and pressures from international lenders to implement austerity measures, has been particularly hard hit as a frontline state. Hungary responded to its refugee crisis by building "a 110-mile fence along its border with Serbia and enact[ing] new, more stringent border control laws."[33] In October 2014, Italy ended its massive program to rescue refugees at sea, the Mare Nostrum, which was replaced by a smaller EU mission called Triton.[34] Like the US response to the Haitian crisis, the EU has tried to stem the flood of immigrants at the source by providing additional financial aid, particularly to Turkey, Lebanon, and Jordan,[35] and pushing for a resolution to the Syrian Civil War.

The route from Turkey to the EU has been particularly popular in refugee smuggling. Consequently, on March 18, 2016, the European Union and Turkey decided to end the "irregular migration" (migration taking place outside the regulatory norms of the sending, transit, and receiving countries) from Turkey to the EU. The agreement targets the refugee smugglers' business model and attempts to remove the incentive to seek irregular routes to the EU.[36] The stated aim is to replace disorganized and dangerous migratory flows by "organized, safe and legal pathways to Europe for those entitled to international protection in line with EU and international law."[37]

The EU and Turkey agreed, first, that all new irregular migrants crossing from Turkey to the Greek islands as of March 20, 2016—whether persons not applying for asylum or asylum seekers whose applications have been declared inadmissible—would be returned to Turkey. Second, for every Syrian returned to Turkey from the Greek islands, another Syrian would be resettled to the EU from Turkey. Third, Turkey would prevent new sea or land routes for irregular migration opening from Turkey to the EU. And, fourth, the EU would speed up the disbursement of the initially allocated three billion euros for the Facility for Refugees in Turkey. Once these resources near depletion, the EU agreed, it would provide an additional three billion euros funding for the facility by the end of 2018.[38]

In practice, the EU and Turkey have thus agreed on a mechanism that outsources a large part of measures aimed at tackling the most difficult dimension of the crisis to Turkey. Unsurprisingly, the agreement has been criticized heavily. For instance, the agreement has been condemned because "it proposes a collective expulsion that debases the value of respect for human rights that Western Europe has prided itself on since the end of World War II, and that the narrative of the EU has been constructed around." Moreover, "swapping desperate human beings one for one, treating people as if they are commensurable and tradable" has been lamented as morally bankrupt.[39] The United Nations High Commissioner for Refugees (UNHCR) said that the agreement undermines the principles of asylum law and nonrefoulement.[40]

Critics charge that the EU is using Turkey as a "refugee camp" and neglecting the very basis upon which it has been built, namely freedom of movement and equal human rights. Moreover, the EU is contradicting international laws pertaining to asylum seeking and its own announced aims.

The most recent international dimension of the refugee crisis is related to superpower politics. NATO officials have accused Russia and Syria of using migration as a strategy in order to destabilize and undermine the European continent by hiding criminals, extremists and fighters in the flow of migrants.[41] Not surprisingly, Russia has an alternative account: Prime Minister Dmitry Medvedev pointed out that because Russia is continuously being described as the worst threat to NATO and to Europe, the world has entered a new cold war.[42] Consequently, this crisis is interwoven with national and international strains as well as legal and moral tensions. Unsurprisingly, the crisis has sparked a diverse and complex discourse about immigration and refugees.

The Rhetorical Form and Functions of Discourse about Refugees

Public understanding of the refugee crisis is influenced by many factors. For frontline countries, the experience of direct interactions with refugees and the crisis that it has created have shaped the perceptions of their citizens and of foreign aid workers. For most of the world, even those in such countries, it is the filtering of the crisis through the news media and its complex interaction with people and events on the ground, international agencies, commentators, and national leaders who seek to shape perceptions of what is happening and what they are doing to address it. As Kenneth Burke has noted, the use of symbols shapes how we "gauge the historical situation."[43] In short, rhetoric shapes, or attempts to shape, perceptions of situations such as the current refugee crisis.

The implications of such shaping are stark for refugees. For example, an incident in Cologne, Germany on New Year's Eve, December 31, 2015, reportedly involved North African or Arab Muslim men who assaulted European women. A number of right-wing European parties began warning that the refugees were less victims than victimizers who threatened Europeans.[44] As noted earlier, leading Republican Party presidential candidate, now president Donald Trump, referred to illegal Mexican immigrants as "rapists."[45] Obviously, such constructions undermine efforts to provide humanitarian relief to desperate refugees.

Among the rhetors in this crisis, the rhetoric used by national political leaders is particularly important because, in the end, it is individual states that are responsible for taking care of the people knocking at their gates. And what one country does (or refuses to do) will influence what others can or are willing to do. The discourse of national political leaders in this crisis has served a number of rhetorical purposes: It serves as a domestic discourse to explain and justify the policies of the country or, alternatively, for those dissenting from those policies to criticize them. It responds to domestic critics. It also addresses organizations (such as the EU) and the world with an explanation or justification of a country's role in this international crisis. It particularly sends a message to refugees, encouraging or discouraging their efforts to seek passage through or refuge in a country.

There are certainly other rhetorical discourses to be examined in this crisis. The media's coverage of this crisis has important implications for how it is perceived by national and international audiences. It shapes perceptions of the nature, extent, and effects of the crisis; it supports or challenges attitudes toward refugees. For example, when three-year-old Syrian refugee Aylan Kurdi washed ashore at a resort in Turkey, the shocking photo of his lifeless body was widely circulated, leading to calls for a greater commitment to resettling refugees.[46] Social media also served to shape attitudes toward the crisis and its victims, as reposts of news and original posts from those on the various fronts of this crisis spread.

Our decision to focus on the discourse of national leaders limits the reach of our study while getting at some unique rhetorical challenges raised by this shared crisis. We wanted to identify *national* discourses—official discourses of nations—to tease out differences and similarities in the way leaders responded to their very different rhetorical situations. While all countries weighed humanitarian, economic, and security concerns, only Turkey (among countries examined here) had an Islamic tradition of "ansar-muhajir," or a guest-host relationship that shaped expectations about their reception of fellow Muslims. Hungary, on the other hand, was dominated by the Ottoman Empire for 150 years; it viewed itself as a historic bulwark protecting European Christianity against Islam, underwriting hostility to these refugees. Serbia, with an average annual income less than a third of that in Germany, could assure its citizens that refugees were only passing through to greener pastures, while showing the European Union that it was a worthy contributor to addressing the crisis that deserved EU membership. Germany, the economic and aspiring political leader of Europe (and perhaps the world, given President Trump's pullback from European allies), itself is led by a prime minister raised in East Germany who is deeply empathetic with the plight of the refugees. The United Kingdom, which kept its own currency after joining the EU, had been growing unhappy about the free movement of Europeans after more than one million Poles relocated to better jobs on its shores, raising concerns among those who faced new competition for jobs and fueling the Brexit vote. Thus, our concern is not merely for how perceptions were shaped by those who talked about the refugee crisis. Rather our interest is in how political leaders in rhetorically unique situations adapted to domestic and international audiences as they were forced to take action (or stand idle, which carried its own significations). The analyses in this book reveal much about the common topoi of rhetoric about refugees as well as the inventional adaptations of rhetors to their particular circumstances.

For both internal and external audiences of national rhetorics of the refugee crisis, such discourse constructs refugees, the refugee crisis, and the character, interests, and efforts of the nations in that crisis. Such constructions work together: thus, if refugees are constructed as potential terrorists, then that supports a cautious policy that depicts a nation as concerned about security rather than simply lacking humanitarian concern. At the level of political decision-making, such a construction also lends support to demands aimed at allocating more resources to the military and police. If refugees are characterized as not victims of brutality so much as victims of bad economic conditions back home, that may support the sort of distinction used against other recent immigrants to the West.

Balancing the demands of various audiences and rhetorical purposes can be complicated. For example, a nation that stresses its openness to granting asylum to refugees might need to take care in representing that openness to prevent any and all immigrants from flooding into the country, or from making risky journeys across the Mediterranean.

Economic interests can become complicated when connected to refugee issues. Humanitarian rhetoric aimed at refugees might find a domestic counterpart that emphasizes the positive effects of immigration for a nation's economy; the latter is easy to merge with neoliberal policies aiming at lowering labor expenses, exploiting refugees.

The discourse of national leaders on the Syrian immigration crisis features three prominent rhetorical strategies: characterization, identification, and scapegoating. As Kenneth Burke has noted, the power of language derives to a great extent in its ability to focus attention, highlighting things while hiding other things and, in some cases, creating "observations" about the world that are merely implications of the "terministic screens" employed.[47] For example, the terministic choices for naming the Syrians in this crisis shaped an understanding of them and attitudes toward them. Thus, in this crisis we find customary terms such as "refugee" and "immigration," but also terms such as "assisted voluntary return," "asylum seeker," "internally displaced person," "forced migration," "irregular migration," "orderly migration," and "facilitated migration" that each endow a different legal status on the persons in question and also subject them to different measures, legal and political.

Rhetors examined here have characterized refugees through nonhuman, metaphoric terms by describing them as "flooding" over national borders and coming in "waves"; or calling them part of EU "quotas" or elements that make up a "crisis"; they are also referred to as "victims" as well as potential "terrorists." They are constructed with qualities that may endear or estrange them from publics, being "mothers," "children," "Muslims," "foreigners," "human beings," who are "dangerous" or "desperate." The various terms deployed by different national rhetors highlight the choices deployed in their strategic rhetoric.

Depending upon the level of support various rhetors desire for Syrian refugees, they typically seek identification with them, or push its opposite, disidentification. That is, they attempt to demonstrate how those refugees are more like the audiences the rhetors address or less like them, preparing them to be embraced or shunned.[48] The terministic screens previously noted help to support or confound such identification, depending upon the audiences to whom they are addressed. For example, for a nation such as Hungary that prides itself on its Christian identity, using the term "Muslim" creates distance from the refugees; but the opposite is the case for Muslim-friendly Turkish audiences. And identification and disidentification function together insofar as highlighting religious differences between a national audience and the refugees, as we see in Hungarian and other national leaders' discourses, disidentifies with the Muslim "others" while bringing together the Christian national audience on the basis of shared religious belief.

Identification and disidentification serve a third rhetorical strategy of scapegoating that is found in many national rhetorics involving the Syrian refugee crisis. President Trump of the United States, for example, tried to ban immigrants from seven Muslim-majority nations and warned Americans of the dangers of Islamic terrorists hiding amid Syrian immigrants. The disidentification from Christian-majority Americans wrought by emphasizing the religious "otherness" of Syrians made it easier to lump desperate refugees in with violent extremists who happen to share the religion of most Syrians, which is "mysterious" to Westerners.[49] Other versions of this scapegoating include blaming refugees for pretending to flee danger when they actually are seeking economic opportunities, suggesting they are culturally incompatible with host nations and will cause problems, or blaming them for the economic burden they create for the nations that would help them.

As Kenneth Burke has explained, scapegoating is a ready rhetorical option in times of disorder. Whatever the order that is idealized—cultural, economic, religious, political, etc.—when that is seen or characterized as in disarray, then guilt arises (for it *should not* be that way), and mortification (blaming oneself) or scapegoating (blaming others) often ensues.[50] It is easier to scapegoat others than accept blame, and those already depicted as troublesome "Others" make good candidates for scapegoating. The chaos surrounding the Syrian refugee crisis for Syria's neighbors, Europe, and even remote countries, such as Japan, which are pressed to accept responsibility for helping to address the crisis, ensures that those who want to close their nation's doors to refugees can find a way to blame the victims. And that makes it doubly difficult for political leaders, such as Germany's Angela Merkel, who want to take the humanitarian high road.

As this introduction suggests, national discourses addressing the current refugee crisis are fraught with rhetorical complexities that implicate local circumstances and international responsibilities. These discourses attempt to make countries appear humane and responsive and their leaders as engaging the interests, capacities, and traditions of those they represent. These are discourses that play against a cacophony of rhetorical responses from other nations and feed into the media's daily coverage of this international crisis. At stake are the lives of millions of refugees, but also the interests of a more than a billion citizens in countries through which the refugees pass and in which they hope to find safe harbor. The chapters that follow examine how national leaders address this issue for the refugees, their citizens, and an anxious world.

Notes

1. While there have been some communication-related studies of the Syrian immigration crisis, only two we have found offer a comparative analysis of national rhetorics. Edina Lilla Mészáros distinguishes the discourses of leaders in Germany, Austria, and Hungary, as well as of supranational organizations (such as the EU), in "A Deconstruction of the Immigration Rhetoric during the Current Refugee Crisis," *Eurolimes* 22 (Sept. 2016): 95–120. Marc Helbling looks at how six European countries frame immigration in political debates in "Framing Immigration in Western Europe," *Journal of Ethnic & Migration Studies* 40, no. 1 (Jan. 2, 2014): 21–41.

Using a Habermasian framework, he notes a number of similarities (such as appeals to transnationalism) as well as differences in their immigration rhetoric based upon "political actors' . . . general commitments and constraints" (37). He codes a large number of statements reprinted in newspapers, though he does not examine distinct rhetorical contexts for particular speeches.

There have been some studies of rhetorical responses to the crisis in particular nations, including Mette Wiggen, "Rethinking Anti-immigration Rhetoric after the Oslo and Utøya Terror Attacks," *New Political Science* 34, no. 4 (Dec. 2012): 585–604 (Norway) and Lia Figgou, "Constructions of 'Illegal' Immigration and Entitlement to Citizenship: Debating an Immigration Law in Greece," *Journal of Community & Applied Social Psychology* 26, no. 2 (Mar.–Apr. 2016): 150–163 (Greece).

Immigration has emerged in recent years as a key interest for rhetoric scholars. For example, see E. Johanna Hartelius, ed., *The Rhetorics of US Immigration: Identity, Community, Otherness* (State College: Pennsylvania State University Press, 2015); Vanessa B. Beasley, ed., *Who Belongs in America? Presidents, Rhetoric, and Immigration*, (College Station: Texas A&M University Press, 2006); David G. Levasseur, J. Kanan Sawyer, and Maria A. Kopacz, "The Intersection between Deep Moral Frames and Rhetorical Style in the Struggle over U.S. Immigration Reform," *Communication Quarterly* 59, no. 5 (Nov. 2011): 547–568; Josue David Cisneros, "(Re)Bordering the Civic Imaginary: Rhetoric, Hybridity, and Citizenship in La Gran Marcha," *Quarterly Journal of Speech*. 97, no. 1 (Feb. 2011): 26–49; Jennifer Wingard, "Some of the People, All of the Time: Trump's Selective Inclusion," *Women's Studies in Communication* 40, no. 4 (Oct. 2017): 330–333; and Jason A. Edwards and Richard Herder, "Melding a New Immigration Narrative? President George W. Bush and the Immigration Debate," *Howard Journal of Communications* 23, no. 1 (Jan.–Mar. 2012): 40–65.

Other scholarly work related to such rhetorics (broadly conceived) from outside of the communication field includes Davide Però, *Inclusionary Rhetoric/Exclusionary Practices: Left Wing Politics and Migrants in Italy* (New York: Berghahn, 2007); Katie E. Oliviero, "The Immigration

State of Emergency: Racializing and Gendering National Vulnerability in Twenty-First-Century Citizenship and Deportation Regimes," *Feminist Formations* 25, no. 2 (Summer 2013): 1–29; Inés Valdez, "Punishment, Race, and the Organization of U.S. Immigration Exclusion," *Political Research Quarterly* 69, no. 4 (Dec. 2016): 640–654; Jamie G. Longazel, "Rhetorical Barriers to Mobilizing for Immigrant Rights: White Innocence and Latina/O Abstraction," *Law & Social Inquiry* 39, no. 3 (Summer 2014): 580–600; Andrea Lawlor, "Local and National Accounts of Immigration Framing in a Cross-National Perspective," *Journal of Ethnic & Migration Studies* 41, no. 6 (May 2015): 918–941; Viktor Varjú and Shayna Plaut, "Media Mirrors? Framing Hungarian Romani Migration to Canada in Hungarian and Canadian Press," *Ethnic & Racial Studies* 40, no. 7 (June 2017): 1096–1113; and Charlotte Laarman, "Family Metaphor in Political and Public Debates in the Netherlands on Migrants from the (Former) Dutch East Indies 1949–66," *Ethnic & Racial Studies* 36, no. 7 (July 2013): 1232–1250.

2. One of the authors discusses the role of Paul Bremer, President Bush's "viceroy" in Iraq, in dissolving the Iraqi army in Clarke Rountree, *The Chameleon President: The Curious Case of George W. Bush* (New York: Praeger, 2011), 39. Milena Sterio, "The Applicability of the Humanitarian Intervention 'Exception' to the Middle Eastern Refugee Crisis: Why the International Community Should Intervene against ISIS," *Suffolk Transnational Law Review* 38 (Summer 2015): 326–327.

3. "Why Is EU Struggling with Migrants and Asylum?," *BBC News*, March 3, 2016.

4. United Nations High Commissioner for Refugees, *UNHCR Mid-Year Trends 2015* (Geneva: United Nations High Commissioner for Refugees, 2015), 4.

5. United Nations High Commissioner for Refugees, 6–7.

6. "Why Is EU Struggling with Migrants and Asylum?," *BBC News*, March 3, 2016.

7. "Hundreds Rescued from Cargo Ship Abandoned in Greek Waters," *BBC News*, December 31, 2015. Alison Smalesept, "A Day after 71 Migrants Died, 81 Escaped the Back of a Truck in Austria," *New York Times*,

September 4, 2015.

8. Pertti Ahonen, Gustavo Corni, Jerzy Kochanowski, Rainer Schulze, Tamás Stark, and Barbara Stelzl-Marx, *People on the Move: Forced Population Movements in Europe and Its Aftermath* (London: Bloomsbury, 2008); Pertti Ahonen, "On Forced Migrations: Transnational Realities and National Narratives in Post-1945 (West) Germany," *German History* 32 (2014): 599–614.

9. Andrew L. Schoenholtz, "The New Refugees and the Old Treaty: Persecutors and Persecuted in the Twenty-First Century," *Chicago Journal of International Law* 18 (Summer 2015): 85.

10. Schoenholtz, 85.

11. Schoenholtz, 85.

12. Schoenholtz, 85.

13. Charges of racism were made as late as the 1990s as President Clinton continued to return refugees to a country he admitted was hostile to human rights. See, for example, Denise M. Bostdorff, "Rhetorical Ambivalence: Bush and Clinton Address the Crisis of Haitian Refugees," in Beasley, 227–228.

14. Bostdorff, 208.

15. Bostdorff, 208–209.

16. Bostdorff, 209.

17. Bostdorff. Bush supported a democratic election and Clinton invaded the country to expel a military junta that had overthrown the democratically elected president.

18. Bostdorff, 219–222.

19. Schoenholtz, 87. Liav Orgad, "Illiberal Liberalism: Cultural Restrictions on Migration and Access to Citizenship in Europe," *American Journal of Comparative Law* 58 (Winter 2010): 57–58.

20. Schoenholtz, 86.

21. Schoenholtz, 87.

22. "1980 and Today: Trump's Immigration Plan: Deport the Undocumented, 'Legal Status' for Some," *CNN*, January 19, 2016.

23. One of the authors has documented this polarization and the reasons for its growth in Clarke Rountree, "Introduction: Strained Voices in

American Political Discourse," in *Venomous Speech: Problems with American Political Discourse on the Right and Left*, ed. Clarke Rountree (Santa Barbara, CA: Praeger, 2013), 1:xix–xl. The Republican presidential primary particularly highlighted the use of immigration as a wedge issue, with front-runner Donald Trump making the most radical claim, that he would deport all eleven million illegal immigrants and build a wall across the entire southern border with Mexico. See, for example, "1980 and Today."

24. Arnie Seipel, "Sweeping Reactions from Politicians over Syrian Refugees in U.S.," *CNN*, November 16, 2015. Donald Trump, the leading Republican presidential candidate, called for a ban on all Muslims entering the country. Eugene Scott, "Trump: My Muslim Friends Don't Support My Immigration Ban," *CNN.com*, December 13, 2015.

25. "Donald Trump's Long History of Racism, from the 1970s to 2016," *Vox*, November 8, 2016.

26. Michael D. Shear and Helene Cooper, "Trump Targets Muslim Areas in Refugee Ban," *New York Times*, January 28, 2017, A1. This ban has been the subject of many challenges. See the chapter on the United States.

27. Orgad, 61.

28. Orgad, 59–60.

29. Orgad, 61.

30. "So What Will Brexit Really Mean? Britain and the European Union," *The Economist*, September 10, 2016, 47.

31. "Charlie Hebdo Attack: Three Days of Terror," *BBC News*, January 14, 2015. "Paris Attacks: What Happened on the Night," *BBC News*, December 9, 2015. Steve Almasy, Kyung Lah, and Alberto Moya, "At Least 14 People Killed in Shooting in San Bernardino," *CNN*, December 3, 2015. Jon Henley and Kareem Shaheen, "Suicide Bombers in Brussels Had Known Links to Paris Attacks," *The Guardian*, April 1, 2016.

32. Neha Bhat, "'My Name is Khan' and I Am Not a Terrorist: Intersections of Counter Terrorism Measures and the International Framework for Refugee Protection," *San Diego International Law Journal* 15 (Spring 2014): 301.

33. Kristin Archick and Rhoda Margesson, "Europe's Migration and

Refugee Crisis," *Congressional Research Service*, October 28, 2015.

34. Andrew Drwiega, "Tragedy in the Mediterranean," *Armada International*, May 2015, 10.

35. Archick and Margesson.

36. EU Commission, *EU-Turkey Agreement: Questions and Answers*.

37. EU Commission.

38. EU Commission, *Implementing the EU-Turkey Agreement—Questions and Answers*.

39. Bridget Anderson, "Why the EU-Turkey Migrant Deal Is a Moral Disaster," *Fortune*, March 17, 2016.

40. The UN Refugee Agency, "UNHCR Expresses Concern over EU-Turkey Plan," March 11, 2016.

41. "Russian PM Medvedev Says New Cold War Is On," *BBC*, February 13, 2016.

42. "Migrant Crisis: Russia and Syria 'Weaponising' Migration," *BBC*, March 2, 2016.

43. Kenneth Burke, *A Grammar of Motives* (1945; Berkeley: University of California Press, 1969), 172; Kenneth Burke, *Language as Symbolic Action* (Berkeley: University of California Press, 1966), 44–52; Kenneth Burke, *Permanence and Change: An Anatomy of Purpose*, 3rd ed. (Berkeley: University of California Press, 1984), 5.

44. Ishaan Tharoor, "The So-Called 'Islamic Rape of Europe' Is Part of a Long and Racist History," *Washington Post*, February 18, 2016.

45. Michelle Ye Hee Lee, "Donald Trump's False Comments Connecting Mexican Immigrants and Crime," *Washington Post*, July 8, 2015.

46. Helena Smith, "Shocking Images of Drowned Syrian Boy Show Tragic Plight of Refugees," *The Guardian*, September 2, 2015.

47. Burke, *Language as Symbolic Action*, 44–47.

48. On identification and disidentification, see Kenneth Burke, *A Rhetoric of Motives* (1950; Berkeley: University of California Press, 1969).

49. We are using "mysteriousness" in a Burkean sense to highlight its strangeness to Christians and their lack of knowledge about it. As Burke says: "The conditions for 'mystery' are set by *any* pronounced social distinctions, as between nobility and commoners, courtiers and king, leader and people, rich and poor, judge and prisoner at the bar,

'superior race' and underprivileged 'races' or minorities. Thus even the story of relations between the petty clerk and the office manager, however realistically told, draws upon the wells of mystery for its appeal, since the social distinction between clerk and manager makes them subtly mysterious to each other, not merely two different people, but representing two different *classes* (or 'kinds') of people. The clerk and the manager are identified with and by different social *principles*" (*Rhetoric of Motives*, 115).

50. Kenneth Burke, *A Rhetoric of Religion* (Berkeley: University of California Press, 1961).

Immigration Rhetoric of Political Leaders in Turkey

FROM GUEST METAPHOR TO EMPHASIS ON NATIONAL INTEREST

İnan Özdemir Taştan and Hatice Çoban Keneş

The antigovernment protests that, after the Arab Spring, began in Syria turned into a civil war and caused a massive refugee crisis. One of the countries that has been affected most by the crisis is Turkey. Turkey has welcomed asylum seekers from Syria, its largest neighbor geographically, by adopting "an open-door policy," that is to say, without imposing any conditions on their entrance. It was initially predicted that one hundred thousand asylum seekers would be accepted and that they would be harbored for a while and return after the civil war ended. By 2016, however, three million Syrian refugees were living in Turkey for their fifth year under a "temporary protection regime" that recognized their status as refugees. As a result, millions of Syrians, initially labeled as "our guests" by the government, struggle to live in Turkey. While some of them are at provisional sheltering centers spread out over ten provinces, most of them are scattered in precarious conditions in cities close to the Syrian border.

1

The current refugee crisis is shaped by Turkey's history of immigration, the origin of the asylum seekers, their ethnic background, and the sheer numbers involved. This crisis has incited a major public debate, in fact, one of the most fundamental issues in political and public debates in Western democracies since the 1970s. Immigration generally, and the Syrian immigration crisis specifically, have become topics on which the political parties have had to take a stand in general elections for the first time in the history of Turkey. Immigration has occupied a central position in the campaign pledges of political parties, in policies related to the subject in election manifestos, and in the campaign rhetoric of political leaders.

As noted, early in the crisis, Syrian refugees were defined as "guests" by the government and Prime Minister Recep Tayyip Erdoğan upon their entry into the country. The definition also was substantially accepted by the public. However, President Erdoğan opened a new dimension to the debate on July 3, 2016, by announcing his plan to confer citizenship on the refugees. The citizenship of Syrian refugees became the first item on the public agenda, from national and local media to social media users, arts communities, the business world and politicians. Thus, immigration and the granting of Turkish citizenship became a contested—and unavoidable—topic for Turkish political parties and their leaders.

After Erdoğan's promise of citizenship, racist, discriminatory, and hateful rhetoric against Syrian refugees was circulated intensively. Several clashes occurred between Syrians and local people in various parts of the country. Actual attacks against Syrians became a pressing issue. While social media featured these attacks, discriminatory discourse also was circulated in the national media. For example, Turkey's third best-selling newspaper, *Sözcü*, criticized the promise of citizenship to Syrians with a headline, "Will You Confer Citizenship on Those?" The newspaper described Syrians in racist and discriminatory terms as "a bad lot, murderers, fanatics" and claimed that while the Turks pay taxes, join the army, and get killed, the Syrians live as "freeloaders." Social media users also criticized Erdoğan and the promise of citizenship with tweets, using the hashtag #ÜlkemdeSuriyeliİstemiyorum

(#IdontWantSyriansInMyCountry).[1] This was the popular climate in which the rhetorical struggle of the political leaders over this issue took place.

Shaped by a humanitarian perspective and the guest-host metaphor, the immigration rhetoric of Erdoğan and the AK Party (Adalet ve Kalkınma Partisi), which has been in power for fourteen years, caused a public uproar. This chapter focuses on the immigration rhetoric of Erdoğan and the leaders of the AK Party. We also will discuss the immigration rhetoric of leaders of other political parties in Grand National Assembly of Turkey (Türkiye Büyük Millet Meclisi). In order to analyze the criticisms voiced against the ruling party led by Erdoğan, we also focus on the speeches and statements of Erdoğan and Ahmet Davutoğlu, as well as Kemal Kılıçdaroğlu, leader of the main opposition party, the Republican People's Party (Cumhuriyet Halk Partisi, CHP); Devlet Bahçeli, leader of Nationalist Movement Party (Milliyetçi Hareket Partisi, MHP); and People's Democratic Party (Halkların Demokratik Partisi, HDP) cochairs Figen Yüksekdağ and Selahattin Demirtas. The material consists of speeches of leaders at the parliament and in media.

Our theoretical focus is on understanding the key metaphors in recent Turkish political rhetoric related to the refugee crisis. As, for example, George Lakoff and Mark Johnson have stressed, metaphors not only are stylistic ornaments but structure our most basic understandings of our experiences and shape our perceptions and actions even without our noticing it. Metaphor, "understanding and experiencing one kind of thing in terms of another," is conceptual in the sense that human thought itself is metaphorical. For example, time, space, morality, emotions, and even life itself are grasped in terms of metaphors: time is money, life is empty, love is burning. Metaphors are crucial to political language. By hiding some aspects while highlighting others, they construct a certain kind of world and imply actions proper to it. For instance, there is a huge difference between immigrants as "threat" or as "workforce."[2]

We will focus on the milestones of the refugee crisis that began in 2011 in Turkey. They include the very beginning of the crisis, that is, the speeches and statements made by leaders when Syrians started to come to Turkey in masses, the 2015 general election campaign, the process of signing a readmission agreement with the European Union (EU), and finally the period after the promise of citizenship was declared publicly. Before analyzing the leaders' immigration rhetoric, we will describe the basic structure of Turkey's government, then examine briefly Turkey's history in relation to immigration and immigration policy in order to understand the background of the issue, with a focus on the rupture caused by the admission of Syrian asylum-seekers to Turkey.

The Turkish Republic

Turkey is a republic that was founded on October 29, 1923, on the territory of the dispersed Ottoman Empire. On April 16, 2017, with a referendum on a constitutional amendment, Turkey's government system switched from parliamentary democracy to an executive presidency, a kind of "one man" regime, where the president retains ties to his or her political party, becomes the head of state and executive, and has sweeping powers from appointing ministers and choosing senior judges and bureaucrats to preparing the budget.[3]

In the period covered by this study (2011–2016), Turkey was ruled by a parliamentary democracy based on the separation of legislative, executive, and judicial powers. Legislative power was held by the Grand National Assembly. The government consisted of a Council of Ministers formed by the prime minister, who was appointed by the president and is usually the leader of the party that received the most votes. There were 550 elected deputies in the parliament, with a 10 percent threshold for political parties to be in the parliament.

The 1982 constitution is still in force, though with many amendments. It was drafted by the National Security Council, which seized power after a military coup in 1980.[4] With this coup, military forces took power and the National Security Council (NSC) governed the country for three years. In 1982, the new constitution, which had an oppressive perspective on democratic rights, was accepted by means of a referendum. The transition to the parliamentary system occurred with the 1983 general elections, won by Turgut Ozal's Anavatan Partisi (Motherland Party). Ozal and his party ruled the country till 1991, a period in which neoliberal transformation of the economy was initiated under the conditions of a full-fledged suppression of leftist politics and labor organizations.[5] The 1990s saw coalition governments and socioeconomic turmoil.[6] After economic crises in 1994 and 1999, the Turkish economy was hit very hard by crisis in 2000–2001, which led to a fundamental change in the political landscape in the 2002 elections. Recep Tayyip Erdoğan's newly established AK Party came to power in the 2002 general elections, in a political atmosphere fierce contest over all current political parties and economic policies. Erdoğan and his party, as we mentioned, remain in power.

During 2003–2014, Erdoğan ruled the country as the prime minister. With the constitutional amendment adopted in 2007, the president was directly elected by the people instead of being elected by the parliament. Following this critical reform, Erdoğan became president by taking 51.79 percent of the votes in the August 10, 2014, election. Erdoğan announced that his status was different from that of his predecessors because he had been elected directly by the people. He continued his engagement with his party informally, appointing a puppet government and prime minister in his administration. He reiterated his claim that Turkey should be governed by a presidential system and held a large number of rallies prior to the general elections of June 7, 2015, demanding a two-thirds majority of parliament (367 seats), which would be able to change the constitution. However, his efforts did not pan out, and for the first time in its history, the AK Party lost its majority in the parliament. As president, Erdoğan gave the task of forming the government to AK Party leader Ahmet Davutoğlu. When Davutoğlu was unable to do so, Erdoğan scheduled so-called reelections, held on November 1, 2015. The AK Party triumphed, receiving 49.5 percent of the votes. The social democratic CHP received 25.3 percent, the nationalist-conservative MHP 11.9 percent, and the HDP 10.8 percent.

The resulting distribution of the 550 seats in the Grand National Assembly was as follows: the AK Party with 317, the CHP with 132, the

HDP with 59, and the MHP with 42. After these elections, Erdoğan forced Davutoğlu to resign both from the prime ministry and the AK Party leadership. He appointed the "low profile" Binali Yildirim, who was more closely aligned with Erdoğan, as prime minister.

Immigration in Turkey: A Brief History

The immigration policy of Turkey can be divided into three historical periods. The first period, from the collapse of the Ottoman Empire until the 1990s, is characterized by the homogenization of the empire's multiethnic and multireligious structure—in other words, the "nationalization" of the population. The second is the "global" period shaped by the disintegration of the Soviet Union, the end of the Cold War, and globalization with its attendant economic and political problems. The third period, involving the recent crisis, is a "postnationalist and neo-Ottoman" period, with the Syrian immigrants at the center. This period constitutes a significant break in Turkey's immigration regime influenced by Ottomanism and Muslim conservatism.[7]

As mentioned previously, the phenomenon that marked the first period is the nationalization of the population. From the collapse of the Ottoman Empire in the 1920s up to the 1990s, immigration functioned as one of the main tools for nationalization and the purification of the population.[8] Nationalization was carried out in two basic ways: first, the emigration of the non-Muslim population and, second, ensuring the immigration of Turk and Muslim populations who had been left out of modern Turkey's borders and were living in countries that were previously part of the Ottoman Empire.[9]

Deportation, commutation, and forced migration were used against the non-Muslim population to push them out of the country.[10] These practices include the 1915 Armenian deportation and the 1923 Lausanne Treaty between Greece and Turkey, which aimed at exchanging Muslims in Greece for the Christian Greek population in Turkey. The result of these practices was a decrease in the non-Muslim population of Turkey from 19 percent in 1914 to 3 percent in 1927 and, eventually, to 0.2 percent by the 1980s.[11]

During this period the Turkish and Muslim population outside the country was allowed to enter Turkey as another means to increase and nationalize the population. Adopted on June 13, 1934, Resettlement Law No. 2510 was an important measure in the operation. It opened the way for persons "of the Turkish race or ones bound to the Turkish culture" to enter Turkey as immigrants or refugees; it also aimed to prevent the arrival of persons who did not fit this description. The law revealed how assimilation practices would be enforced against those citizens who, as stated in the law, were "of non-Turkish origin or . . . not bound to the Turkish culture" (for example, a person whose mother tongue was not Turkish) by forcing them to live in specific regions.[12] The remainder of the Armenians were removed from Central Anatolia and subjected to forced migration to Istanbul.[13] This law remained in effect until 2006.

This resettlement law was an example of the immigrant policies of the newly established Republic of Turkey: international migration was accepted by the state only as a means to incorporate people of Turkish origin. Between 1923 and 1950 about 850,000 Muslims and Turks from countries including Greece, Bulgaria, Romania, and Yugoslavia were allowed to immigrate to Turkey.[14] Turkey held on to the policy while acknowledging the Geneva Convention Relating to the Status of Refugees of 1951. Turkey accepted the Convention with a proviso recognizing that the Convention related to "the events before 1951 and that occurred in Europe." A protocol added to the Convention in 1967 that was approved by Turkey in 1968 removed the earlier time limit but retained the geographical limitation to Europe. Thus, Turkey still recognizes as refugees only those who come from European countries. Turkey evaluates the applications made by people coming outside Europe together with United Nations High Commissioner for Refugees (UNHCR) and channels to the UNHCR the applications of those to whom refugee status in a third country has been granted.

Turkey accepted around 400,000 Bulgarian Turk immigrants fleeing the oppressive and assimilationist policies of the Bulgarian government, in accordance with the Geneva Convention of 1989. These immigrants were later naturalized by an amendment to the Citizenship Law.[15] As well as the admission of "cognates" (that is, those related by blood) left in the Balkans, various kinship groups in the Middle East and Asia have been accepted to the country by tailor-made laws in line with their demands— despite the geographical limitation discussed earlier. For example, when the Soviet Union invaded Afghanistan in 1979, Turkish-Afghan immigrants were allowed to enter Turkey and settle in the various provinces of the country by Law No. 2641, enacted in 1982.[16]

Altogether, from 1923 until 1997 more than 1.6 million immigrants were allowed to settle in Turkey. The vast majority of this population were cognates who were quickly naturalized.[17] The breakup of Yugoslavia led to waves of migrations to Turkey: 20,000 people fled Bosnia between 1992 and 1998; 17,000 came from Kosovo in 1999, and 10,000 people from Macedonia in 2001.[18]

The policy stressing ethnic, religious, and cultural bonds, recognizing cognates coming from both Europe and Central Asia as immigrants, and naturalizing them swiftly changed during the 1990s.[19] The second period in Turkey's immigration history includes globalization as a major determining factor. Now the migration of non-Turkish and non-Muslim people to Turkey took place for the first time. In short, the migration of those considered "foreigners" may be mentioned for the first time.[20] The main reasons for this are globalization and political and economic problems in Turkey's neighborhood in the Middle East, especially in Afghanistan, Iran, Iraq, and Syria.[21]

While Turkey was trying to limit international immigration in this period to only "Turks," new arrangements had to be made due to immigration for reasons including work, transit, and suitcase trading (whereby goods for trade are carried in suitcases rather than shipped). Consequently, on November 30, 1994, Turkey issued the Refuge and Asylum Regulation regulating the procedures pertaining to asylum seekers and refugees. According to the regulation, individuals with refugee status coming from European countries are defined as "refugees," whereas individuals from countries outside Europe are labeled "asylum seekers."

In accordance with these regulations, those coming from outside Europe are allowed to stay in Turkey until they have obtained refugee status from a third country, and they are expected to be granted permission to remain until they have resettled in a third country.[22]

In 2003 the Law on Working Permits for Foreigners was enacted. It brought new regulations on the working conditions of foreigners in Turkey.[23] The EU harmonization process also imposed new regulations on Turkey's immigration legislation. Although the geographical limitation clause derived from the Geneva Convention was repealed by the 2005 National Action Plan on Asylum and Migration Areas, the limitation still de facto holds.[24] Turkey's admission of around three million Syrians and debates over citizenship over several years have created a rupture in historical migration practices. This crisis marked the beginning of a new era.

Syrian Refugees as a Break in Turkey's Migration Admission Policy

The massive migration of Syrians forced to leave their country from April 2011 onward due to the civil war started a new era in migration admission in Turkey. First of all, it was the largest number of people Turkey had ever agreed to accept. Another feature that separates this period from the previous ones is the "implementation of a positive admission policy" that the government did not apply to any other group except persons who were considered as kin of Turks.[25]

The first group of 250 people that escaped the civil war in Syria reached the Yayladağı district of Hatay, one of the border cities between the two countries, on April 29, 2011. These Syrians were placed in a temporary shelter center (camp) established at the location. Turkey applied an "open-door policy" to meet asylum requests and accepted everyone coming across the Syrian border without restrictions or conditions. As the number of those arriving has risen, the number of temporary accommodation centers has increased. In June 2016, twenty-six temporary shelter services served ten provinces, and 2,733,850 Syrians, 256,230 of them in these camps, were staying in Turkey.[26]

As mentioned earlier, Turkey regards individual immigrants from Europe as refugees under the framework of its immigration law, while people from other regions are not recognized as refugees. This creates a legal discrepancy in the adoption of nearly three million Syrian war victims. To resolve this contradiction, Syrians were placed under a "temporary protection regime" in October 2011 in accordance to Article 10 of the regulation of the Ministry of Interior that administers the applications of asylum seekers. However, when the large number of Syrian refugees revealed that the issue could not be handled by simply amending existing legislation, new laws became mandatory. Both the status of Syrian refugees and the ongoing accession negotiations with the EU were addressed with the passage of the Law on Foreigners and International Protection in 2013. The General Directorate of Migration Administration under the Ministry of Interior was established by the law, and a temporary protection regime was enacted. A Temporary Protection Directive regulating the implementation of the law came into force in October 2014. A temporary provision for the Syrians was added, stating that they were under temporary protection.[27] Accordingly, Syrians lived in Turkey as guests under a "temporary protection regime" for five years without being granted refugee status, until July 3, 2016, when Prime Minister Erdoğan suddenly announced that citizenship would be granted to them.

This important shift in immigration policy is related to the so-called axis shift in the country's foreign policy.[28] Turkey began to practice a proactive policy aiming to be a "soft power" problem solver and a Middle East leader when Ahmet Davutoğlu was the foreign minister, and this approach continued when he became prime minister in 2014. The foreign policy sought to make Turkey a regional political and economic actor that can influence, shape, and control Eurasia.[29] Emphasizing Ottoman geography and cultural partnership, the policy positioned Turkey as a Eurasian force in a form of "neo-Ottomanism."[30] This policy is one of the key reasons why Turkey opened its doors to the influx of refugees after the civil war in Syria begun.[31]

Religion has emerged as an important tool in Turkey's new foreign policy, touting multiethnic coexistence in the Middle East based on shared religion. Though the emphasis was effective in the eyes of the Sunni community in the Middle East, it did not show the expected overall effect due to the different denominational composition of the region.[32] Turkey's support for the anti-Assad opposition in Syria's civil war was mostly led by the Sunnis. Because Assad is a Nusayri (Alawite), and the support he received in the civil war was from Iran, another major Alawite country in the Middle East, the issue began to take on the character of a sectarian disagreement. Turkey's support for the opposition in this conflict made its Middle East strategy appear to support the Sunni sect.[33] This perspective was reinforced through Turkey's appeal to religious brotherhood as a new basis for immigration, accepting those fleeing Assad and the civil war. As will be examined subsequently in more detail, the "Ansar-muhajir"/guest-host metaphor, deriving from the history of Islam and religious brotherhood, emerges as an important element in the admission process.

Erdoğan's Humanitarian Immigration Rhetoric and the Power of the Guest-Host Metaphor

The founder of the policies and rhetoric on the Syrians in Turkey is no doubt the AK Party, which has been in power since 2002. Its leaders include Ahmet Davutoğlu, who was the minister of foreign affairs between 2009 and 2014, then prime minister between 2014 and 2016, and Recep Tayyip Erdoğan, the president. Erdoğan, former prime minister and president as of August 10, 2014, and the ruling AK Party–led government have used humanitarian rhetoric since the beginning of the refugee crisis. This rhetoric is closely associated with neo-Ottoman foreign policy of the AK Party government, as we mentioned earlier. The Ottoman Empire, which ruled for over six hundred years, is an important reference point for this foreign policy. In addition, the notion of religious brotherhood in relation to non-Turkish people in the areas of old Ottoman Empire has been used as an important element in Turkey's "soft power." Turkey as a country and Erdoğan as its leader have been presented as always welcoming, defending, and protecting the oppressed folks of Muslim countries in the Middle East, Africa, and Asia with a humanitarian rhetoric including a religious emphasis. In addition, the notions of neighborhood and friendship also support the guest-host metaphor.

It should be noted that the "guest" metaphor, which is used to name the Syrian asylum seekers entering into the country, does not refer to an ordinary guest-host relationship, but a relationship based on religious brotherhood drawing from the Islamic tradition. In the early years of Islam, when it began to spread in the Arabian Peninsula region, Muslims fleeing persecution in Mecca were forced to migrate to the city of Madinah. Muslims in Madinah welcomed them and hosted them as "guests" in their homes. The Islamic prophet Muhammad, calling on both guest and host Muslims and naming them "brothers," created a brotherhood law between them. He referred to Muslims that were forced to migrate as *muhacir* (*muhajir*, pl. *muhajirun* in Arabic), and the Muslims of Madinah who welcomed the others as "ensar" (*ansar* in Arabic), which means "the ones who help."[34] The fraternity between *ensar* and *muhacir* provided the solution to such problems as sheltering, adaptation to a new city, and maintaining life. It placed religious brotherhood before status based on tribal membership or economic prosperity, and also laid the foundations of the imagination of a new Islamic society.[35]

When applied to the current crisis, the guest-host metaphor used by Erdoğan treats millions of Syrians fleeing from the civil war and taking refuge in Turkey as *muhacir*, and those in Turkey as the *ensar*. With such a function, it is a powerful ontological metaphor.[36] It treats the phenomenon essentially in religious terms. In this way a complicated web of events and actions can be comprehended with a model of religious and moral obligations adopted from the Islamic tradition. The functions of the metaphor will be discussed next in more detail.

The *ensar-muhacir* metaphor was adopted and disseminated particularly by President Erdoğan and representatives of the ruling AK Party, including leaders in positions in the government, nongovernmental organizations, foundations, associations, and the press.[37] The following statement by Erdoğan while visiting and addressing the Syrians at a refugee camp in Gaziantep after being elected president in 2014 is a good example of the way the *ensar-muhacir* metaphor has been constructed and used:

> We are pleased, proud, and glad here to host you for about four years in Turkey. *You guys have become muhacir.* You were forced to leave your country. *We also have become the ensar.* We have used all the means available for you. Whatever anyone says, you are not a burden for us.[38]

We claim that the guest-host/*ensar-muhacir* metaphor has fulfilled three major functions in the ruling party's and Erdoğan's humanitarian rhetoric on the Syrian refugee crisis while serving the needs of Turkey's political agenda. First, the guest-host metaphor helped to resolve conflicts arising from Turkey's immigration legislation and provided a wide range of options for the government's policy on Syrian refugees. Second, it softened the reaction of the Turkish public to the Syrians and the government by pointing to the impermanence of both the civil war in Syria and the refugee crisis. Third, consonant with the AK Party's "new Turkey" project and neo-Ottoman foreign policy, it stressed that responsibility for the Syrian asylum seekers belongs to the public and the opposition, not only to the government. This idea was emphasized because the metaphor referred to the generosity and hospitality that "our glorious history" required.

These functions can be explained as follows. As mentioned earlier, Turkey's refugee law grants refugee status to refugees only from the European countries. The government, accepting millions of Syrians into the country with its open-door policy, placed the asylum seekers in camps, identifying them as "guests" as a way to bypass the legal contradiction, which does not correspond with national and international laws.[39] In November 2011, the interior minister of Turkey attended a UN meeting and declared that Syrians who took refuge in Turkey were taken under a "temporary protection" regime. While the government declared to the international community that it gave to Syrians an identified status, it implied for the Turkish public that they were temporary guests. In fact, the name "temporary protection" regime implies the adoption within the national territory of masses who seek refuge, the principle of nonrefoulement, and meeting the basic and immediate needs of that people, but it does not imply arrangements to sustain their lives in the long run. This short-term solution continued until the Syrians finished their fifth year in Turkey, still defined as "guests" in the rhetoric of the AK Party leaders. For example, Syrians are described as "our guests" in the web page and publications of the official organization, the Disaster and Emergency Management Presidency (AFAD), responsible for the construction and administration of the camps. The title of a 2014 booklet created by AFAD on Syrians in Turkey is a good example of such rhetoric: *Syrian Guests in Turkey*.[40] The words of government representatives who visited the camps are also reported in the book: the common emphasis is the guest position of the Syrians.[41] Prime Minister Erdoğan, visiting the Akçakale camp in Şanlıurfa, addressed the people there: "At the moment, you are in the lands of your brothers; you are in your own home. You are most welcome, hopefully until security is established in Syria and you wish to return voluntarily."[42] Deputy Prime Minister Besir Atalay explained "how the guests were hosted": "We are accommodating all Syrians crossing the border under our 'Open Door' policy. We are hosting our guests under good conditions in Turkey and meeting their needs. All services are provided to our Syrian guests."[43]

Their prolonged guest status, leaving the Syrians without a status recognized by international law, also provided flexibility for the government to maneuver in accordance with its political aims at home and abroad. Although the Syrians were defined as guests, they were also used as pawns in the readmission debate with the EU. This strategy is reflected in Erdoğan's words criticizing the EU that promised but did not pay three billion euros to be used for the refugees:

> In the past we have stopped people at the gates to Europe, in Edirne we
> stopped their buses. This happens once or twice, and then we'll open

the gates and wish them a safe journey. . . . We do not have the word "idiot" written on our foreheads. Don't think that the planes and the buses are there for nothing. We will show patience up to a point and then we'll do what's necessary.[44]

What is clearly seen in this quotation is the collapse of the humanitarian rhetoric that Erdoğan had constructed since the beginning of the Syrian refugee crisis. The way the humanitarian rhetoric based on the guest metaphor sentenced the Syrians to the authority of the host and the close relation between the interests of the landlord and this visit is revealed explicitly by the statement, "We do not have the word 'idiot' written on our foreheads." This idiom in Turkish, used to stress that someone is not so naive and idiotic as to be fooled, not only clarifies that there is a cost for Turkey in being the "host" for millions of Syrians, but also demands that Turkey be compensated. Syrians who were accepted in Turkey with humanitarian emphasis and defined as "our *muhacir*" have now been turned into an instrument that is deprived of legal rights in bargaining with the EU. In other words, Erdoğan implied that if the aid promised by the EU was not given, the Syrians would be sent into EU territory by planes and buses.

As seen in Erdoğan's rhetoric, while the lack of status of the Syrians concealed by the guest metaphor renders them a tool that can be used in foreign policy,[45] in domestic policy it makes them dependent on the "host," namely the AK Party government and President Erdoğan because they accepted and welcomed the Syrians. More importantly, the requests of Syrians are blocked because of the "guest feeling" and their dependence. That is to say, their claims are not considered to be based on human rights, and the Syrians are expected to be content with what is given to them by the "landlord" in the host-guest relationship and "keep their place."[46]

The second function of the guest metaphor at the center of Erdoğan's humanitarian rhetoric is the emphasis on transience; that is to say, it implied that the civil war in Syria would end soon and the Syrians would return to their country. When the first Syrian march to Turkey began, the AK Party government and Prime Minister Erdoğan's predictions about the matter followed the guest model: those arriving were called "our guests" and placed in the camps built for them. But it was also specified that their residency had quantitative limits. For the foreign minister at that time, Ahmet Davutoğlu, the "psychological threshold for Turkey is 100,000." When Davutoğlu mentioned this threshold in his meeting with the United Nations High Commissioner for Refugees, Antonio Guterres, in August 2012, he suggested creating a safe zone in the north of Syria for Syrians fleeing the war if that threshold were exceeded.[47]

In September 2012, Prime Minister Erdoğan, in response to the CHP's leader, Kemal Kılıçdaroğlu, who criticized the government's policy on Syrian refugees, stated that the war in Syria would soon end and that Turks would celebrate victory with "our brothers and sisters":

> The CHP will not dare to go to Damascus tomorrow, you will see it. But we will go there in the shortest possible time, if Allah wills it; and embrace our brothers. That day is close. We will pray near the grave of Salahaddin Ayyubi and pray in the Umayyad Mosque. We will pray for our brotherhood freely in Hejaz Railway Station.[48]

On the one hand, these words show Erdoğan's belief that the civil war in Syria would be over in a very short time; on the other hand, they reflect the bond of religious brotherhood constructed in Erdoğan's humanitarian rhetoric. Criticized by the opposition leader as being too involved in the war in Syria, Erdoğan drew the defensive line on whether to stand by the Sunni Muslims or not. According to Erdoğan, those who do not support Muslims resisting the Assad regime in Syria will not have the courage to go to Damascus after the victory, but they will be able to pray in front of the great Muslim leader Saladin Ayyubid's tomb (who ended the Crusader rule in Jerusalem) and to perform *salaat* in the Ayyubid mosque. Rhetoric that relates the Crusader invasion of Egypt with Assad's rule in Syria also legitimizes Turkey's intervention in the Syrian Civil War in terms of religious brotherhood.

Although the number of Syrians taking refuge in Turkey rose to two million in 2014, Erdoğan continued to emphasize the transient character of the visitors he initially defined in terms of religious brotherhood. In his rally ahead of presidential elections in Hatay, one of the border provinces, Erdoğan stated that he was aware that Syrians had created some difficulties in a few provinces and added: "Sooner or later our Syrian guests will return to their homes. This is what *ensar* is supposed to be."[49] Moreover, although the number of Syrian asylum seekers exceeded the "psychological threshold" voiced by Davutoğlu dozens of times and even five years after the war started in Syria, Erdoğan and representatives of the government continued to define Syrians as "guests."

The third function of the guest metaphor, preferred instead of a legal status based on universal human rights, is to make the refugee problem not a legal issue but a humanitarian one and a matter of conscience, and to ensure that the Turkish people share the government's responsibilities to the Syrian refugees.[50] Both the president and AK Party representatives praised the nation for the hospitality shown the Syrian people, and they criticized the opposition parties for lacking the Ottoman and Turkish tradition of hospitality. In his speech in September 2012 at the party's general assembly, Erdoğan praised Turkey's hospitality culture that stems from the Ottoman Empire and the people maintaining this culture and attacked CHP and its leader Kılıçdaroğlu, who criticized the policy of the AK Party on Syrian refugees by saying that they lacked the culture of the Ottoman Empire. Erdoğan posed the following question: "We are the grandsons of our ancestors. Mr. Kılıçdaroğlu, whose grandson are you?"[51] Recalling in his speech that in 1945 the CHP-led government had turned its back on Muslim Azeri intellectuals who were escaping Stalin's rule, Erdoğan linked his own history with the Ottoman tradition that took refugees from various parts of the world under its wing. In this way, at the same time, he also implied that the CHP was rootless and unreligious. It must be stressed here that Erdoğan reproduces the rupture between the nationalist, secular political tradition that adapted to the modernization project underway since the establishment of Turkey, and the religion-based Ottomanist political line against it. In other words,

Erdoğan defines the appropriate ways to discuss the refugee crisis by linking it with Turkey's history, traditions, and Islamic past dating back to the Ottoman Empire, with the crucial distinction drawn between the country's modernist secular wing and the Ottoman Islamic wing.

Another AK Party leader who thanked the public for their help, their tolerance toward Syrian refugees, and their Ottoman hospitality was Ahmet Davutoğlu. Davutoğlu traveled throughout the country in preparation for the 2015 general elections. Particularly in the border cities with heavy Syrian populations he thanked the people of the region for their hospitality, patience, and sacrifice. Importantly, he voiced his gratitude using familiar rhetoric: by emphasizing the Ottoman tradition and religious brotherhood. On the other hand, Davutoğlu also criticized opposition leaders, particularly the main opposition party, for lacking humanistic values:

> Doesn't it clash with us reading Yasin-i-Sharif[52] and refusing the oppressed who are knocking [on] your door and giving them to the tyrants? ["Yes" sounds]. . . . Now Mr. Kılıçdaroğlu said, "We will return these Syrians." Dear people of Hatay, I kiss the forehead of each one of you, *we owe thanks to you, owe a debt of gratitude, you saved the honor of our history.* You, the children of Habib-i Najjar, *you ensar Hatay people*, you received the oppressed ones with open arms. . . . Look, the Ottoman Empire opened its doors when Jews, Muslims were slaughtered in Spain 500 years ago.[53] Whenever the ones who suffer arrived at our door, we opened our door, our table, and our home to them as Haci Bektas Veli said.[54] You, Hatay people, *you gave a lesson to humanity.* You gave tyrant Assad a lesson in humanity and you gave the world a lesson. . . . *We are proud of Hatay*, to be sure.[55]

By referring to past religious figures of the provinces he visited (Habib-i Najjar), Prime Minister Davutoğlu emphasized that the region duly fulfilled the obligation stemming from a tradition of hospitability. The prime minister used similar rhetoric in his speeches in other border provinces. He thanked people in the border regions for "saving the honor" of Turkey's glorious history based on the Ottoman tradition while reminding them of the responsibility of being the host/*ensar*.

Erdoğan's and the AK Party's humanitarian refugee rhetoric, emphasizing conscience, brotherhood, neighborly feelings, with the guest metaphor as the binding element of such rhetoric, created an important frame for recognizing and comprehending the presence of three million Syrians in Turkey, with the three functions discussed earlier. However, the boundaries of "being a guest" were reached when President Erdoğan announced that the government might grant citizenship to the Syrians: the public reaction was immensely critical. Consequently, the immigration rhetoric of both Erdoğan and the government began to shift from humanitarianism toward pragmatism. We will discuss this transformation in what follows.

From Guest for Five Years to Citizenship in One Night: Erdoğan's Shift from Humanitarian Rhetoric to National Interests

When the day before the Eid al-Fitr (the holiday marking the end of Ramadan) on July 3, 2016, President Erdoğan announced on behalf of his party that Syrians might be granted citizenship, a large public debate ensued. The president's administration had already prepared the draft bill describing the steps in the naturalization process that would make the Syrians citizens, without subjecting that proposal to public and parliamentary debate.

With this announcement, the rhetoric that Erdoğan and the ruling party had used for the last five years changed overnight. As we have noted, it was emphasized for many years that, the effort being made for the Syrians was a matter of opening the doors to refugees who were in a difficult situation, but hosting them temporarily. But the refugees' fundamental rights according to international migrant law were never discussed properly, and the geographical distinction pertaining to non-European countries was kept intact in the migration law. President Erdoğan and government representatives tried to describe the framework and the rationale for citizenship to justify this development, which departed from the guest rhetoric they had sustained for years. The humanitarian rhetoric addressing emotions was replaced by a rational interest rhetoric. This meant a dramatic change in the metaphorical conceptualization of the phenomenon: the ontological basis was transformed from religion and morality to that of pragmatics, national interest, and legality.

Six arguments to support the new policy can be gleaned from Erdoğan's discourse. First, not all Syrians, just those who would be most beneficial for the country, could become new citizens of Turkey. This implication may be drawn from the following figures: the number of Syrians to be naturalized would be limited to three hundred thousand people, many fewer than the three million who might have been naturalized. Citizenship would not be granted suddenly; first a group of thirty or forty thousand people would be naturalized, and then up to three hundred thousand gradually.[56]

Second, as is stated also in the Turkish Citizenship Law,[57] those eligible for naturalization must meet certain criteria. Three of the criteria listed in the law were emphasized: having a good moral character, not threatening national security and public order, and speaking Turkish sufficiently. These criteria, highlighted in statements made by the government, were intended to answer critiques suggesting that the Syrians could not adapt to life in Turkey and that they constituted a problem in terms of public order and national security. As we will discuss in more detail in the next section, the criticisms directed against the government's Syrian refugee policy by the opposition parties draw on these themes.

Third, conferring citizenship to the Syrians would enrich Turkey and contribute to the infrastructure of science and technology.[58] After Erdoğan's statement on naturalizing Syrians, in the Salat el Eid prayer, he also expressed this argument as follows:

Western nations open their doors to such skilled individuals and they have no choice but to go [to the West] when we do not open the gates [of citizenship] ourselves. We would like to benefit from their knowledge. . . . Why let them go to England or Canada, instead of taking them in?[59]

What is striking here is that the Syrians in the "guest" position, who have depended on the care and support of the owner of the house (i.e., *ensars*) for five years and cost Turkey a great deal of money, are suddenly rhetorically transformed into an opportunity that will slip through Turkey's fingers if the country does not take the necessary action. In fact, it is implied that if Turkey does not naturalize qualified Syrians, developed Western countries will steal them.

Fourth, Erdoğan claims that endowing the Syrians with citizenship would benefit both Syrians and Turkey. This common interest is emphasized in the following:

> Will we sentence these refugees to shelter in these camps for years or to the basement of the apartments they find empty? . . . For example, most of them are working illegally now. We say that there must be a solution for this situation. There are doctors, engineers, lawyers, health personnel, teachers among these people, all of whom can beneficial for our country; these people can be naturalized.[60]

Erdoğan stresses the alleged national interest in including Syrians in the legal labor market instead of spending money for refugee camps. Thus, the skilled migrants can also be utilized.

Another argument that justifies Erdoğan's policy of conferring citizenship is the claim that there is a similarity between another country's granting citizenship to Turks and naturalization of the Syrians by Turkey.[61] Turkey is a country of emigration to many countries, Europe in particular—since the 1960s, about 6 percent of the population in the country have been emigrants[62]—and the analogy is assumed to engender empathy toward the Syrians.

The last argument put forward by Erdoğan continues the analogy. According to Erdoğan, Turkey is as strong as Germany or America, both of which accept many Turkish immigrants. Turkey has the power both geographically and economically to naturalize Syrians: "There's no need to hesitate. This nation, with its seventy-nine million people, is occupying an area of 780,000 square kilometers. Germany, which has a surface area that is half of ours has currently eighty-five million people living there. We are a country that can easily manage these numbers."[63] Therefore, naturalization of the Syrian refugees will demonstrate the power of Turkey. The argument supports Turkey's foreign policy's soft-power aims.

These arguments, repeated in President Erdoğan's and the government's official rhetoric, did not garner widespread support from the Turkish public. Harsh responses arose from both the leaders of opposition parties and civil society after the policy of naturalization was announced. We will focus next on the rhetoric of the leaders of the opposition parties before and after the naturalization statement.

Opposition Leaders Test Humanitarian Rhetoric and the Citizenship Promise: Major Themes of the Debate over Immigration

As we pointed out earlier, Recep Tayyip Erdoğan's and his party's humanitarian rhetoric revolved around the guest metaphor and created an atmosphere that legitimated Syrian presence in the country in terms of morality and religion. The immigration rhetoric of the opposition parties in the parliament criticizing the government's refugee policies stressed national interests against Erdoğan's emotional emphasis on humanitarianism and religious fraternity.

The rhetoric of the chairman of the main opposition party, the CHP, Kemal Kılıçdaroğlu, who promised to send Syrians back to their own country, turned a critical gaze on the government's role. CHP disparaged the AK Party's foreign policy on Syrian refugees in the party's 2015 election manifesto. The CHP considered Syria's conflict an internal matter and strongly criticized Turkey's involvement as stemming from the AK Party's policies: it was partly due to ineffective Turkish foreign policy that Syrians had been forced to take refuge in Turkey. Thus, the CHP promised to implement a better foreign policy that would bring peace to the Middle East, sending the Syrians back home as soon as peace was achieved.[64] Kılıçdaroğlu stressed national security, public order, Turkey's economic losses, and the privileges granted to the Syrians.

National interests and security concerns came to the fore in the rhetoric of another opposition party in the parliament, the political representatives of Turkish nationalism since the 1960s, the MHP. The MHP's leader, Devlet Bahçeli, criticized the government on the grounds that accepting immigrants with an uncontrolled open-door policy posed a threat to national security. Another objection to the AK Party's policy was based on a claim about inadequate support to the Turkmen living in the Bayırbucak area in northern Syria near the Turkish border. However, Bahçeli developed a more moderate rhetoric on refugees than the CHP leader Kılıçdaroğlu, at least until the announcement of the promise of citizenship. Although his party's 2015 election manifesto promised that Syrians would be sent home as soon as the civil war ended,[65] Bahçeli did not emphasize the promise. Instead Bahçeli, accepting Erdoğan's guest metaphor, stressed that the presence of Syrians exceeded any idea of their being guests and needed to be kept within "reasonable boundaries."[66]

The HDP, representing the Kurdish political movement in the parliament,[67] differed radically from the other parties on the Syrian issue. Only the HDP discussed the immigration issue from the perspective of rights in its 2015 election bulletin. HDP cochair Selahattin Demirtas was the first political leader who expressed the need to grant citizenship to Syrian refugees.[68]

Next we will discuss in more detail the most important themes in the immigration rhetoric of the opposition leaders.

NATIONAL SECURITY AND PUBLIC ORDER

In the Syrian refugee debate, national security was an often-voiced theme, particularly by CHP and MHP leaders. They claimed that border security was weak and that Turkey's open-door policy had allowed ISIS militants to enter the country. After suicide bomb attacks made by ISIS in Turkey, CHP leader Kılıçdaroğlu accused the government of shutting its eyes to the presence of militants.[69] MHP leader Bahçeli, arguing that the government supported terrorist organizations just because they were anti-Assad, claimed that the refugees constituted a national security threat: "The exporting of the uncertainty of the neighboring regions into our country, thus infecting us by means of transmission, is becoming increasingly apparent and is accelerating."[70] That is, the Syrians who had been allowed to enter the country were vessels carrying Syria's uncertainty into Turkey.

Both Kılıçdaroğlu and Bahçeli voiced their concerns pertaining to public order, securitizing the refugee issue. According to Kılıçdaroğlu, Syrians living in Turkey, without national control, threatened Turkey's social order. Kılıçdaroğlu, addressing young businessmen in Izmir, defended himself against criticism about his promise to send the Syrian refugees back: "'When you say, 'Return the Syrians,' they say, 'Well, why do you say this, sir?' . . . We do not know what the Syrians are costing us yet.' You'll see tomorrow that important actors in the underground world will emerge among these people. Our public order will be disturbed."[71] In Kılıçdaroğlu's security rhetoric, the Syrians were constructed as a threat to Turkey's social order. Importantly, they were also seen as causing the deterioration of the traditional Turkish family structure through their violence against women, prostitution, marriage for money, and polygamy.[72] A similar concern also was raised by MHP leader Bahçeli, who harshly criticized granting citizenship to the Syrian refugees in a speech delivered to the parliamentary group of his party. Like Kılıçdaroğlu, he defined Syrians as those who create trouble, disturb the public order, and weaken morality.[73]

ECONOMIC BURDEN

The economic cost of aid to Syrian refugees emerges as another theme expressed by Kılıçdaroğlu and Bahçeli, the chairmen of the social democratic and nationalist parties. Both have often asserted that three million Syrians are a big burden for the Turkish people and economy—which is, they say, already in trouble. In a speech addressed to the MHP's parliamentary group, Bahçeli stated that the costs exceeded Turkey's economic power. He defined these expenses using dramatic rhetoric: the prime minister and the government were "squandering and wasting our nation's elbow grease and our people's labor." Stressing that the government was behaving in opposition to the "Turkish nation," Bahçeli criticized the government: "While we have millions of poor and unemployed people who eke out existence by relying poor relief, transferring the state treasury to serve a global, bloody plan, distributing it to everyone like *ulufe*, is folly and reckless."[74]

CHP leader Kılıçdaroğlu also argued that while the government spent large amounts on asylum seekers, disadvantaged groups, such as the unemployed, pensioners, and the poor, were ignored. Kılıçdaroğlu claimed that privileges not given to the citizens were, in fact, granted to Syrians: "A man from Kilis cannot get treatment at a hospital. The hospital serves the Syrian. . . . Syrians start businesses in Kilis. They do not pay taxes. They have no insurance registry; they do not pay insurance premiums. How will Kilis people compete with them? When Kilis people claim their rights, their claim is repressed with TOMAs [antiriot water cannons]."[75] Kılıçdaroğlu added a more detailed financial criticism: "You find 5.5 billion dollars for two million Syrians, you find money for the horse farm, but there is no money when it comes to the pensioners."[76]

These comparisons between disadvantaged segments of the Turkish people and the refugees feature alienating and discriminatory language. It is ironic that Kılıçdaroğlu, the leader of a social democratic party, does not blame corporate capitalists, financial monopolies, or militaristic and imperialist actors, but instead scapegoats war-ravaged Syrians for the plight of the workers, retirees, and the poor in Turkey. Kılıçdaroğlu's rhetoric echoes that of the MHP, a nationalist conservative party, and is in line with the rhetoric of right-wing parties and their leaders in Europe and the United States. Again, as he did when the Syrians were constructed as a threat to national security, Kılıçdaroğlu reminded his audience about his election promise to send the Syrians back to their country: "I promise, we will bring peace to the Middle East. . . . And we will send our Syrian brothers back. Sorry. Every person will be happy on the place she was born on earth, everyone is happy in their own country."[77]

ETHNICITY

Ethnicity was another theme expressed by Bahçeli. Bahçeli discussed the ethnic theme in two ways. First, he alleged that the Turkmen living in Bayırbucak in Syria were not adequately supported by the government and the "sensitivity" shown to Syrians was not shown to Turkmen: "Somehow, being a party to the conflict does not come to the prime minister's mind when our Turkmen brothers are getting hurt; Turkmen cities are plundered, destroyed, and continuously bombed. For some reason, the prime minister has decided to remain neutral when Turkey and the Turkish nation are in jeopardy—and this seems to be his habit."[78] According to Bahçeli, the government was actually friendly to terrorist groups in Syria, instead of supporting Turkmen hurt by them who were living in Syria and Iraq.

The second approach to ethnicity in the immigration rhetoric of Bahçeli is revealed in discussions on granting citizenship to Syrians. According to Bahçeli, naturalizing around three million Syrians "will turn our final homeland, which is the eternal heritage of our ancestors and our martyrs, into an ethnic boiler room."[79] Bahçeli considered the citizenship project a blow to Turkey's Turkishness; what was at stake was protection of the "final homeland." He further warned the government: "Whoever thinks of giving our final homeland to ethnic masses and degrading Turkishness—my advice to them is to mind their step."[80] As we can see here, Bahçeli's immigration rhetoric is a manifestation of a nationalist discourse that sees Turkishness in mythic and homogenous terms, that is, as something lacking differences or variations. Consequently, Syrians, who comprise various ethnic groups, would disrupt this purity, and authentic Turkishness would be jeopardized.

HUMAN RIGHTS

Among the parties in the opposition, only the leaders of the HDP have emphasized human rights explicitly. In its 2015 general elections bulletin, the HDP promised that Turkey's geographical proviso in the Geneva Convention restricting its obligations to refugees from Europe would be revoked and work on treating migrant workers as "compatriots" would begin. The bulletin also included pledges to provide immigrants safe shelters and transportation channels. Combating hate speech directed against immigrants was also among the promised measures.[81]

Interestingly, HDP cochair Selahattin Demirtaş offered a perspective quite different from that of other leaders. Its philosophical roots were in the Kantian model of a universal world citizenship that transcends national and international regulations.[82] In his speech addressing students of Boğaziçi University during his election campaign, Demirtas said:

> Everyone is a world citizen and has the right to enjoy its resources equally. This land is theirs, as it is ours. Syrian territory is also ours, as theirs. It is the common property of humankind. We cannot treat them as foreign refugees. Everyone who was forced to take refuge in our country should get decent human treatment. Humanity is trampled in Syria. Those who were forced to migrate should not be treated as refugees and migrants; they should feel free here. There should be a policy to improve the situation in Syria. Turkey must cease fire as soon as possible, and if the Syrians want to stay here, they can, and those who want to go should be helped.[83]

Consistent with this perspective, Demirtaş was the first leader among the Turkish parliamentary parties to state that citizenship should be granted to Syrian refugees. According to Demirtaş, repatriating Syrians "without ensuring stability and peace in Syria will be inhumane. Maybe they will never go, or maybe they will never be able to go. They will be staying here. For that reason, the status of citizenship should be given and their integration must be begun quickly."[84] Although Demirtaş announced in his speech to the parliamentary group of his party that he was against Erdoğan's plan to grant citizenship to Syrians and suggested that a referendum be held on the issue, he later retracted his statement with an apology: "I misspoke. This is not an official policy of our party. I committed an injustice to these people [Syrians] when I called for a referendum. Referendums cannot be held on fundamental rights and liberties."[85] What is more, Demirtaş emphasized that everyone can become a Turkish citizen by fulfilling all the requirements and criticized the government's plans to naturalize only highly skilled Syrians. According to him, such a proposal was contrary to human rights.[86]

VISA EXEMPTION AND THE READMISSION
AGREEMENT WITH THE EU

The indignation that erupted when the body of a three-year-old Syrian boy washed up on a beach on September 2, 2015, made tangible to the world how dangerous refugees' efforts to seek a better life in Europe could be. The outrage that followed this tragedy led EU countries to accelerate negotiations on implementation of the readmission agreement signed in 2013, in order to prevent illegal migration of refugees under poor conditions and via hazardous roads to the EU from Turkey.

Two new policies were discussed in the negotiations. First, Turkey would readmit the refugees who had illegally entered to the EU from Turkish territory, with financial help from the EU. Second, Turkey would allow visa-free passage to the Schengen area for Turkish citizens. President Erdoğan and Prime Minister Davutoğlu presented the agreement as a great success. Referring to Kayseri people, admired for their trade intelligence, Davutoğlu proclaimed that a "Kayseri bargain" was made with the EU.[87] Although in Davutoğlu's rhetoric the bargain had been favorable to Turkey, CHP and MHP leaders criticized it harshly. CHP leader Kılıçdaroğlu claimed that the deal was a bad one and that the government had "foolishly" damaged Turkey: "Now Erdoğan states that 'We are not foolish.' . . . Yes, you are a fool for signing the readmission agreement with the EU. How in the world can you sign such a deal when there are already 2.5 million Syrian refugees in Turkey?"[88] Kılıçdaroğlu also claimed that the agreement would make Turkey "an inn" for refugees. The bargain was a "violation of human rights" because Europe was taking the skilled immigrants and sending the less-skilled ones to Turkey, an act of discrimination. He also combined human rights concerns with the economic interests of Turkey. "Let's give them 6 billion euros; then they should take all the Syrians, Afghans, and Pakistanis. . . . Which Syrians will they take? They will accept the ones with a university degree and other professionals. No matter how you slice the rest. This attitude is contrary to human rights,"[89] Kılıçdaroğlu said. In this way the agreement with the EU was disparaged for stamping on human rights and for being against the interests of Turkey—exactly the opposite of what Erdoğan and Davutoğlu had claimed.

Similar arguments were presented by MHP leader Bahçeli. He claimed that the EU was aiming to transform Turkey into a refugee house, with the cooperation of the government. Bahçeli claimed that the seventy-two articles set forth under the readmission and visa exemption agreement were an attack on Turkish sovereignty. Bahçeli claimed that the articles were actually part of a political game: they were used to obstruct Turkey's fight against terrorism conducted by Kurdish fighters. As a result of the readmission agreement, Turkey was put in the position of a "rental guard waiting at the EU border." Consequently, Turkey's "national dignity and rights as a sovereign nation" were undermined.[90]

POLITICAL OPPORTUNISM, NOT CITIZENSHIP

The leaders of the opposition parties shared a common view that naturalizing Syrian refugees did not support Turkey's interests, as Erdoğan and the AK Party had argued; instead, the policy simply supported Erdoğan's political agenda. If the Syrians were naturalized, one and a half million of them would vote in the next elections, helping Erdoğan's presidential regime. Kılıçdaroğlu's statements are the most extreme examples of this strand of rhetoric. He stated that the naturalization of the Syrian refugees was treasonous: "If the government is doing this in order to design a new regime, it is a betrayal to Turkey. If it is doing this in order to gain votes to introduce the presidential system, it is a betrayal."[91]

MHP leader Devlet Bahçeli, favoring a conservative immigration policy based on kinship, also claimed that naturalizing three million

Syrians would "cheapen" Turkish citizenship. Bahçeli, who considered Erdoğan's promise of citizenship to be a political ploy, brought into play an economic concern by alleging that citizenship would "make benefits available [*peşkeş çekmek*]" to Syrians. *Peşkeş çekmek* means "to donate someone's property to anyone else," and Bahçeli was constructing citizenship as a privilege belonging only to those who are Turkish by ethnicity. "Offering" this privilege to three million Syrians would dim the honor of Turkish citizenship. According to Bahçeli, "no state or political man" could argue against this fact. It is worth noting that the citizenship issue was not approached in terms of legality subject to certain criteria or as a human right; it was rather used to emphasize that authentic Turkishness is defined, first and foremost, in terms of ethnicity.

Although the HDP advocates that Syrians be recognized as refugees and naturalized when necessary, HDP cochairs shared other political leaders' view that Erdoğan had an ulterior motive behind his promise to grant citizenship to Syrians. HDP cochair Figen Yüksekdağ stated that naturalizing the refugees without even granting them refugee status, as required by international law, showed the insincerity of the government. He claimed that Syrians in the country were being used to establish "AK Party colonies" that could vote for Erdoğan's presidency.[92]

Except for a few statements made by Demirtaş, political leaders neglected to discuss citizenship as a status based on rights; instead, their rhetoric focused on economic burdens, national security, and public order. The suspicion voiced by all the opposition leaders—that the AK Party and President Erdoğan had a hidden agenda and were not sincere about citizenship—could constitute one of the biggest obstacles to dealing with the subject from a perspective based on rights. Another obstacle in this regard was the statement that Syrians, who had been discussed for five years within a framework based on the guest metaphor, would be naturalized in a night, without discussing it publicly and in the parliament. This shows that a democratic debate on refugee and citizenship issue is of vital importance, as it is in many other policy areas.

Conclusion

Turkey was one of the countries that developed moderate policies on the admission of refugees fleeing the Syrian Civil War. In 2011, the then-prime minister, Recep Tayyip Erdoğan, and his ruling AK Party government accepted all Syrians to the country in an open-door policy, without any conditions. The practice, which contradicted Turkey's previous immigration policy, together with Erdoğan and the government's humanitarian rhetoric and the guest metaphor, set the scene for handling and discussing the crisis in Turkey. The humanitarian perspective and the guest metaphor were effective in building public support for accepting Syrians into the country. But as the civil war in Syria dragged on and the number of asylum seekers increased, this humanitarian rhetoric of neighborhood, religious brotherhood, conscientious support, and the guest metaphor, emphasizing the transience of Syrians in the country, prevented negotiations on a solution to the long-term presence of asylum seekers in the country. In other words, the rights-based perspective was marginalized as a result of the government's open-door policy and its rhetorical strategy in framing the issue.

Opposition leaders have taken their own approach to the government's rhetorical choices. CHP leader Kılıçdaroğlu, adopting the rhetoric of national security and economic burden, stressed that Syrian "guests" should be sent back to their country. Similarly, emphasizing national security, economic burdens, and decomposition of ethnic structure, MHP leader Bahçeli accepted the limited relationship offered by a "guest" definition. At the same time, however, he criticized the presence of Syrians who were exceeding all limits as guests and suggested a temporary residence restricted to certain camps and cities. Even HDP leaders, approaching the issue from the perspective of rights and stressing that the Syrians should be naturalized because "the world is our home," did not produce any policy on the issue. Consequently, when naturalizing the Syrians was announced by President Erdoğan, the public, which had not discussed the subject before and had considered the issue in terms of temporary "residency," reacted strongly. As Erdoğan and the ruling party's immigrant rhetoric was shifting from a humanitarian perspective to a rhetoric of national interest, other leaders had to retune their arguments as well. Accordingly, while CHP and MHP leaders strongly protested the citizenship proposal, HDP leaders, having a rights-based approach, supported naturalizing the Syrians. But they also were concerned that naturalized Syrians would be pro-Erdoğan and vote in favor of his presidential regime.

Because the citizenship debate is a relatively fresh item on the Turkish political agenda, the rhetoric of political leaders on the subject is open to new developments and conversions. However, at this point it can be stated that Erdoğan's humanitarian rhetoric and the guest metaphor that form the basis of Turkish refugee discourse have made it easy for the government to maneuver amid various political situations: hosting millions of Syrians as guests over a long period of years without granting them refugee status, conducting EU visa exemption negotiations, and imposing Syrians' presence on the public without, for example, removing Turkey's geographical proviso attached to the Geneva Convention. Indeed, our analysis shows how changes in the ontological foundation of political metaphors are connected to a reorientation of policy.

Humanitarian rhetoric built on the guest metaphor made a permanent contribution to Turkey's nationalist and conservative discourse about immigration. Although it sustains conservative Islamic rhetoric by stressing religious brotherhood, the AK Party's humanitarian rhetoric has transformed traditional views in which citizenship is limited to persons of Turkish ethnicity. Hence, from a rhetorical perspective, immigration in Turkey cannot be constructed and discussed in terms of ethnicity and geographical boundaries alone, as it used to be.

Notes

We wish to thank Ulku Doganay for her insightful comments and advice on the first draft of this chapter.

1. Semih İldiz, "Erdogan's Citizenship Offer Fans Flames of Anti-Syrian Sentiment in Turkey," *Al Monitor*, July 12, 2016.

2. George Lakoff and Mark Johnson, *Metaphors We Live By* (1980; Chicago: University of Chicago Press, 2003), 5, 244–245; also Kenneth Burke, *A Grammar of Motives* (Berkeley: University of California Press, 1969), 503–505.

3. This new government regime, according to the Venice Commission, "leads to an excessive concentration of executive power in the hands of the president and the weakening of parliamentary control of that power." Venice Commission, "Opinion on the Amendments to the Constitution Adopted by the Grand National Assembly on 21 January 2017 and to be Submitted to a National Referendum on 16 April 2017," http://www.venice.coe.int/webforms/documents/default.aspx?pdffile=cdl-ad(2017)005-e. With the presidency and general elections of June 24, 2018, Erdoğan became the first president of the Republic of Turkey, with 52.6 percent of the votes. His AK Party became the first among other parties, with the 42.6 percent of the votes and 290 out of 600 seats. Four other parties have formed the parliamentary group in the Grand National Assembly: the CHP, with 144 seats; the HDP, with 67 seats; the MHP with 49 seats, and newly established Good Party, also nationalist but from a more secular viewpoint, with 42 seats.

4. Turkey's democracy was interrupted by several military coups, the first of which occurred in 1960 against the rising authoritarian tendencies of the Democrat Party government led by Adnan Menderes. After this coup d'état, a new and more libertarian constitution came into force in 1961. With this constitution parliamentary democracy was empowered, the principle of a separation of powers was accepted, and many political, civic, social, and democratic rights attained constitutional status. Another military intervention took place with the military memorandum issued on March 12, 1971, against the government of the Adalet Partisi of the Justice Party, a center-right party and successor of the Democrat Party. After this memorandum the ruling government resigned and a new government mainly composed of technocrats was established. Some constitutional amendments restricted democratic rights (Carter Vaughn

Findley, *Turkey, Islam, Nationalism, and Modernity: A History, 1789-2007* [New Haven: Yale University Press, 2010]). The last military intervention was against Erdoğan and his government, which faced a failed coup d'état on July 15, 2016. Once an ally of Erdoğan and the AK Party, religious leader Fethullah Gülen was accused of leading this attempt. On July 20, 2016, a state of emergency was declared that lasted until July 18, 2018. Under the state of emergency, Turkey was governed under strict security policies and social, economic, and legal pressures and prohibitions.

5. Findley; Feroz Ahmad, *The Making of Modern Turkey* (New York: Routledge, 2005).

6. The Kurdish issue came to the fore in this decade with armed conflict between the Turkish state and the PKK (Kurdistan Workers Party). The government chose strict and oppressive security policies on the Kurdish issue. The rise of Political Islam was another important feature of this decade. The coalition government formed by the Islamist Welfare Party (Refah Partisi) resigned following another intervention by the Turkish army on February 28, 1997. Finally, the 1990s were turbulent years for the Turkish economy.

7. Didem Danış, "Türk Göç Politikasında Yeni Bir Devir: Bir Dış Politika Enstrümanı Olarak Suriyeli Mülteciler," *SAHA Dergisi* 1, no. 2 (2016): 6–11.

8. Danış; Ahmet İçduygu et al., *Türkiye'nin Uluslararası Göç Politikaları, 1923-2023: Ulus-devlet Oluşumundan Ulus-Ötesi Dönüşümlere* (Istanbul: MiReKoç, 2014), 53–55.

9. İçduygu et al., 56–57.

10. Mesut Yeğen, "Müstakbel-Türkten Sözde Vatandaşa: Cumhuriyet ve Kürtler," May 23, 2009, obarsiv.com.

11. İçduygu et al., 53–57.

12. Soner Çağaptay, "Reconfiguring the Turkish Nation in the 1930s," *Nationalism and Ethnic Politics* 8, no. 2 (2014): 71–75.

13. M. Çağatay Okutan, *Tek Parti Döneminde Azınlık Politikaları* (Istanbul: Istanbul Bilgi Universitesi Yayınları, 2009), 250.

14. Kemal Kirişçi, "Disaggregating Turkish Citizenship and Immigration Practices," *Middle Eastern Studies* 36, no. 3 (2000): 8.

15. Kirişçi, 13.

16. Kemal Kirişçi, "Refugees of Turkish Origin: 'Coerced Immigrants' to Turkey since 1945," *International Migration* 34, no. 3 (July 1996): 385–412.

17. Danış.

18. Kirişçi, "Disaggregating Turkish Citizenship"; Republic of Turkey Ministry of Interior Directorate General of Migration Management, "History of Migration," goc.gov.tr.

19. Didem Danış and Ayşe Parla, "Nafile Soydaşlık: Irak ve Bulgaristan Türkleri Örneğinde Göçmen, Dernek ve Devlet," *Toplum ve Bilim* 114 (2009): 131–158.

20. Içduygu et al., 57.

21. Içduygu et al., 58; Yılmaz Demirhan and Seyfettin Aslan, "Türkiye'nin Sınır Ötesi Göç Politikaları ve Yönetimi," *Birey ve Toplum* 5, no. 9 (2015): 39.

22. Ahmet Hamdi Topal, "Geçici Koruma Yönetmeliği ve Türkiye'deki Suriyelilerin Hukuki Statüsü," *Journal of Istanbul Medipol University School of Law* 2, no. 1 (2015): 10.

23. Kemal Kirişçi, "A Friendlier Schengen Visa System as a Tool of 'Soft Power': The Experience of Turkey," *European Journal of Migration and Law* 7, no. 4 (2005): 358.

24. Içduygu et al., 62.

25. Danış, 10.

26. The Turkish government reports the following figures for various camps: Şanlıurfa (102,692), Gaziantep (38,672), Kilis (32,245), Hatay (18,654), Kahramanmaraş (18,401), Adana (10,315), Adıyaman (9,663), Osmaniye (9,089), Mardin (8,766), Malatya (7,733). "Kampların Bulunduğu Iller ve Barınan Suriyeli Sayısı Şöyledir," goc.gov.tr.

27. Hakan Ataman, "Yazılı Basında Ayrımcı Söylem, Suriyeli Mülteciler," in *Medyada Nefret Söylemi ve Ayrımcı Dil Eylül–Aralık 2014 Raporu*, Hrant Dink Foundation, 61–105, nefretsoylemi.org.

28. N. Ela Gökalp Aras and Zeynep Şahin Mencütek, "The International Migration and Foreign Policy Nexus: The Case of Syrian Refugee Crisis and Turkey," *Migration Letters* 12, no. 3 (2015): 193–208.

29. Göktürk Tüysüzoğlu, "Milenyum Sonrası Türk Dış Politikası: Yeni Osmanlıcılık ve Türk Avrasyacılığı Ekseninde İnşa Edilen Bir

Pragmatizm," *Alternatif Politika* 5, no. 5 (2013): 309.

30. Tüysüzoğlu, 299.
31. Özge Bilgili and Melissa Siegel, "Policy Perspectives of Turkey towards Return Migration: From Permissive Indifference to Selective Difference," *Migration Letters* 11, no. 2 (2014): 218–228; Selcen Öner, "Soft Power in Turkish Foreign Policy: New Instruments and Challenges," *Euxeinos: Governance and Culture in the Black Sea Region* 10 (2013): 7–15; Gökalp and Mencütek; Tüysüzoğlu.
32. Tüysüzoğlu.
33. Tüysüzoğlu.
34. Zeki Sarıtoprak, "The Qur'anic Perspective on Immigrants: Prophet Muhammad's Migration and Its Implications in Our Modern Society," *Journal of Scriptural Reasoning* 11, no. 1 (2011): n.p.
35. Sarıtoprak.
36. Lakoff and Johnson, 25–30.
37. For example, the Ansar Foundation, founded in 1979, one of Turkey's oldest religious foundations, of which Erdoğan's family are members and economically sponsor, organizes Iftar meals in various parts of the country in Ramadan month, under "Ansar-Muhajir Fellowship Table." See http://www.ensar.org/haber-beykozdaensarvemuhaciriftardabul utu_h986.html.
38. "Cumhurbaşkanı Erdoğan: Bizler Ensar Sizler Muhacir," Haber7.com, October 7, 2014, haber7.com (emphasis added).
39. The UNHCR defines people that are forced to leave their homeland in five categories: (1) refugees, (2) asylum seekers, (3) returnees, (4) internally displaced persons (IDPs), and (5) stateless persons. See UNHCR at unhcr.org/who-we-help.html.
40. AFAD, *Syrian Guests in Turkey*, afad.gov.tr.
41. AFAD, 78–89.
42. AFAD, 78.
43. AFAD, 79.
44. "Turkey Threatens to Open the Gates and Send Refugees to Europe," *The Telegraph*, February 11, 2016.
45. Danış.

46. It has been emphasized in in the local press of the cities on southern border, where the number of refugees living in refugee camps and outside camps is massive, that the Syrians were not content with the opportunities provided to them. For example, some news and social media outlets featured claims that the refugees have "endless demands," suggesting that some demanded sunscreen, sunglasses, or air conditioners, causing trouble or even riots. See, for example, "Sığınmacılar Güneş Gözlüğü de Istiyor Mu?" ["Do Refugees Also Demand Sunglasses?"], İskenderun Ses Gazetesi, http:// iskenderunses.net; "Suriyeli Muhalifler Türk Bayrağını Indirdi" ["Syrian Opponents Took Down the Turkish Flag"], Medya Güne Bakiş, www. medyagunebakis.com; "Suriyeli Derdi Bitmiyor" ["The Syrian Problem Does Not End"], *Yeni Güney Gazetesi*, yeniguneygazetesi.com.

47. "Turkish Foreign Minister Ahmet Davutoglu Met with United Nations High Commissioner for Refugees Antonio Guterres in New York," *AK Parti*, August 31, 2012, akparti.org.tr.

48. "Premier Vows to Pray in Damascus Mosque 'Soon,'" *Hurriyet Daily News*, September 5, 2012, hurriyetdailynews.com.tr.

49. "Başbakan'dan Kritik Hatay Mesajları," *Milliyet*, July 20, 2014, millyet. com.tr.

50. Ulku Doganay and Hatice Coban Kenes, "Yazılı Basında Suriyeli Mülteciler: Ayrımcı Söylemlerin Rasyonel ve Duygusal Gerekçelerinin İnşası," *Mülkiye Dergisi* 40, no. 1 (2016): 172.

51. "Premier Vows to Pray in Damascus Mosque 'Soon.'"

52. Yasin-i Şerif is one of the most important surahs in the Koran, the holy book of Muslims.

53. Habib Al-Najjar was a carpenter who lived in Antioch at the time of Jesus. According to the legend, Al-Najjar, believed Jesus's apostles, who were sent to the people of Ja-Sin, and was martyred for his faith. Muslims believe that his story is described in the Ja-Sin surah of the Koran. The Habib Al-Najjar mosque was the first mosque in the Ottoman Empire. The graves of John, Pavlos, and Shem—the apostles—are also in this mosque. It is therefore considered a symbol of interreligious dialogue and tolerance.

54. One of the most important saints and philosophers of Anatolian Alevits, Haci Bektas Veli is famous for his tolerant and humanistic thoughts. As a considerable part of Hatay's population is Alevit, Davutoğlu refers to Hacı Bektas Veli.

55. "Başbakan Davutoğlu: 8 Haziran'da Iktidar Olamazsam Istifa Ederim," *Hürriyet*, May 9, 2015, hurriyet.com.tr (emphasis added).

56. "Up to 300,000 Syrians Could Get Turkish Citizenship: Report," *Hurriyet Daily News*, July 10, 2016, hurriyetdailynews.com.

57. According to Article 11 of the Turkish Citizenship Law (Law No. 5901), "(1) An alien who wishes to acquire Turkish citizenship shall (a) be in the age of majority and have the capacity to act either according to his/her own national law or, if he/she is stateless, according to Turkish law, (b) have been resident in Turkey without interruption for five years preceding the date of his/her application, (c) verify his/her determination to settle down in Turkey with his/her manners, (d) have no disease constituting an obstacle in respect of public health, (e) be of good moral character, (f) be able to speak a sufficient level of Turkish, (g) have income or profession to provide for maintenance for himself/herself and his/her dependents in Turkey, (h) have no quality constituting an obstacle in respect of national security and public order." *Official Gazette*, no. 27256, June 12, 2009.

58. "Turkey's Erdogan Moots Plan to Grant Citizenship to Syrians," Reuters, July 5, 2016, reuters.com.

59. "Turkey's Erdogan Moots Plan to Grant Citizenship to Syrians."

60. Verda Özer, "Suriyeli'ye TOKİ Konutları," *Hürriyet*, July 7, 2016, hurriyet.com.tr.

61. Özer.

62. *Migration and Remittances Fact Book, 2011*, 2nd ed. (Washington, DC: World Bank, 2011), 246.

63. Özer.

64. "CHP's Latest Election Promise of Sending Back Syrian Refugees in Turkey Comes under Criticism," *Daily Sabah*, April 23, 2015, dailysabah.com.

65. *MHP 7 Haziran 2015 Seçim Beyannamesi: Toplumsal Onarım ve Huzurlu Gelecek*,

May 3, 2015, 230, mhp.org.tr.

66. Devlet Bahçeli, "Speech in MHP Group Meeting in Turkish Grand National Assembly," November 5, 2013, mhp.org.tr.

67. The process of building a nation-state with the Ottoman Empire's multiethnic and multireligious population has been quite harsh on non-Turkish and non-Muslim citizens. While the non-Muslim Greek Cypriots and the Armenian minorities were targeted in the first step of the establishment and domination of the Turks as nation of the state, in the second step Kurds as non-Turkish Muslims were faced with various assimilation practices. The Kurds have been "categorically" denied in the state discourse since the late 1920s. It has been argued that the Kurds were actually "mountain Turks" and that Kurdish riots were an "incitement of external enemies," or the Kurdish issue was reduced to a "regional backwardness" problem (Mesut Yegen, *Devlet Soyleminde Kurt Sorunu* [Istanbul: İletisim, 1999]). The second period of the ruling AKP governments (2007–2011) created a significant break in this discursive tradition. The government under the leadership of Erdoğan initiated a "negotiation and democratic opening" process in 2009, arguing that Turkey could solve the Kurdish issue not by war but by recognizing some of the ethnocultural rights of Kurdish citizens on the basis of a brotherhood of religion. However, this process became clogged before the 2015 general elections and then suspended. Erdoğan and the ruling AKP have assumed a nationalist outlook on the Kurdish issue and have formed an alliance with the Nationalist Movement Party. In 2016, Selahattin Demirtaş and Figen Yüksekdağ, cochairs of the parliament's third-largest party, the HDP, and some members of parliament were arrested. In the cities where the Kurds live extensively, mayors elected by popular vote were arrested and their municipal governments began to be governed by *kayyım* (officials appointed by the government). On the other hand, when the military conflicts intensified again in Kurdish provinces, twenty-two hundred scholars, including us, released the petition "We Will Not Be a Part of This Crime," calling on the Turkish state to return to the negotiation table. Some of the petitioners were arrested; many others got fired from universities. Later, terrorist investigations and

lawsuits were opened against all petitioner-scholars. Many scholars who signed the declaration were dismissed from the public service by decree laws issued during the state of emergency that began after the coup attempt of July 15, 2016.

68. "Demirtaş: Suriyelilere Mülteci Muamelesi Yapamayız," *Hür Bakiş*, May 11, 2015, hurbakis.net.

69. "CHP Leader Accuses Gov't of 'Protecting' ISIL, Laying Ground for Ankara Massacre," *Hurriyet Daily News*, October 20, 2015, hurriyetdailynews.com; "At Least 42 Killed in Terror Attack on Istanbul's Atatürk Airport," *Hurriyet Daily News*, June 28, 2016, hurriyetdailynews.com.

70. Devlet Bahçeli, "Speech in MHP Group Meeting in Turkish Grand National Assembly," November 4, 2013, http://88.255.31.62/htmldocs/genel_baskan/konusma/4063/index.html.

71. "Kemal Kılıçdaroğlu: Suriyeliler Bütün Düzenimizi Bozacak," *Habertürk*, March 12, 2016, haberturk.com.

72. Kılıçdaroğlu.

73. Bahçeli.

74. Bahçeli. *Ulufe* refers to the service pay distributed by sultans, especially to janissary soldiers.

75. "CHP lideri Kılıçdaroğlu'ndan sert Kilis Tepkisi," *Milliyet*, April 22, 2015, milliyet.com.tr.

76. Kılıçdaroğlu refers to Erdoğan's farm in İstanbul-Çatalca, which was constructed for his horses. "Yargıyı Kim bu Hale Getirdi," *Hürriyet*, April 29, 2016, hurriyet.com.tr.

77. "CHP's Latest Election Promise of Sending Back Syrian Refugees in Turkey Comes under Criticism."

78. Bahçeli.

79. "Bahçeli'den 'Suriyelilere Vatandaşlık' Tepkisi," *Aljazeera Turk*, July 4, 2016, aljazeera.com.tr.

80. "Bahçeli'den 'Suriyelilere Vatandaşlık' Tepkisi."

81. *HDP 2015 Seçim Bildirgesi: Büyük İnsanlık Çağrısı* (2015), 45, hdp.org.tr.

82. Immanuel Kant, *Perpetual Peace: A Philosophical Essay*, trans. M. Campbell Smith (London: George Allen and Unwin , 1795).

83. "Demirtaş: Suriyelilere Mülteci Muamelesi Yapamayız."
84. Muharrem Sarıkaya, "Suriyelilere Vatandaşlık Hakkı Verilmeli," *HaberTürk*, May 24, 2015, haberturk.com.
85. "Syrians Should Be Recognized as Refugees: HDP Co-chair Demirtaş," *Hurriyet Daily News*, July 14, 2016, hurriyetdailynews.com.
86. "Syrians Should Be Recognized as Refugees."
87. Owen Matthews, "Why the EU's Deal with Turkey to Stem Migrants Flow Is Deeply Flawed," *Newsweek (Europe)*, March 28, 2016, europe. newsweek.com.
88. "Opposition Says Turkey's National Security at Risk," Cihan News Agency, February 16, 2016, cihan.com.tr.
89. "CHP Chairman Suggests Turkey Gives €6B to EU to Take All Refugees," *Daily Sabah*, March 11, 2016, dailysabah.com.
90. Devlet Bahçeli, "Speech in MHP Group Meeting in Turkish Grand National Assembly," April 26, 2016, _http://88.255.31.62/htmldocs/ genel_baskan/konusma/4063/index.html.
91. "Turkey Should Hold Referendum on Offering Citizenship to Syrians: CHP Leader," *Hurriyet Daily News*, July 12, 2016, hurriyetdailynews.com.
92. "HDP Eş Genel Başkanı Figen Yüksekdağ," Habert7.com, July 3, 2016, habert7.com.

Serbian Migration Rhetoric

THEY ARE ONLY PASSING THROUGH

———•◆•———

Ivana Cvetković Miller

I n 2015 the number of migrants arriving in Europe reached the highest ever recorded in the post–World War II period. Frontex, the European Union Agency that coordinates European border management, recorded that over 910,000 migrants reached Europe in the first nine months of 2015.[1] Without a centralized response to the newly emerged situation on the European Union level, EU and non-EU member countries embraced different strategies toward migrants. Germany and Sweden welcomed migrants, especially those who were fleeing war-devastated Syria, but later closed their borders in order to exercise tighter frontier management.[2] Eastern EU member Slovakia announced that it would take in only Christians.[3] On the other hand, Hungary, which is positioned on the southern EU frontier, built a barbed-wire fence along its borders to protect both its own territory and the EU common space.[4] Given these conditions, migration has become a prominent topic in the

European media, part of the political discourses across Europe, and a key topic in parliamentary debates.

After the most recent EU enlargement in 2013, Serbia became positioned as a transit country for migrants from the Middle East and Africa. Its position on the EU southern border strategically placed Serbia as the final link in the Western Balkans route, the second most frequent entry point for migrants to the EU. Finding their way in overcrowded cars, buses, trains, or on foot, over 760,000 migrants traveled through Western Balkan countries in 2015 to reach the Schengen zone of free movement.[5]

This chapter explores the discourse of Serbian politicians in addressing the immigration crisis. As a postcommunist, postsocialist border country seeking to join the EU, Serbia's political discourse is shaped by complex rhetorical goals. Additionally, Serbia is a "pass-through" country (rather than a country of final destination) for most of these immigrants, creating different domestic concerns relating to this crisis. Indeed, Serbia's own citizens have sought to migrate to more prosperous Western countries, creating identification between the domestic audience and those who would use the country as a gateway to the West. This chapter focuses on Serbian political speeches and documents from 2013 to 2015 to reveal how Serbian officials position immigrants and construct the ongoing crisis.[6] It seeks to contribute to a broader understanding of the migration crisis and of constructions of mobility and access to mobility.

Historical and Political Context: Serbia and the European Union

The modern Republic of Serbia is the state successor of the post–World War II creations—the Socialist Federal Republic of Yugoslavia, the Socialist Republic of Yugoslavia, and the State Union of Serbia and Montenegro, which briefly lived in the 2000s. After the post-World War II Communist and socialist period, the breakup of the Federal Republic of Yugoslavia along ethnic lines led to political pluralism in the 1990s and further democratization of Serbia in the 2000s. In its democratic era,

Serbia is a parliamentary republic with a unicameral multiparty National Assembly whose members are elected in a proportional representation vote. The chief of state is the directly elected president, though the position is largely ceremonial. The executive power lies in hands of the prime minister, traditionally appointed by the president. The National Assembly elects the prime minister's cabinet, and since 2000 the Serbian government usually has been a coalition of several political parties.

In the twentieth century, democratic governments reframed the postcommunist and postsocialist country's foreign policy to gain EU membership. Leaving behind its Communist past, Serbia embraced European values and promoted Europeanness as the country's prominent feature. The European Union identified Serbia as a potential candidate for the EU membership in 2003, and in 2012 it was granted EU candidate status. In December 2015, as a part of the accession negotiation process with the EU, Serbia opened the first two accession negotiation chapters—the chapter on financial control and the chapter on needed normalization of relations between Serbia and Kosovo.[7] As a Balkan Peninsula country with an EU future, Serbia still confronts the Western historical representation of the Balkans as a primitive, racially and culturally inferior territory between the Orient and Europe that is burdened with violent nationalism.[8]

After the former Yugoslavian Republic of Croatia joined the EU in 2013, Serbia became positioned outside of the EU's external frontiers, bordering four EU member states, Croatia, Hungary, Romania, and Bulgaria, each with a different Schengen Agreement status. The existing Schengen Agreement guarantees free movement of people in the EU area and abolishes internal borders, while a single external border was tightened. The Agreement enables migrants' mobility to increase once they cross the external frontier.[9] With the exception of Hungary, the more recent EU members, including Croatia, Bulgaria, and Romania, are still not full members of the Schengen area. They maintain their internal borders while, at the same time, face pressure to manage tightly their external borders in order to meet the conditions for Schengen membership.

Serbia's History of Immigration and Asylum Policies

Geographical position on the periphery of Europe and a complex historical, political, and economic context have shaped Serbia's weak and underdeveloped immigration and asylum policies. There are three distinct migration patterns in Serbia's history that affect migration policy institutionalization: labor emigration, Yugoslavian war-caused migration and internal displacement of people, and migration the country has been facing during the democratic rule period since 2000.

The labor emigration pattern characterized the soft-communism approach of the 1950s, 1960s, and the 1970s. Illegal labor emigration from the Socialist Federal Republic of Yugoslavia to Western European countries started around 1954 following strictly forced and politically motivated migration in the aftermath of World War II.[10] In the 1950s, workers left the then predominately agricultural country in search of employment and better economic conditions in industrialized Western Europe, especially the German Federal Republic and France.[11] It took a decade for Yugoslavia's political elite to institutionalize ostensibly temporary labor emigration through a set of employment agreements with individual countries of immigration. Those bilateral agreements regulated the employment and the rights of Yugoslav workers in the countries where they were considered temporary workers. The labor emigration rate kept increasing, and in 1971 the estimated emigration rate reached 4.2 percent, positioning Yugoslavia as the country with the second highest emigration rate in Europe, with 920,000 workers who were employed abroad.[12] The most desirable labor destination for Yugoslavian workers was the German Federal Republic, with 66.1 percent of all labor emigration.

Over the next decades Serbian citizens have continued to migrate to more prosperous countries of the Western world. The emigration increase peak was reached during the 1990s when around 415,000 people left the country following the breakup of the Socialist Federal Republic of Yugoslavia.[13] Many of them were granted legal immigrant status or asylum, as they were treated as people who came from an area of humanitarian crisis. The main factors that influenced massive migration in the 1990s was the war's devastation along with a severe political and economic crisis followed by high unemployment rates.

Economic factors remain the main driver for further emigration in this century. Alongside the labor migration, the trend of highly educated and qualified people leaving the country (the brain-drain phenomenon) was intensified at the end of the last century. The data on Serbian people who live abroad are incomplete; however, the 2014 data estimate that Serbia's diaspora comprises over 5.1 million people who live in about one hundred countries around the world.[14] Nevertheless, Germany remains the top destination county.

In the 1990s the EU countries implemented tighter migration and asylum regulations. The outcome of those tighter policies was twofold. First, the EU countries stopped treating migrants from Serbia as eligible for asylum status, and consequently in 2009 the EU granted Serbia a visa-free status.[15] However, economic hardship continued to be an important incentive to migration—in 2000 Serbia's GDP per capita was only US$5,777.[16] Serbia's insignificant increase in GDP per capita in 2014 to US$13,698 from the previous year's US$13,668 (compared to Germany's US$46,393 GDP per capita in 2014),[17] led to a 14 percent increase in the number of asylum seekers from Serbia to the EU. Serbia became a leader in asylum requests among the Balkan countries, with the most requests claimed in Germany.[18]

Second, as an aspiring EU member state, Serbia was forced to harmonize its immigration regulations with the EU laws. The Law on Ratification of Readmission Agreement for Irregularly Residing Persons between Serbia and the EU from 2009 enforced acceptance and reintegration of deported persons who were illegally staying in the EU.[19] The acceptance and reintegration of returnees is an ongoing process, and the European Council made an assessment that between fifty thousand and one hundred thousand people will be returned to Serbia from Western Europe in the upcoming decades, solely on the basis of the readmission agreement. In 2014, 8,130 people returned to Serbia, mostly from Germany and Hungary; 76 percent of returnees were Roma people.[20]

In the aftermath of the 1990s civil war in the former Yugoslavia and NATO's military intervention in 1999, Serbia faced an influx of refugees and internally displaced persons, creating a second migration pattern. A refugee data census from June 1996 reported 598,000 refugees and war-affected persons who came to Serbia fleeing from the former Yugoslav republics, mainly Croatia and Bosnia and Herzegovina.[21] Six years later, in 2002, 762,000 refugees from the former Yugoslavian republics of Slovenia, Croatia, and Bosnia and Herzegovina remained in Serbia. Forcefully moved refugees were predominantly ethnic Serbs, including over 200,000 internally displaced persons from Serbia's autonomous region of Kosovo.[22]

While the existing regulations treat as internally displaced persons only those who left Kosovo during and after the NATO military action in 1999, the Law on Refugees, first adopted in 1992 and revised in 2010, very narrowly defines the term *refugee* as applying only to persons who are by origin from the territory of the former Yugoslavian republics and who fled the war in the territory of the former Socialist Federal Republic of Yugoslavia in the period between 1991 and 1998.[23] Additionally, under the Law on Refugees *refugee* includes every person who does not want to go back or who wants to be integrated into Serbian society. The ambiguity of the narrow definition of the term *refugee* has caused many terminological inconsistencies when it comes to the overall migration policies. The 2007 Law on Asylum is considered an expansion of the refugee definition to as include people from outside of the former Yugoslavia.[24]

The number of refugees decreased over the years as they returned or integrated into society by choosing to seek Serbian citizenship. Yet in 2014 almost 44,000 refugees still resided in Serbia. A majority of them were ethnic Serbs who were forced to leave Croatia in the 1990s. On the other hand, in 2014 there were 204,049 internally displaced people from Kosovo residing in Serbia. Despite the country's effort to prove the sustainable return successful, only 310 persons returned to Kosovo in 2014.[25]

The constant flow of migrants in the last few years, especially those who are fleeing armed conflicts in Africa and the Middle East, marks the third migration pattern. The significant increase in the numbers of both immigrants and asylum seekers in Serbia confirmed the country's importance on the route of migrants' transition to the West.[26] Moreover, the increased numbers of immigrants challenged Serbia's fragile, underdeveloped, and inefficient migration system.

Serbia's migration policies enforced in the democratic era are based on the definitions of immigrants adopted from the EU legislation about immigration.[27] The development of the Strategy for Management of Migration and the asylum system was established only in 2008 when the Assembly of the Serbian parliament adopted the Asylum Law.[28] The 2009 management of migration strategy and the 2012 Integrated Border Management Strategy contributed to the conceptualization and improvement of the existing migration policies, which are both based on the EU standards.

Immigrants, defined as people who legally stay in Serbia for at least a year, are coming mainly from China, Russia, and Romania; along with immigrants from Macedonia and Libya, they comprise almost 54 percent of total immigration in Serbia.[29] The main reasons for immigrating to Serbia are work and family reunification. Chinese immigrants were welcomed to Serbia in the late 1990s during the regime of Slobodan Milošević. Almost six thousand Chinese people resided in Serbia in 2014, comprising almost a quarter of all immigrants.[30] The share of immigrants who choose to live and work in Serbia shows that Serbia is a much less desirable final destination than the former Yugoslavian republics of Slovenia, Croatia, and Montenegro.

The right to asylum was recognized by the constitution of the Socialist Federal Republic of Yugoslavia in 1974. However, the option of asylum seeking did not exist until the Law on Asylum that was implemented in 2008 as a consequence of Serbia's regulative coordination with the EU.[31] The Law on Asylum expanded the Law on Refugees regulating the "conditions and procedure for the granting and cessation of asylum, as well as the status, rights and obligations of asylum seekers and persons granted the right to asylum in Serbia."[32] The law also promoted the principles of nondiscrimination and deportation prohibition. However, the Law on Asylum and related bylaws still need further clarification and development to improve the efficiency of the asylum procedure, the response time to asylum applications, the competence of the official departments dealing with asylum seekers, the integration of persons granted asylum, and the capacity of accommodation facilities.[33]

In the first five years following the Law on Asylum's enactment, around ten thousand people sought asylum and only ten were granted the right to legally stay in Serbia.[34] Around 40 percent of that number sought asylum in 2013. The largest numbers of immigrants who sought an asylum were from Syria (20 percent), Eritrea (16 percent), Somalia (10 percent), and Afghanistan (9 percent).[35] Armed conflict was listed by 63 percent of the asylum seekers as the main reason for fleeing their country of origin.[36] The share of asylum seekers tripled in 2014, with 16,500 migrants seeking asylum in Serbia. The majority were immigrants from Syria (58.8 percent), followed by Afghans (18.4 percent) and migrants from Eritrea (4.8 percent).[37] Furthermore, the number of the asylum requests increased more than seven times compared to the requests submitted in 2010.[38] Migrants who ask for asylum in Serbia are registered as asylum seekers, receive a legal status, and are provided with shelter in an asylum center, given an asylum ID, permitted freedom of movement in Serbia, and granted free healthcare and free primary and secondary education.[39] However, out of 16,500 migrants who in 2014 expressed an intention to seek asylum, only 388 filed asylum claims.[40] Migrants do seek asylum in Serbia so that they do not get deported, but they usually leave Serbia as soon as they are able, looking for better opportunities elsewhere in the EU and not waiting for the end of the asylum approval process. The misbalance in the share of those who express intention to seek asylum and migrants who file asylum claims suggests that majority of migrants are only in transit through Serbia. In 2014, 307, or 79 percent of, asylum claims were suspended before the final stages of the asylum decision, because asylum seekers left Serbia and migrated further to the West.[41] Migrants confirmed that traveling through Serbia, after leaving Greece and Macedonia to reach the Schengen zone, is shorter than the route through Bulgaria and Romania.[42] It is important to bear in mind that the numbers of those who seek asylum in Serbia is not equivalent to the numbers of migrants who pass through Serbia on the Balkan route. The share of migrants who entered Serbia unnoticed by the state authorities was six to seven times larger than the number of asylum seekers.[43]

Tensions between Domestic and International Audiences

As the preceding history shows, Serbia has faced significant immigration challenges recently. The country's aspiration to EU membership and its spatial proximity to the EU borders are important in the migration institutionalization processes. Also significant is Serbia's political history as a country whose citizens have escaped the civil war of the former Yugoslavia, who have traditionally been migrating to developed countries seeking better economic opportunities, or who have escaped from the Communist and later socialist regimes. These crucial factors shape the construction of immigration and of migrants by the Serbian government and its leaders.

As a Communist and socialist country, Serbia enforced laws that regulated labor migration in the 1960s, 1970s, and 1980s. The Socialist Party of Serbia (SPS), as a leading faction of the government in the 1990s, formulated the Law on Refugees, whereas the modification of the refugee law and enforcement of the new laws on readmission, asylum, and the Strategy for Border Management were projects carried out by different EU-oriented democratic governments in the 2000s. Serbia's first multiparty democratic governments were mainly formed around the Democratic Party and the Democratic Party of Serbia. In 2008, Serbia's very fragmented political scene affected the alliance of the Democratic Party and the Socialist Party of Serbia, bringing socialists (without Milošević) back to the political limelight. However, the government's inability to execute desired and timely political and economic changes, as well as severe budget cuts forced upon Serbia by the International Monetary Fund, strengthened nationalist parties. In 2012 the Socialist Party of Serbia became the leading political force, followed by the empowerment of the Progressive Party of Serbia (SNS) in 2014. Being pro-EU oriented and at the same time preaching nationalistic values, both parties only tinkered with weak migration policies to meet the EU requirements.

During the period of 2013–2015, when the migration caused by the conflict in Syria significantly increased, two multiparty Serbian governments were formed around the aforementioned two nationalistic political parties—the Socialist Party of Serbia and later the Progressive Party of Serbia. Major political figures were the former prime minister, Ivica Dačić, and since April 2014, the new prime minister, Aleksandar Vučić, and his cabinet members. Dačić is also a leader of SPS, and Vučić is a party leader of SNS. Even though the Socialist Party of Serbia is left wing, whereas the Progressive Party of Serbia is a right-wing party, both political parties support the Serbia's EU path, and both are thought to promote Serbia's nationalist interests. Additionally, both Dačić and Vučić were supporters of and held prominent positions in the autocratic government of Slobodan Milošević, who was charged with war crimes including genocide and crimes against humanity related to the wars in Bosnia and Herzegovina, Croatia, and Kosovo. Milošević passed away in his prison cell in 2006, and his trial was terminated without a conviction. Vučić and current Serbian president Tomislav Nikolić used to be the highly ranked members of the ultranationalistic far-right-wing Serbian Radical Party. In 2008 Vučić and Nikolić parted ways with that party's leader, Vojislav Šešelj, who at the time was awaiting trial at the International Criminal Tribunal for the Former Yugoslavia (ICTY) for crimes against humanity and violations of the customs of war.[44] Vučić and Nikolić formed the Progressive Party and had significant successes in both 2012 presidential and 2014 parliamentary elections. Šešelj was acquitted of all charges by the ICTY in 2016.

Prime Minister Dačić's government continued with the politics of close relationship with the EU and further implementation of the EU requirements. Dačić recognized the need to expand the capacity of the only two asylum facilities in Serbia and opened four additional temporary facilities (two of them in towns settled predominantly by citizens of the Muslim faith).[45] Faced with twice as many asylum seekers as in 2012, and protests against migrants in the city of Obrenovac, where a temporary asylum center was erected, Dačić's government "harshly condemned the outbreak of violence and the setting on fire of the asylum facility in Obrenovac."[46] With the need to demonstrate the government's control of the situation and to manage public fear of and protests against migrants, Dačić's rhetoric stressed the right to freedom of movement over charges that migrants had crossed the borders illegally. The prime minister addressed the citizens' protests in Obrenovac, pointing out that "illegal migrants are not supposed to cause any problems," and that "in spite of the local population's right to disagree with the asylum center location, illegal migrants have to be provided with accommodations somewhere."[47]

Prime Minister Aleksandar Vučić has faced challenges from the increase in the number of migrants using Serbia as part of the Balkan route to reach the EU zone of free movement; thus, he and his cabinet members developed a nuanced rhetoric balanced between pleasing the EU, especially its leader, Germany, while still insisting on strong nationalist ideas to please the party's voters. The tensions between domestic and international audiences shaped the official rhetoric, which was built around strategies such as focusing on migrants' presence as temporary, valorizing Europeanness, collaborating with the EU and regional countries, and protecting national interests.

Focusing on Migrants' Presence as Temporary

"They are just passing through" is the dominant narrative of Vučić's government. It is built around the notion that migrants, who are looking for a better future, do not see Serbia as their final destination. Serbia is a "transit country," and discourse describes "brief voluntary retention of migrants on Serbia's territory" and "the temporary character of asylum camps."[48] The prime minister employs this strategy of positioning migrants as temporary visitors both when addressing the public and in conversations with foreign diplomats. For instance, after meeting with the US secretary of state John Kerry, Vučić stated that "refugees do not want to stay, neither in Serbia nor in Hungary, but are proceeding toward Germany and the Scandinavian countries."[49] Vučić also said that "Serbia is assisting migrants as much as the country can by providing medical and other aid and facilitating their stay in Serbia for a few days, which is how long they usually sojourn in Serbia."[50]

The "temporary presence" narrative is a part of a broader strategy of reassurance in which the government comforts Serbian citizens with the idea that Serbia should and will help migrants in their transit toward EU member states, and that migrants will not stay permanently or cause any problems. This strategy reinforces nationalism for the domestic audience by justifying the humanitarian treatment of migrants only in light of their temporary presence, which will not endanger the nation, its economy, or its security. At the same time, this discursive move dismisses migrants' importance, since their presence in Serbia is only temporary and Western European countries will provide a permanent residence for them; it implicitly suggests that Serbia is not attractive enough to entice migrants to remain. By employing this strategy the Serbian leadership affirms Serbia's backwardness and economic inferiority to Western Europe, highlighting its lack of development, wealth, and power relative to EU countries.

The reassurance strategy is supported by arguments built around "Migrants do not cause any trouble" narratives. For instance, the Prime Minister Vučić said, "Serbia will continue taking care of refugees, who are in many cases good people forced to leave their home countries by terrorist threats and other causes."[51] The argument draws on memories of Serbian refugees' sufferings during and after the civil war. "Twenty years ago we also faced hundreds of thousands of refugees coming to Serbia from Krajina and Bosnia and Herzegovina," Vučić said.[52] Even though the prime minister draws a parallel with Serbian refugees who were forced to leave their homes, his characterization of immigrants as "in many cases good" implies that there are those who are not. While he carves out from the mass of immigrants those who are acceptable because they are good, he also implies that immigrants are not acceptable and desirable generally. He leaves open the possibility that those judged as "good people" are worthy of care.

The construction of migrants as temporary visitors is frequently presented in an active voice, assigning migrants agency in their mobility. Vučić assigns agency to migrants by saying, "They have their own routes, and they want to stay in groups and to reach the border as soon as possible."[53] Similarly, Aleksandar Vulin, minister of labor, employment, veteran, and social affairs, said, "Those people do not want to stay in Serbia. Those people will not stay in Serbia; they have their own routes and plans."[54] By assigning migrants agency to decide where they are going, the Serbian leadership employs a rhetorical strategy that suggests that the good people among migrants, who are welcome to stay, nonetheless will leave Serbia to reach more prosperous countries. At the same time, the Serbian leadership speaks for immigrants, describing not only what they are doing but also the motives behind their actions.

Valorizing Europeanness

European Union membership and Europeanness have been Serbia's political goals since 2000. European values of solidarity, humanity, and responsibility, and Serbia's willingness to act according to those values, are often emphasized in political messages. Serbian leadership emphasizes that the country belongs to Europe and the EU, and that by playing by EU rules Serbia passes the test of Europeanness. Ironically, this discourse of progress appeals to Serbian aspirations for cultural and racial superiority.

A claim that Serbia behaves in a European way is evident in an excerpt from the prime minister's address after a meeting with European Commission officials: "Our country is behaving in a constructive and European manner in terms of finding solutions for the migrant crisis the whole of Europe is facing."[55] The prime minister often states that Serbia, even though not an EU member, is capable of behaving in a more

European way than some member states. After meeting with a United Nations High Commissioner for Refugees official, Prime Minister Vučić emphasized "Serbia's willingness to act even more responsibly than some EU countries by applying the quota system."[56] Without explicitly naming other countries, Vučić implicated EU members such as Poland, the Czech Republic, and Hungary, which disagree with the suggested system of migrant redistribution to each EU state. Moreover, by obeying EU rules, Serbia presents itself as an overachiever that "registers and fingerprints more migrants on daily bases than the whole EU."[57]

The European norm of Christianity as distinct from other religions, especially Islam, is also evident in the rhetorical strategies of Serbian politicians. Once an officially atheist Communist country, contemporary Serbia embraces Orthodox Christianity. Christianity undergirds European standards and human rights, which shapes the ways Serbia deals with migrants. For example, the deputy speaker, Vladimir Marinković, said after a meeting with the Austrian delegation, "As a country with serious intentions that respects European standards and human rights, and also as Christians, we will continue to treat migrants fairly."[58] Even though a member of the Socialist Party of Serbia, Marinković identifies Christianity as an important value of Europeans, and does not specify Orthodox Christianity. Catholicism and Protestantism are valued in the core European countries, while the new, eastern members on the EU periphery, incorporate Orthodox Christianity from the EU margins.[59] By stressing Christianity and Christian values, rather than the Orthodox Christianity associated with Eastern Europe, Serbian leaders identify more broadly with Europe.

Moreover, Christianity is placed higher on a religious hierarchy in Europe by othering Islam and identifying it with insecurity and threat. After the Paris attacks in November 2015, the Serbian prime minister said, "I am proud of the fact that nobody in Serbia attacked citizens of Muslim faith."[60] This type of rhetoric implies also tolerance, an acceptable European value.

The strategy of valorizing Europeanness suggests that the politicians are aware of power relations between Serbia and the EU, and it positions the EU as the more powerful partner, with certain expectations about Serbia. Therefore, Serbia's official voice implies that the Balkan country strives for European belonging and portrays itself as acceptably European. Serbia is not an EU member state, and therefore Serbian politicians claim the values associated with Europeanness, European culture, and European identity as a way to break out of the subjugated position of an outsider. Therefore, the public discourse about migrants and Serbia assistance, politicians in Serbia often link to the goal of furthering Serbia's accession negotiations with the EU.

Proclamations of humanity, humanitarian attitudes toward migrants, Christianity, and neighborly conduct may be "European," but they are often in conflict with discourses of fear of migrants, otherizing, and exclusion. Overemphasizing Europeanness acts to silence different voices present in Serbia's diverse political scene, in which twenty-three political parties have representatives in the parliament.

Collaborating within the Region and the EU

The third strategy based in the European value of solidarity is evident in the sequential reasoning that starts with "We did not cause that problem" and "Therefore, we deserve cooperation from our neighbors and the EU." The strategy calling for collaboration maneuvers within the contested space of supranationalism and Europeanness on the one side, and national interests on the other. For instance, Vučić called on the EU to assist in providing a solution: "Serbia will never close its borders to migrants, but we expect that the EU leaders will come up with a plan defining the ways in which we should respond to the influx of hundreds of thousands of people to the Balkans."[61] The value of neighborly solidarity is tightly linked with Europeanness, and therefore Serbia's politicians in their statements highly value European values of partnership and maintaining good neighboring relations. An example is the prime minister's statement issued after a meeting between representatives from Serbia, Bulgaria, and Romania: "Serbia will put into effect all decisions made by the three countries, because Serbia is a loyal partner and a good neighbor."[62]

This strategy builds on discursive modes that position Serbia as a good host country that acts according to international laws and EU norms: Serbia provides refugees and asylum seekers needed assistance and allows free movement. Employing this strategy, politicians often mention the EU, UNHCR, or, most frequently, Germany, as the EU power state whose opinion matters the most and who is currently content with the ways Serbia deals with migrants.[63] Serbia's organization and support are evaluated, both according to the measurement of the international organizations and what Serbia considers appropriate assistance. However, migrants' needs and voices are absent from the picture; they are the problem causing the need for collaboration.

Moreover, two narratives are present in the "collaborating" strategy that supplement and contest each other, reproducing ideologies of Europeanness and nationalism. The narrative "We are helpful in the migration process but are not the ones who caused the migration," and the narrative "We are helpful, but we cannot do it on our own and need support and international monetary assistance" are evident in Vulin's statement: "We appeal to the international community to understand that this problem was not caused by Serbia, and, therefore, Serbia cannot solve the problem. We need aid in dealing with the problem, and we need it now."[64]

Protecting Our National Interests

The strategy of protecting national interests is built around a discourse of national security, border controls, and access to citizenship, and it is aimed at protecting the nation both from migrants and from actions taken by neighboring countries and the EU. This strategy reinforces nationalism and threatens the European values of solidarity and unity. Prime Minister Vučić raises the issue of protecting national interests but does not identify the actions that will be taken in that regard. Vučić does say, "Serbia will not erect walls and barbed-wire fences on its borders but will take security precautions to protect its citizens."[65] This discursive mode positions migrants as invaders and as threats both to the body of the nation and to the individual bodies of citizens. Xenophobia is at the heart of this strategy, but it is tempered by the fact that there will not be fences and walls.

Migrants and porous borders are the focus of the protection of national interests when it comes to relations with Serbia's neighbors Croatia and Hungary. Serbia officially frames any obstruction of migrants' flow to the EU countries as a matter of protecting national interests. Vučić stated, "Serbia will react by protecting national and state interests only if Germany and Austria reinstate border control."[66] Similarly, when referring to a blockade of transport traffic on the Serbian-Croatian border initiated by Croatia's decision to seize traffic coming from Serbia, he claimed that good relations with Croatia are in Serbia's interest; however, he insisted that "in instances of border-crossing closures, Serbia could not be allowed to be humiliated, and therefore we carried out measures to protect and defend the nation."[67]

Critical Standings of Minority and Oppositional Parties

The tension between pleasing international audiences and national audiences is especially present in the parliamentary debates, where both the ruling majority and opposition parties create dynamic and competitive constructions of the migrant crisis. On one side, the oppositional, ultraright, nationally oriented Serbian Radical Party's rhetoric expresses skepticism about the government's overall competence to control borders and manage migrants' identities and mobility on Serbian territory.[68]

On the other side, even parties that support the government deploy complex rhetorical tactics when migrants affect their electorate. Parties such as the Alliance of Vojvodina Hungarians (SVM) rely on naming and specific word choices when raising concern about migrants' presence.

Balint Pastor of the SVM, referring to migrants during a parliamentary discussion, complained: "Between 1,000 and 1,500 migrants arrive daily to Kanjiža. Those people settle in the park only fifty meters from the Municipality Building." Aleksandar Vulin responded, "We will provide for them as much as we can, but we have no right to stop and hold up those people."[69]

The rhetorical strategy of otherizing uses strategic word choice while explaining the kinds of problems migrants are causing. Critics of immigration note a decline in the number of tourists, compromised public safety, migrant intrusions into fields and the destruction of crops, and the disrupting of "normal life" and social order. Pastor's party does support the official pro-EU policy, but he is vocal when migrants affect public order in towns close to the Hungarian border, among which population the SVM (an ethnic minority party) is popular:

> Migrants are walking through crop fields, orchards, and they are severely damaging crops and agriculture. Who will make that up to our citizens and agricultural producers? . . . Because of the huge number of migrants, two tractor trailers full of trash are emptied daily. All restaurants are occupied. . . . Migrants are also standing in lines alongside our citizens at the post office, where people withdraw their money. . . . Public buses are occupied with migrants, and our citizens cannot get onto those buses. Big monetary losses in tourism are expected. In Kanjiža, for instance, four cultural events are scheduled for August, and we are expecting approximately four thousand visitors, who are now canceling their hotel reservations.[70]

This statement to the Serbian parliament exemplifies the complexity of the rhetoric in which politicians balance the country's national interests (which include attaining EU membership) against the local interests of citizens who feel insecure and see migrants as dangerous others. The rhetoric also reproduces power relations between those who decide what is normal and must be maintained and those who are disrupting the existing order, suggesting that they have to be controlled and removed to the bounded space outside of what is considered normal, domestic, and safe. The discursive move of naming, when connected to specific problems that "others" may cause or are causing, accomplishes the positioning of migrants as threatening and undesirable.

The most extreme critic of the governmental migration policies, and also the most extreme and xenophobic constructor of migrants, is the pro-Russian People's Party of Serbia (SNS), with its leader, Nenad Popović. The party, which did not garner enough support to hold seats in the parliament, criticized the government's loyalty to Germany as undesirable when it comes to solving the migrant crisis.[71] Popović proposed Trump's model of fences as the most effective strategy:

> The United States built a thousand kilometers of walls and barriers on the border with Mexico with almost two thousand towers and around twenty thousand guards to protect the US territory from illegal and loosely controlled migrants' access. . . . Therefore, Serbia should follow the US example and erect a physical barrier accompanied with army forces on the border with Macedonia. That is the only way to stop illegal access and provide a peaceful life for the citizens of Serbia.[72]

This rhetoric treats immigrants as intruders into nationally owned spaces. The rhetoric of the Hungarian minority party depicts immigrants as a threat to the prosperity of the local communities where SVM voters live. At the same time, this otherizing discursive strategy is aimed at government officials, urging them to solve the migrant problem and financially support the community in its efforts to deal with immigrants. Otherizing as a part of border control and management discourse is also used in the opposition party critique of the government. Finally, some opposition parties, such as the SNS, employ otherizing as a tool to dehumanize migrant bodies as a threat to the nation-state and Serbian citizens.

Overcoming the Binary of Europeanness and Nationalism

The official discourse on migration produces, reproduces, and legiti-mizes three ideologies: Europeanness, nationalism, and xenophobia. These three ideologies simultaneously build on each other and are con-tested. They emerge through multiple levels and enable Serbian political elites to construct migrants, the body of the nation-state, and citizenship through complex discursive strategies. The evident ideologies contest each other by claiming diametrically opposite values and attitudes, for example, European openness and humanitarianism versus a national-istic desire to protect the nation, its spaces, and its economic interests. Rhetorically, the "Europeanized" appeals of the government appear even more humanitarian in contrast to the anti-immigrant complaints of the minor parties. However, even those defending immigration policies concede the challenges posed by the immigrant masses.

Serbia's political and economic aspiration toward EU membership shapes immigration regulation, immigration rhetoric, and Serbia's self-identification within Europe. Europe is constructed as an entity that signifies peace, cooperation, and freedom,[73] and is confined to particular geographical spaces, shaped by legal treaties, and defined by moder-nity, Christianity, and an ambiguous idea of "European values."[74] In opposition to its definition as a peace-signifying, overarching entity of cooperation, solidarity, and unity, the EU is also defined in regard to the "other," those who are positioned outside of the boundaries and the strict criteria for membership in the club called the European Union.[75] Serbia's leaders recognize that their country is outside this "club," while using its humanitarian message to emulate the ideals of the EU. Yet as a "pass-through" country for immigrants, it stands apart from the more economically developed EU countries with which it seeks to identify.

At the same time, Serbia also features a national rhetoric that high-lights its position as a nation-state, its nationhood, and its national identity. This rhetorical emphasis emerges especially in the discourse on control of national borders and unregulated migration.[76] Unlike the rhetoric identifying with Europe, this is a rhetoric of division whereby nationhood and national identity rely on defining who belongs and who does not belong to the nation-state and national identity. While minority parties stress nationalism more than the government, neither can ignore issues of identity and how national actions and attitudes reflect and reinforce it.

While Serbia's immigration rhetoric is built on and reinforces Europeanness and nationalism, it is not simply a discourse that balances those polarized categories. The immigration discourse is a site of contested meanings, competing values, representations, and rhetorical moves of the government to please the EU, by simultaneously welcoming immigrants and shouldering the looming refugee problem, and by otherizing outsiders who are compromising both national and EU borders. Immigrants are ripe for construction as victims of war—a familiar role for Serbians, given the country's tumultuous history—and also as threatening outsiders, whose religion, ethnicity, and ready association with violence and terrorism make them targets for scapegoating.

A rhetorical advantage of Serbia's front-door role in the immigration crisis carries ironic implications for its identity. Leaders can calm fears of threatening outsiders by reminding Serbians that the immigrants are only passing through. That sets up a distinction between desirable EU countries in the West and Serbia's own less desirable status. The government can play the humanitarian while avoiding thorny issues of settlement and multicultural tensions by suggesting that no one—not even desperate refuges—wants to live here.

Serbia's immigrant rhetoric in the twentieth century relates to the complex political, historical, economic, and cultural context of a country on the geographical and political edges of the EU, creating a discursive space in which the Serbian leadership, in nuanced, diplomatic, and sometimes ambiguous ways, moves between Europeanness and nationalism and passes through the existing binary.

Notes

1. "FRAN3 2015, Frontex Risk Analysis Network Quarterly Report," *Frontex*, 2015, frontex.europa.eu.
2. Melissa Eddy, "As Germany Welcomes Migrants, Some Wonder How to Make Acceptance List," *New York Times*, September 5, 2015.
3. Laura Smith-Spark, Vasco Cotovio, and Arwa Damon, "Slovakia Says It Will Take Only Christian Migrants as Europe's Crisis Mushrooms," *CNN*, August 20, 2015.
4. "Serbian PM 'Shocked" at Hungary's Plan for Migrant Fence," *BBC*, June 18, 2015.
5. "Migratory Routes Map," *Frontex*, 2016, frontex.europa.eu.
6. All translations from Serbian are by the author.
7. "Serbia 2013 Progress Report," European Commission, 2013, ec.europa. eu.
8. Maria Todorova, *Imagining the Balkans* (New York: Oxford University Press, 2009).
9. "The Schengen Area and Corporation," *EU-Lex Access to European Union Law*, 2009, eur-lex.europa.eu.
10. Ivo Baučić, *The Effects of Emigration from Yugoslavia and the Problems of Returning Emigrant Workers* (The Hague: Martinus Nijhoff, 1972), 2.
11. Baučić, 2.
12. Baučić, 3.
13. Vesna Lukić et al., "Dynamic Historical Analysis of Longer Term Migratory, Labor Market and Human Capital Processes in Serbia," Country Report Developed within the Project SEEMIG Managing Migration and Its Effects—Transnational Actions Towards Evidence Based Strategies, 13, seemig.eu.
14. "Migracioni Profil Republike Srbije za 2014 Godinu," *Vlada Republike Srbije* (2014): 36.
15. Lukić et al., 12.
16. GDP per capita (Serbia), World Bank, data.worldbank.org.
17. GDP per capita (Germany), World Bank, data.worldbank.org.
18. "Migration and Migrant Population Statistics," European Commission,

ec.europa.edu.

19. Lukić et al., 20.

20. Roma people, or Gypsies, have been historically marginalized when it comes to opportunities for employment, education, health insurance, and quality dwelling. See "Migracioni Profil Republike Srbije za 2014 Godinu," 53, 54, 56.

21. Lukić et al., 13.

22. Lukić et al., 14.

23. The number of refugees in Serbia in 2002 represented 8 percent of Serbia's population (without Kosovo population data). See "Pregled Pravnog i Institucionalnog Okvira Republike Srbije u Oblasti Upravljanja Migracijama," International Organization for Migration (2011), 36.

24. "Pregled Pravnog i Institucionalnog Okvira Republike Srbije u Oblasti Upravljanja Migracijama," 36.

25. "Migracioni Profil Republike Srbije za 2014 Godinu," 57, 62.

26. Sena Marić, Snežana Petijević, and Jana Stojanović, "Analysis: Asylum Seekers in Serbia and Serbian Asylum Seekers in Europe" (2013), 7, https://www.academia.edu/7648815/Analysis_-_asylum_seekers_in_ Serbia_and_Serbian_asylum_seekers_in_Europe.

27. Mirjana Bobić, "Imigracija u Srbiji: Stanje i Perspektiva, Tolerancija i Integracija," *Demography* 10 (2013): 107.

28. Marić et al., 7.

29. "Migracioni Profil Republike Srbije za 2014 Godinu," 13, 14.

30. "Migracioni Profil Republike Srbije za 2014 Godinu," 18, 21, 22.

31. Branislava Knežević and Vojin Vidanović, "Problemi Azilanata u Srbiji," *Srpska Politička Misao* 4 (2011): 425, 426.

32. Lukić et al., 20.

33. Marić et al., 19, 20.

34. Marić et al., 7.

35. Marić et al., 8.

36. Marić et al., 10.

37. "Migracioni Profil Republike Srbije za 2014 Godinu," 46.

38. "Migracioni Profil Republike Srbije za 2014 Godinu," 48, 49.

39. Marić et al., 7.
40. "Migracioni Profil Republike Srbije za 2014 Godinu," 49.
41. "Migracioni Profil Republike Srbije za 2014 Godinu," 50.
42. Marić et al., 15, 16.
43. Marić et al., 8.
44. "Case Information Sheet: Vojislav Šešelj," International Criminal Tribunal for the Former Yugoslavia, icty.org.
45. "Osuda Podmetanja Požara u Objektu aa Smeštaj Tražilaca Azila," *Vlada Republike Srbije*, November 28, 2013, srbija.gov.rs.
46. "Osuda Podmetanja Požara u Objektu aa Smeštaj Tražilaca Azila."
47. Fonet/Beta, "Azilanti Moraju da se Smeste," *Blic*, December 12, 2013, blic.rs.
48. "Usvojena Strategija za Rešavanje Pitanja Izbeglica u Srbiji," *Vlada Republike Srbije*, July 10, 2015, srbija.gov.rs; "Srbija Pokazala Evropsko Lice u Odnosu Prema Migrantima," *Vlada Republike Srbije*, October 1, 2015, srbija.gov.rs; "Srbija Neće Biti Ostavljena Sama da Rešava Problem Migranata," *Vlada Republike Srbije*, September 25, 2015, srbija.gov.rs.
49. "Srbija se Ponaša u Skladu sa Evropskim Vrednostima," *Vlada Republike Srbije*, September 16, 2015, srbija.gov.rs.
50. "Srbija Spremna da Preuzme Svoj Deo Odgovornosti za Migrante," *Vlada Republike Srbije*, September 4, 2015, srbija.gov.rs.
51. "Srbija će Očuvati Bezbednost Svojih Građana," *Vlada Republike Srbije*, November 17, 2015, srbija.gov.rs.
52. "Oko," *RTS*, September 10, 2015, youtube.com.
53. "Oko."
54. Institut Poslaničkih Pitanja Poslednjeg Četvrtka u Mesecu, *Skupšina Srbije*, July 30, 2015, parlament.gov.rs.
55. "Budućnost Briselskog Dijaloga Zavisi od Sprovođenja Sporazuma," *Vlada Republike Srbije*, October 30, 2015, srbija.gov.rs.
56. "Srbija Spremna na Dijalog u Regionu Zbog Migranata," *Vlada Republike Srbije*, October 19, 2015, srbija.gov.rs.
57. "Privremeni Prihvatni Centar za Migrante u Beogradu," *Vlada Republike Srbije*, August 19, 2015, srbija.gov.rs. "Neophodno Sveobuhvatno Rešenje za Migrantsku Krizu," *Vlada Republike Srbije*, September 21, 2015, srbija.

gov.rs. "Srbija Neće Biti Ostavljena da Sama Rešava Problem Migranta," *Vlada Republike Srbije*, September 25, 2015, srbija.gov.rs.

58. "Delegacija Poslaničke Grupe Prijateljstva Austrija-Srbija u Poseti Narodnoj Skupštini," *Skupština Republike Srbije*, October 27, 2015, parlament.gov.rs.

59. Ruth Wodak, "Discourses in European Union Organizations: Aspects of Access, Participation and Exclusion," *Text & Talk* 27 (2007): 655–680.

60. "Srbija će Znati da Zaštiti Svoje Interese," *Vlada Republike Srbije*, November 16, 2015, srbija.gov.rs.

61. "Neophodno da EU Utvrdi Plan za Rešavanje Problema Migranata," *Vlada Republike Srbije*, August 27, 2015, srbija.gov.rs.

62. "Saradnja sa Bugarskom i Rumunijom u Rešavanju Migrantske Krize," *Vlada Republike Srbije*, October 24, 2015, srbija.gov.rs.

63. "Neophodno da EU Utvrdi Plan Za Rešavanje Problema Migranata," *Vlada Republike Srbije*, August 27, 2015, srbija.gov.rs. "Srbija Spremna na Dijalog u Regionu Zbog Migranata."

64. Institut Poslaničkih Pitanja Poslednjeg Četvrtka u Mesecu, Skupšina Srbije.

65. "Srbija će Očuvati Bezbednost Svojih Građana."

66. "Dijalog Ključ Regionalne Stabilnosti," *Vlada Republike Srbije*, September 28, 2015, srbija.gov.rs.

67. "Dijalog Ključ Regionalne Stabilnosti."

68. "Srpski Radikali Zahtevaju Zaštitu Granica Srbije Zbog Nekontrolisanog Ulaska Migranata," *Srpska Radikalna Stranka*, August 13, 2015, srpskaradikalnastranka.org.rs.

69. Institut Poslaničkih Pitanja Poslednjeg Četvrtka u Mesecu, *Skupšina Srbije*.

70. Institut Poslaničkih Pitanja Poslednjeg Četvrtka u Mesecu, *Skupšina Srbije*.

71. "SNP: Zašto 'lojalnost' Srbije Nemačkoj u Migrantskoj Krizi," *Srpska Narodna Partija*, December 6, 2015, srpskanarodnapartija.rs.

72. "Nenad Popović: Primeniti Američka Iskustva u Zaštiti Granica od Migranata," *Srpska Narodna Partija*, February 4, 2016, srpskanarodnapartija. rs.

73. Bo Strath, "Belonging and European Identity," in *Identity, Belonging and Migration*, ed. Paul Jones, Ruth Wodak, and Gerard Delanty (Liverpool:

Liverpool University Press, 2008), 21–37.

74. Wodak.

75. Kati Tonkin, "Opening Borders, Framing Identities: The 'Return to Europe' in Jan Gogola's *Ceske Valenice Evropske*," *Journal of European Studies* 45 (2015): 122–136.

76. Emily Ironside and Lisa M. Corrigan, "Constituting Enemies through Fear: The Rhetoric of Exclusionary Nationalism in the Control of "un-American" Immigrant Populations," in *Rhetoric of U.S. Immigration: Identity, Community, Otherness*, ed. E. Johanna Hartelius (University Park: Penn State University Press, 2015).

Political Rhetoric
in the Refugee Crisis in Greece

Yiannis Karayiannis and Anthoula Malkopoulou

growing concern about the ongoing refugee crisis in the Mediterranean lies at the heart of current public discussions and controversies in Europe. It is estimated that over a million people arrived to Europe by sea in 2015 alone, while many hundreds lost their lives attempting to do so.[1] The impact of massive arrivals on the economic, social, and cultural life of EU nation-states often has been interpreted negatively, giving rise to xenophobic and anti-immigrant political attitudes. Exploiting these attitudes, far-right parties and extreme political movements have soared across the EU countries, embodying a serious threat for democratic viability.[2] Under these circumstances, the EU has been struggling to manage the crisis in a manner that is effective and compatible with its political values. But so far the refugee crisis has exposed the difficulties of EU consolidation, and the union's limited ability to play a leading role in a rapidly changing global order.

If we add to the huge numbers of refugees the difficult domestic economic situation in the main receiving states like Greece and Italy, divisions and inequalities among EU member-states are intensified. Especially regarding Greece, the refugee crisis constitutes "a crisis within the crisis," as it has been aptly noted,[3] since it hit during a deep financial depression that entered its eighth consecutive year in 2016. The urgent need to address the financial crisis simultaneously with the refugee crisis was exacerbated by the "entrapment" of a significant number of refugees in Greek territory.[4] According to data from the Greek police, in 2015 no less than 911,471 arrests of undocumented immigrants were recorded, an extremely high number compared to previous years (77,163 in 2014).[5] Very fast the refugee/migrant issue has become a political one,[6] which parties frame either in a manner that favors the social integration of immigrants or in a manner that encourages xenophobia and anti-immigrant attitudes.

Following the general increase in research on anti-immigration attitudes, these issues have been systematically explored also in Greece.[7] Some of these studies have focused on Greek immigration discourse, including parliamentary and media discourse.[8] However, little attention has been paid to *how* political party discourse and speeches by party leaders frame this issue, especially in the midst of the ongoing crisis. In other words, what is missing is a comprehensive account of Greek political leaders' rhetoric on the refugee/migrant crisis, which shapes domestic policies and public attitudes and promotes specific perceptions, evaluations, and judgments. Our aim is to fill this gap by studying the ongoing refugee/migrant crisis in Greece from the point of view of "rhetorical political analysis," that is, how political discourse forms arguments and shapes meanings concerning this issue, in order to justify and promote specific goals.[9]

We will pay special attention to metaphors, which are a key rhetorical device used in order to establish specific meanings. In their seminal work George Lakoff and Mark Johnson underline that metaphors do not primarily constitute properties of language but rather of thought.[10] According to Lakoff and Johnson, "Metaphors . . . are conceptual in nature. They are among our principal vehicles for understanding. And they play a central role in the construction of social and political reality."[11] The metaphorical association of an abstract notion with a concrete thing establishes specific meanings about it, by highlighting some aspects and hiding others. For example, the metaphorical definition of politics as "power struggle" highlights the contentious character of politics at the expense of the collaborative one. In that sense, metaphors may function strategically, as tools of persuasion, since they favor specific views and understandings; as such, they can also enhance partisan ties and feelings of belonging.[12] Especially, so-called discourse metaphors[13] decisively frame issues and the language used in connection to them, and function as keys to broader patterns of thinking. In sum, metaphors perform multiple cognitive, emotional, and ideological functions and are an integral part of political discourse,[14] which is why our analysis pays special attention to them.

The chapter proceeds as follows: First, we offer a brief overview of Greek political culture and immigration policy that serves as a background to understand recent developments. This part includes also a short description of rhetorical differences between the main political actors. Second, we concentrate on the immigration and refugee rhetoric of two main political parties in the current historical conjuncture, that is, Nea Dimokratia (New Democracy, ND) and Synaspismos Rizospastikes Aristeras (Coalition of the Radical Left, SYRIZA).[15] During the ongoing refugee/migrant crisis these two political parties have been the main players in government and opposition respectively; most importantly, they express diametrically opposed views regarding the nature and solutions of this crisis. We examine speeches of their political leaders (namely, Alexis Tsipras for SYRIZA and Antonis Samaras for ND) that were given in different contexts and moments in the lifetime of the crisis. In the conclusion, we outline and compare the main metaphors and rhetorical descriptions used in these speeches and sketch the general contours of the current refugee/immigration rhetoric in Greece.

An Overview of Greek Asylum and Immigration Politics

The Greek state favors a strictly defined national, religious, and linguistic identity. Based on the conservative principle of *jus sanguinis*, Greek citizenship law is one of the least generous in the European continent: it requires seven years of residency for adult foreigners (it was 10 years before 2010) and had until recently denied citizenship to children of noncitizens born, raised and schooled in Greece.[16] The Greek Orthodox Church is per the constitution recognized as the country's official creed and enjoys extensive institutional privileges. Further, despite a continuous presence of traditional non-Greek speakers, the Greek state has never recognized the presence of linguistic minorities on Greek soil. In other words, through these policies, Greece is neither very welcoming nor accommodating as a receiving state for foreigners.

Indeed, the immigration policies in Greece have been haphazard and ill disposed. In 2011, the foreign population amounted to roughly 11 percent of the overall population, including coethnic, legal, and illegal immigrants at roughly equal proportions. The first category comprised Greek co-ethnics, who arrived in the 1990s from the dismantled Soviet Union and were granted citizenship almost automatically; co-ethnics from Albania were also granted special status after 2007. The second category, legal immigrants, also came mostly from Albania—the ethnicity that makes up 60 percent of the foreign population in Greece (in 2011)—as well as other Balkan and southern Asia countries. Despite the growing number of legal arrivals through the 2000s, however, the country did not develop a comprehensive program of immigration management and integration. Regulations were ad hoc, reacting to actual migration flows through regularization programs; or instrumental, aimed at creating a cheap and temporary labor force.[17] Stay permits, granted mostly to seasonal workers, were short and hard to obtain. Social, cultural, and political marginalization was the norm. As a final blow, the economic crisis that hit the country in 2008 has seriously aggravated the state of insecurity and unemployment of Greece's migrant stock.[18]

After 2007, the stark increase of arrivals at its eastern land and sea border forced Greece to change its policy and redirect resources and targeted EU funds to the management of illegal migration. Border controls were given priority, and the number of apprehensions became overwhelming, as Greece became by far the main entry point for unauthorized entry to the EU.[19] The joint European force Frontex reinforced policing resources, and a 10 km fence was built at the Evros land border with Turkey. Despite these changes the pressure continued, not least because of the Dublin II Regulation that assigned responsibility for examining EU asylum applications to the country of entry of the applicants. This led to an extensive use of detention in notoriously overcrowded facilities with appalling living conditions (such as the Amygdaleza center). Detention policy was complemented with a feeble program of forced and voluntary returns.[20]

Meanwhile, the EU adapted its asylum policy to the urgent realities. Screening and first reception centers were set up in main spots of entry into Greece after 2013. Asylum services were also bolstered, and several EU countries unilaterally suspended implementation of the Dublin II regulation, thus offering some relief to Greek authorities. In response to the dramatic increase of Syrian refugees and smuggled migrants arriving to Greece by sea in 2015, the EU reached an infamous agreement with Turkey on March 18, 2016: illegal immigrants would be readmitted to Turkey and Syrian refugees from Turkey resettled directly to EU countries.[21] In reality, however, the category of persons to be returned was defined in a manner that could include refugees and asylum seekers; further, considering political turmoil in Turkey, the success of this new policy is in question.[22]

Although Greece's refugee/migrant policy is to a large extent determined by EU decisions, political parties are key actors in shaping public opinion. Immigration rhetoric is therefore best understood in connection to the national political context. Greece is a multiparty, parliamentary democracy, with an electoral system of reinforced proportionality that allocates one-sixth of seats as a bonus to the party receiving the largest number of votes. This creates a majoritarian government-opposition effect, parallel to the presence of smaller parties. Following the elections of September 2015, the Greek parliament featured eight parties. The leading government party is democratic socialist SYRIZA, and the leading opposition party is the liberal conservative ND. Together they hold 219 out of 300 seats in the parliament. Among the six minor parties that share the remaining 81 seats, one is communist, one social democratic, two liberal/centrist, one national conservative, and one ultranationalist.[23] Altogether, Greek parties represent a broad array of immigration-related ideological viewpoints that range from ethnic nationalism and racism to inclusive humanitarianism.

Is anti-immigration rhetoric prevalent in Greece? Despite the significant migration flows in the country from the 1990s onward, the issue of immigration had not caused intensive political debates and new party cleavages as in other European countries before the late 2000s. Anti-immigration rhetoric was first used by LAOS, a minor ultranationalist party present in the Greek parliament only from 2007 until 2012. Xenophobic talk was then taken over by ultranationalist Golden Dawn (GD), which embraces biological racism and violence and describes foreigners as "subhuman carriers of disease."[24] It has had a steady 7 percent electoral support since 2012, despite the trial of its leader and many of its MPs and party members on grave criminal charges (ongoing as of early 2019). Another nationalist actor is the Independent Greeks (ANEL), currently a minor government coalition partner.[25] In addition to them, the main conservative party, ND, is also highly critical of immigration, as this paper aims to show. To give a picture of the general scope of anti-immigration party attitudes in Greece, these three parties voted against granting citizenship to second-generation immigrant children in July 2015: New Democracy, the Independent Greeks, and Golden Dawn.[26]

In what follows, we will present an overview and analysis of the political rhetoric pertaining to immigration used by the leaders of the two dominant Greek parties, SYRIZA and ND. One can discern a clear and qualitative differentiation between the two parties in terms of ideology, rhetoric, and policy. Antonis Samaras, ND prime minister from 2012 until 2015, has in general favored a tough stance against immigration, justified through appeals to security and public order. On the other hand, the subsequent prime minister since 2015 and leader of SYRIZA since 2009, Alexis Tsipras, has promoted a paradigm of humanitarian solidarity and inclusion, often posited against a parsimonious EU policy on asylum and immigration. The presentation of Greek political rhetoric through the perspective of two political parties may strike the reader as a binary construction that overlooks gray zones and more nuanced perspectives. Despite such appearances, our goal is not to present the rhetorical playing field as black and white, but simply to narrow the scope of analysis. By focusing on two diametrically opposed descriptions of the refugee/ migrant crisis, we hope to allow for a more in-depth understanding of the qualitative divide between government and opposition on this policy field and the discourse that surrounds it.

New Democracy's "Security" Rhetoric

As mentioned earlier, the main conservative party, New Democracy (ND), is very skeptical of immigration, and, as a result, immigrants figure in its rhetoric in a mostly negative light. Most of the time, the refugee/ migrant crisis is approached in terms of "smuggled immigration" (*lathro-metanastefsi*), rather than a question of refugees and asylum seekers. The unlawful activity of "smuggled immigrants" is conceived as a threat to national security, social cohesion, and the national economy. It is argued that Greece's society and economy have no capacity to integrate a high number of immigrants, only a (minor) part of them who legally enter the country.

This line of argument was first adopted by the previous leader of the ND Konstantinos Karamanlis (1997–2009) and was significantly expanded by Antonis Samaras, who succeeded the former in the party leadership (2009–2015). Samaras called more attention than before to the question of immigration, which he tout court associated with illegal smuggling, a move that deliberately neglects distinctions between legal immigrants, illegal immigrants, and refugees entitled to international protection. "The issue is not whether you would call it illegal immigration or smuggled immigration," he said. "Whatever you call it, it is something that we must address immediately."[27]

According to Samaras, "smuggled immigration" has a serious negative impact on national economy, which becomes more acute due to the financial crisis. As he argued, "Today, when the country cannot cover the basic needs of its own taxpayers, they [SYRIZA] promise to millions of illegal smuggled immigrants unemployment benefits."[28] In addition, "smuggled immigrants" are involved in the "black economy" and "black trade," which "kills," as he asserted, the legal trade and the economy.[29]

> Smuggled immigrants export currency from Greece to countries outside the Euro. This cannot continue. They cannot legally export currency from illegal work! This will be checked. And will be taxed. We cannot chase those working legally for the last euro, while illegals are completely unchecked."[30]

By conflating all immigrants with illegal immigrants and, more importantly, by juxtaposing them to legally working nationals, he articulated the common topos "immigrants are stealing our jobs," which underlies most anti-immigrant populist rhetoric today.

In addition to being associated with illegal economic activities, "smuggled immigrants" are also claimed to threaten social security and public order since the country has no capacity to integrate the entire number of immigrants. In Samaras' words:

> The . . . dilemma that we face . . . is between security and fear. Today, when criminality is rampant, they [SYRIZA] want to disarm the police! Today, when Greece is swarming with illegal smuggled immigrants they invite them to bring their . . . families too![31]

And elsewhere he notes:

They [SYRIZA] never explained to us how social cohesion will be maintained if we give legalizing papers to all smuggled immigrants, if we disarm the police, if we hand out money that does not exist even to those who entered the country illegally.[32]

In this tone, the policy of "open borders" that is supported by SYRIZA is rejected on the grounds that it will cause significant problems in Greece's relation with other EU countries. As Samaras stated, "SYRIZA wants an *internally broken* Greece, with millions of smuggled immigrants, now legal, together with their families. And *externally isolated*, with no international support."[33] According to Samaras, addressing the problem of "smuggled immigration" implies a reform of the existing legal framework;[34] it also requires cooperation between EU countries since a single member state cannot sufficiently address it. As Samaras noted, "We are trying to repatriate them [the smuggled immigrants]. And this has already started. But to continue, it requires a common European policy and decisive support from Europe's side."[35]

The policy of "open borders" is denounced not only for its detrimental effects on the country but also for nourishing political radicalism and far-right movements. Especially with reference to Greece, Samaras argues that this policy fuels the rise of the neo-Nazi party Golden Dawn. He states, "When their [SYRIZA's] position is that we need to legalize all smuggled migrants, are they thus not serving the neo-Nazis?"[36]

All in all, immigrants themselves are described in very negative terms. Samaras's presentation of the refugee/migrant crisis as primarily a matter of "smuggled immigration" that has terrible effects on Greek society and economy portrays immigrants as agents of danger and harm. Although it is at times recognized that "smuggled immigrants" are "desperate people" who risk their life for a better future, it is stressed that they do participate in and in essence serve an illegal and harmful activity. As Samaras stated,

As you saw, human tragedies occur like a few fortnights ago with the shipwreck in Italy's Lampedusa, where hundreds of lives of smuggled migrants were lost. Only if there are incentives and facilitations for mass repatriations will these "caravans of the desperate" stop. We must and can as Europe fully shield our borders . . . [and] give prospects and hope to these peoples to stay in their countries. . . . Smuggled migration does not solve any problem. It merely allows—and we must be saying this straight—the most hideous trade to flourish: the human trade that is [properly] called slave trade! It allows traffickers to make a fortune. And it transfers the unrest from the most destabilized regions to the rest of the world.[37]

With this line of argument, which presents immigrants as agents of harm, Samaras seeks to discourage immigration to Greece. It does so by associating immigration to aggression and illegality. In his own words,

Desperate people from various troubled areas are trying to get into Europe. They enter Greece because it is geographically possible. And then they get trapped in Greece, since no other European country accepts them. We look at these people with love and compassion. We understand [their] anxieties and despairs. But they cannot stay in our Country. Neither our society nor our economy can bear them. *Our cities cannot be under occupation anymore. Our citizens cannot abandon their neighborhoods and feel absolute insecurity.* Greece cannot become a reception center for millions of smuggled immigrants from around the world! This is simply not possible. Make no mistake; this is not an issue of ideology or obsession. It simply cannot be done and we are not discussing it.[38]

Rhetorically, the conception of "smuggled immigration" as a threat to national security and social cohesion is highlighted through the use of certain metaphors. As has already been noted, the commonplace perception promoted is that of the limited capacity of the national economy and of the country to accept a large number of foreign citizens. The metaphor used to give this impression of limited capacity is that of a "container," a box with restricted space and limited air inside, which is a common topos of anti-immigration rhetoric in Europe.[39] As Samaras argued, "Greece is *overflowing* with smuggled immigrants," and "We are gradually clearing the neighborhoods that were *suffocating*."[40] These metaphors of spatial limits seek to support a specific view of immigration as intrusive, unwelcome, and eventually harmful, all the while promoting the idea of legitimate native residents versus illegitimate newcomers.

Further, "smuggled immigration" is given a negative signification by being designated as a threat. Metaphorically this is expressed with references to catastrophic events such as "floods" and "waves" that disturb the tranquility of the sea. As Samaras argued, "There is no Greek, or any serious party, that objects to ending and reversing the *waves* of smuggled immigrants."[41] In another occasion he stated: "Until a few years ago, my friends, the Country's borders were full of holes from the *waves* of smuggled immigrants . . . [enabled by] the ones who want to *flood* the country with smuggled immigrants."[42]

The rhetorical framing of "smuggled immigration" as a threat is not limited to the vocabulary of natural disaster. Precisely in order to reflect the immigrants' agency in a process that undermines national security and the country's social cohesion, the threat is represented metaphorically also in terms of a war situation. In this context, migrants are classified as "invaders" that need to be confronted. As Samaras stated:

> In the last year we have done a lot! We stopped the influx of smuggled immigrants. And we have started slowly to limit them. In the domain of public safety we've done in the last year things that have not been done for many years. And we did all these in line with all preconditions of humane treatment. We do not shoot unarmed women and children at the borders, or sink boats with smuggled immigrants. We do not do such things. Yet, we cannot accept an "unarmed invasion."[43]

The metaphorical representation of the immigration crisis with war terms was repeated on several occasions. For example: "My New Democracy brothers, in recent years our Country suffered an 'unarmed invasion' of hundreds of thousands of smuggled immigrants. . . . And we cannot let the seismic waves of upheaval in our [regional] neighborhood dismantle the Country."[44] In such warlike conditions, the proposed government policies are justified in order to restrain the enemy. This offers a chance to claim credit—"In the last two and a half years, we curbed the flow of smuggled immigrants"[45]—which is often done through the infamous bellicose motto of "recapturing" the cities from illegal immigrants:

> We began a real campaign to strike a blow against illegal immigration systematically and at all levels. We have managed only the first steps so far. And the picture is changing everywhere, mainly in city centers, which have been occupied by smuggled immigrants and had surrendered to their illegal activities. The "recapturing" of our cities, which we had promised, began. When we took over, Greece was a country without a capital city! Today the law is in place and is applied in each square meter of downtown Athens.[46]

In addition to recapturing the inner cities, the image of "unarmed intruders" implies a need to defend the national territory from external attacks and threats. This rhetorical circumscription of the national land is made through the overused metaphor of an "unfenced vineyard" (*xefrago ampeli*), a colloquial phrase that describes uncontrolled access to private property. As Samaras stated:

> Greece is no longer an "unfenced vineyard." . . . And the road is open also for the repatriation of smuggled immigrants and for the distribution of those who cannot be repatriated in all [European] Union countries, so they do not get trapped in Greece, which cannot accommodate more, and they cannot go elsewhere, and nobody else wants them.[47]

Similarly, Samaras accused the opposition party SYRIZA of wanting Greece to be an "unfenced vineyard."[48] The interesting aspect to this metaphor is that it performs at least three functions. First, the complaint that Greece is reduced to an "unfenced vineyard" reinforces the identification of Greek nationals with their national territory, which should be closed to outsiders. Second, it emphasizes the importance of private property and ownership, which are high priorities and values for the liberal conservative party ND. Third, and perhaps more important, this specific metaphor familiarizes the public with the idea and the policy of actual fencing; this is an important bridge to the debate on the construction of a 10 km border fence in the Evros land border with Turkey. In other words, the description of Greece as an "unfenced vineyard" serves at once as a nationalist, neoliberal, and anti-immigrant argument.

In sum, Samaras's use of metaphors and political rhetoric represents the general strategy of his party, ND, to securitize the immigration issue. Immigrants are portrayed as a threat equivalent to floods and wars or abusive intruders, which reinforces rhetorically the binary construction of "us"—the legitimate residents of the country under attack—and "them"—the ill-motivated criminal newcomers. The racist ideological construct underlying this classification will become clearer when compared with the opposite rhetorical strategy of solidarity and integration adopted by ND's rival, SYRIZA.

The Solidarity-Humanitarian Argument

As in the case of ND, SYRIZA's arguments for the refugee/migrant crisis are presented in several institutional contexts (parliament, election campaigns, party conventions, etc.), and remain consistent during the party's terms both in opposition and in government. Like ND, SYRIZA also considers the refugee/migrant crisis as a matter of utmost importance. But, unlike ND, it does so not because of security concerns but because it constitutes a major humanitarian problem and highlights the asymmetries within the EU.[49] It is "the most important issue threatening Europe today" and "one of the most serious regional and global challenges to be faced by the EU in years," threatening the very political credibility and identity of the EU.[50] In general, it "brings to the surface major questions with a deep ideological and humanistic content."[51]

According to SYRIZA, the refugee/migrant crisis is particularly acute in host countries such as Greece. As explained by PM Tsipras, the number of arrivals more than doubled between 2013 and 2015 and would continue to increase. Yet he noted that "over 80 percent of new arrivals are people with a refugee profile (Syrians at 60 percent, Afghans, Somalis, and Eritreans)." Nevertheless, he added, the amount of new arrivals "by far exceeds the capacity of our hosting infrastructure, especially in a period of deep economic and social crisis."[52]

There are several reasons why this large number of refugees and immigrants is difficult to control and accommodate successfully. One is the need to respect human rights, especially socioeconomic rights, which is difficult to do given the economic crisis that the country faces, but also the security crisis stemming from the political instability in the region.[53] But a key factor influencing how the refugee crisis is being dealt with, according to SYRIZA, is the deep division within the EU that is currently dominated by a political ideology alien to its proclaimed values. In these conditions, major coordination problems arise from the conflicting policies adopted to address the refugee crisis.[54] As Tsipras stated, "We need to manage a huge refugee crisis, which brings to the surface the great political conflicts that divide Europe from one end to the other, but also each country separately."[55]

It is argued that the prevailing EU policy on the refugee/migrant crisis is unable to tackle it effectively. As Tsipras stated, "A common Europe of peoples with a social orientation cannot exist as long as immigration is treated as a problem of external border security and as long as police repression is prioritized."[56] This handling of the refugee crisis clashes, according to SYRIZA, with the values and political ideals of the European Union. As Tsipras stated,

> When the Mediterranean becomes a wet grave, when the Aegean is washing up dead children, then European civilization itself is in crisis, the very concept of a united Europe. Because when a united Europe has a respected set of rules involving fiscal discipline and does not have solidarity as a supreme value, leaving each member state alone in front of a major European crisis, then this Europe cannot have anything to do with the Europe of its founding values, nor can it even have a future.[57]

Likewise, he noted: "Our humanity is being tested, our effectiveness is being tested, Europe's ability to share the burden and act as a real Union is being tested."[58] To sum up, a large part of SYRIZA's rhetoric goes to criticizing the EU for handling the refugee crisis in a nonhumanitarian manner.

Conversely, the party denounces the EU's policy as a springboard for racist and xenophobic attitudes that facilitate the rise of far-right political parties.[59] In response, Europe "must show its open, humanitarian face against the crisis that has developed and close the door to the far right, racism, and xenophobia, which raise their head all over Europe."[60] As Tsipras stated in another occasion:

> Against the logic of fortresses, walls, and fences, against the logic that wants to turn European borders into a battlefield, we firmly believe that we must work hard to prove that humanity, solidarity, hospitality are not utopias of some romantics but are still the dominant values of the European edifice and can become political practice.[61]

In addition, the current EU policy is unable to tackle the refugee/migrant crisis effectively because it is based on an approach that does not correspond to the real causes that created it.[62] In Tsipras's words, the vast majority of people who move to Europe via Greece are "refugees fleeing wars and conflicts . . . that we as a global community failed to manage and resolve effectively."[63] It is a "global drama," he concludes, "created by an erratic foreign policy and military interventions of the West."[64] Elsewhere he states: "People who are stacked and die at our borders are not immigrants but refugees. This means that Greece has an international and European obligation to secure human conditions of reception and living [for these people]."[65]

In other words, SYRIZA's rhetoric constructs an identity of new arrivals as refugees rather than immigrants. It paints the picture of people whose lives are at risk, rather than people who greedily seek a better lifestyle. They are innocent victims who must be protected without exception, since "Protecting the refugee figure is a historical legacy of

European civilization, and one of the most important issues at stake concerning the future of our societies."[66] In sum, Tsipras builds the following narrative: the European Union and frontline countries like Greece are facing a refugee and not an immigration crisis; as a result, there is a need for a shared, pan-European response when dealing with global humanitarian emergencies. In response, SYRIZA claims to have launched appropriate policy initiatives and adopted special measures, and it has also communicated the problem to the EU, which has led to an adjustment of refugee management strategies.[67]

To change the mental representation of the crisis cultivated by ND rhetoric from a dangerous national threat to a humanitarian crisis, SYRIZA PM Tsipras deployed a different set of metaphors. First of all, the view of the refugee/migrant crisis as a problem caused by cruel wars and civil strife is metaphorically conveyed by the term "refugee flows" (*prosfygikes roes*). This term replaced the party's own earlier references to refugee and immigration "waves" (*kymata*), or "undocumented immigration."[68] The replacement was a strategic move by SYRIZA to change the terms of the debate set by ND and rid it of negative connotations of natural disaster and criminality that were alien to SYRIZA's own approach to the refugee crisis.[69] In other words, the use of the new term "refugee flows" neutralizes the perceived impact of refugees on the domestic economy and society, as it creates an impression that new arrivals are temporary and transitioning (i.e., flowing) through Greece. At the same time, the reference to "refugee flows" makes the phenomenon impersonal, since it puts the emphasis on the products of a larger process and not on the individual agency of each refugee/immigrant. For SYRIZA, refugees are the innocent victims of wars and of the destructive policies of the West in various parts of the world, rather than agents of the problem they seem to cause.

Conversely, it is implied that the policy of closed borders is unnatural and inhuman and only serves to shape conditions of capture and death. As Tsipras argued:

> Greece in recent years, due to policy choices that were not aimed
> at distributing responsibility—because Europe above all means

solidarity—has unfortunately turned into a negative example of a warehouse of human souls, which of course suits those who want to criticize Greece, but this does not give any solutions to the problem.[70]

The closed-border policy is for SYRIZA a disgrace for European civilization. On the occasion of the much-reported drowning of a three-year-old Syrian refugee boy, washed up on a Turkish beach, Tsipras made a forceful statement: "The Aegean Sea yesterday washed ashore the European civilization on the coast of Bodrum."[71] Trying to link this failure of European values to the rise of racist and far-right parties, he connected the unwillingness to address the refugee problem in a coordinated and humane way to memories from the deplorable European past of Nazi atrocities:

> When every country is left alone to face what it cannot, then the trains of shame appear, the trains of the hunted, that Europe would like to have erased forever from its collective memory. Then even the most bigoted, the most dangerous far-right cries from the heart of Europe can be heard loudly.[72]

In sum, addressing the refugee crisis can be recapped, according to SYRIZA, in two opposing images of Europe and its values. On one side is the tendency to undermine the logic of solidarity between EU member states, to promote the "enclosing" of the European area and to adopt policies for containing refugees. On the other side is the logic of solidarity between member states, an attempt to do justice to European civilization and its values with immigrant integration policies and respect for human rights. The conflict between these two sets of policies is underlined by Tsipras:

> Which is the Europe that we envisage? The Europe of the baker from Kos, who distributes his remaining bread to refugee children? Or the Europe of the Hungarian prime minister, who builds fences and distributes bullets? The Europe of poor [islands of] Lesvos and Kos, which despite the crisis hosted tens of thousands of refugees, or the

Europe of the wealthy state of Bavaria that, despite its prosperity, does not accept to host even thirty thousand of them? A fortress Europe that will have its eyes closed to the disasters that itself causes?[73]

SYRIZA is of course passionately supporting "the baker from Kos," a figure of humanitarian sacrifice in support of the victims of war even in conditions of domestic poverty. This is a conscious choice from a left-wing party that stands in stark contrast to hostile language against refugees by right-wing governments at home and abroad. SYRIZA's distinct political and ideological stance on the refugee/migrant crisis is represented not only through the very meaning of its arguments, but also through the rhetorical framing of these arguments. The party leader deliberately introduces keywords that are either neutral or positive toward refugees and migrants. In this way, Greece's left party tries to change the terms through which the refugee/migrant crisis is debated and perceived in the national context.

Conclusions

The analysis of recent Greek political rhetoric shows that the ongoing refugee/migrant crisis is not a matter locked into one "objective" perspective. Instead, it is a field of contentious politics and antagonistic meanings and interpretations attached to specific arguments. Indeed, apart from a few points of convergence, the two leading political parties under examination frame the refugee/migrant crisis in a completely different manner. These differences are connected to their broader disagreements about the European Union, economic development, and social cohesion; they also reflect two distinct value systems and political visions. Therefore, it is plausible to argue that the perception of this crisis is basically conditioned by various and often opposed ideological viewpoints.

The case of Greece demonstrates how political parties formulate their views about the refugee/migrant crisis into competing arguments based on their broader political and ideological beliefs. From the rhetorical point of view, these arguments involve distinctive metaphorical schemes, appeal to different commonplaces and acceptances, and are based on alternate types of reasoning. Through these arguments, political leaders seek to promote specific meanings and perceptions. They are also used to enhance partisan ties and mobilize the public toward specific political actions.

Despite the deep-seated antagonism between the two parties, they also share some common points. First, both political parties agree that the current unprecedented refugee/migrant crisis must be immediately and drastically addressed. This is the case especially for Greece, because it is a geographical entry point of refugees and migrants to the EU, and because it suffers from a deep financial recession that minimizes its capacity to integrate and support newcomers effectively. Second, both political parties acknowledge that Greece has no capacity to address this issue alone; instead, it needs the EU's contribution. Thus, the government must urgently put the issue at the top of the EU policy agenda.

However, these points of convergence are combined with a directly opposed set of proposed solutions. Moreover, both parties accuse the other of having policies that encourage extreme-right political movements and enhance xenophobic attitudes and anti-immigrant feelings. First of all, the two parties identify different causes for the emergence of the refugee/migrant crisis and, by extension, adopt different views about the identity of new arrivals. ND perceives the issue mainly as the result of illegal activity of immigrants and their smugglers. From this point of view, they argue that most new arrivals are "smuggled immigrants" (*lathrometanastes*) rather than refugees, a pejorative term that represents them as agents or willful participants in organized crime (smuggled immigration). On the contrary, for SYRIZA the new arrivals are mostly refugees, innocent victims fleeing wars and military interventions in several countries, unwillingly driven out of their homelands.

Second, the two parties detect different risks that arise from the influx of foreigners. For ND the illegal activity of traffickers and immigrants constitutes a threat to internal security and social cohesion. It has also a significant impact on economic development since these il-legal activities undermine the national economy and discourage private investments. On the contrary, for SYRIZA the refugee/migrant crisis generates a very different concern. What is at stake, rather, are the politi-cal integrity of the EU—its ability to solve the problems it is confronted with in a manner that distributes the burden fairly among member-states and is in accordance to its commitment to human rights, humanitarian protection, and international peace.

Third, the two parties adopt very different policy discourses regard-ing the refugee/migrant crisis. The proposed policies by ND focus on preventing refugees from coming to Greece and, by synecdoche, to Europe. To this end, its political discourse is replete with proposals of punitive measures that block illegal immigration. On the contrary, in the political discourse of SYRIZA, proposed policies favor solidarity activities and actions that promote the social inclusion of refugees and by extension their social and economic development. Especially for host countries like Greece, this policy of "open borders" is acknowledged as necessary in order to prevent the entrapping of refugees against their will.

Fourth, the arguments we have mentioned imply a dissimilar narra-tive about the EU's role and EU-Greek relations. For ND, the EU must protect its borders in order to safeguard its role as a key international player. The specific role of Greece is to ensure its national security, not only for Greece's own benefit, but also because the borders of Greece are the (southeast) borders of the EU. On the contrary, for SYRIZA the refugee/migrant crisis is a chance for Europe to corroborate its values and political principles, that is, the spirit of solidarity and humanity. The same principles should also animate a new, alternative political ap-proach to the financial and humanitarian crisis that resulted from the EU-condoned austerity measures in Greece. In other words, while ND sees Greece as the border guard of EU, SYRIZA sees it as the good ambassador and executer of EU's humanitarian values.

These differences in the political rhetoric of the two parties are vis-ible in the metaphors they use. ND's metaphorical scheme of "unfenced vineyard" (*xefrago ampeli*) is a rhetorical configuration of "ownership" of national land that is at risk from external threats and must therefore be sealed off. Other metaphors used by the conservative party are those of the "country as a container" and of "immigration as a natural disaster." To the contrary, in order to underline the crisis as a process of forced uprooting, the term used by SYRIZA, "refugee flows" (*prosfygikes roes*), turns attention to the systemic and structural factors that produce refugees rather than illegal immigrants. Thus, it neutralizes the negative connotations and eliminates any reference to the agency of the individuals concerned. Ultimately, the metaphors used by both parties function as key reflections of broader cultural and political worldviews.

In sum, the Greek experience indicates that refugee/immigration policy, like any other policy, is conditioned by disparate worldviews articulated by argumentative discourse, rather than by the unmediated application of rational solutions. Language is thus a tool that shapes power relations and underlines important political and ideological differences between the main parties in this debate. This illuminates the importance of political rhetoric as an integral part of a political struggle that crucially affects the life of millions of displaced and migrating people, and to a lesser extent the life of people in the countries where they arrive.

Notes

1. United Nations High Commissioner for Refugees (UNHCR), *Global Appeal 2016-2017*, unhcr.org. It is estimated that 3,771 refugees and migrants lost their lives trying to reach Europe in 2015, and almost as many in 2014 and in 2016. See also *Operational Portal, Refugee Situations: Mediterranean Situation*, unhcr.org.

2. It should be noted at this point that the so-called far-right parties are not necessarily identical to those with an anti-immigration stance. See Joost van Spanje, "The Wrong and the Right: A Comparative Analysis of 'Anti-immigration' and 'Far Right' Parties," *Government and Opposition* 46, no. 3 (2011): 293–320.

3. See Georgia Spyropoulou and Dimitris Christopoulos, *Refugee Issue: "'Will We Succeed?': A Management Review and Comprehensive Proposals* [Προσφυγικό: "Θα τα καταφέρουμε;". Ένας απολογισμός διαχείρισης και προτάσεις διεξόδου] (Athens: Papazisis Publications, 2016), 18.

4. Spyropoulou and Christopoulos, 14–15.

5. Spyropoulou and Christopoulos, 19.

6. We use the composite term "refugee/migrant" throughout the text to indicate that the crisis concerns neither refugees nor immigrants alone. Among the thousands of daily arrivals to Greece there are both refugees (i.e., asylum seekers, mainly from war-torn Syria) and economic immigrants fleeing poverty and other hardships. This is why official political rhetoric also mixes the two terms "refugees" and "migrants." Of course, this mixing can also be a deliberate political move to downplay the international obligations of a receiving country toward refugees, as we shall show in our analysis. Still, the two issues are closely interconnected from a rhetorical point of view, which is why we chose to use the composite term.

7. Georgios Karyotis and Stratos Patrikios, "Religion, Securitization and Anti-immigration Attitudes: The Case of Greece," *Journal of Peace Research* 47, no. 1 (2010): 43–57; Stefania Kalogeraki, "The Upsurge in Intolerance against Migrants during the Greek Recession," *International Journal of Diverse Identities* 13 (2015): 1–16; Lia Figgou, Antonis Sapountzis, Nikos Bozatzis, Antonis Gardikiotis, and Pavlos Pantazis, "Constructing the Stereotype of Immigrants' Criminality: Accounts of Fear and Risk in Talk about Immigration to Greece," *Journal of Community & Applied Social Psychology* 21 (2011): 164–177.

8. We primarily refer to the work by Anna Triandafyllidou and her colleagues. Anna Triandafyllidou, "The Political Discourse on Immigration in Southern Europe: A Critical Analysis," *Journal of Community & Applied Social Psychology* 10 (2000): 373–389 (focusing on the discourse of NGOs, trade unions, and public employees); Anna Triandafyllidou and Ruby Gropas, "Constructing Difference: The Mosque Debates in Greece," *Journal of Ethnic and Migration Studies* 35, no. 6 (2009): 957–975 (focusing on media and parliamentary debates); Thanos

Maroukis, "Irregular Migration in Greece: Size and Features, Causes and Discourses," in *Irregular Migration in Europe: Myths and Realities*, ed. Anna Triandafyllidou (Abingdon: Routledge, 2016), 93–113.

9. James Martin, *Politics and Rhetoric. A Critical Introduction* (New York: Routledge, 2014); Allan Finlayson, "From Beliefs to Arguments: Interpretive Methodology and Rhetorical Political Analysis," *Political Studies Association* 9, no. 4 (2007): 545–563.

10. George Lakoff and Mark Johnson, *Metaphors We Live By* (Chicago: University of Chicago Press, 1980); Jonathan Charteris-Black, *Politicians and Rhetoric: The Persuasive Power of Metaphor* (New York: Palgrave, 2005).

11. Lakoff and Johnson, 159.

12. Charteris-Black; Paul Chilton, *Analysing Political Discourse. Theory and Practice* (New York: Routledge, 2004).

13. Jörg Zinken, Lina Hellsten, and Brigitte Nerlich, "Discourse Metaphors," in *Body, Language and Mind. Volume 2: Sociocultural* Situatedness, ed. Roslyn M. Frank, René Dirven, Tom Ziemke, and Enrique Bernárdez (New York: Mouton de Gruyter, 2008), 363.

14. Andreas Musolff, *Metaphor and Political Discourse: Analogical Reasoning in Debates about Europe* (New York: Palgrave, 2004); Elena Semino, *Metaphor in Discourse* (Cambridge: Cambridge University Press, 2008); Terrell Carver and Jernej Pikalo, eds., *Political Language and Metaphor: Interpreting and Changing the World* (New York: Routledge, 1998).

15. All translations of quotes to English are our own.

16. After long political and legal struggles, the situation was partly alleviated by Law 4332/2015, which granted access to citizenship for second-generation immigrants.

17. Anna Triandafyllidou, "Greek Immigration Policy at the Turn of the 21st Century: Lack of Political Will or Purposeful Mismanagement?," *European Journal of Migration and Law* 11, no. 2 (2009): 159–178.

18. Charalambos Kasimis, "Greece, Migration 1830s to Present," in *The Encyclopedia of Global Human Migration*, ed. Immanuel Ness, vol. 3 (Oxford: Wiley-Blackwell, 2013), 1602–1609.

19. In 2010, 90 percent of all apprehensions for unauthorized entry in the EU were made in Greece. "Frontex Deploys Rapid Border Intervention

Teams to Greece," Frontex News Releases, October 25, 2010, frontex.
europa.eu.

20. For a more detailed account of Greece's irregular immigration
    control policies, see Danai Angeli, Angeliki Dimitriadi, and Anna
    Triandafyllidou, *Assessing the Cost Effectiveness of Irregular Migration Control
    Policies in Greece*, Midas Report (Athens: ELIAMEP, 2014).

21. European Commission, "Fact Sheet: EU-Turkey Agreement: Questions
    and Answers," europa.eu.

22. Laura Pitel and Jim Brunsden, "Blow for Migrant Deal as Turkey Rejects
    EU Terror Law Demands," *Financial Times*, August 9, 2016, ft.com.

23. We use these party-ideological labels with caution, on the basis of the
    parties' official self-identification, and not their actual rhetoric or policy
    lines.

24. Antonis A. Ellinas, "The Rise of Golden Dawn: The New Face of the Far
    Right in Greece," *South European Society and Politics* 18, no. 4 (2013): 543–
    565.

25. For many observers, it is surprising how a nationalist party (Independent
    Greeks) is in a stable government coalition with a humanist party
    (SYRIZA), considering how opposed the two parties are on
    immigration. Suffice it to say here that the coalition is sustained mainly
    by a joint opposition to austerity economics and a common populist
    language.

26. "Greece Votes to Grant Citizenship to Immigrants' Children," *Daily Star*
    (Lebanon), June 24, 2015, dailystar.com.lb.

27. Response of Prime Minister Antonis Samaras to the programmatic
    statements of the new government, July 8, 2012, primeminister.gr.

28. Speech at a campaign rally in Athens, June 15, 2012, antilogos-gr.
    blogspot.com.

29. Response of Prime Minister Antonis Samaras to the programmatic
    statements of the new government.

30. Speech at the opening of Seventy-Seventh Thessaloniki International
    Fair, September 8, 2012, primeminister.gr.

31. Speech at a campaign rally in Athens.

32. Speech at the opening of Seventy-Seventh Thessaloniki International Fair.

33. Speech at a campaign rally in Athens. In another occasion he argues: "In the platform of the conference of parties involving the European Left, there is a position that you must abolish Frontex, which prevents free immigration in Europe. So, to let in all smuggled immigrants" (Speech in parliament on the occasion of SYRIZA's proposal for a vote of no confidence to government, November 10, 2013, primeminister.gr).

34. Speech during the programmatic statements of the new government, July 7, 2012, primeminister.gr.

35. Speech at the preparatory meeting for the Party Convention in Thessaloniki, June 9, 2013, primeminister.gr.

36. Speech at the preparatory meeting for the Party Convention in Thessaloniki, June 9, 2013.

37. Speech to the Political Committee of ND, October 12, 2013, primeminister.gr.

38. Speech at the Ninth Ordinary Convention of ND, June 28, 2013, primeminister.gr; our emphasis.

39. Jonathan Charteris-Black, "Britain as a Container: Immigration Metaphors in the 2005 Election Campaign," *Discourse & Society* 17, no. 5 (2006): 563–581.

40. Speech to the Political Committee of ND; our emphasis.

41. Speech at the Parliamentary Group of ND, July 24, 2012, primeminister. gr.

42. Speech at the opening of the Seventy-Ninth International Fair in Thessaloniki, September 6, 2013, primeminister.gr. Speech in a campaign rally in Tripoli, May 20, 2013, primeminister.gr; our emphasis.

43. Speech at the preparatory meeting for the Party Convention in Thessaloniki, June 9, 2013.

44. Speech at the Ninth Ordinary Convention of ND.

45. Speech at a campaign rally in Komotini, January 5, 2015, primeminister. gr.

46. Speech at the Parliament Group of ND, November 4, 2012, primeminister.gr.

47. Speech at a party event on the occasion of forty years of ND, October 4, 2014, primeminister.gr.

48. Speech in parliament on the occasion of SYRIZA's proposal for a vote of no confidence to government, August 10, 2014, primeminister.gr.

49. Speech by Tsipras at the Parliament Group of SYRIZA, October 3, 2015, primeminister.gr.

50. Comment by the president of SYRIZA for refugees, September 4, 2015, primeminister.gr. Speech by Tsipras at the EU Summit on Immigration, April 24, 2015, primeminister.gr.

51. Speech at a campaign rally in Athens, September 18, 2015, primeminister. gr.

52. Speech at a campaign rally in Athens, September 18, 2015.

53. Speech at a campaign rally in Athens, September 18, 2015. We refer mainly to the unstable regimes that were put in place following the Arab revolution, the ISIS attacks across the Maghreb, but also the Turkish domestic troubles and its involvement in the Syrian war. Speech by Tsipras at the Summit for Immigration and Migration Flows, October 1, 2015, primeminister.gr.

54. Policy statements of government by Tsipras, February 8, 2015, primeminister.gr. See also speech by Tsipras at the EU Summit on Immigration, April 24, 2015.

55. Policy statements of government by Tsipras, October 5, 2015, primeminister.gr.

56. Statements by Tsipras after meeting with European Commissioner for Immigration Dimitris Avramopoulos, April 7, 2015, primeminister.gr.

57. Speech at a campaign rally in Athens, September 18, 2015.

58. Comment by Tsipras for refugees, September 4, 2015, www.syriza.gr.

59. Speech at a campaign rally in Athens, September 18, 2015.

60. Speech by Tsipras at the Parliament Group of SYRIZA.

61. Policy statements of government by Tsipras, October 5, 2015.

62. Speech by Tsipras at the Parliament Group of SYRIZA.

63. Speech by Tsipras at the Summit for Immigration and Migration Flows.

64. Comment by Tsipras for refugees.

65. Comment by Tsipras for refugees.

66. Speech by Tsipras at the EU Summit on Immigration, April 24, 2015.

67. Policy statements of government by Tsipras. Comment by the president

of SYRIZA for refugees. See also speech in a campaign rally in Levadia, September 4, 2015, syriza.gr.

68. Speech at a campaign rally in Korinthos, June 10, 2015, syriza.gr, and speech in a campaign rally in Kalamata, January 11, 2015, syriza.gr. Speech in a campaign rally in Komotini, January 13, 2015, syriza.gr.

69. To be fair, we must note a shift in the type of arrivals at the Greek border, which became predominantly Syrian refugees only after SYRIZA came to power in January 2015.

70. Statements by Tsipras after meeting with European Commissioner for Immigration Dimitris Avramopoulos, April 7, 2015.

71. Speech at a campaign rally in Levadia.

72. Speech at a campaign rally in Levadia.

73. Speech at a campaign rally in Athens, September 18, 2015.

Viktor Orbán's Anti-Brussels Rhetoric in Hungary

BARELY ABLE TO KEEP EUROPE CHRISTIAN?

———•◆•———

Heino Nyyssönen

According to Prime Minister Viktor Orbán, Hungarians do not like empty talk or waffling, but prefer straight talk. The migrant crisis is no exception, and this chapter studies the crisis in Orbán's rhetoric. The chapter looks at characterizations of migrants and the immigration crisis as it is understood through the historical conception of Christian Europe and its opponents. The emphasis is on Viktor Orbán's speeches in 2015 and 2016 on the anniversary of the Hungarian Revolution of 1848. My argument is that Orbán used the migrant crisis to strengthen his position in the struggle against "Brussels" (i.e., the European Union) and its supposed "cosmopolitan immigration policy." Hungary has been a key player and on the front line in the migrant crisis, and it is striking how the crisis is strengthening critical sentiments concerning democracy and the EU.

A key source for Hungarian national anniversaries is poet Sándor

Petőfi, who penned these opening lines in the beginning of the 1848 revolution in Pest (the eastern part of present-day Budapest):

On your feet, Magyar, the homeland calls!
The time is here, now or never!
Shall we be slaves or free?
This is the question, choose your answer!—By the God of the Hungarians
We vow,
We vow, that we will be slaves
No longer![1]

This is perhaps the best agitation poem ever written. It has depicted not only Hungarian radicalism but Hungary's political culture as well. The current prime minister, Orbán, used some of these sentiments in his National Day speech on March 15, 2016; indeed, I will show that these lines are directly relevant to his response to the ongoing migrant crisis.[2] In the present case, Orbán, who has dominated recent Hungarian politics, is the agent, history the frame, and immigration the case to be interpreted.

If Orbán uses the migrant crisis against "Brussels," his critics blame him for the backlash against Hungarian democracy. My aim here is twofold: on the one hand I construct a background narrative based on Orbán's statements in 2015. On the other hand, I offer a careful analysis of two subsequent speeches, which I consider crucial to understanding Orbán's position in Europe-wide political debates. The two speeches are the first large occasions on which Orbán evaluated recent political developments. The first address was delivered in February 2016 to evaluate the year's political developments; the second was given on March 15, 2016 (this practice continued in 2017, as well).

Anniversary as such is a setting for ceremonial speeches. It is repetitive in its nature and, thus, makes it possible to stop for a while, to recall the past, and to envision the future. However, such ceremonial addresses do not necessarily take place only on national holidays but can be delivered on any anniversary. Thus, the Hungarian yearly evaluation, *évértékelő*, is comparable to other speeches concerning the state of the nation, such as the US State of the Union address. For continuing politicians, the rhetor is de facto defending and praising his own achievements in front of the national public. Interestingly, this yearly evaluation speech was initiated by Orbán himself in the late 1990s.

Such ceremonial addresses vary in their length and can be rich in details—Orbán's evaluation of 2016 took more than an hour. Even if Hungarians could expect "revolutionary" speeches on March 15 (the date of the 1848 revolution), this time the March speech was rhetorically exceptionally harsh; the migration crisis made its appearance in both the 2015 and 2016 anniversary speeches.[3] Orbán's primary audience was his loyal supporters, although through news distribution and translations the message was potentially global. Extraordinary in 2016 was an audience of several thousand Polish guests, who visited Orbán in the aftermath of the conservative victory in Poland.

To set the stage for analyzing these speeches, I will offer background on Hungarian immigration policy leading up to Orbán's term in office. Next, I will focus on two discursive strategies of the PM: Orbán's use of "us" and "them" distinctions in defining Hungarians and, next, his construction of "Christian Europe." I will conclude with an analysis of Orbán's views on the current EU, the EU's relation to migrants, and the future of immigration policy. I will show that Orbán's speech on March 15, 2016, in particular developed a clear anti-Brussels agenda.

Background on Hungarian Immigration Policy and the Current Crisis

Traditionally Hungary, like many other postcommunist countries, is a country of emigration more than immigration. The collapse of Austria-Hungary and the Trianon Peace Treaty (1920) forced many people leave. Since World War II there have been several waves of emigration, such as the one after the 1956 uprising. Globally, the resettlement of 170,000 Hungarian refugees in 1956 and 1957 constitutes the first large-scale resettlement undertaken within the framework of the contemporary refugee law regime, that is, the 1951 Convention and the Statute of United Nations High Commissioner for Refugees.[4] Much less known are the Greek immigrants: because of the Greek Civil War, Communist-led Hungary resettled more than seven thousand men, women, and children, particularly in a small village, Beloiannisz.

In the EU optimism of 2004, Hungarians calculated that they could receive ten thousand more immigrants than the annual number of emigrants. A kind of mass migration had already taken place in the 1990s: about half a million ethnic Hungarians had either moved to Hungary or to the West; almost half of them (230,000) were from Romania. Thus, because ethnic Hungarians form a reserve for the Hungarian labor markets, a typical discourse of refugees as a labor force has not emerged in Hungary.[5] Despite this potentiality, the main aim of immigration policies was to keep compatriots in their birthplaces, and not to persuade them to move to Hungary.

Nowadays most foreigners staying in the country come from Romania. However, it would be a half-truth to call them all Romanians, as many of them are ethnic Hungarians, mainly from Transylvania. According to data from 2000, the number of foreigners is some 1.3 percent of the population, among the smallest percentages in Europe. In 2004 there were approximately 150,000 foreigners with temporary or permanent residence permits. The highest number of refugees arrived during the Yugoslavian wars: 53,359 refugees were registered in 1991. Ten years later the number had dropped, and the refugee population in total was some six to nine thousand people in Hungarian territory before the EU accession.[6]

The situation changed drastically in 2015 with the Syrian Civil War's escalation and the flow of refugees peaking. According to Eurostat, Hungary rose to the top three in receiving of first-time asylum applications, though illegal immigrants pushed this peak even higher. Germany received the lion's share at 35 percent, with Hungary second at 14 percent. Surprisingly, 174,000 first-time applicants is almost the same number of Hungarians who were resettled after 1956.[7] Despite these numbers, it was clear that Hungary was a transit country due to Hungary's policies during the crisis. Geopolitically Hungary is a border country in the EU; but according to Dublin regulations, which determine the member state responsible for examining an application by an asylum seeker—normally the state through which the person has first entered the EU—Hungary faces a potential risk that migrants might be returned to them.

Politically the crisis has strengthened Prime Minister Viktor Orbán's position.[8] Orbán has dominated Hungarian politics since 2010, when his national conservative party Fidesz-KDNP won a two-third's majority in the parliament. Since 2010 the nature of the Hungarian "majoritarian democracy" has been debated in the European Parliament. Significant changes followed Orbán's rise, beginning with a new constitution in 2011, which was enacted by a two-thirds governmental majority. Orbán praised the idea of "illiberal democracy," which was distancing itself from the EU's "liberal democracies."[9] After the 2018 parliamentary election, there were four primary parties in the opposition: the Hungarian Socialist Party, its splitter party the Democratic Coalition, the liberal-green Politics Can Be Different, and the extreme nationalist Jobbik.

Given these developments, Hungary's position in the EU was controversial even before the migrant crisis. When Orbán explained the state of democracy in Strasbourg in May 2015, he insisted that Hungary had a right to close the door to migrants: of the 43,000 asylum applications, Kosovars submitted 24,000 in the first quarter of 2015.[10] The Hungarian government frequently raised the right of the member states to defend their own borders, insisting that power should be restored to national jurisdictions. Orbán condemned as a crazy idea the proposal to let asylum seekers into Europe and to apportion them on the basis of quotas.[11] Politically this address in Strasbourg took place only a few weeks after Fidesz had for the first time lost a constitutional seat to Jobbik. In the aftermath Orbán demanded that the death penalty should be kept on the agenda—a position defying the prevailing stance in the EU. Thus, this topic reached the European Parliament in the same speech as immigration and made the subsequent months more difficult.

In Strasbourg Orbán announced that the Hungarian government had launched a domestic consultation on immigration. In May the government circulated a questionnaire and a letter by the prime minister. Citizens were expected to answer twelve questions and submit their responses to the PM's office by July 1. Unlike the Strasbourg speech, the letter included no numbers or references to the immigrants' risky trips across the Mediterranean, Greece's challenges on the front lines of the immigration crisis, or the origins of the migrants. Instead, the PM stated that the recent terror attack in Paris had revealed the EU's inability to manage migration in a responsible manner. As the number of economic migrants had become twenty times as large in a few months, he insisted, Brussels had failed, requiring Hungary to act unilaterally.[12]

In general, the "National Consultation" can be labeled a mode of populism, which had been used, for example, to legitimize the new constitution in 2011.[13] In the case of migrants the government utilized the results on billboards: "People have decided: the country has to be defended." The turnout in the consultation remained low, as indicated by Orbán's explanation to a German audience: "One million members of our eight million strong electorate returned completed questionnaires, and eighty-five per cent of them said that the EU has failed in its attempts to manage immigration."[14]

The idea to close Hungary's southern border was not raised in the National Consultation, but it emerged in public discussions in June 2015, before the deadline for returning the questionnaires of the consultation. On the seventeenth the government announced that it was building a four-meter-high, 175 kilometer fence on the Serbian border—an "Iron Curtain," as the leading oppositional daily *Népszabadság* called it.[15] This piece of news divided the parties: the foreign minister, Péter Szijjártó, referred to existing fences on the Turkish-Bulgarian and Greek-Bulgarian borders. The leftist and liberal opposition reminded readers about Israel's wall between the Palestinians and the Jewish population, and said it preferred cooperation with the EU. The leader of Jobbik, Gábor Vona, suggested that Fidesz was dancing to Jobbik's tune and carrying out its policy.[16]

A by-product of the 2015 consultation was a "poster war." The government ordered a billboard campaign to support its National Consultation.

In the billboards there were texts such as, "If you come to Hungary, don't take the jobs of the Hungarians!" and "If you come to Hungary, you have to obey our laws." Usually the texts were in Hungarian; thus the audience was domestic rather than newcomers. The provocative campaign resulted in a countercampaign, in which the texts were repainted or changed: "Come to Hungary—we're already working in London."[17]

In August 2015 Hungary became a flashpoint in the European-wide crisis. The focal question was whether Hungary should stop asylum seekers, even by hard measures, or respect their will and let them continue their journey through Hungary. In particular, the Keleti Railway Station in Budapest played a role in these competing campaigns, with civilians helping newcomers and the police preventing their departure from Hungary. Because of political hesitation, around twelve hundred migrants started to march by foot to the Austrian border. In the autumn a new European axis emerged, when other Visegrad countries—Poland, Czech, and Slovakia—joined Hungary to oppose refugee quotas.[18] For Orbán quotas were not the answer: "Quotas are an invitation for those who want to come." In February 2016 he announced a referendum on immigration, which was later scheduled to be held in October 2016. According to Orbán, the referendum represented the people's will and Brussels could not dictate an immigration quota against that will. There are different views on whether Orbán "won" or "lost" the battle: a vast majority, 98 percent, supported the PM's views in the referendum, but only 43 percent of those entitled to vote did so.[19]

Constructions of Immigrants by Viktor Orbán

Viktor Orbán aimed to distinguish between the free movement of workers within Europe and migration coming from outside. As regards the latter, he further distinguished "genuine refugees" from "immigrants" who were simply seeking a better life. However, this did not clarify who should be considered part of each group. It functioned rhetorically as a synecdoche, one of Kenneth Burke's four master tropes, in which a part of something is used to represent the whole and vice versa; thus, immigrants and refugees alike were potentially painted as questionable migrants. The government already had created such juxtapositions, such as in the questionnaire's name: "National Consultation on Immigration and Terrorism," which connected immigration and terrorism. It is noteworthy that the Orbán letter and the questionnaire discussed only economic immigrants, using the term *megélhetési bevándorlók* (economic migrants), which implied corruption and criminality and people who are swindlers.[20]

In addition, Orbán said that migrants "looked like an army," drawing on the fact that the majority of the migrants were young men. The media, in contrast, often showed women and children. Different representations agitated people on the competing sides. Two covers of pictorial magazines clarify the problematic distinction: the government-leaning *Heti Válasz* interpreted the newcomers as a mass, which was using a "human shield" in their march to the Austrian border, while the more critical *HVG* presented Orbán with a sword in his hand, accompanied by the text, "One against all."[21] While the former referred to cowards, the latter questioned the PM's stubborn struggle against aliens.

This discourse of aliens is influenced by perceptions, which Robert Jervis noted in his famous *Perception and Misperception in International Politics*. Often decision-makers see others' behavior as more purposeful, planned, and coordinated than it actually is. They tend to dismiss coincidence and see coherence in others' actions even when they are uncoordinated. Experience matters, as humans tend toward cognitive consistency by assimilating new information into preexisting images.[22] Obviously, Orbán could play on those perceptions in painting refugees as not escaping a crisis so much as seeking economic advantage.

In *German Focus Magazine* Orbán repeated that the government was defending "European values" and insisted that Islam "has never been part of Europe. . . . It's the rulebook of another world." In the *Frankfurter Allgemeine Zeitung* (September 3, 2015) Orbán raised the question of migrants and Europe in relation to representation of difference, notably in culture and religion:

Let us not forget, however, that those arriving have been raised in another religion, and represent a radically different culture. Most of them are not Christians, but Muslims. This is an important question, because Europe and European identity is rooted in Christianity. Is it not worrying in itself that European Christianity is now barely able to keep Europe Christian? If we lose sight of this, the idea of Europe could become a minority interest in its own continent.[23]

Rhetorically, this dualist view works through inclusion and exclusion, by which the speaker constructs alliances in terms of opposition. A version of such a distinction was used, for example, by President George W. Bush in 2001: "Either you are with us, or you are with the terrorists." This either-or functions two ways: first, persuading bystanders to join the rhetor's group, and second, providing a Manichaean dualism that frames an understanding of the world.

Occasionally Orbán's statements became too sharply anti-Muslim, and he had to withdraw or rephrase them (especially in front of international audiences). For example, in front of the European People's Party in October he said: "Let me draw your kind attention to the fact that [the] European Christian democratic approach doesn't tolerate any anti-Muslim policy. Muslim faith which we honor and respect is not responsible for the root causes of this mass migratory movement." On the other hand, he insisted that the current situation was not a refugee crisis, but a migratory movement. He admitted there were refugees, but stressed the presence of economic migrants and also foreign fighters.[24]

For a domestic audience on March 15, 2016, he spoke in the name of Europe. There are many taboo topics in the current Europe, at least according to politician Viktor Orbán:

In Europe today it is forbidden to speak the truth. . . . It is forbidden to say that today we are not witnessing the arrival of refugees, but a Europe being threatened by mass migration. It is forbidden to say that tens of millions are ready to set out in our direction. It is forbidden to say that immigration brings crime and terrorism to our countries. It is forbidden to say that the masses of people coming from different civilizations pose a threat to our way of life, our culture, our customs, and our Christian traditions. It is forbidden to say that, instead of integrating, those who arrived here earlier have built a world of their own, with their own laws and ideals, which is forcing apart the thousand-year-old structure of Europe.

In this National Day speech Orbán used repetition in the style of classic propaganda. But he also said what he claimed could not be said, even as he argued that a discourse dominates in Europe that excludes critical voices and criticism. For the domestic audience he depicted the future as full of threats caused by mass migration, which also threatened "our" way of life and Christian traditions. This is the theme I will examine next.

Viktor Orbán's Christian Europe

In Viktor Orbán's rhetoric different civilizations pose a threat for the Christian Europe. "We" (Hungarians) are the citizens of historical and spiritual Europe, like Charlemagne, Leonardo, Beethoven, King Saint Ladislaus, Imre Madách, and Béla Bartók. In this discourse "Europe" means a unity of Christians, free and independent nations with common roots, values, and history.[25] On March 15, 2016, he urged that "Europe is a community of Christian, free and independent nations; it is the equality of men and women, fair competition and solidarity, pride and humility, justice and mercy."[26]

Contrary to this idealism, however, states are obviously also rivals in relation to each other. Orbán's political views on Europe became particularly clear in the summer of 2013, when the European Parliament stated that Hungary had a problem in its democracy as defined in the EU's Lisbon Treaty. In Brussels Orbán hailed a Europe of free nations, while in Budapest the Fidesz-controlled parliament passed a resolution insisting that Hungarians are against a union in which the greater misuse power and insult sovereignty and the small have to obey. According to the resolution, Hungarians were acting in the name of European values.[27] In other words, Orbán is contesting the current liberal language of values: according to him, it is Hungary that has already acted on the basis of European values, not the EU.

In Orbán's rhetoric Christianity and its relation to Islam are based on a historical approach. In Hungary Ottoman domination lasted 150 years until the Christian forces subdued it for Austria. Orbán used this seventeenth-century experience in September 2015, when he replied to the president of the European Council, Donald Tusk. Tusk had argued that Christianity carries a duty to help those in distress, "a duty to our brothers in need," regardless of race, religion, or nationality. In his response Orbán claimed the view that Hungarians "are the only ones who have experience [living together with Muslim communities] because we had the possibility to go through that experience for 150 years."[28]

This kind of rhetoric has much in common with Slobodan Milošević, a former president of Yugoslavia charged with genocide during the Yugoslavian wars of 1991–2001, who also constructed himself as a defender of Europe in the manner of the battle of Kosovo Polje of 1389. Orbán highlights the first sentences of the new Hungarian constitution: "We are proud that our king Saint Stephen built the Hungarian state on solid ground and made our country a part of Christian Europe one thousand years ago."[29] Here the phrase *Christian Europe* refers to a connection between the origins of the state and Catholic religion, still the largest denomination in Hungary—under Stephen the country was recognized as the Catholic Apostolic Kingdom.

Thus, in addition to Christian Europe, there is the discourse of defending Europe in Orbán's rhetoric. Orbán constructs himself as defending all of Europe, in comparison to which potential mistreatment of refugees is a minor issue: in September 2015 Orbán defended the Schengen Area as one of Europe's greatest achievements. However, he insisted that Schengen only works if individual member states fulfill their obligations under the Schengen Agreement—namely the protection of external borders and thereby ensuring the possibility of free movement within Europe: "What is happening now is overwhelming. This is why the fence which we Hungarians are building is important. . . . The fence as a line of defense is a consequence of the Schengen Agreement, and is thus a necessity for Europe."[30] In this way Hungary is constructed as the defender of both Europe and Christianity, a modern bulwark of Christianity, *antemurale Christianitatis*, as Pope Leo X defined Croatia in the sixteenth century against the Ottoman Empire.

The slogan "Christian and national" is crucial in the Orbanian discourse examined here.[31] The slogan has ambiguous connotations in Hungarian political culture. For example Paul A. Hanebrink, who has studied the Christian national ideology between 1890 and 1944, warns that the stress on *Christian* Hungary is little more than anti-Semitic code. He notes that in Hungary in the aftermath of the catastrophes of World War I, "the new religious nationalism went hand-in-hand with the more exclusive vision of nationhood." Then emerged stereotypes, many of them anti-Semitic and nationalistic, that the political elites had resisted before 1914.[32] Consequently, although the "Christian National Course" became a pejorative doctrine in Communist-led Hungary, the post–World War I Christian-national ideology was not promoting democracy but limiting it—contrary to contemporary claims.

Unlike in the West, different understandings of anti-Semitism are a matter of constant political debate in Hungary. Interestingly, in Viktor Orbán's 2016 yearly evaluation speech, "evil"—anti-Semitism for example—originates from outside and enters the country as a consequence of international immigration: "We do not want and we will not bring criminality, terrorism, homophobia and anti-Semitism to Hungary."[33] Unfortunately, this rhetorical maneuver is only a half-truth: for example, a few months before the speech, a private foundation was planning a statue for a pro-Nazi minister Bálint Hóman, a move that was condemned by the US special envoy against anti-Semitism. The mayor of Székesfehérvár, representing the Fidesz party, had another view: in a democracy the foundation has a right to erect a statue, but the foundation has to return the funding it received from the city and the government.[34] Although criticism of Islam seems to be a unifying factor in the European extreme Right, the Hungarian far-right party Jobbik was recently excluded from the Europe of Nations and Freedom group in the European Parliament, which was dominated by right-wing French politician Marine Le Pen, because of its anti-Semitism.[35] Thus an exclusive form of Christian nationalism is an integral part of Hungarian rightist political discourse: Europe is a community of Christian nations, and protecting such an order justifies policies that contradict its core values.

Domestic 'Them' and the "Host Animal"

In Viktor Orbán's 2016 yearly evaluation speech the present EU is divided into two camps: on one hand, there are the unionists and, on the other hand, those who favor sovereignty. According to Orbán the unionists favor the "United States of Europe" and mandatory migrant quotas. Those who are for sovereignty prefer a Europe of free nations, and will not even hear about quotas, the symbol of the time. In the latter group there are "the proud nations," like Poland after the conservative election victory in late 2015.[36]

Distinctions between "us" and "them" can be found not only on the international but also on the European and domestic levels, too.[37] Thus, there is a "snake" in the Christian paradise, and particularly in the EU capital of Brussels. For Orbán "Brussels" is a metonymy of failure, a rhetorical enemy—however Orbán, unlike David Cameron, has until now never suggested leaving the EU. According to the yearly evaluation in 2016, the main opponent is not migrants but Brussels, which has the power to organize Europe's defense but lacks the will. In front of his supporters Orbán was de facto presenting a coherent "Other" group in the EU, even an international conspiracy, in which there was no room for coincidence:

There is not better word than absurd to what happens in Brussels. In my view in Brussels and in a few European capitals the political and spiritual elite is cosmopolitan (*világpolgár*), contrary to the national-minded majority. The most bizarre coalition of human traffickers, human rights activists, and top politicians plan and bring here several million migrants.[38]

Despite Orbán's own party family, the European People's Party (EPP), being the largest political group, Brussels in general is the metonymic venue in which the common adversary can be located (2016):

> It is forbidden to say that this is not accidental and not a chain of unintentional consequences, but a planned, orchestrated campaign, a mass of people directed towards us. It is forbidden to say that in Brussels they are constructing schemes to transport foreigners here as quickly as possible and to settle them here among us. It is forbidden to say that the purpose of settling these people here is to redraw the religious and cultural map of Europe and to reconfigure its ethnic foundations, thereby eliminating nation states, which are the last obstacle to the international movement. It is forbidden to say that Brussels is stealthily devouring ever more slices of our national sovereignty, and that in Brussels today many are working on a plan for a United States of Europe, for which no one has ever given authorisation.

In this way Orbán is turning the current crisis against his European critics by employing a version a rhetorical figure called *apophasis*: he makes public what is (allegedly) forbidden by repeating the topic prohibited. In the EPP summit Orbán made further clarifications to the rhetorical enemy construction. His political opponents outside the EPP group were in fact responsible for fomenting the migrant crisis:

> We cannot hide the fact that the European left has a clear agenda. They are supportive of migration. They actually import future leftist voters to Europe hiding behind humanism. . . . They attack core values of our European identity: family, nation, subsidiarity and responsibility.[39]

The political Left in particular is the Hungarian prime minister's target. As we have seen, according to Orbán, there is a European-wide leftist conspiracy to bring more voters to Europe—all this under the guise of humanism. It is true that the Left, but also greens and liberals, have expressed their concern about democracy in Hungary. Moreover, such institutions as the Venice Commission, the Economist's Democracy Index, and Freedom House have recorded signs of concern over Hungary's democratic institutions. Even the European Parliament has critically evaluated Hungary five times since 2010 concerning the freedom of media, the constitution, and the country's political situation.[40]

In the face of such criticism, Orbán's own party group, the EPP, has been divided. Orbán has had disputes with German chancellor Angela Merkel, and he was the only one, in addition to David Cameron, who opposed the EPP's nominee for the president of the European Commission, Jean-Claude Juncker.

On March 15, 2016, Orbán identified another enemy: the international media, which do not recognize Hungary's tolerance for new "family members":

> Today's enemies of freedom are cut from a different cloth than the royal and imperial rulers of old, or those who ran the Soviet system; they use a different set of tools to force us into submission. . . . Today the international media's artillery bombardments, denunciations, threats and blackmail are enough—or rather have been enough so far. . . . It is claimed that we are xenophobic and hostile, but the truth is that the history of our nation is also one of inclusion and the intertwining of cultures. Those who have sought to come here as new family members, as allies or as displaced persons fearing for their lives have been let in to make a new home for themselves. But those who have come here with the intention of changing our country and shaping our nation in their own image, those who have come with violence and against our will, have always been met with resistance.[41]

As a politician Orbán has favored confrontation, and also here he uses sharp either-or rhetoric that divides people into goats and sheep. The good guys belong to the family and are expected to uphold the status quo, whilst the bad ones challenge the present national order. However, it is difficult to say whether Orbán's words are aimed at strengthening the spirit of those who already share this "civil religion," launching trial balloons, or are laying the groundwork for an even more aggressive policy. Moreover, it seems clear that all these aforementioned quotations reflect bitterness and feelings of injustice felt by a relatively small East Central European country.

In May 2015 Orbán defended the current Hungarian policies in the European Parliament. According to him, "The only reason these issues [the death penalty and immigration] should come up in the context of my country is that the Hungarian people like to talk about difficult issues in a straightforward manner. This is our nature; we do not like empty talk, and we do not like to waffle." Orbán continued insisting that Hungarians "are speaking our mind when we say loud and clear that we Hungarians would like to keep Europe for the Europeans, and we also wish to keep Hungary as a Hungarian country."[42]

Orbán's "Hungarian nature" is obviously connected to Hungary's political culture. Traditionally the debate concerning political culture has focused on whether the "culture" and the "political" are stable variables or in a constant change. I would suggest that, drawing on Almond and Verba's rough typology, Hungary's political culture has recently moved from participatory culture toward the category of subject political culture: citizens are aware of the central government and heavily subjected to its decisions with little room for dissent. Archie Brown, who studied the socialist countries in 1970s, has in turn claimed that political culture is complex and indeed in a constant state of change. For him the concept referred to several topics like perceptions of history, beliefs and values, identification, political knowledge, and expectations.[43]

Orbán discussed expectations in his speech in February 2016, painting a rather gloomy picture:

> The main danger to Europe's future does not come from those who want to come here, but from Brussels' fanatics of internationalism. . . . We shall not allow it to force upon us the bitter fruit of its cosmopolitan

immigration policy. We shall not import to Hungary crime, terrorism, homophobia and synagogue-burning anti-Semitism. . . . In the end we find ourselves being told to pack up and leave our own land.

Here, then, the prospective change is negative, but not in a way explicated by the traditional democratic criteria pointed out previously. Rather, according to Orbán, the change seemed to be toward further curtailment of national sovereignty and all the possible side-effects that that reduction presumably brings. The prime minister reveals the main culprit using rhetoric familiar from far-right propaganda, that is, "internationalism" and its "fanatics"; the immigrants who enter the country are merely tools for this devious ideology. History is again an important factor in Orbán's rhetoric, and he extracts the essence of the Hungarian nation by referring to important anniversaries.[44]

> Yes, we Hungarians have two revolutionary traditions: one leads from 1848, through 1956 and the fall of communism, all the way to the Fundamental Law and the current constitutional order; the bloodline of the other tradition leads from Jacobin European ancestors, through 1919, to communism after World War II and the Soviet era in Hungary. Life in Hungary today is a creation of the spiritual heirs and the offspring of the '48 and '56 revolutions. Today, as then, the heartbeat of this revolutionary tradition moves and guides the nation's political, economic and spiritual life. . . . Today, as then, the ideals of '48 and '56 are the pulse driving the life force of the nation, and the intellectual and spiritual blood flow of the Hungarian people.[45]

Suitably, the present day—and hence the speaker himself!—represent a culmination of history, in other words, the true ideals of Hungary. However, the opponent is still present in the form of internationalism. First of all, 1919 refers to the short-lived Soviet Republic in Hungary:

> Not even the uplifting mood of a celebration day can let us forget that the tradition of 1919, too, is still with us—though fortunately its pulse is

just a faint flicker. . . . But without a host animal, its days are numbered. It is in need of another delivery of aid from abroad in the form of a major intellectual and political infusion; unless it receives this, then after its leaves and branches have withered, its roots will also dry up in the Hungarian motherland's soil, which is hostile to internationalism.

According to the prime minister, internationalism, the counterforce to the true spirit and ideals of Hungary, keeps haunting the nation. In Orbán's rhetoric even a "tradition" is organic, a tree that dies without foreign assistance. Thus the critical problem is that although the "Hungarian soil" is a naturally hostile environment to internationalism, the ideology has infiltrated the country using a "host animal." The "host animal" metaphor particularly caught the public attention, and observers asked whether it referred to Jews, liberals, Orbán's opponents in general, refugees, or even to Hitler's parasites, which kill the host in the end.[46]

To analyze the metaphor in more detail we have to go back to Orbán's 2016 speech, in which he was using a language of political realism and discussing both balancing and bandwagoning.[47] Thus, for Orbán "regional balancing" is more difficult and complicated but more valuable than "hiding in the soft, warm and hairy back of the host animal."[48] Seemingly Orbán supported the former, which is "more valuable to 1100 years old Hungary," while those who hide are bandwagoners, and align with stronger, even adversarial, powers. Consequently, based on the yearly evaluation speech, the "host animal" is the European Union. In Orbán's rhetoric it has favored the domestic opposition with its "humanistic" and "international" aims more than his nationalistic government.[49] Thus, Orbán implies that the Soviet rule of 1919 and the EU represent essentially the same enemy.

Perhaps not that shockingly, Viktor Orbán's critique of the European Union employs rhetorical tropes similar to those Adolf Hitler deployed in his *Mein Kampf*, as illustrated by Kenneth Burke. The irony of course is that Orbán, whose rhetorical unification devices resemble Hitler's, has frequently opposed (Muslim) immigrants based on their alleged anti-Semitism.

First, there is the symbol of common enemy against whom people must unite. Men who can unite on nothing else can unite on the basis of a foe shared by all, as Burke noted. In this way one may divert attention from internal problems to an external threat. Without a united voice the outside enemy will gain the upper hand, and by the same token all voices opposing this unity become dangerous. Furthermore, in our case immigrants are a deux ex machina, which has helped Orbán politically to underline the gravity of the situation. Whereas for Hitler the enemy was "natural" in being based on race, in Orbán rhetoric the adversary is an ideology that has appeared in various forms during Hungary's history. In any case, after such essentialization of the opponent, all "proof" is henceforth automatic. It is always "internationalism" and its "fanatic" supporters who are plotting against Hungary, now using even immigrants for their political purposes.

Second, "Brussels" serves as an "anti-Mecca." It is a geopolitical symbol for the common enemy, an international a nest of all the ill, chaotic forces that threaten Hungary and its sovereignty. Third, internationalism represents the appropriate scapegoat, an all-around panacea. A symbolic rebirth of the nation will follow when the scapegoat is "eliminated." What is also important is that in this way Orbán can emphasize his image as the strong man who will save Hungary. He is a link in the long chain of historical heroes that have defended the nation (and Europe), and it is through identifying with him that the audience can move forward toward a better future.[50]

What Is To Be Done?

As we have seen, the Hungarian political culture is overtly historical: it is not unusual to refer to the first king or the medieval state, which, for example, in the German context would sound odd. The way Viktor Orbán constructs the present as a crucial, kairotic moment is derived from this peculiar trait.

As early as 2011 Orbán surprised many when he said on March 15 that Hungarians do not let the EU dictate, as they did not let Vienna dictate in 1848 or Moscow in 1956 or 1990. This cyclical perception of history in which Brussels is likened to Moscow is common among EU critics but usually highly contested.

Instead of differences, such rhetoric stresses continuities, similarities, and repercussions. An example of this is the way Orbán depicted history as having an essentially immutable character (2015):

> We know that one hundred and sixty-seven years ago Hungary's relative weight was greater than it is today. . . . We are part of Europe, and together with the continent's other nations we wish to shape its future. Today Europe is full of questions, and Hungary is full of answers. . . . One hundred and sixty-seven years have flown past, but the essence has not changed. The struggle for Hungary's sovereignty will never end, and in this cause we have only ourselves to rely on. . . . Only the strong survive.[51]

Interestingly, the Hungarian prime minister uses a device Kenneth Burke called "inborn dignity." According to it, a people—Hungarians—are innately superior to others and hence entitled to privileged treatment. The device can be used to instill a sense that others, in this case the leading EU countries, have treated "us" badly. All this has to do with the ongoing migrant crisis, which in Orbán's rhetoric is a planned and orchestrated campaign—yet another obstacle that history has thrown in Hungary's way.

History is both a resource and a burden, which demands current generations to act. Accordingly, in 2016 the prime minister presented a dramatic set of questions to his audience:

> Three weeks before his death in battle, in his last letter to János Arany, Sándor Petőfi asked the following question: "So what are you going to do?" When we, his modern descendants, read this, it is as if he is asking us the same question. So what are you going to do? How will you make

use of your inheritance? Are the Hungarian people still worthy of their ancestors' reputation?

Classically, ceremonial addresses either praised or censured, but Viktor Orbán's speech was full of agitation, urging his audience either to do or not to do something—hence very much a political speech in the Aristotelian sense.[52] Indeed, it would be wrong to limit ceremonial actions only to praising or blaming, as they, indeed, recall the past and make guesses of the future, as "the time has come" (2016):

> The time has come to ring the warning bell. The time has come for opposition and resistance. The time has come to gather allies to us. The time has come to raise the flag of proud nations. The time has come to prevent the destruction of Europe, and to save the future of Europe.

According to Orbán, the future of Europe stands or falls in the question: "Shall we live in slavery or in freedom? That is the question—give your answer!" Thus, in the end of the March 15, 2016, speech, Orbán, currently the best pupil of the national poet Petőfi, raised the question found in the opening quotation of this article. A year earlier, in 2015, a quotation from Petőfi's "National Song" made its appearance. For Orbán a symbolic rebirth is possible someday, as Petőfi's famous lines included a promise that Hungary will be worthy of the old glory: "We Hungarians are on the threshold of a great era. The name of Hungary will be great again, worthy of its old, great honor."[53]

Conclusion

Hungary, a border country in the EU, has been one of the key players in the recent migrant crisis. In this chapter I have studied Prime Minister Orbán's rhetoric during the crisis. Viktor Orbán is one of the most colorful European politicians who favors confrontation and whose policies divide Hungarians and European audiences. The migrant crisis has strengthened his popularity, and the conservative victory in Poland has opened more international space for him.

As regards immigrants, in Orbán's rhetoric they were depicted most often as economic migrants, foreign fighters, and refugees. Importantly, in his separation of "genuine refugees" from those merely seeking better life he did not specify in detail the criteria for such a distinction. As a result, potentially any immigrant could be an "impostor." On the other hand, because Orbán repeatedly stressed the Christian origins and nature of Hungary and Europe, the category of people who are not seen as belonging there is obvious. Consequently, a crucial part of Orbán's rhetoric related to the crisis in the notion of Hungary—and the prime minister—as the legitimate defender of "Christian Europe." If this nation falls, the rest of Europe is in peril, as the traditional bulwark argument used by many different leaders throughout history states.

Maybe even more important than naming and identifying the newcomers and their motives (in the prime minister's rhetoric) is to notice the usage of the crisis, which has been a tool in Orbán's struggle against his critics, particularly those in Brussels. The immigration crisis of 2015–2016 has been depicted as yet another act in a struggle that runs throughout history against forces threatening Hungary. In the twentieth century the enemy was most often Moscow; now it is "the capital" of the EU. Crucially, Viktor Orbán's rhetorical construction of the crisis allows him to criticize the European Union for acting against its core values; in other words, here the EU is depicted as perverse. Ironically, however, in this construction Orbán's own antidemocratic policies are claimed to be justified to save European democratic order.

Orbán is a political chameleon, whose rhetoric is rich and has varied in the course of years. In 2011 WikiLeaks revealed that Orbán had said to ambassadors to the EU: "Pay no attention to what I say to get elected."[54] Accordingly, there is also the question how much we may generalize based on the metaphor "host animal" or expressions such as "empty talk," "waffling," or "warning bell" used by a single politician. Almond and Verba have discussed political cultures on the national level. Brown referred most frequently to groups, too. However, in Hungary the case seems to be somewhat different. As an individual politician, Viktor Orbán has contributed to the Hungarian political culture perhaps more than any other politician since 1990. In addition to his rhetorical presence, Orbán is the longest-serving PM since 1990.

According to critics, the quality of Orbán's speeches has deteriorated during the last years. They insist it is not possible to speak about his style anymore except on a low intellectual level, in which Orbán is breaking moral codes and making the exceptional the normal.[55] However, in this Orbán is not alone, as this kind of rhetoric has spread in many countries. In the United States Donald Trump's rhetoric concerning Muslims, fences, and Mexicans is as exclusionary as Orbán's. In Hungary Orbán's rhetorical enemy is "Brussels," its "fanatics of internationalism," and particularly in this case study, its "cosmopolitan immigration policy." There the archetype is an international liberal, and even better, one who had leftist views in his youth.

Demands for ending political correctness may mean backlash in rhetorical skills—and soon in the standard of politics. I would suggest that instead of interpreting dubious metaphors, we should read the speeches literally, too: it is time to find out what the "host animal" looks like. On an illocutionary level an imminent association from "host animal" is "parasite," but saying it loud was hypocritically left to "slanders" and opponents (i.e., to "them"). How can one argue for defending "European values" and demand capital punishment be kept on the agenda at the same time?

The particular speech on March 15, 2016, may have been the most radical a post-1990 Hungarian prime minister has delivered so far. As a ceremonial speech it did not concentrate only on the present, but also praised and blamed the past and the future. To broader contextualize Viktor Orbán's addresses, we need both vertical and horizontal comparisons, from Donald Trump to Ian Farage, and so on, but also from the Soviet system to the Hungarian history. One may blame Orbán and his brutal abuse of history. However, further research may also ask in which sense Orbán is a product of Hungarian culture, too. Petőfi belongs to cultural treasures of Hungary, and his reputation has survived through generations. Nowadays March 15 is one of the official national days in the Hungarian democracy. Do they have similar speeches in France on July 14?

Notes

1. There are several translations of the poem, and this one is taken from "Poetry of Revolution," politicalworld.org. Cf. "The National Poem" ("Nemzeti dal"), lyricstranslation.com.

2. Here I use the term "migrant crisis," as I consider it the most neutral concept in use, as it does not define the nature or motives of a person in advance. The term "refugee crisis" is also in use, but being a refugee, to be precise, is a status that can be granted to an asylum seeker.

3. Viktor Orbán, "Orbán Viktor ünnepi beszéde," March 15, 2016, kormany.hu; Emilia Palonen, "Rupture and Continuity: Fidesz and the Hungarian Revolutionary Tradition," *La Révolution Française*, June 1, 2016, lrf.revues.org. "Európa és a menekültválság: egy mindenki ellen," *HVG*, March 5, 2016, hvg.hu; "Anita **Élő**, "Gyerekarcú honfoglalás," *Heti Válasz*, September 24, 2015, valasz.hu.

4. Marjoleine Zieck, "The 1956 Hungarian Refugee Emergency, an Early and Instructive Case of Resettlement, " *Amsterdam Law Forum* 5, no. 2 (2013): 46.

5. Zieck.

6. Heino Nyyssönen, "Foreigners, Labour Force and the Decrease in Population. Fragments and Rhetoric from Political Discussion in Finland and Hungary," in *The 2004 Enlargement's Influence on the Labor Market in the European Union*, ed. Jerzy Bubiak (Poznan: Adam Mickiewitz University, 2007), 40–41; Péter Stepper, "The Visegrad Group and the Agenda on Migration: A Coalition of the Unwilling?," *Corvinus Journal of International Affairs* 1, no. 1 (Feb. 2016): 63–71.

7. Eurostat, "Asylum in the EU Member States: Record Number of over 1.2 Million First Time Asylum Seekers Registered in 2015; Syrians, Afghans

and Iraqis: Top Citizenships," March 4, 2016, ec.europa.eu.

8. [Orbán's popularity], *Népszabadság* October 29, 2015, 1; Neil Buckley, "Orbán's Hard Line on Migrants Proves a Ratings at Home," *Financial Times*, September 20, 2015.

9. Stephan Löwenstein, "Merkel in Ungarn: Revolution, Ohne den Rasen zu Betreten," *Frankfurter Allgemeine Zeitung*, February 2, 2015, faz.net; Heino Nyyssönen and Gábor Szabó, "Unkarin 'Illiberaali Demokratia' ja Politiikan Luottoluokittajat," *Politiikka* 57, no. 3 (2015): 178–189. Hungarian sociologist and former liberal minister Bálint Magyar calls Hungary a mafia state: the small ruling elite behaves like a mafia. Bálint Magyar, *The Post-Communist Mafia State: The Case of Hungary* (Budapest: CEU Press, 2016).

10. Viktor Orbán, "Orbán Viktor Felszólalása az Európai Parlamentben" ("Prime Minister Viktor Orbán's Speech in the European Parliament"), May 19, 2015, kormany.hu.

11. Orbán, "Orbán Viktor Felszólalása az Európai Parlamentben."

12. *Nemzeti Konzultáció* (National Consultation) (2015).

13. In 2017 there were even two consultations, the first to "Stop Brussels," and the second against the "[George] Soros Plan," both in line with the topics analyzed in the present chapter. Heino Nyyssönen, "Kansallinen Konsultaatio Aivopesee Unkarissa," *Kaleva*, October 4, 2017.

14. Viktor Orbán, "Those Who Are Overwhelmed Cannot Offer Shelter to Anyone," *Frankfurter Allgemeine Zeitung*, September 3, 2015.

15. "Lehúzzuk a Vasfüggönyt," *Népszabadság*, June 22, 2015, 1.

16. [Border Barrier], *Népszabadság*, June 18, 2015, 1, nol.hu; [Vona's view], *Népszabadság*, June 22, 2015, 1, nol.hu.

17. Nick Thorpe, "Hungary's Poster War on Immigration," *BBC*, June 13, 2015; Dan Nolan, "'Come to Hungary—We're Already Working in London' Says Pro-Immigration Billboard Campaign," *The Telegraph*, June 17, 2015.

18. [Keleti Railway Station], *Népszabadság*, September 2, 2015, 1; [Keleti Railway Station], *Népzsabadság*, September 5, 2015, 1; Stepper.

19. Ian Traynor, "Migration Crisis: Hungary PM Says Europe in Grip of Madness," *The Guardian*, September 3, 2015; Viktor Orbán, "Speech by

Prime Minister Viktor Orbán on 15 March," March 16, 2016, kormany. hu; Heino Nyyssönen, *Tasavallan loppu? Unkarin Demokratian Romahdus* (Jyväskylä: Atena, 2017), 194–195.

20. Miklós Haraszti, "The Intricacies of Translation," *Hungarian Spectrum*, April 26, 2015, hungarianspectrum.org.

21. [Cover], *HVG*, October 16, 2015; Élő.

22. Robert Jervis, *Perception and Misperception in International Politics* (Princeton: University Press, 1976).

23. Orbán, "Those Who Are Overwhelmed"; "Ungarns Ministerpräsident Viktor Orban Bleibt Hart: Muslimische Einwanderer Gehören Nicht Nach Europa," *Focus*, October 16, 2015, focus.de.

24. Viktor Orbán, "Speech of Viktor Orbán at the EPP Congress," October 22, 2015, kormany.hu.

25. Viktor Orbán, "Orbán Viktor Évértékelő Beszéde," February 28, 2016 (speech by Prime Minister Orbán, kormany.hu).

26. Viktor Orbán, "Orbán Viktor ünnepi Beszéde," March 15, 2016 (speech by Prime Minister Orbán, kormany.hu).

27. [Orbán's EU visit], *Népszabadság*, July 3, 2013, 1; [Resolution of the Hungarian parliament], *Magyar Nemzet*, July 9, 2013, n.p.

28. Robert Mackey, "Hungarian Leader Rebuked for Saying Muslim Migrants Must Be Blocked 'to Keep Europe Christian,'" *New York Times*, September 3, 2015.

29. The Fundamental Law of Hungary 2011, parlament.hu.

30. Orbán, "Those Who Are Overwhelmed."

31. "A Jobbik Magyarországért Mozgalom Értékelvű, Konzervatív, Módszereiben Radikális, Nemzeti-Keresztény Párt," October 24, 2003 (Jobbik Party Founding Declaration, jobbik.hu).

32. Paul Hanebrink, *In Defense of Christian Hungary: Religion, Nationalism, and Antisemitism, 1890-1944* (Ithaca, NY: Cornell University Press, 2007), 2–3.

33. "Nem Akarunk és Nem Fogunk Bűnözést, Terrorizmust, Homofóbiát és Antiszemitizmust Importálni Magyarországra," kormany.hu; Orbán, "Orbán Viktor Évértékelő."

34. Rishi Ilyengar, "US Envoy Slams Plans by Hungarian City to Erect Statues of Wartime Anti-Semite," *Time*, December 13, 2015; "US Joins

Hungary Protest over Pro-Nazi Homan Statue," *BBC*, December 14, 2015.

35. J. Arthur White, "Jobbik to Wilders and Le Pen: Liberalism and Zionism Are the Enemies, Not Islam," *Budapest Times*, February 22, 2014, n.p.; Heino Nyyssönen, "Euroopan Oikea Laita on Lavea," *Kaleva*, August 14, 2015, n.p.

36. Orbán, "Orbán Viktor Évértékelő."

37. Heino Nyyssönen and Mari Vares, "Introduction," in *Nations and Their Others: Finland and Hungary in Comparison*, ed. Heino Nyyssönen and Mari Vares (Helsinki: East and West Books, 2012), 9–33.

38. "Magam úgy látom, hogy Brüsszelben és néhány európai fővárosban a politikai és szellemi elit világpolgár, szemben az emberek nemzeti érzelmű többségével. Így jött létre a világtörténelem legbizarrabb koalíciója az embercsempészek, a jogvédő civil aktivisták és az európai csúcspolitikusok között arra, hogy tervezetten ideszállítsanak sok millió migránst" ("Orbán Viktor Évértékelő").

39. Orbán, "EPP Congress."

40. Nyyssönen and Szabó; [EU and Hungary], *Népszabadság*, December 17, 2015, 1; Löwenstein.

41. Viktor Orbán, "Orbán Viktor Ünnepi Beszéde," March 15, 2016, kormany.hu.

42. Viktor Orbán, "Orbán Viktor felszólalása az Európai Parlamentben" (Speech by Prime Minister Orbán in the European Parliament), May 19, 2015, kormany.hu.

43. Archie Brown, "Introduction," in *Political Culture and Political Change in Communist States*, ed. Archie Brown and Jack Gray (London: Macmillan, 1979), 10–25; Heino Nyyssönen, "Political Cultures in Urho Kekkonen's Finland and János Kádár's Hungary," in *Bridge Building and Political Cultures: Hungary and Finland, 1956–1989*, ed. Anssi Halmesvirta and Heino Nyyssönen (Jyväskylä: University of Jyväskylä, 2006), 13–76.

44. Heino Nyyssönen, *The Presence of the Past in Politics. "1956" after 1956 in Hungary* (Jyväskylä: SoPhi, 1999).

45. Orbán, "Orbán Viktor Ünnepi Beszéde."

46. "Viktor Orbán's Speech: War against the World," *Hungarian Spectrum*,

March 16, 2016, hungarianspectrum.org.

47. Kenneth N. Waltz, *The Theory of International Politics* (Long Grove, IL: Waveland Press, 2010).

48. "Én is tudom, hogy nehezebb és bonyolultabb, mint láthatatlanul meglapulni egy gazdaállat puha, meleg és szőrös hátán, de biztosan méltóbb 1100 éves Kárpát-medencei történelmünkhöz. . . . És most szeretném okát adni annak, miért mondtam el mindezt. Röviden: azért, mert ezt most mind veszély fenyegeti. . . . Veszély fenyegeti a gondosan felépített nemzeti külpolitikát" ("Orbán Viktor évértékelő").

49. Daniel Chandler, *Semiotics: The Basics* (London: Routledge, 2007).

50. Kenneth Burke, *The Philosophy of Literary Form: Studies in Symbolic Action* (Berkeley: University of California Press, 1974), 191–203.

51. Viktor Orbán, "Viktor Orbán's Speech on the Anniversary of the Hungarian Revolution of 1848," March 15, 2015, kormany.hu.

52. Aristotle, *Rhetoric*, trans. W. Rhys Roberts (Blacksburg: Virginia Tech University Press, 2001), books 1–3.

53. Orbán, "Speech on the Anniversary."

54. [WikiLeaks about Orbán], *Népszabadság*, September 6, 2011, 1.

55. Anna Kertész, "Orbán Nagyon Fél, Mondja a Pszichológus," *Vasárnapi Hírek*, April 2, 2016, vasarnapihirek.hu.

Why Do Poles Oppose Immigrants?

THE POLISH POLITICAL ELITE'S
(ANTI-)IMMIGRATION RHETORIC

————— • ◆ • —————

Jarosław Jańczak

During the European immigration crisis in 2015, Poland initiated a debate on refugees, immigrants, and cultural and religious homogeneity, but also (and consequently) on national sovereignty and the model of European integration. This debate took place amid parliamentary and presidential elections. Those discussions were deeply rooted both in the low level of national diversity of contemporary Polish society and in the legacies of multi- and monoculturalism, as well as the historical experience of dealing with "others." These have been visibly reflected in the discourses of political and national leaders.

The aim of this chapter is to examine the (anti-)immigration rhetoric in Poland, analyzing public statements by leaders of the main political parties, as well as key officials in the period 2015–2016 in Poland. To interpret them, however, they have to be contextualized in relation to Polish history and experiences with "non-Poles." First, I will discuss Polish political culture with an emphasis on historical legacies and current political divisions. After that I will present the development of Poland's immigration policy. Then I will analyze how immigrants and immigration have been discussed in Polish political rhetoric.

Polish Political Culture

In order to understand the current immigration rhetoric of key politicians and national leaders, investigating the contexts of their approaches is of utmost importance. It will be claimed here that two factors contribute to current attitudes of Poles toward incomers: historical legacies and current political life. Both not only frame the political debate on immigration but also affect the creation of beliefs regarding immigration as a phenomenon, as well as the immigrants themselves. These are explored in the sections that follow.

HISTORICAL LEGACIES

Historical legacies contributing to how immigration and migrants are perceived in Poland and by Poles, including the political elites, result from the historical developments of the Polish state and Polish nation. Three components are of primary relevance here: the ethnopolitical shape of the Polish state, Christianity in its Catholic form, and the political concepts related to Poland's geopolitical location on the edge of Western civilization.

The ethnopolitical shape of Poland can be presented in four main phases of the development of Polish statehood. The early-medieval Polish state, whose borders corresponded to contemporary Polish territory, was an assembly of Slavic/Polish tribes, baptized in the Latin rite and relatively homogenous with regard to the socioeconomic, cultural, and political order. This tradition of homogeneity exists in Polish political thought as the *Piast* concept, named after the ruling dynasty of the time. Together with the union of Poland and Lithuania, a new ethnopolitical reality emerged and soon dominated the era between the fifteenth and eighteenth centuries. This is expressed by the *Jagiellonian* concept (again, after the ruling dynasty of the time), as Poland became a multiethnic European empire, containing the territories of most of the present Baltic States, Belarus, and Ukraine.[1]

The Polish-speaking, Catholic nobility, constituting about 10 percent of the population, ruled this multiethnic and multilingual state from its capital in Kraców. This imperial era and status has been remembered in the Polish tradition as resulting from openness and tolerance between various ethnic groups (slightly less than 50 percent were Polish speakers; the rest encompassed Ukrainians, Belarusians, Germans, Jews, Lithuanians, Armenians, and others) and religious groups (Catholics, Protestants, Orthodox, Muslims) and the ability to successfully uphold relations between them.[2] After a century of political nonexistence that followed, Poland was resurrected after World War I, and its ethnoterritorial shape resulted from a national dispute between the supporters of the Piast and Jagiellonian conceptions. The question was whether a newly reborn Poland should be limited to its core ethnic territories, aiming at being a coherent nation-state, or whether it should form a multiethnic empire dominating the central part of Europe. Eventually, a hybrid form was created with about 70 percent Poles, 15 percent Ukrainians, 8 percent Jews, 4 percent Belarusians, and 4 percent Germans.[3]

This multiethnic structure, settled in the conflicting international environment of interwar Europe, resulted in the political instability of the state and serious tensions between national groups. World War II brought not only changes in the location of Polish borders (moving the state westward) but also created an almost exclusively Polish cultural and political space (the Jewish population was largely exterminated by Nazi Germans during the war, the German population was expelled based on the Potsdam Conference provisions, and the remaining Ukrainians were dispersed by the Polish Communist authorities), resulting in the Piast model, ironically, being implemented by the Communist regime. Consequently, the collapse of communism and the beginning of the reconstruction of a new free Poland after 1989 happened in a homogeneous Polish environment, with almost no national minorities (less than 3 percent Silesians, Kashubians, Belarusians, Ukrainians, and Germans).[4] Entering a globalized world and European integration was even more difficult, after over four decades of political and economic isolation.

Christianity in the Polish culture is not only of a religious character, but also of a cultural and political nature. Accepting Western Christianity was a civilizational choice and constituted entry to the civilized world in the tenth century. Most of the conflicts in Polish history were marked by religious aspects (Russians were Orthodox, Germans and Swedes were Protestant, Turks were Muslim), where Catholicism was an element of Polishness. The fight for independence in the nineteenth and twentieth centuries was supported by the Catholic Church in Poland, often being the only organizational structure substituting for the nonexistent Polish state (in the nineteenth century and during World War II) or representing the Polish nation (during the Communist period, 1945–1989).[5] Despite secularization processes after 1989, it still remains one of the indicators of national identity.[6] This is about Poles declaring themselves to be Catholic, and with regard to the rest, it is widely accepted that "the Catholic faith continues to be fundamental for the shape of Polish culture and even avowed atheists who want to fully participate in the Polish cultural community recognize that Catholic and Christian culture is a shared national value."[7]

Finally, the geopolitical location of Poland on the edge of Western civilization resulted in another contextual factor relevant for understanding Polish attitudes toward immigrants. The Polish political and cultural tradition is deeply rooted in the Latin civilization. However, contrary to France or Germany, Poland has always been located on its periphery. This has resulted in two historical processes: (1) the never-ending necessity of confirming its Western belonging and identity (manifested, among other things, by the European Union accession process), but also in (2) defining its own role and position in the West as a defender of Western civilization. Poles believe that the West exists (and has been constantly developing) because it is well protected by its defender and bulwark. Poles believe they have saved Europe several times in history, including from the invasion of the Mongols (in the thirteenth century), the Turks (the fifteenth–seventeenth centuries), the Bolsheviks (1919–1921), and so on.[8] European Union membership in 2004 and entering the Schengen zone in 2007 (after tightening border procedures and proving to be able to effectively control the eastern boundary) located Poland again on the periphery and allocated it the task of protecting the European Union's second longest land border against many unwanted phenomena, especially organized crime, illegal migration, and so on.

Hence, the Polish approach to immigration is rooted in the historical context, framing the perception of "us" versus "not us." It is influenced by ethnoterritorial developments that have made Poland a homogeneous state and Poles a homogeneous nation that, after several decades of isolated homogeneity, was again exposed to "others." The religious factor is a part of national identity and belongs to the very core of Poland's self-definition. At the same time, the perception of its historical role as Europe's defender was reimposed on Poland in modified form in the context of the European integration process and the necessity of protecting the external Schengen boundary.

CURRENT POLITICAL LIFE

The second factor framing the approach toward immigration is current political life. Both domestic (the presidential and parliamentary elections held in 2015) and European components (the network of alliances) may be enumerated here.

In 2015, both presidential and parliamentary elections were held in Poland.[9] The results were an accumulation of a long-lasting conflict between liberal and conservative forces. The liberals, Civic Platform (Platforma Obywatelska, PO) and their ally, the Polish People's Party (Polskie Stronnictwo Ludowe, PSL), representing mainly the beneficiaries of the transformation living in the western part of the country, as well as in urban areas, had held power from 2007, and had held the presidency since 2010. Their political program was based on the middle class, economic freedom, and openness, especially to Western Europe.

The conservatives, Law and Justice (Prawo i Sprawiedliwość, PiS), acted especially on behalf of the poorer part of the population, living mainly in the eastern part of Poland and in rural areas. PiS opted for a national solidarity that was to be reflected especially in a significant strengthening of social policies. It also supported maintaining traditional values, especially stressing the Christian foundations of the normative, cultural, and political systems in Poland, and distancing itself from liberal developments in the Western world in favor of a traditionally understood national community. In the presidential elections held in May 2015, the conservative candidate Andrzej Duda received 51.5 percent of the votes, which was followed by Law and Justice winning the parliamentary elections in October, getting a majority of seats in the parliament and forming a conservative government in due course.

The European level of political developments forms the second factor contextualizing the immigration debate. Domestic political splits were reflected on the EU's scene.[10] Civic Platform (PO) was a part of the European People's Party, and a strong ally of Angela Merkel's Christian Democrats in Germany. It was in favor of deepening and accelerating the European integration process. Poland's active role in the European project was aimed at strengthening Poland's position as a reliable and relevant partner, aware of and sensitive to Europe-wide problems. The strategy of close collaboration with Germany, and promoting European solidarity were the key tools of this strategy. Part of this tactic was filling the post of the president of the European Council. Donald Tusk, Polish prime minister from 2007, was chosen—with the significant support of Angela Merkel—to hold the post in 2014. Law and Justice, on the other hand, joined the European Conservatives and Reformists, opting for a more nation-state-oriented EU, supporting and re-equipping national authorities with some of the prerogatives already transferred to Brussels, and at the same time opposing the dominant role of Germany in the community.

Thus, to sum up, Polish political discourses on immigrants took place in the context of the lively political debate related to the national elections and a class of openness-oriented liberals and nationally oriented conservatives. Additionally, it was framed by European politics and different visions of the role of nation-states and Germany in the EU project.

Polish Immigration Policies

Polish immigration policies over recent years have been determined by the fact that over the last two centuries Poland has been a source of several huge waves of emigration and—with some exceptions, especially recently—has never attracted large groups of foreign immigrants. In contrast to the states of Western Europe, Poland never possessed overseas colonies (a source of economic and cultural connections, and the creation of migrational networks), its economy neither boomed enough to create demand for a new labor force (with the exception of the years 2015–2018) nor offered the social security that attracts settlers (as in the welfare state systems of Western Europe).

It is estimated that nowadays there are about twenty-one million people of Polish origin living outside Poland, compared to the population of thirty-eight million residing in the country. With the exception of those Poles who decided to stay in Lithuania, Belarus, and Ukraine after the border shift in 1945 (over one million people), and those sent in exile to Siberia and Kazakhstan by the Russian and Soviet authorities in the nineteenth and twentieth centuries (about half a million people), all the others (or their ancestors) migrated because of political or economic reasons to the West. This includes almost two million Poles who moved mainly to the United Kingdom after Poland's entry to the European Union in 2004, as part of the principle of the free flow of people.[11]

The first years after the end of World War II were marked by policies aiming at the reintegration of the masses of Polish nationals from the territories lost to the Soviet Union (almost two million people), as well as Polish slave workers from Germany (about half a million people), and Polish soldiers fighting in Western Europe against Germany.[12] This, however, was not an immigration but a repatriation policy, where the

newcomers did not represent foreign cultures, languages, and denomi-
nations; but, quite the opposite, belonged to the very core of the Polish
nation. Two groups of refugees formed a tiny exception. About twelve
thousand Greek political refugees, who had to leave their state after
the civil war were accepted in 1949 by the Polish Communist regime;
some of them left Poland, while the rest integrated well with the Polish
society. In 1973, about six thousand Chilean supporters of the deposed
Salvador Allende were received; most of them, however, fled. Additionally, in the 1970s the Vietnamese started to arrive in Poland, but on a
smaller scale.[13]

The first visible groups of foreigners appeared in Poland after the
change of political system in 1989. However, due to the fact that Poland's GDP level has remained (despite significant progress over the last
two decades) three to five times lower than that in Western Europe, the
unemployment level has been (with the exception of recent years) higher
than the EU average, and the social security system has been very poor,
there have been almost no pull factors attracting migrants. Those who
moved to Poland have been rare. Some of them belong to the group of
managers of foreign companies investing in Poland; others were military
conflict refugees from the post-Soviet territory, especially from Caucasus
states, including Chechnya.

The only larger groups of immigrants, this time of economic character, were the Vietnamese. Based on earlier contacts, they started to settle
down and bring their families after 1989. This group has been very active
economically in trade (especially textiles) and ethnic catering services.
The exact size of the group is not officially known, the estimates are that
there are between twenty and forty thousand of them, living mainly in
Warsaw.[14] The Vietnamese have never been considered a problematic
group of immigrants and have never become a matter of a wider public
or political debate. In the wider perception, they are a well-assimilating,
hardworking, and unproblematic minority. The second biggest group
is Ukrainian immigrants; after 2004, they became visible on the Polish
labor market, especially in the eastern part of the state. Following the
war in Donbas, 2015 brought a sharp influx of Ukrainian workers to

Poland. Almost one million visas with work permits were issued in 2015; additionally, workers started to come illegally to Poland from Ukraine on a massive scale.[15] Most of the Ukrainians found seasonal and low-paid jobs across Poland (filling the gap left after many Poles migrated to the west, and meeting the demand created by a booming economy and unemployment level significantly below the EU average).[16] At the same time, many Ukrainians are studying at Polish universities or are employed as specialists. Due to their linguistic and cultural proximity, Ukrainians tend to easily integrate into Polish society. Warm feelings toward them, resulting from the Polish support for Ukraine's pro-European attitudes and its struggle against Russian-backed separatists, contrast, however, with the still unresolved historical issue of the Volhynia massacre during World War II, which is a source of anti-Ukraine attitudes among Polish right-wing supporters.

It is important to note that after 1989 Poland was granted the status of a safe country; in 1991 Poland signed the Refugee Convention, and a limited but constant flow of refugees started to enter Poland. These were mainly citizens of the former Yugoslavia, after its bloody disintegration, as well as of the former Soviet Union, representing the Caucasian nations: Chechens, Armenians, as well as some Iraqis and Somalis.[17] Up to 2003, the annual number of refugee status applications was about three to four thousand; later (after the entry of Poland to the European Union, but also due to new conflicts) it rose to seven to ten thousand per year, with Chechens dominating among the applicants.[18] Since 2013, the number of applicants has been at the level of about fifteen thousand per annum. At the same time, however, the number of positive decisions has been stable over the last decade, ranging between two hundred and three hundred persons; a similar number of applicants are granted "subsidiary protection" or "tolerated residence" status.[19]

These numbers reveal that, in comparison to Western European states, Poland has been of minimal interest among immigrants, as well as refugees.[20] Additionally, a visible share of those coming to Poland treated it only as a transit state, and sooner or later moved further to the west or north of the continent.

Polish immigration policy is relatively recent. It came into being only in the new millennium as a result of external pressure. In the interwar period and during the Communist times, it was based on state control and concentrated on the emigration of Polish citizens, not on the influx of foreigners.[21] In 2012, the Polish government finally accepted a national strategy on immigration, "Polityka migracyjna Polski—stan obecny i postulowane działania" (Poland's immigration policy—current state and proposed activities),[22] fitting Polish solutions to the new circumstances resulting from Poland's membership in the European Union. It resulted from intensive work initiated in 2007, but was kept behind governmental doors in the initial phase and involved highly limited consultations with other interested partners, such as nongovernmental organizations.[23] It was operationalized in 2014 with an implementation plan.[24]

It is interesting to see how official documents describe and structure Polish immigration policy priorities. First of all, they stress that (large scale) immigration is a new challenge for Poland and the Western experience in this regard is—due to the different circumstances—of limited use here. At the same time, EU regulations apply, and the necessity of designing the forms for the access of foreigners to the Polish labor market follows from Polish membership of the EU.[25] Second, there are chapters devoted to persons of Polish origin, students, and scholars coming for educational purposes, businesspeople and delegated workers, and EU citizens using the freedom of work, and only then are other categories discussed. The former groups are given preferences with regard to immigration to Poland. This principle seems to be based on the historic-national approach, as well as the labor market's demands, especially in the context of a booming economy, the aging of society, and Polish emigration to the west. At the same time, the integration of immigrants into Polish society is stressed as one of the principles of the policy. Illegal immigration is another element that has to be monitored and prevented as a part of the general policy.[26] The implementation of these policies is monitored, and the relevant institutions are to publish reports on the advancement and pace of work, usually every three months.[27]

In 2015, the Polish liberal government agreed to participate in the allocation of migrants from Syria after their massive influx to Greece, Italy, and Germany. Seven thousand persons were to be transported to Poland; 6,100 of them were to come from the camps in Greece and Italy, and a further nine hundred directly from the Middle East.[28]

This decision was gradually modified and, ultimately, suspended by the new conservative government. In February 2016, the head of the Office for Foreigners declared than only four refugees could be accepted that year. But due to the November 2015 terrorist attacks in Paris, the government announced that no refugees would be accepted unless security concerns were resolved.[29]

In 2015, a nongovernmental organization, the Estera Foundation, established by a group of Syrian migrants of Christian origin, invited fifty Syrian-Christian families to Poland, organizing financial support to host them. By the beginning of 2016, most of them had gone, however, mainly migrating further to the western part of Europe.

National and Political Leaders about Immigrants

The last part of this chapter investigates the discourses of national and political leaders on immigrants in Poland. Its most significant properties have already been described. First, most of these discourses concentrate on refugees, due to the influx of over one million people to the EU, especially in 2015. The category of immigrants consequently appears mainly as an argument to explain or justify a specific approach to refugees. Second, the focus is on statements of the main political parties. Due to the elections in 2015, many of them are quoted in their roles as the leaders of the state (the liberals before the elections and the conservatives afterward) or as representatives of the opposition parties (in the reverse order).

What is striking in the discourses is that most of the leaders not only construct categories of immigration and immigrants, but also use these discourses to construct Poles and Poland. I will discuss both dimensions later. In general, most of the political parties have not been enthusiastic about newcomers; they differ, however, significantly in how they express their hesitance and what compromises they have been able to make in this field.

Immigrant and Refugee Rhetoric

Probably the first and the most relevant element in the debate over the last two years has been that of distinguishing between the categories of refugees and immigrants. Since hosting refugees has been considered a legal and moral obligation (although the conservatives have at the same time been particularly against accepting them), the key construct has been to label them as economic immigrants in order to reject them. Prime Minister Ewa Kopacz (PO) mentioned several times that Poland cannot afford economic immigrants and that the EU has to prepare a "policy of return."[30] Rafał Grupiński, PO spokesman, claimed that "the principle of voluntarism and working out how to distinguish economic migration from actual refugees is crucial."[31] Jarosław Kaczyński (PiS leader) stressed in September 2015 that "considering this issue we have to clearly differentiate between refugees, who are fleeing from war, and economic migrants. And who created the social magnet that attracts immigrants? Germany did. [Hungarian prime minister Viktor] Orbán was right here saying that it is their problem, not ours."[32] Przemysław Wipler (member of parliament from the liberal-conservative party KORWIN), observed: "This is an invasion of illegal immigrants on Europe."[33] Prime Minister Ewa Kopacz (PO) tried to persuade her opponents to be more open, while stressing at the same time that "it is necessary to tighten the borders and distinguish refugees from economic migrants."[34] President Andrzej Duda (PiS) claimed that "if we combine the tragedy of refugees with the needs of economic migrants, we are unable to help any of these groups effectively."[35] Consequently, refugees from the Middle East have been constructed as not "true refugees," victims of wars trying to save their lives, but rather as economic migrants looking for a better future in Europe. Additionally, the legality of their entry into the EU was put into question.

Second, refugees have been classified as a threat to the security of Poland and Poles. Two lines of argumentation have been visible here: the principle of security and refugees as a threat of various kinds.

The refugee issue is contextualized within the wider problem of security in an unstable world. For example, after the Paris terrorist attacks in November 2015, one of the conservative politicians, Konrad Szymański (PiS), said that Poland should condition its implementation of the declaration on refugees on "guarantees of security."[36] Jarosław Kaczynski (PiS) appealed to Prime Minister Kopacz to "protect Poland's own citizens." He asked in September 2015 "if the government has the right to yield to external pressure and, without the clearly expressed attitude of the nation, make decisions that are most likely to have an adverse impact on our everyday lives, public space and our real liberty zone. And, our safety, as has already been indicated."[37] The candidate to become the next prime minister, Beata Szydło (PiS), also stressed in 2015 that "a Prime Minister should have citizen's security in mind, first and foremost."[38] When debating the number of refugees Poland was to accept, then-prime minister Ewa Kopacz (PO) declared the following: "I will do nothing to destabilize our country."[39] She added that "we want Poland to monitor who comes here. Negotiations on this topic are already underway at a ministerial level in Europe."[40] Tomasz Siemoniak (PO), minister of defense, stressed the dual nature of the arguments influencing public opinion: "One day we see tragic pictures of children dying in desperate attempts to cross the sea, and another day we see riots triggered by refugees."[41] At the same time, however, Prime Minister Kopacz (PO) warned the conservative opposition: "Stop threatening Poles that we are going to be flooded with crowds of refugees one beautiful day. We do not have to put up walls and razor-wire fences on our borders today. Our borders are safe at present."[42]

This general discourse on immigration and the relocation of refugees as a threat to the state and nation has been translated more precisely into a picture of the specific threats refugees bring with them.

Terrorism and diseases tend to dominate here. President Duda (PiS) stated that the Polish government shall "ensure that Poles are well protected against epidemiological risks."[43] Witold Waszczykowski (PiS), minister of foreign affairs, stressed in an interview that "the fewer circles there are that can support terrorists, the easier it is to defend ourselves. This is how Poland is defending itself, by refusing to accept immigrants."[44] Zbigniew Ziobro (PiS) stated that "we should not admit followers of Islam, as some of them are extremists who will become a very serious and real threat to the security of our citizens, as the experience of rich EU countries shows."[45] Patryk Jaki (PiS) claimed that "there will be terrorists among refugees. [Furthermore,] 90 percent of immigrants do not want to work and are aggressive. Your naïveté with respect to Islamic State is reminiscent of the naïveté of people who in 1938–39 believed that Hitler was good. King Jan III Sobieski is turning in his grave."[46] Consequently, refugees are constructed as carriers of exotic diseases, as well as potential terrorists. Islam and aggression are amalgamated, and all the refugees are pictured as Muslims. Poland's role as a defender is stressed by the reference to King Jan III Sobieski, who saved Vienna, along with Poland and the entire West, from the Turkish-Muslim invasion in 1683.

If refugees are mainly economic migrants and they constitute a threat to Poland, where are the true "refugees," should they be helped, and how? In the politicians' discourse the answer seems to be clear: they should be helped at their original location, and Poland has a moral obligation to support them, while additionally discouraging them from coming to Europe. Tadeusz Iwiński (one of the leading social democratic politicians) asked the conservative opposition about the compatibility of their standpoint with the Catholic principles of mercy: "Did the United Right listen to Pope Francis?"[47]

In September 2015, Jarosław Kaczyński (PiS) proposed a principle that should determine the logics of providing assistance to refugees:

> Such a principle does exist—it is the order of compassion. Under this
> principle, our nearest and dearest come first, then there is the nation,

and then—others. Does this principle say that we should not help? No! But we should do so in a safe manner—financially. It was said here that USD 2.8bn are required to maintain the camps from which such enormous masses of people trickle into Europe. Let us assume such a portion of the obligation that corresponds to our GDP. This will be our true solidarity and a way to resolve this problem.[48]

"We suggest that refugees are helped, but this help is offered where there really are refugees, namely where war is being waged," added Mariusz Błaszczak (PiS), minister of domestic affairs and administration.[49] President Duda claimed that "the international community has the obligation to liquidate the true reasons for this refugeeism and to restore the right everybody has to live in their own homeland."[50]

In other words, helping refugees was to be carried out in their homelands in a way that would not be too much of a financial burden to Poland. This was "true solidarity." In this way moral and economic aspects were combined with a key concept, solidarity, of Polish political history. In the early 1980s, Solidarity became the first independent labor union in a Soviet-bloc country. It was a hugely popular, nonviolent, anti-communist social movement that contributed significantly to the fall of communism. In addition, solidarity is an important aspect of Catholic social thought.

Another way of constructing the picture of refugees was related to the issue of the influx of Ukrainians to Poland in 2015. In this case, despite the fact that they were economic (but culturally and linguistically close) immigrants, the conservative (as well as—to some extent—liberal) option tried to construct them as refugees to demonstrate Polish openness to a Europe-wide problem, as well as the fact that Poland had been affected by it in its local variation and was able to address the challenge in the European way. President Duda (PiS) stated: "As concerns refugees, we have a particular problem due to the conflict in Ukraine: as long as the war continues, thousands of Ukrainians will continue to flee the country, mainly to Hungary and Poland." Minister of Foreign Affairs Grzegorz Schetyna (PO) claimed that "Poland is a model, which we

are all stressing, of securing the eastern border of the European Union.
. . . We may face the threat of a migration crisis any time the situation
in Donbas escalates. I keep reminding about it every time we talk to the
EU."[51] Prime Minister Kopacz (PO) stressed that "for any government
the problem of refugees will not end on October 25 . . . on account of
the developments in Eastern Ukraine Poland may need the solidarity
of Europe. Solidarity should work both ways."[52] Finally, the new prime
minister, Beata Szydło (PiS), said in the European Parliament: "I am
here today because I feel the sense of profound responsibility for what is
happening in Poland and in Europe. Speaking about migration and migrants, Poland has taken in around one million refugees from Ukraine.
One million people nobody was willing to help."[53]

Construction of Poles and Polishness with the Help of Immigration Discourses

The case of Ukrainian migrants, and presenting them as refugees, leads
to a more general discourse on Polish openness to representatives of
foreign nations and cultures. As this discourse contradicts both the
current ethnic situation in Poland, as well as the position of most of
the leaders toward immigrants from the Middle East, historical arguments are usually presented. For example, then President Bronislaw
Komorowski (PO) stressed that "we have very rich experience, both
positive and negative, of living next to people of different cultures. We
also have enormous experience in building integration mechanisms—
the assimilation practice in the Republic of Poland used to be said to
be exceptionally praiseworthy. All this is in our historic genes."[54] John
Godson (member of parliament from PSL) stressed that "it is natural
to have concerns and fears. Fear is a bad councilor, though. We should
be slightly more open towards refugees. Poland is famous for its solidarity and hospitality. Poland has always offered shelter to the oppressed.
All this can be easily destroyed by fear and irresponsible behavior."[55]
Zbigniew Girzyński (member of parliament from PiS) claimed that

"Poland was strong because it was tolerant, and also because it had Jan III Sobieski as a king, who protected it against the expansion of other cultures. We have a problem bringing 200 persons from Donbas and we are talking about bringing thousands of refugees?"[56]

Rarely does this mythologized historical openness translate into current proposals. Prime Minister Ewa Kopacz (PO) observed that

> we are in Poland, which decided to take in 200 Syrians, most of whom have already left. Not so long ago, we took in 86,000 Chechens and have you seen any threats to the security of Poles? Therefore, I am asking today if we can afford to make a gesture of solidarity with those who flee out of fear. Can a nation of 40 million afford a gesture of solidarity? We are comparing the actual fears of Poles and the situation of these people. We have to be ready to take them in. Poland has the lowest rate of immigrants in Europe—0.3%. Our borders are secure. We are ready to implement a comprehensive plan and we are ready to talk about it at the European Council's sessions. The one condition we demand is the supervision over the allocation of people arriving in Europe. We are on the better side of the world.[57]

Another set of arguments went in a similar direction, referring to Poles still living in the former Soviet Union territories and waiting for repatriation. Beata Szydło (PiS) asked: "Now, when Poland is discussing taking in immigrants, the government is making a decision to bring immigrants and sees no obstacles, I have a simple question: why isn't the Polish government doing anything to facilitate the return of Poles to Poland?"[58]

When analyzing the discourse of state and political leaders in Poland, one of the notable facts is that refugees are also presented as a symbol of continental processes: the moral and cultural collapse of the West as well as the inappropriate policies of the European Union. At the same time, both of these processes allow Poland to present itself in a wider context, using refugees as an argument and illustration. In this context, Poland is one of the last defenders of European values and

Europeanness based on nation-states, Christianity, national unity, and cultural homogeneity.

Refugees are consequently pictured not only as aggressive destroyers and representatives of what is alien and barbarian, but also as the forerunners of processes that are visible in Western Europe: the erosion of the nation-state and the disintegration of cultural unity and even of public order. A small group of newcomers will not cause these processes but will initiate what will be inevitable and unstoppable later on. Jarosław Kaczyński (PiS) claimed in September 2015:

> The thing is that there is a serious threat that the following process will be initiated: first, the number of refugees soars dramatically, then they do not observe our laws and customs and, eventually, they impose their sensitivity and their requirements on the public space in many different aspects. And they do so in a most aggressive and violent manner. If somebody says this is not true, let them take a look around Europe. Let them look at Sweden, at the 54 zones with Sharia law. At Swedish concerns about displaying the national flag, because it features a cross. Female Swedish students are not allowed to wear short skirts because it is disapproved of.[59]

He went on, asking: "What is happening in Italy? Churches have been taken and are treated like toilets now. And in France? The ongoing riots, Sharia law and patrols ensuring it is being observed. . . . Do you want the same thing to happen in Poland? Do you want us to stop feeling like the hosts in our own country?"[60]

Mariusz Błaszczak (PiS), minister of domestic affairs and administration, stated that "no lessons were learned from previous attacks in Paris and Brussels. Ms. Federica Mogherini burst into tears, when the Eiffel Tower was lit up, Hanna Gronkiewicz-Waltz lights up the Palace of Culture. . . . This is a consequence of the policy of multi-culti, politics, political correctness. You cannot envisage how this situation could be resolved. . . . We will not make the mistakes of the West."[61] Refugees symbolize, then, an unwanted aspect and form of westernization. Poland consequently becomes an exemplification of pure, classical European-ness and one of its last bastions. It has to guard European values against an external threat; moreover, ironically, Poland cannot count on the West when protecting Westernness.

Finally, the debate over refugees embodies the debate over the future and form of the European Union, including its supranational or intergovernmental character and the role of sovereignty executed by member states. Refugees that were to be compulsorily relocated from Germany and Italy or Greece symbolize the power of Brussels or Berlin being imposed on Poland. On the one hand, President Duda (PiS) confirmed that Poland would accept two thousand refugees while opposing compulsory quotas. On the other hand, during the Twenty-Fifth Economic Forum in Krynica, he said: "I will not agree with the dictates by the strong [members] of the EU."[62] He stressed that every EU member "should meet the quotas in proportion to the capabilities of a state to provide help."[63] Mariusz Błaszczak (PiS) assessed Polish immigration policy during the conference on the first year of conservative government, labeling it as "sovereign." He claimed that the EU's policy was

> mistaken . . . and will cause successive waves of immigrants from Africa and Asia to enter Europe. This is what the proposal of the European Commission to assign permanent quotas to individual states will result in. This defies the EU treaties which define what the European Union should be and leads to threatening its security. We are consistent in our solidarity with other European Union states, delegating Polish border guards to the external borders of the EU.[64]

One year earlier he claimed that "Germany is trying to share the cost of maintaining immigrants with other member states."[65]

Beata Szydło (PiS) added that "Germany wants to blackmail Europe" and stressed that most refugees want to get to Germany.[66] Jarosław Gowin (PiS) also talked about "German blackmail."[67] In September 2015, Jarosław Kaczyński (PiS) referred to the argument about EU subsidies for states accepting refugees, claiming, "There is also this argument that we get paid by the EU. These are European resources. What do we get paid for? For transferring a huge part of our capacity to decide about our matters to great and strong EU states."[68] Conservative leaders stressed that it was Germany that created the immigration crisis and was responsible for it. Prime Minister Beata Szydło said that

> the problem of refugees makes us realize that the issue of solidarity needs to be clarified. Solidarity is about sharing what is good and about being ready to offer help when something extraordinary or dangerous occurs. For instance, great natural disasters, terrorist threats or even warfare. The term solidarity cannot be applied, however, to the attempts to sort of export the problems some states created for themselves and without any participation of other states that are supposed to share their burden now.[69]

The liberals, on the other hand, saw solidarity as a necessity of accepting the relocation of refugees. Prime Minister Kopacz warned in September 2015 that "turning our backs on those who need help from our European family means that we morally and mentally exclude ourselves from this community."[70] Rafał Grupiński claimed that "our European community needs to demonstrate solidarity on two levels: on the fundamental level of solidarity with refugees . . . ; [and] the second level of solidarity is intra-European solidarity, or sharing the responsibilities and expenses related to this problem."[71] Minister of Foreign Affairs Grzegorz Schetyna (PO) argued that "turning our backs on our partners who take these people in is against our own interests."[72] Therefore, refugee quotas represented the domination of the EU, especially of Germany. In the liberal view, the principle of European solidarity required that the quotas be accepted by countries concerned, or they would not implement them, blaming Germany for the problem of refugees. Refugees symbolize, then, the view of the European Union where the conservatives are trying to regain power from Brussels and from Berlin. Ludwik Dorn argued that "we are demonstrating our solidarity not to refugees but to the countries that are flooded by them. What the opposition is doing will make Poland a lonely island nobody will care for when the moment of truth comes."[73]

Conclusions

In October 2016, 54 percent of Poles declared they were against accepting refugees from conflict zones; 40 percent were in favor. A vast majority of the latter would prefer refugees to be sent back when the conflict is over. Perplexingly enough, the fact that Poland has accepted practically no refugees from the Middle East contrasts with the rather warm feelings toward the approximately one million economic migrants from Ukraine. Those attitudes are reflected in the rhetoric of the political and state leaders in Poland, but have also been created by them. None of the leading political parties has been particularly enthusiastic about accepting larger groups of refugees from the Middle East in 2015–2016. In part, this reflects the traditionally strong stress on homogeneity and unity present in the Polish culture.

In terms of ideological divisions, the conservatives (fighting to take power and then governing the state) stressed the threats caused by immigrants, especially those resulting from cultural differences. They stressed national community and unity against alleged negative external influences. The liberals, in turn, considered refugees an additional cost that could be paid in the name of European solidarity. On the other hand, they usually constructed refugees in a similar, albeit more moderate, manner, in other words, more or less as a burden or a nuisance in any case.

As regards the rhetoric of Polish national leaders, three important factors emerge. First, the Polish political language examined here often draws on "natural" metaphors. For example, the metaphor of "flood" is a common one: immigrants "are flooding us," and they are like "waves" that "are pouring in." Such rhetoric emphasizes the widespread Polish sentiment about the crisis: it is as though immigration would be suffocating or drowning the nation. This is, however, not the only approach.

Politicians also tend to securitize the phenomenon: immigration is a threat. Accordingly, although solidarity was an important argument for accepting refugees, it was implied that an overdose of it would destabilize the nation. Interestingly, in addition to terrorism and incompatibility of Islam, in Polish rhetoric there was conspicuously present also a concern related to biological hazards. Here the argument was that the diseases immigrants bring constituted a grave danger for the original population.

Second, the refugee crisis was used to discuss the country's problematic relation to its neighbor in the west, Germany. The countries have a long and complicated history, beginning in the tenth century and "culminating" in the invasion of Poland by Nazi Germany in September 1939. A common argument was that it was Germany that was the main culprit for the crisis: it had created a "social magnet" for immigrants. Thus, the crisis was essentially Germany's problem, and other EU states should not be put to pay for its mistakes. The implication was clear: Germany was again causing problems for the whole of Europe.

Third, the analyzed Polish discourses were politicized in relation to time. First, they were deeply rooted in the historical legacies of national and cultural homogeneity, predominantly based on Catholicism, as well as in the self-perception of Poles as a defender of Europe against external threats. Second, electoral campaigns brought to the fore the question of the future. They additionally heated up the debate that eventually moved from the topic of immigrants and refugees to the problem of the Polish position in the EU and the shape of the continental integration project. In this context, ironically, it was also claimed that Poland in fact was one of the last remnants of the authentic West, which the EU was about to wreck with its ill-conceived understanding of solidarity.

All in all, contemporary Polish immigration rhetoric with national unity as the key element reflects the two fundamental processes at the beginning of the chapter: namely, the necessity of confirming Poland's Western belonging, while at the same time defining its own indispensable role as *the* defender of authentic Western civilization. From these factors followed the discussion of immigration and immigrants, which turned swiftly into a debate about what Poland, Polishness, and Europeanness actually are. To be sure, the construction of political identities drawing on history and religion is a particularly intense issue because the issue at stake is the immutable essence of "us."

Notes

1. Norman Davies, *God's Playground* (Oxford: Oxford University Press, 2005).
2. Marceli Kosman, "The Polish Res Publica of National and Ethnic Minorities from the Piasts to the 20th Century," *Przegląd Zachodni* 2 (2014): 19.
3. Kosman, 21.
4. Kosman, 21–22.
5. Zdzisław Mach, "The Roman Catholic Church in Poland and the Dynamics of Social Identity in Poland," in *The Religious Roots of Contemporary European Identity*, ed. L. Faltin and M. J. Wright (New York: Continuum, 2007).
6. Lucyna Stetkiewicz, "The Role of the Catholic Church and Polish Religiosity," *Journal for the Sociological Integration of Religion and Society* 3, no. 2 (2013): 1–17.
7. Archibishop Stanisław Gądecki, Speech during the Polish Catholic School Forum, Częstochowa, Poland, November 4, 2016, episkopat.pl.
8. Jarosław Jańczak, "Why Go beyond EU Borders? Historical and Structural Reasons for the EU Eastern Edge States' External Initiatives," in *Beyond Borders: External Relations of the European Union*, ed. Jarosław Jańczak (Poznan: Wydawnictwo Naukowe INPiD UAM, 2008), 62–64.
9. Radoslaw Markowski, "The Polish Parliamentary Election of 2015: A Free and Fair Election That Results in Unfair Political Consequences," *West European Politics* 39, no. 6 (2016): 1311–1322.
10. Melchior Szczepanik, "The 2014 European Elections in Poland: Are We in for Another Uninspiring Campaign?," *European Policy Institute Network*, *Commentary* 15 (Dec. 2013): 1–5.
11. "Migracje Zagraniczne Ludności: Narodowy Spis Powszechny Ludności i Mieszkań 2011," Główny Urząd Statystyczny, Warsaw 2013.

12. Norman Davies, *Heart of Europe: A Short History of Poland* (Oxford: Oxford University Press, 2001), 108-109.

13. "Uchodzcy Info," *Uchodzcy Info*, uchodzcy.info.

14. Teresa Halik, *Migrancka Społeczność Wietnamczyków w Polsce w Świetle Polityki Państwa i Ocen Społecznych* (Poznan: Uniwersytet im. A. Mickiewicza w Poznaniu, 2006).

15. Jagienka Wilczak, "Milion Ukraińców w Polsce: Kim są? Gdzie Pracują?," *Polityka*, June 14, 2016, polityka.pl.

16. Marta Jaroszewicz and Tomasz Piecha, "Ukrainian Migration to Poland after the 'Revolution of Dignity': Old Trends or New Exodus?," in *Ukrainian Migration in Times of Crisis: Forced and Labour Mobility*, ed. Dušan Drbohlav and Marta Jaroszewicz (Prague: Charles University, 2016).

17. Paweł Hut, "Repatrianci i Uchodźcy po 1991 r.w. Polsce," *Problemy Polityki Społecznej: Studia i Dyskusje Rocznik* 24, no. 1 (2014): 47-60.

18. Anita Adamczyk, *Społeczno-polityczne Implikacje Imigracji do Polski w latach 1989-2007* (Poznan: Wydawnictwo Naukowe WNPiD UAM, 2012).

19. "Uchodzcy Info."

20. Konrad Pędziwiatr, "Imigranci w Polsce i Wyzwania Integracyjne," *INFOS, Biuro Analiz Sejmowych* 184 (2015): 1-4.

21. Anna Kicinger, *Polityka Migracyjna Polski 1918-2004* (Warsaw: Uniwersytet Warszawski, 2011).

22. "Polityka Migracyjna Polski—Stan Obecny i Postulowane Działania" Dokument Przyjęty Rrzez Radę Ministrów w dniu 31 lipca 2012 r., Ministerstwo Spraw Wewnętrznych, Departament Polityki Migracyjnej ["Immigration Policy of Poland—State of Art and Proposed Activities," document accepted by the Council of Ministers on July 31, 2012, Ministry for Foreign Affairs, Department of Migration Policy], mswia. gov.pl.

23. Mikołaj Pawlak, "Imitacja w Tworzeniu Polskiej Polityki Integracji Cudzoziemców," *Studia Migracyjne—Przegląd Polonijny* 39, no. 3 (2013): 104.

24. "Plan Wdrażania dla Dokumentu 'Polityka Migracyjna Polski—Stan Obecny i Postulowane Działania,'" Dokument Przyjęty Przez Radę Ministrów w dniu 2 grudnia 2014 r. Opracowanie: Zespół do Spraw Migracji ["Implementation Plan for the Document 'Immigration Policy

of Poland—State of Art and Proposed Activities,'" document accepted by the Council of Ministers on December 2, 2014, prepared by Unit for Migration Issues].

25. "Polityka Migracyjna Polski," 5-7.

26. "Zasady i Rekomendacje Polityki Migracyjnej dla Polski," in *Polityka Migracyjna Polski Wobec Wyzwań Demograficznych, Biuletyn Forum Debaty Publicznej* 36 (2015): 72.

27. "Sprawozdanie z Realizacji Planu Wdrażania dla Dokumentu 'Polityka Migracyjna Polski—Stan Obecny i Postulowane Działania w Roku 2014,'" Warsaw, dnia 22 maja 2015 r. ["Report of Realization of the Implementation Plan for the Document 'Immigration Policy of Poland—State of Art and Proposed Activities in 2014,'" Warsaw May 22, 2014]; "Sprawozdanie z Realizacji Planu Wdrażania dla Dokumentu 'Polityka Migracyjna Polski—Stan Obecny i Postulowane Działania' w III kwartale 2015, Warszawa, dnia 30 grudnia 2015 r. ["Report of Realization of the Implementation Plan for the Document 'Immigration Policy of Poland—State of Art and Proposed Activities' in 3rd quarter 2015," Warsaw, December 30, 2015].

28. Artur Dragan, "Polska Jako Kraj Migracji," *Biuro Analiz i Dokumentacji, Zespół Analiz i Opracowań Tematycznych*, Kancelaria Senatu Luty (2016): 9.

29. "Rząd: Polska Nie Jest w Stanie w tej Chwili Przyjąć Imigrantów," *Gazeta Prawna*, March 23, 2016, gazetaprawna.pl.

30. Renata Grochal and Agata Kondzińska, "Polscy Politycy Grają Uchodźcami w Kampanii: Szydło: Niemcy Chcą Szantażować Europę," *Gazeta Wyborcza*, September 10, 2015, wyborcza.pl.

31. Rafał Grupiński, Statement in Parliamentary Debate, September 9, 2015 in the lower chamber, Sejm. The original protocol is available at sejm.gov.pl.

32. Jarosław Kaczyński, Statement in Parliamentary Debate, September 9, 2015, sejm.gov.pl.

33. Przemysław Wipler, Statement in Parliamentary Debate, September 9, 2015, sejm.gov.pl.

34. Ewa Kopacz, Statement in Parliamentary Debate, September 9, 2015, sejm.gov.pl.

35. Andrzej Duda, "President's Speech during the UN Summit for Refugees and Migrants," Permanent Mission of the Republic of Poland to the United Nations in New York, September 19, 2016, nowyjorkonz.msz.gov.pl.

36. "Przyszły Minister: Przyjmiemy Uchodźców, Jeśli Będziemy Mieć Gwarancje Bezpieczeństwa," *Dziennik Wschodni*, November 14, 2015, dziennikwschodni.pl.

37. Kaczyński, Statement in Parliamentary Debate, September 9, 2015.

38. "XXV Forum Ekonomiczne. Beata Szydło o Uchodźcach: "Premier Powinien Myśleć Przede Wszystkim o Bezpieczeństwie Obywateli," *Gazeta Wyborcza*, September 9, 2015, wyborcza.pl.

39. "Polscy Politycy Grają Uchodźcami w Kampanii. Szydło: Niemcy Chcą Szantażować Europę," *Gazeta Wyborcza*, September 5, 2015, wyborcza.pl.

40. "Polscy Politycy Grają Uchodźcami w Kampanii."

41. "Siemoniak o Rządach Kopacz: 'W tych Ostatnich Ośmiu Latach Koalicji PO-PSL Był to Rok Najtrudniejszy'," *wPolityce.pl*, September 22, 2015, wpolityce.pl.

42. Kopacz, Statement in Parliamentary Debate, September 9, 2015.

43. "Poland's President Warns of Refugees Bringing Epidemics," *Al Jazeera*, October 18, 2015.

44. "Waszczykowski: Im Mniej Środowisk, Które Mogą Dawać Pożywkę Terrorystom, Tym Łatwiej Jest Się Bronić. 'Tak Broni Się Polska, Nie Chcąc Przyjmować Imigrantów,'" *wPolityce.pl*, March 25, 2016, wpolityce.pl.

45. "'Nie Ulegać Niemieckiemu Szantażowi,' 'Muzułmanie Ekstremiści,' 'Współpracować z UE,' Czyli Polskie Partie o Uchodźcach [ANKIETA]," *Gazeta Wyborcza*, September 9, 2015, wyborcza.pl.

46. Patryk Jaki, Statement in Parliamentary Debate, September 9, 2015, sejm.gov.pl.

47. Tadeusz Iwiński, Statement in Parliamentary Debate, September 9, 2015, sejm.gov.pl.

48. Duda, "President's Speech during the UN Summit."

49. "Szef MSWiA: Naszą Dewizą Zero Tolerancji dla Chuligaństwa i Łamania Prawa," *PAP Polish Press Agency*, November 15, 2016, pap.pl.

50. Duda, "President's Speech during the UN Summit."

51. Grzegorz Schetyna, Statement in Parliamentary Debate, September 9, 2015, sejm.gov.pl.

52. Kopacz, Statement in Parliamentary Debate, September 9, 2015.

53. "Szydło: 'Polska Przyjęła Milion Uchodźców z Ukrainy.' A co Pokazują Liczby?," *Gazeta Wiadomości*, January 20, 2016, wiadomosci.gazeta.pl.

54. Bronisław Komorowski, "Opening Speech, Polityka Migracyjna Polski Wobec Wyzwań Demograficznych," *Biuletyn Forum Debaty Publicznej* 36 (2015): 9.

55. John Godson, Statement in Parliamentary Debate, September 9, 2015, sejm.gov.pl.

56. Zbigniew Girzyński, Statement in Parliamentary Debate, September 9, 2015, sejm.gov.pl.

57. Kopacz, Statement in Parliamentary Debate, September 9, 2015.

58. Beata Szydło, "MP's Speech," Polish Press Agency, July 7, 2015, pap.pl.

59. Kaczyński, Statement in Parliamentary Debate, September 9, 2015.

60. Kaczyński.

61. "Zamach Terrorystyczny w Nicei: Wiele Ofiar [Relacja]," *Onet Wiadomości*, July 15, 2016, wiadomosci.onet.pl.

62. Andrzej Duda, "President's Speech at 25th Economic Forum in Krynica," *Daily Sabah Europe*, September 9, 2015, dailysabah.com.

63. Duda, "President's Speech at 25th Economic Forum."

64. "Zamach Terrorystyczny w Nicei."

65. Grochal and Kondzińska.

66. Grochal and Kondzińska.

67. Grochal and Kondzińska.

68. Kaczyński, Statement in Parliamentary Debate, September 9, 2015.

69. Beata Szydło, "Exposé Premier Beaty Szydło—Stenogram," November 18, 2018, premier.gov.pl.

70. Kopacz, Statement in Parliamentary Debate, September 9, 2015.

71. Grupiński, Statement in Parliamentary Debate, September 9, 2015.

72. Schetyna, Statement in Parliamentary Debate, September 9, 2015.

73. Ludwik Dorn, Statement in Parliamentary Debate, September 9, 2015, sejm.gov.pl.

Flüchtlingsrepublik Deutschland

DIVIDED AGAIN

———•◆•———

Julia Khrebtan-Hörhager and Elisa I. Hörhager

A mong various Western societies, Germany represents a very interesting and fertile research field with regard to immigration as a host country, with a unique cultural past and an even more challenging present and future with regard to cultural diversity and global leadership. The "German question"—about the role of a country too big for Europe and too small for the world—has been on the agenda for quite some time.[1] Many in Europe fear that Germany is becoming too bossy; some newspaper cartoons in southern Europe portrayed Chancellor Angela Merkel with a Hitler moustache. Notably, the German word for leader is *Führer*, the title previously adopted by Adolf Hitler—an additional reason for German ambivalence and discomfort with regard to European leadership.[2]

On the other hand, German moral guilt toward the world, together with a unique cultural phenomenon of *Vergangenheitsbewältigung* (coping with the past)[3] and a relatively recent national attempt to create a new, positive image of the country on the world stage, significantly contributes to the ongoing development of relationships between the German self and the non-German Other. Importantly, as recently as 2015—the year in which the publication (the first time since World War II) of Hitler's infamous *Mein Kampf* (*My Struggle*) coincided with the outburst of the refugee exodus from the Middle East—as many as 75 percent of Germans said that Hitler's crimes mean Germany still cannot be a "normal" country and must play a "special international role."[4]

Furthermore, the status quo of the European Union as well as the ongoing discussions of potential Turkish membership make the study of immigration in Germany significant, particularly since Germany is home to the largest Turkish immigrant population among European countries (around three million), and it is a key player in the ongoing humanitarian crisis. The partisanship over immigration has only sharpened with the current refugee crisis, caused by the instability in the Middle East.

A look at the statistics on asylum applications in Germany shows that the general instability in the Middle East, and specifically the civil war in Syria, is not the only factor behind the rapid influx of refugees into Germany. After declining radically as the result of the legislative reforms on asylum in 1993 and remaining at low levels through the following two decades (down to under twenty-five thousand first applications in 2007), the number of asylum applications in Germany began rising again in 2009 and significantly in 2013 (above one hundred thousand first applications).[5] Syrian refugees initially flocked to the neighboring countries of Lebanon, Turkey, Jordan, Iraq, and Egypt, with about one hundred thousand entering Europe in 2013. As the numbers fleeing the civil war and the unrest increased and the conditions for refugees in the neighboring countries worsened, so did the number of Syrian and Afghan asylum applicants in Germany. In 2015, there were 441,899 applications in Germany, while the number of people registered at the German borders reached almost 1.1 million.[6] Of those registered refugees, only 39.2 percent were Syrian, 14.1 percent Afghans, and 11.1 percent Iraqis. The other half of the asylum applicants came from the Balkan region:

Albania, Kosovo, Serbia, and Macedonia. However, as a result of intergovernmental efforts and an asylum recognition rate of almost zero,
this situation has shifted. Beginning in January 2016, most applicants
came from Syria, Iraq, and Afghanistan. Despite this increase, the rate
of rejection of asylum status also steadily decreased from 32.4 percent in
2015 to 25.8 percent in the first months of 2016.[7]

Overall, the aforementioned situation has led Germany and Europe
more generally to grapple with shifting geographical, political, and
rhetorical borders. With the European Union facing a rising humanitarian crisis—a crisis that in fact challenges the very idea of an (arguably)
united Europe—the task of the EU has been to critically rethink and
reconsider its own nature, its multicultural dynamics, and the pressing
matter of its fast-growing diversity. Nicknamed "Europe's hegemon,"
Germany stands in the epicenter of a multicultural debate—a sobering
fact that once again invites a thorough revisiting of German intercul-
turality, multiculturalism, and the immigration situation. We will begin
with a brief overview of the German political system and the country's
immigration policies.

A Brief Historical Overview of Immigration and Asylum in Germany

The reunited Federal Republic of Germany is a parliamentary democracy and a multiparty republic, in which voting is done by proportional
representation. There are two legislative houses: the Bundestag and the
Bundesrat (the parliament and the federal council, respectively). The
president is the head of state, yet is largely overshadowed by the chancellor as the head of the government. The current government's preoccupa-
tions include the so-called German-German question (of Eastern and
Western Germanies), the ongoing energy and grid transition dynamics,
and the current humanitarian/refugee crisis, due to which the Bundesrepublik Deutschland (Federal Republic of Germany) was nicknamed
Flüchtlingsrepublik Deutschland (Refugee Republic of Germany).

Immigration matters in Germany are quite complex and frequently controversial. In order to understand the specificities of the recent political debate in the midst of the huge influx of refugees from North Africa and the Middle East, a brief glance at the history of immigration and asylum politics in Germany is necessary. On July 4, 2001, the newly constituted German Commission on Immigration announced its recommendations for the future of Germany's migration policy. In its report, the commission finds that "even though Germany has long been, de facto, a country of immigration, a concept for immigration in line with the interests of society is lacking."[8] It explicitly rejects the "decades old political and normative assertion that 'Germany is no country of immigration.'"[9] At the turn of the century, this commission spoke out about the reality of German immigration during a time where much of the political world was still not ready to accept the facts of permanent immigration. It is odd that Germany (formerly West Germany) would self-identify as a country of nonimmigration, when the influx of foreigners into the country has been on a steady rise from half a million, or 1 percent of the population, in 1961 to seven million, or 9 percent, since 1995.[10] Tracing the legal framework of immigration and the positions of the country's political parties' stances on this issue helps explain the political hesitancy of leaders to actively form a policy of immigration by denying the very reality of immigration.

The following brief overview is divided into three chronological phases according to the advancing institutionalization of migration and asylum policies. The first phase is one of *state-controlled "temporary" immigration* (1955 to 1973). Germany, historically a country marked mostly by emigration, experienced an initial population influx during and after World War II consisting of 12.5 million displaced Germans from eastern European territories having become part of Poland or the Soviet Union.[11] It was followed by a first wave of foreign migrants in the form of *Gastarbeiter* (guest workers) as a solution to the shortage of workforce in West Germany.[12] The history of that period of immigration into Germany was shaped by economic forces: in order to supply a workforce able to fuel economic growth in the postwar times, Germany opened up its frontiers to poorer foreigners in need of employment. Specifically, in order to sustain the so-called economic miracle following its reconstruction, the Federal Republic of Germany (FRG) signed nine recruitment agreements (*Anwerbeabkommen*) from 1955 to 1968 with Italy, Greece, Spain, Turkey, Morocco, South Korea, Portugal, Tunisia, and the former Yugoslavia.[13] These agreements allowed the recruitment of *Gastarbeiter* to work in the industrial sector for jobs that required few qualifications. Despite the erection of the Berlin Wall putting a halt to workforce immigration from East Germany in 1961, the foreign workforce started to gain in numbers until it reached 11.9 percent of the total workforce in 1973.[14] Their denotation as guest workers implied an economic and social classification as temporary workers mainly employed in industrial production at the bottom rung of the job market.

After economic downturns, briefly in 1966–1967 and with the oil crisis in 1973, the policies of workforce immigration were brought to an abrupt halt. At that point, there were 2.6 million *Gastarbeiter* working in West Germany, compared with no more than 72,900 foreign workers in 1954.[15] In November 1973, the government decided to end the recruitment of workers from outside the European Community through the so-called recruitment moratorium (*Anwerberstopp*). This moratorium has remained in place until today, with a few exceptions mainly aimed at highly qualified workers.[16]

The recruitment of foreign workers was supposed to be on a temporary basis through the principle of rotation (*Rotationzprinzip*), in which workers from one country were meant to be periodically replaced in shifts. This policy failed to consider the reality of migrant workers who increasingly saw Germany as their home and wanted to remain there and then reunite with their families. The moratorium of 1973—whose effects were both the reduction of the numbers of new foreign workers as well as the loss of mobility for these migrant workers to come and go—significantly contributed to the decision of many *Gastarbeiter* in Germany to settle there permanently with their families. Based on the Aliens Act of 1965,[17] which provided the domestic legal framework for the recruitment agreements, the spouses and children of *Gastarbeiter* received residence permits. This piece of legislation framed the resulting policy as a "policy of foreigners" (*Ausländerpolitik*) that encompassed all aspects regulating the entry and exit as well as the sojourn of foreigners on German territory. The effects of this initial framing persist until today, as Germany still does not have a more comprehensive immigration law (*Einwanderungsgesetz*)—this despite the fact that one in five foreigners living in Germany (1.34 million people) was born on German soil and belongs to the second or third migrant generation, with almost one in three being Turkish, Italian, or Greek.[18]

The legislative reforms that would pave the way to increased civil protection and eventually citizenship for these de facto permanent migrants and their descendants were only put in place starting almost two decades later. During this first phase, despite large-scale, long-term or permanent immigration, the latter was not yet accompanied by corresponding institutions or policies.

During the second phase, Germany became a country of *informal immigration* (1973 to 2005). In the first decade after the recruitment moratorium, the slow increase in the foreign population of Germany was mainly due to family reunification. This form of migration brought with it a whole set of problems that had not been considered by the legislature under the umbrella of temporary workforce migration. Those included the legal uncertainty of immigrants in terms of their resident permit status, and the issue of integrating immigrant children into the education system. Especially for the so-called second generation (children of immigrant families born in Germany), this situation of legal uncertainty became increasingly untenable. In the 1980s, legislative efforts repeatedly yet unsuccessfully sought reform and modernization of the Aliens Act. The debate remained defined by the questions of how to minimize new immigration into Germany, whose economic need was reaching its saturation; how to encourage *Gastarbeiter* to leave and thus promote voluntary emigration; and how to reduce the family-reunification-based immigration of *Gastarbeiter* relatives. However, the only legislation passed on the matter was the 1983 Law on the Determinable Facilitation of the Willingness to Return of Foreigners.[19]

The Aliens Act of 1965 was finally reformed on January 1, 1991. The new law represented a compromise between, on the one hand, the recognition of the factual situation faced by immigrants in Germany, creating a legal immigration status and the possibility of the acquisition of citizenship for the second generation and long-term foreign residents.[20] On the other hand, it increased bureaucratic leeway for the control and repatriation of immigrants and continued to restrict new immigration. Having emerged as a long-sought-after compromise between different political positions, this law was criticized for "causing new contradictions."[21] According to a legal commentator, the law is difficult to understand for nonexperts and continues to treat foreigners as a "potential source of danger for the German society," subjugating them to "official reporting and monitoring requirements that border on totalitarian surveillance."[22]

During the first decades, foreigners-related politics in Germany focused primarily on the immigrants due to the extremely low levels of actual asylum seekers. This situation eventually changed during the 1980s, when the numbers of asylum seekers started rising (from 57,379 in 1987 to 438,191 in 1992).[23] However, the political debates on the subject of asylum seekers remained embedded in the discourse about *Gastarbeiter*. Although the legal right to asylum in accordance with the German constitution remained relatively uncontroversial, what was critically debated was what would happen once asylum status was recognized and the asylum seekers remained in Germany. As the mainstream political attitude of the time was that even those foreigners the Germans had voluntarily allowed into the country as economically valuable assets were not supposed to stay, the chances of asylum seekers receiving the privilege of permanent residency looked rather bleak. Furthermore, conservative and nationalist discourses blurred the distinction between voluntary immigration and immigration related to asylum seekers and focused mainly on various social issues related to both aforementioned groups in an undifferentiated manner. They were framed as social parasites, undermining the very core of the German culture, namely, its Christianity.

Eventually, such lack of distinction between different groups of immigrants in the political debates fostered extreme opinions and was accompanied by the rise of xenophobic incidents. During 1991 and 1992, right-wing extremists attacked homes and small businesses of immigrant workers and the initial reception facilities for asylum seekers. At the same time, political parties negotiated the so-called asylum compromise, which introduced two new pieces of legislation in 1993 restricting the right to political asylum in Germany: the Asylum Procedure Act (Asylverfahrensgesetz) and the Asylum Seekers Benefits Act (Asylbewerberleistungsgesetz).[24] As the legal basis for the right to asylum, Article 16 of the federal constitution, previously stating that "politically persecuted persons have the right to asylum," was supplemented by four additional paragraphs introducing new limitations to the laws. Those involve the exclusion from the right to asylum of anyone entering Germany from a "safe third country," and the identification of "safe countries of origin."[25] The Asylum Procedure Act also introduced accelerated asylum procedures (the so-called Airport Procedures), and the Asylum Seekers Benefits Act extracted asylum seekers from the welfare system by reducing their benefits. As mentioned earlier, this compromise was reached in a context of extremely violent acts against asylum seekers, which also occur in the current refugee crisis and feature the rhetoric against the "glut of asylum seekers."[26]

The xenophobic attacks of the early 1990s came up in the current discourse again as 2015 saw a record number of attacks on facilities housing asylum seekers. The number of attacks on housing facilities for refugees rose dramatically from 24 documented cases in 2012 to 1,005 attacks in 2015.[27] An important example is Hoyerswerda in eastern Germany, the city in which a housing facility for Vietnamese immigrants was attacked and vandalized five nights in a row in 1991. In 2015, despite the mayor's appeal to "not let 1991 be repeated," the newly built refugee facility was vandalized by right-wing extremists before refugees could even be housed there.[28] Despite the indignation among mainstream politicians, who quickly took to Twitter to condemn the attacks and demand the incarceration of those responsible, the rate of solved cases where those responsible could be identified is no higher than one in four incidents.[29]

Furthermore, since the 1990s, immigration has also become a policy concern at the European level. With the Maastricht Treaty in 1994 and the consolidation of the European Single Market and the Schengen Agreement on the mobility of persons, immigration policy was recognized as a European challenge; yet it became part of the intergovernmental Justice and Home Affairs pillar, meaning it remained on the level of national regulation. In western European countries, legal migration has taken on four forms: family unification; traditionally privileged migration relations (in Germany for late repatriates and Jews from the Commonwealth of Independent States); workforce immigration; and restricted immigration of asylum seekers.[30] In 1999, the EU's competence in this domain was officially recognized by the Treaty of Amsterdam.[31] Despite this recognition, so far immigration has been regulated by the respective national laws of the EU members, and there has been little progress made in the area of a common asylum policy. This problematic and still unresolved controversial issue plays a prominent role in shaping current German national rhetoric on the subject of the necessity of an "'All-European solution' to the refugee crisis."[32]

Finally, the Law on Citizenship was reformed in 2000,[33] opening up the possibility for the acquisition of citizenship by immigrants in accordance with European standards. Up until this reform, German citizenship had been based solely on the ethnonational principle of *jus sanguinis*," or "law of blood." Historically, Germany has been among those nations that determine citizenship based on parentage. Except for minor amendments, Germany's existing *Blutsrecht (jus sanguinis)* laws date back to 1914, a time when the population was much more homogeneous and relatively free of *Ausländer* (foreigners). The *Blutsrecht* principle itself goes back to Bavaria in 1818 and went into effect in the German Reich in 1870.[34]

Critics of strict naturalization laws viewed them as a relic of the past and an obstacle on the way to successful integration. Change came with Chancellor Gerhard Schroeder in late 1998. Schroeder and his Socialist Party of Germany/Green coalition government pushed through more liberal naturalization laws. The time required before a foreigner can apply for citizenship was reduced from fifteen to eight years. A foreign spouse of a German citizen can apply for citizenship after only three years. Naturalized citizens must prove an absence of criminal records, financial sustainability, and knowledge of the German language and culture, and pledge to uphold the German constitution and the democratic system. After 2000, children born to immigrants on German territory could acquire citizenship if at least one of their parents had their permanent residence in Germany for at least eight years. This law gave many second- and third-generation children of migrant workers the opportunity to become officially recognized as German nationals.

The final phase is one of Germany as a country of *ongoing and growing migration* (2005 to today). At the turn of the century, the single reform of the 1965 Aliens Act in 1990 had not provided for an updated, less contradictory aliens policy. However, political initiatives in 2000 and 2001 brought the "policy of foreigners" back to the political agenda. This included the "Green Card initiative" for temporary work permits given to highly qualified workers from outside the EU, as well as the constitution of the Commission on Immigration, referred to in the introduction to this section, which recommended a fundamental transformation toward a true policy of immigration and integration. The rationales mentioned include the responsibility of Germany toward the international community in times of ongoing globalization, combined with the economic necessity of attracting more highly qualified foreign workers (and creating a brain drain for other countries), replacing an aging population, and a concern over the population movement from small and rural areas in eastern Germany to growing and mostly western German cities.[35]

In the context of these initiatives, a legislative project for a comprehensive law on immigration (*Zuwanderungsgesetz*),[36] reforming the existing legislation on immigration, asylum, and citizenship, was first proposed by Chancellor Schroeder in 2001. It aimed at an immigration policy better aligned with the needs of the German economy and was the subject of intense debates, criticized, if on different grounds, by opposition parties as well as by nongovernmental organizations.[37] Importantly, after 9/11, this reform project was modified to exclude the security aspects from the immigration law and integrate them into another legislative project focused on security instead. The law was rejected by the parliamentary opposition and, due to issues with the voting procedure exploited by the opposition, its passage was delayed for years until a modified version finally went into force in January 2005, forming the current legal basis of Germany's immigration policy. It reduced the various types of residency into two permits (temporary and indefinite) and placed the focus on measures of integration. It also placed more responsibility on the federal office for migration and refugees in terms of harmonizing and accelerating the administrative procedures, as well as allowing for better protection of asylum seekers' families. In an analysis of the policy outcomes conducted by Klaus Stüwe, the law is not very positively evaluated in terms of increased control over immigration or improved integration of foreign residents (which is, of course, difficult to measure).[38]

As has become obvious since the beginning of the current refugee crisis, the legislation already in place provided an inadequate basis for dealing with large-scale immigration into Germany. However, the discussion on updating Germany's policy on immigrants was abruptly marginalized by the advent of the refugee crisis.

The division and the polarization of political standings and opinions, as well as the corresponding tendencies in the German national rhetoric, can be best understood when embedded in the framework of German political culture, summarized in the following brief overview of the country's leading parties and their representatives.

German Political Parties: Divided Standings on Immigration

The two largest parties, which form the current governmental coalition, are the conservative Christian Democratic Union (CDU), which partners with its even more conservative Bavarian counterpart, the Christian Social Union (CSU), on the federal level, and the Social Democratic Party of Germany (SPD). The right-of-center liberal Free Democratic Party (FDP) has been present in the federal parliament since 1949 and often participated in the ruling coalition as the minor partner of the conservatives; yet since 2013 it has been unable to make the cutoff of 5 percent of votes needed to gain seats and has therefore lost much of its political relevance. The left-of-center Green Party (Bündnis 90/Die Grünen) grew out of environmentalist social movements in 1980 and participated in a ruling coalition with the Socialists for two legislative periods from 1998 to 2005. Finally, the Left Party (Die Linke) resulted from the fusion of the two anticapitalistic socialist parties in 2007 and is very strong in the *Länder* of the former German Democratic Republic. Despite being one seat stronger than the Greens in the current Bundestag, it has never formed part of the government.

Political positions on immigration and asylum seekers have been divided from the beginning.[39] In accordance with the legislative situation, no clearly defined "immigration policy" existed in partisan programs in the 1960s and 1970s, and for some observers even into the 1990s.[40] In addition, the political debates on immigration were marred by racist discourses in the 1980s and beyond.

Being rather reactive on the issue of immigration historically, in the 1980s parties from across the political spectrum were finally forced to recognize what they had been previously denying, namely that the *Gastarbeiter* and their families were there to stay in Germany. Since then, the Socialists have been demanding relatively progressive reforms of the laws governing resident status, naturalization (with the limited possibility of dual citizenship), and participation in municipal elections. Their initiatives were often backed by the Liberals—a collection of parties that includes people from Die Linke, from *Bündnis 90/Die Grünen*, and from the SPD. Their policies on immigration ranged from a progressive policy of integration to the facilitation of emigration together with the prevention of new immigration. Both Socialists and Liberals wanted to accelerate asylum-related procedures. The Greens emphasized the need for liberal policies toward asylum seekers, advocating for an acceptance of asylum seekers without proof of persecution or on the basis of economic hardship and ecological catastrophes, promoting the idea of inclusive multiculturalism, and conceptualizing Germany as a country of immigration. While the Greens recognized the reality of German immigration as permanent from their very founding period in the 1980s, they were followed by the Liberals in the early 1990s, and eventually by the Socialists in 2005. However, immigration reforms demanded by these parties experienced only moderate success due to the opposition of the conservative parties. The latter formulated their views on immigration as temporary in the 1970s and rejected any reforms suggesting an alternative standing. Only in 1994 did the conservative parties recognize the permanent nature of *Gastarbeiter* immigration and the need for a policy of integration on the federal level, while further advocating for reducing the number of foreigners in Germany. Since the turn of the century, all parties represented in the Bundestag have focused on the issue of integration, with an emphasis on the "naturalization of Islam"[41] as a religion that, alongside Christianity, should belong to the German *Nationalbild* and constitute and integral part.

Before the current refugee crisis hit Germany in the spring of 2015, the grand coalition government between the conservatives and the Socialists (CDU/CSU-SPD) had reached an agreement on limited immigration reforms. The Socialists were criticized for not pushing through their demand for dual citizenship and for adopting the rhetoric of their conservative partner on migrants and refugees. This meant "reducing the incentives for migration into social security systems," rejecting "the freedom of changing country in order to receive more social benefits,"[42] and strengthening the measures for returning illegal refugees and migrants. In early 2015, the leader of the Socialist faction proposed an immigration law (*Einwanderungsgesetz*, different from the current *Zuwanderungsgesetz*) for targeted immigration and a better integration of migrants and refugees into the German workforce. This proposition caused discord among the coalition partners. Initially, Merkel rejected the need for a new law in light of the "urgent question of the multitude of refugees," yet has expressed her willingness to negotiate such a legislative project of state-led immigration in order to reduce the pressure on the asylum system.[43] Most important, however, Merkel's attention and rhetoric focused on refugees coming from hot spots, whom the chancellor is determined to "show Germany's friendly face" (*Deutschlands freundliches Gesicht zeigen*).

That notably humanitarian if not entirely noble goal, however, has been often criticized by other politicians as naive and at times even hypocritical, while revealing the split in contemporary national rhetoric on the subject matter—the split intensified by the initially problematic and still controversial nature of German multicultural relations.

Controversial German Multiculturalism

Although the immigration laws in Germany underwent several reformation attempts and became more liberal, the political and cultural climate in which the refugee crisis intervened has been rife with controversy for quite some time now. In 2010, the now-infamous German politician and historian Thilo Sarrazin published a best-selling book, *Deutschland schafft sich ab* (*Germany Is Abolishing Itself*),[44] where he denounced the failure of German multiculturalism and asserted that of all the minorities in Germany, Turkish and Arab immigrants were the most unwilling to integrate. With regard to those predominantly Muslim immigrant groups, Sarrazin suggested that

> no other religion in Europe makes so many demands. No immigrant group other than Muslims is so strongly connected with claims on the welfare state and crime. No group emphasizes its differences so strongly in public, especially through women's clothing. In no other religion is the transition to violence, dictatorship, and terrorism so fluid.[45]

Although Sarrazin has been denounced as racist, his perspective on Turkish and Arab Muslims reflected the views of many Germans. One of the most recent examples of German Islamophobia is represented by the alarmingly fast-growing anti-Islamic movement Pegida—Patriotische Europaer gegen die Islamisiering des Abendlandes (literally, Patriotic Europeans against the Islamization of the Occident).

In the same year that Sarrazin published *Deutschland schafft sich ab*, German chancellor Angela Merkel shocked her countrymen and the world with the bitterly blunt statement, "German multiculturalism is dead."[46] In December 2015, she qualified her assessment, and instead suggested that multiculturalism remains a "white lie" and does nothing more than producing parallel societies:

> At the start of the 1960s we invited the guest workers to Germany. We kidded ourselves for a while that they wouldn't stay, that one day they'd go home. That isn't what happened. And of course, the tendency was to say: let's be "*multikulti*" and live next to each other and enjoy being together, [but] this concept has failed, failed utterly.[47]

This statement by Merkel can be read politically as a direct challenge to political opposition from the Green Party, which has championed liberal immigration policy under the banner of a "multicultural society" since the party's foundation in the 1980s. Subtracted from political strategy, however, Merkel's statement is representative of the mindset that allowed Germany to refuse, for half a century, its fact-based label as a country of immigration and instead frame the inflow of foreigners according to the instrumental notion of a state-led policy for foreigners under economic imperatives. When it became clear that many *Gastarbeiter* and their families could not be simply sent back home, and as more refugees started to receive asylum status in Germany, the debates surrounding "labor/ workforce migration" (*Arbeitsmigration*) and "asylum" (*Asyl*) were no longer separated, but fused to become the object of ideological and political maneuvering about "foreigners." The two broad aims of the immigration law in force since 2005—limitation and integration—are two sides of the same coin that reflect this ambivalent political stance on immigration. While admitting that labor/workforce immigration, is, in reality, a permanent form of immigration for many of the foreigners concerned and therefore accepting the necessity of integration, the law tries to limit immigration as much as possible and sees this as in accordance with German interests, which as a principle would tend to undermine the liberal and welcoming stance toward immigrants necessary for their successful integration.

Integration is the legislature's response, first developed in a pragmatic manner by communal and provincial levels of government dealing with the *Gastarbeiter*, to balance out the potentially detrimental consequences of this unacknowledged yet permanent immigration by aiming at a conflict-free absorption into German society. In 2015, integration also became the key concept suggested by the main political parties as a way to handle the asylum seekers arriving in Germany—an ongoing process, significantly affected by the lack of a common European policy. Current German standing in the refugee crisis reveals a growing split among European nations regarding the European asylum system (Dublin III), and even more importantly, divided—and often polarized—German attitudes toward the country's drastically changing demographics.

Flüchtlingsrepublik Deutschland: *A Culture of Welcome?*

On August 31, 2015, Angela Merkel gave a comprehensive press conference, focusing on the subject of immigration and, more specifically, the refugee situation.[48] She addressed problematic and much-debated issues such as immigrants' initial reception (*Erstaufnahmeeinrichtungen*), processing time (*Bearbeitungdauer*), and repatriations (*Rückführungen*); the fair distribution of migrants in Europe (*faire Verteilung in Europa*); safe countries of origin (*sichere Herkunftsländer*); and combating the causes of the refugee crisis (*Bekämpfung von Fluchtursachen*). Merkel's rather neutral "fair distribution" term has been amplified into "fair distribution of burdens" (*faire Lastenverteilung*) by numerous politicians, including the minister president of Rhineland-Palatinate Mainz Malu Dreyer in a recent Bundesrat resolution from February 2016.[49] The discursive shift from neutrality to the negativity associated with a "burden" in relation to refugees has developed into a noticeable tendency in the national rhetoric.

From the outbreak of the crisis until now, the main plea of the chancellor to the German citizens has been to be proud of humanity as the leading idea of the German constitution, with the basic right (*Grundrecht*) of the politically persecuted to seek asylum. Importantly, the chancellor often referred to the first sentence of the constitution: "The dignity of a person is unimpeachable" (*die Würde des Menschen ist unantastbar*) and emphasized that the question of dignity equally applies to citizens and noncitizens (i.e., immigrants). She frequently thanks those welcoming immigrants and severely criticizes various xenophobic sentiments also present in contemporary German rhetoric. Merkel defines Germany as a country of hope and opportunity (*ein Land der Hoffnung und der Chancen*), implicitly crafting the idea of the "German dream" for refugees. In line with that, the chancellor conceptualizes proper integration of asylum seekers as today's central national mission, underlining, however, that the latter will be an uneasy, time-consuming challenge, and appealing for patience and flexibility—to add to the traditional German thoroughness (*Gründlichkeit*).

Curiously, the chancellor often references the twenty-fifth anniversary of German unification using the so-called German-German question as an analogy to the refugee crisis as a comparable national challenge. She emphasizes how flexibility, patience, and creativity, in line with the changes of institutional systems, contributed to the success of unification. The significance of the analogy is twofold. First of all, Merkel openly admits the historically created and challenging differences between the western and eastern Germans (the latter considered Germany's very own "others," nicknamed *Ossies*) and the consequential lack of a homogeneous society and a unified political culture. The analogy and the implied synonymy of the others (former East Germans with today's refugees/asylum seekers) frame the current immigration issue as a humanitarian phenomenon that is supposed to extend beyond the national, racial, ethnic, and religious differences so prominent among the current refugees. When confronted with the questions about xenophobia and the right-wing extremism (*Rechstextremismus*) as a typical eastern German phenomenon, compared to the more tolerant and inclusive German West, Merkel prioritized diplomacy, deliberately refusing to "make an East-West conflict out of it" (*daraus einen Ost-West-Konflikt machen*). She sought to bring those debates back to the higher interest of humanity, reminding the audience that every person is first and foremost a person (*jeder Mensch ist ein Mensch*), regardless of his or her origin. A concept of *Willkommenskultur* (the culture of welcome) and Merkel's by now debatable slogan, *Wir schaffen das!* ("We will manage this!") became the central ideas of Merkel's refugee-related rhetoric, with the chancellor continuously emphasizing humanitarian responsibility toward those in need. She keeps reminding her fellow citizens that Germany is a strong country that managed much in the past and should not fail now. In line with that, Merkel addresses the need for a new immigration law that would address the current German need of a labor force (*Arbeitskräften*) in general as well as a qualified labor force in particular (*Fachkräften*), simultaneously emphasizing the relatively young age of many refugees and thus evoking synonymy with the former *Gastarbeiter.* "The fundamental right to asylum does not have a limitation," the chancellor asserted, and "as a strong, economically healthy country we have the strength to do what is necessary."[50] At the same time, Merkel admitted that Germany and Europe face a conflict between freedom and safety.[51]

Another leading concept of CDU/CSU's policy and Merkel's rhetoric is their version of integration. When in 2010 and later in 2015, Merkel declared the death of German multiculturalism, she referred to the *Gastarbeiter* pages of German history as an example of completely failed integration that lead to the existence of "parallel societies." She repeatedly admits that conceptualizing and treating *Gastarbeiter* as guests who would eventually leave and thus do not need to truly integrate into the German society utterly failed and emphasizes how important it is not to make the same mistake with the current refugees. She has said that since the third and the fourth generation of post-*Gastarbeiter* have lived side by side with Germans, that alone has irreversibly transformed Germany into an immigration country (*Einwanderungsland*).

Importantly, acknowledging the fact that the majority of the former guest workers were Muslim Turks, Merkel emphasized that Islam has come to belong to Germany and Germany's so-called "national picture" (*Nationalbild*), and that any kind of Islamophobia would not be tolerated in Germany. The rhetorical implications of the national picture create a model of an inclusive, democratic, multireligious, and multiethnic civil society as a political and cultural antonym of the infamous concept of Arian Germanness during the time of the Holocaust (i.e., a picture with which Germany is commonly associated). In line with that rhetoric, Merkel criticized foreign politicians (e.g., Hungarian and Polish, among others) for their selectivity with regard to those in need (e.g., in their call for no Muslim or no black refugees, or only Catholic refugees) and once again brought back the central idea of the German constitution prioritizing the dignity of people regardless of their origin. The following statement is highly significant: "I am deeply concerned if people start saying 'We don't want Muslims, we are a Christian country.' Maybe tomorrow somebody will say 'Christianity is also not that important any longer, we should be religion-free.' It cannot be right."[52] This statement reveals that in addition to her attempts to promote inclusion, integration, and religious tolerance, Merkel indirectly emphasized the importance of Christianity as the leading religion in Germany. One should not forget, after all, that in addition to being the chancellor, Merkel is the leader of the conservative Christian Democratic Union. On top of that, she is a former East German and the daughter of a Lutheran pastor.

Nicknamed *Mutti Merkel* (Mother Merkel), the chancellor is often applauded for her Christian humanitarian aspirations and her noble ambition of integration and inclusion. She emphasizes that Germans are "not just appalled but horrified by what has been caused in the way of human suffering for tens of thousands of people."[53] At the same time, the growing critique of the chancellor's standing on refugee politics reveals too many pressing issues. Lack of unified European refugee policy is in the center of the concerns. With multiple other EU members closing borders and practicing discriminatory selectivity with regard to those who they are willing to accept, Germany remains in the epicenter of the crisis, with growing numbers of refugees and insufficient resources to accommodate their needs. Furthermore, many approaches the chancellor suggests—including dialogue with Afghanistan's Taliban, ending the war in Syria, finding a shared European solution for the refugee crisis, and a large-scale and speedy transformation of German society that would imply economic, political, and social changes—do not sound either plausible or realistic.

Unsurprisingly, Merkel's open-door policy toward Syrian refugees has caused a number of confusions and controversies, including a November 2015 statement by the interior minister Thomas de Mazière about granting civil war refugees only subsidiary protection, which the minister described as "a win for security and order for Germany."[54] Although de Mazière later backtracked and admitted that procedures will remain unchanged until there is a decision, the polarization of opinions on the subject is growing. One of the much-debated subjects remains family reunification (*Familiennachzug*)—with polarized opinions and propositions about humanitarian responsibility on the matter, the temporary nature of the process, and its legal implications. Nina Warken (CSU/ CSU) emphasizes that although certain procedures are clearly desirable (*wünschenswert*), they must also be entirely legal and in accordance with European and international human rights, as well as the UN Convention of the Rights of Children. Aydan Özoğuz (minister of state by the chancellor/*Staatsministerin bei der Bundeskanzlerin*) addresses another related issue that needs critical reexamination—that the family reunification legislation is valid only for two years and automatically expires after that period.

Importantly, although almost half a million asylum applicants in one year is an unusually high number, it is not unprecedented. In fact, the large number of asylum applicants to Germany in 2015 was previously topped in 1992 by mainly Yugoslav and Romanian refugees. This historical comparison is recurrent at times when the very nature and cause of the current crisis comes under debate. While Merkel argues that her decisions are taken in response to a humanitarian emergency in the Middle East, other politicians and high-profile migration experts openly blame the chancellor for causing a new humanitarian emergency in Germany. For example, Horst Seehofer, Bavaria's premier and leader of its governing party, the Christian Social Union, has repeatedly blamed Merkel for the alarming number of refugees arriving in Germany. "We need a limit to immigration to maintain our internal security. I don't want to be seen as scaremonger, but our security is one of the main reasons why a limit is necessary," he said in October 2015 while also calling for better protection of the EU's borders.[55] In February 2016 Seehofer stated that Merkel's refugee policy amounted to a "reign of injustice" or "illegality."[56] In line with the statement, Seehofer, who previously called Merkel's decision to open the borders to all refugees since September 2016 "a mistake that will keep us occupied for a long time"[57] and demanded fixed "upper limits" to the number of migrants, even entertained the idea of suing the federal government in the constitutional court. The argument that Merkel's "welcome culture" is not only naive but downright illegal is popular among German conservatives, including a former president of the constitutional court and CSU member, Hans-Jurgen Papier, and a well-known former judge of the constitutional court, Udo di Fabio.[58] Their arguments suggest that legally Germany may process asylum claims voluntarily but is not obliged to do so; thus the voluntary decision to proceed with the current policy should have been made by the German parliament and not by the chancellor alone. Another popular critique is based on German federalism and the currently muddled divisions of responsibilities between the nation and its states. The "border issue" also remains unresolved. Gerda Hasselfeldt, a CSU parliamentary leader, suggests erecting transit zones along Germany's borders like those in airports. Markus Soeder, Bavaria's finance minister, has also called for a fence. A group of Christian Democrats, self-identifying as the "security club," debate closing Germany's borders to refugees entirely.[59]

The Social Democratic Party, with its chairman, Sigmar Gabriel—who also serves as the minister for economic affairs and energy and the seventeenth vice-chancellor—shows partial agreement with the CDU on the question of integration of refugees.[60] Gabriel emphasizes, however, that although refugees need help, so do many Germans, especially now that the need for construction of new apartments (*neue Wohnungen bauen*) for the hundreds of thousands of refugees, and enabling their professional training (*ihnen Qualifizierungen anbieten*), competes with the same need for many Germans. Gabriel conceptualizes the situation as a "double integration challenge" (*doppelte Integrationsherausforderung*) and elaborates that Germany is facing massive challenges. At the same time (and in the same sentence) he directly refers to Merkel's slogan "We will manage this" by asking a rhetorical question: "But who else if not us should manage it?" (*Aber wer außer uns soll das schaffen?*). The implications of his question go beyond a simple agreement with the chancellor and suggest that at this point of the refugee crisis Germany does not have a choice but to proceed and carry on with double integration.

Gabriel's harsh critical standing on the ongoing and growing xenophobia and racism (e.g., as in eastern German Heidenau) echo those of the chancellor/CDU, as reflected in his 2015 statement denouncing these groups as "a mob that belongs behind the bars" (*Das Pack, welches eingesperrt werden muss*). The xenophobic group, however, eagerly reappropriated the term.[61] Declaring "We are the mob" (*Wir sind das Pack!*), they criticize both Gabriel and Merkel for alleged double standards regarding the constantly emphasized and constitutionally acclaimed human dignity, claiming that by imprisoning them Berlin would deprive "the mob" of that same dignity it preaches. Gabriel and Merkel were also called "people's traitors" (*Volksverräter*) by the same group.[62] Following Gabriel's visit, Merkel once again emphasized the need for tolerance, as well as legal and humanitarian help during her own visit to Heidenau.[63]

Joachim Gauck, German president, also endorses integration as the one and only course Germany can and should take.[64] In his discourse, Gauck juxtaposes two Germanys: "Dark Germany" (*Dunkeldeutschland*) as the place of xenophobia, intolerance, racism, and an overall déjà vu as a contemporary version of Nazi Germany, and a "bright Germany" (*ein helles Deutschland*) that embraces the culture of welcome and integration. Gauck points out that German society can succeed only with the bright Germany. Symbolically, the metaphor is powerful in its analogical connotation with the times of Enlightenment and the Age of Reason (*Zeitalter der Aufklärung*), famous for the promotion of religious tolerance, logical and unbiased thinking, and respect for human rights. It features the groundbreaking ideas of Enlightenment German philosopher Immanuel Kant, who wrote about the necessity for and the means to perpetual peace (*Zum ewigen Frieden*). Encouraging and praising those volunteering to help the refugees, the president remains cautiously optimistic that Germany can indeed manage, given the right spirit. Furthermore, referring to German history and public memory, Gauck stresses that the country was once in a much worse situation than today, fighting enormous poverty; though challenging, the refugee crisis does not rise to a state of emergency (*Notstand*).[65] At the same time, although the chancellor claims repeatedly that the right to asylum has "no upper limit," the president suggests that "our reception capacity is limited even when it has not yet been worked out where these limits lie."[66]

A new German right-wing oppositional party, Alternative für Deutschland (Alternative for Germany, AfD) however, disagrees with Gauck, Merkel, and Gabriel about the state of emergency in Germany.[67] AfD was born as an antieurozone movement and is now increasingly representative of conservative, white, upper-middle-class, and typically male voters, even though the party is not yet represented on the federal level. Its recent electoral success has been attributed to the "simple solutions" it suggests for the refugee crisis: introducing upper limits, suspending the right to asylum, suspending the Schengen border-free travel regime, and closing national borders.[68] The current AfD leadership has often referred to the current situation in Germany as "asylum chaos." Stuttgart AfD politician Heinrich Fiechtner refers to the refugee crisis as an "attack on the German people." Frauke Petry, head of AfD, suggested that police should use firearms if necessary to stop refugees at Germany's borders, and Petry's fellow AfD board member Betrix von Storch added that if necessary, even women and children should be fired at. AfD has made dramatic gains in local elections, winning 24 percent of the vote in Saxony-Anhalt and more than 10 percent in Baden-Wurttemberg and Rhineland-Palatinate, a victory that Petry described as "a great day for democracy," suggesting that AfD is "the only party in Germany that represents an increased civic participation."[69]

Contrary to the chancellor, AfD emphasizes that Islam does not belong in Germany. AfD rhetoric is often criticized for being too similar to that of the Dresden-based Islamophobic Pegida movement, famous for its hate speech, and similar to the NPD, a neo-Nazi party that state governments are trying to ban. AfD's leaders have often been accused of collaboration with Pegida, whose slogans include "Refugees are invaders," "We want our homeland back," "Send the criminal asylum seekers packing," and "We are the people" (*Wir sind das Volk*). Curiously, it is again Germany's east that seems to have difficulties with open borders and open minds,[70] unmasking the unsolved nature of the German-German question. Importantly, Merkel personally condemned Pegida's misuse of the slogan "We are the people"—the phrase previously adopted by East German anticommunist demonstrators. This unifying phrase, the chancellor complains, is now being used to divide and exclude those with different skin color and religion.[71]

Attacks on women by mobs of young men of North African or Arabic origin on New Year's Eve 2015 in Cologne, Stuttgart, and Hamburg further inflamed Germany's refugee debate.[72] Over one hundred women reported being sexually assaulted (including a reported case of rape) and robbed. Chancellor Merkel called the assaults "disgusting" and demanded justice regardless of the origin of the perpetrators. Alice Schwarzer, Germany's leading feminist and editor-in-chief of the leading German feminist magazine *Emma*, claimed that Germany is "naively importing male violence, sexism, and anti-Semitism."[73] AfD's Frauke Petry framed the events as the "terrible consequences of a catastrophic asylum and migration policy."[74] Eventually, it was confirmed that some of the molesters, muggers, and rapists were asylum seekers; obviously, the incident has created even greater challenges for *Willkommenskultur* (the culture of welcome).

In direct opposition with the AfD, the Greens support refugees and promote integration. In late 2015, Claudia Roth, a vice president of the German parliament, wrote an open letter to Berlin's mayor, Michael Muller. Referring to LaGeSo—the German abbreviation for Berlin's state office for health and social affairs, infamous for its sluggishness— Roth stated that "refugees at LaGeSo are deprived of their human dignity"[75] in violation with the German constitution. Mueller, a center-left Social Democrat, blamed the responsible cabinet member, a Christian Democrat, who as a consequence accepted the resignation of LaGeSo's director. Although the situation at LaGeSo improved somewhat, the event did not change much in the general crisis, revealing Germany's inability to reach agreement on refugee policies and successfully and efficiently integrate the newcomers.

In a 2016 talk show featuring leaders from the Greens, the AfD, and the CSU parties, as well as a right-wing extremism expert Olaf Sundermeyer,[76] Claudia Roth (from the Greens) restated the position of her party in support of refugees. She condemned xenophobia, suggesting that those encouraging hatred against migrants should be prosecuted. Sundermeyer suggested that xenophobia in Germany is geographically limited and rooted in the German east—a region that historically has been culturally isolated from any kind of diversity and is unable to handle it today. When criticizing right-wing extremism, he focused on the "poisonous climate" and "provocation and abuse of people's angst." Petry (AfD) remained firm in her position, accusing the leading coalition, the Greens, and specifically the chancellor, of "creating false hopes and unrealistic encouragement (*Anreiz*)" for the refugees and attracting a huge number of people, "70 percent of whom do not even have the right to asylum, according to the Geneva Convention."[77] She also addressed an increasing number of intercultural conflicts—not only with the local population but also among the different groups of refugees.

In the midst of these political debates, a significant development took place on the legislative front. In February 2016, the Bundesrat approved a second asylum package that focuses on swifter procedures and allows fewer family members to follow asylum seekers.[78] "We will be deciding faster on applications lodged by citizens of safe countries and by individuals who conceal their true identity," said Ole Schröder, parliamentary state secretary in the Federal Ministry of the Interior on February 25, 2016, during the Bundestag's final deliberations on the key measures contained in the asylum package.[79] Overall, the asylum procedure can now be completed within a week (even if this plan has yet to be implemented). To allow Germany to cope better with the massive influx of refugees, the families of asylum seekers entitled to subsidiary protection will not be permitted to follow them to Germany for a period of two years. The new legislation states that deportation will be possible even if medical care in the country of destination is not equivalent to that in Germany (except in cases of life-threatening or serious illness). Furthermore, a new organization will be responsible for procuring replacement travel documents of refugees without papers, as well as providing better protection for legal minors, including a requirement for a full police clearance certificate for people working in reception facilities.[80]

With the hopes and expectations related to the second asylum package, many problems of German integration remain: it is still slow, there are not enough housing opportunities, schools are struggling to integrate refugee children who do not speak German, fights regularly break out inside overcrowded asylum centers (frequently between young men of different ethnic and religious groups), and there have been more attacks on migrant centers.[81] A larger European solution is needed. Therefore Merkel and Gabriel, together with the president of the European Commission, Jean-Claude Juncker, are warning that Schengen could collapse together with Europe's single market. Despite their pan-European appeals, of the 1.1 million refugees who entered the EU in 2015, about 90 percent have ended up in Germany, Austria, and Sweden.[82] Sweden declared it could not cope and reintroduced border controls, while Austria has said it is suspending Schengen—which leaves Germany practically alone in dealing with the influx of refugees.

Chancellor Merkel admits that the course she has chosen is not easy and that sometimes she also despairs. Yet the chancellor always restates that "it is my damn duty to do everything I can so that Europe finds a collective way." Referring to the challenging situation in Germany in particular and in the EU in general, the chancellor asks: "What's right for Germany in the long term? There, I think, it is to keep Europe together and to show humanity."[83] However, despite her emphasis on the urgent need for a unified Europe, Merkel herself has not refrained from taking unilateral decisions, undermining the current EU asylum policy. Nor has she been completely immune from participating in the blame game of the conservative politicians who accuse Greece of a lack of discipline in the refugee crisis, and demand that the "politics of waving through" refugees stop.[84] All in all, the chancellor's often inconsequential if not contradictory decision-making contributes to the fact that Germany is starkly divided on its standing, with the division being so complex that if affects most of the areas of the current political culture, as well as the present and the future role the "reluctant hegemon" will end up playing in the humanitarian crisis in the EU and on the world arena.

Germany in Times of (Humanitarian) Crisis: Divided Again

German division on the subject of immigration reveals a number of thought-provoking controversies that significantly challenge the pronounced national course of *Willkommenskultur* and integration. Despite the prominent positions of Angela Merkel's "open-arms policy," her emphasis on Germany's humanitarian duty to harbor refugees ("Everyone knows what they have been through!")[85] has gone hand in hand with policies aimed at radically reducing the numbers of other types of migrants. Just as the German government has put in place contingencies for accepting Syrian refugees since July 2014, it has been working together with the governments of the Balkan and the Maghreb countries to control and reduce immigration from and through these regions. The minister of the interior, Thomas de Mazière, even emphasized that Afghan refugees could be sent back to the "many safe regions" of their home country.[86] The selective treatment of different refugee groups by the political elite has been applied at the bureaucratic level in asylum procedures. In September 2015, the national administration for migration and refugees suspended the Dublin system for Syrian refugees, but continued to deport refugees from Somalia, Iran, and Iraq back to Bulgaria or Hungary, where they faced worse conditions. Similarly, the representative of the Green parliamentary faction on foreign policy derided the recent asylum deal between the EU and Turkey, saying it offered no real legal channels for refugees from Syria and beyond to enter Europe.[87] Syrian and other refugees trapped at the border between Macedonia and Greece now face a situation similar to that in Hungary, yet Germany's government has not chosen the same solution and is instead insisting on a return to Schengen. The aforementioned division of the refugees into those eligible for asylum in Germany and those less lucky revealed another trend of the current political culture: that of conditional welcome.

Another crucial division of political opinions and legislative policies is present with regard to the demographics of the refugees Germany is willing to accept and integrate. For various reasons, the demographic pattern of the inflow of refugees from the Middle East has taken on a similar pattern to the one during the *Gastarbeiter* era. Up until February 2015, more than 60 percent of refugees were male.[88] This gender imbalance, combined with cultural differences between the immigrants and the host population, played a central role in the alarming attacks on German women in Cologne, Stuttgart, and Hamburg, as well as the consequential media framing of the assaults as a natural outcome of the misogynistic nature of the Islamic patriarchy.

Since January 2016, women and children have constituted the majority of refugees into Europe.[89] However, the new asylum laws specifically restrict family reunification—a controversial policy that entails grave long-term consequences for the desired integration of the migrants and does not provide a stable foundation for a permanent successful stay of those in need. Touching upon this issue, in a speech the chancellor delivered to her fellow party members in January 2016, Merkel directly addressed Syrian and Iraqi refugees. Although she encouraged them to embrace the German welcome, she emphasized its temporary nature and expressed her hope that the currently "affected" would eventually leave: "We expect that, when Syria is again at peace and IS [ISIS/ISIL] has been eliminated in Iraq, you return back home with the knowledge of what you have now received from us."[90] Ironically, this rhetoric of desired temporality strongly resembles the previous national framing of immigrants during the *Gastarbeiter* pages of German history—those same pages that, according to the chancellor, led to the creation of parallel societies and the entire idea of German multiculturalism being a "white lie." Yet even the chancellor's standing is divided in its simultaneous acceptance of two radically opposite political aims—the unconditional acceptance of refugees on humanitarian grounds, on the one hand, and a systematic rejection of permanent and demographically inclusive immigration, on the other.

Finally, the controversial rhetorical mélange of different—and often mutually exclusive—political opinions and public policies reveals the challenging divisions in the desired outcomes for the "German engine," ranging from pursuing the best national interest while maintaining a strong European leadership, to the relatively recent German attempts at repaying its historical guilt and creating a new, positive *Nationalbild* the country and its chancellor attempt to demonstrate to the world. Curiously, that growing trend toward preoccupation with Germany's image could already be observed during numerous political events in this legislature in terms of both domestic politics and foreign policy. With its participation in EU and NATO missions, some observers described the advent of a new era of German foreign policy.[91] Its formerly passive role in world politics has shifted toward active involvement. Notably, Germany's shifting image in the world came under debate during the Soccer World Championship in 2006, when the omnipresent national flag was billed as displaying a "newly self-confident" patriotism.[92] Besides, in the phaseout from nuclear energy and the shift toward renewable energy sources—a radical policy change and Merkel's response to the Fukushima nuclear disaster in March 2011—the discourse once again emphasized how Germany was becoming a pioneering model for other countries.[93] In line with that rhetoric of Germany being a role model in many areas, Merkel's demand that the refugees should be conscious of "what they have received" from Germany in terms of humanitarian assistance also points out the underlying attempts to show proof of a new, changed, and likable country.

Whether or not—and for how long—this image of a humanitarian, welcoming, and kind Germany can withstand the international reality of growing refugee flows from the Middle East and the domestic reality of a growing political challenge from the partisan Right will depend upon the peace talks in Geneva, the stability of Turkey, and a number of other factors beyond Merkel's control. Divided international standings on the matter certainly contribute to the already existing controversy. And in the best (or worst, depending on the interpretation) traditions of Cold War superpower rhetoric, the United States and Russia are also quite divided in their attitudes toward the current German refugee politics. Referring to a highly debated case of a Russian-German girl allegedly abducted and raped by a Middle Eastern refugee in Berlin (which subsequently turned out to have been made up by the girl herself), the Kremlin expressed general dismay at current German refugee politics. On January 26, 2016, Russia's foreign minister, Sergei Lavrov, publicly accused Germany of hushing up the aforementioned case in order "to paint over reality with political correctness."[94] Overall, the Russian political elite has been severely critical of the German course.[95] During his visit to Germany on April 24, 2016, US president Barack Obama, on the contrary, praised the chancellor for being a "courageous" leader "on the right side of history."[96] Rhetorically, Obama's appraisal of the German *Willkommenskultur* in general and the chancellor in particular was as persuasive as its Russian critique.

Just several months prior to Obama's appraisal, the chancellor made a passionate and uncharacteristically decisive and emotion-laden statement: "I have to say in all honesty: If now we even have to apologize for showing a friendly face during an emergency, then this is not my country."[97] Yet it is: Angela Merkel's divided Germany—divided between East and West, the political parties, the need for immigration and the wish to limit it, conservatives and liberals, supporters and haters, the infamous past and the challenging present, the *Vergangenheitsbewältigung* and an attempted multifaceted European leadership. Divided again.

Notes

1. "Europe's Reluctant Hegemon: Special Report Germany," *The Economist*, June 15, 2013.
2. "Europe's Reluctant Hegemon."
3. All translations from German by the authors.

4. "What the Fuehrer Means for Germans Today," *The Economist*, December 19, 2015.

5. Ulf Rinne and Klaus F. Zimmermann, "Zutritt zur Festung Europa? Anforderungen an eine moderne Asyl- und Flüchtlingspolitik," *Wirtschaftsdienst* 95, no. 2 (2015): 114–120.

6. "476.649 Asylanträge im Jahr 2015," *Frankfurter Allgemeine*, January 6, 2016, faz.net.

7. Bundesamt für Migration und Flucht, *Aktuelle Zahlen zu Asyl*, March 2016, bamf.de.

8. Unabhängige Kommission, "Zuwanderung," *Zuwanderung Gestalten, Integration Fördern* (Berlin: Bundesministerium des Innern, 2001), 11.

9. Unabhängige Kommission, "Zuwanderung," 12.

10. Bundesministerium des Innern, Migration und Integration, *Aufenthaltsrecht, Migrations- und Integrationspolitik in Deutschland* (Berlin: Bundesministerium des Innern, 2014), 16.

11. Those of German nationality are considered ethnic Germans. Klaus J. Bade and Jochen Oltmer, *Normalfall Migration* (Bonn: Bundeszentrale für politische Bildung, 2014), 52.

12. Jutta Höhne, Benedikt Linden, Eric Seils, and Anne Wiebel, *Die Gastarbeiter: Geschichte und Aktuelle Soziale Lage* (Düsseldorf: WSI Report, 2014).

13. Jochen Oltmer, "Einführung: Migrationsverhältnisse und Migrationsregime nach dem Zweiten Weltkrieg," in *Das "Gastarbeiter"-System: Arbeitsmigration und ihre Folgen in der Bundesrepublik Deutschland und Westeuropa*, ed. Jochen Oltmer, Axel Kreienbrink, and Carlos Sanz Díaz (Munich: Oldenbourg Verlag, 2012), 9–21.

14. Bundesministerium des Innern, 15.

15. Johannes D. Steinert, *Migration und Politik: Westdeutschland–Europa–Übersee, 1945-1961* (Osnabrück: Secolo, 1995), 281.

16. Bundesministerium des Innern, 27.

17. Bundesrepublik Deutschland, Das Ausländergesetz der Bundesrepublik Deutschland vom 28, April 1965, Sammlung des Bundesrechts, *Bundesgesetzblatt*, II 2600–2601, 1965.

18. Bundesministerium des Innern, 34.

19. Bundesrepublik Deutschland, "Gesetz zur Förderung der Rückkehrbereitschaft von Ausländern," Bonn: *Bundesgesetzblatt*, I 1377–1348, November 30, 1983.

20. Klaus Bade, "Versäumte Integrationschancen und Nachholende Integrationspolitik," *Aus Politik und Zeitgeschichte* 22–23 (2007): 34.

21. Bade and Oltmer, 3.

22. Helmut Rittstieg, *Deutsches Ausländerrecht: Die wesentlichen Vorschriften des deutschen Fremdenrechts* (Munich: Deutscher Taschenbuch Verlag, 1992).

23. Bundesamt für Migration und Flüchtlinge, *Migration, Asyl und Integration*, 14. Auflage, Nuremberg: Bundesamt für Migration und Flüchtlinge, 21.

24. Bundesamt für Migration und Flüchtlinge.

25. Article 16 of the Grundgesetz (German constitution).

26. Bade and Oltmer, 110.

27. Jorg Diehl, "Gewaltwelle: BKA zählt mehr als tausend Attacken auf Flüchtlingsheime," *Spiegel Online Politik*, January 1, 2016.

28. "Brandanschlag auf Flüchtlingsheim: Tröglitz ist überall," *Handelsblatt*, April 12, 2016.

29. "Geringe Aufklärungsquote Angriffe auf Flüchtlingsheime verfünffacht," *Tagesschau*, April 28, 2016.

30. Bade and Oltmer, 122.

31. European Commission, *A Common Immigration Policy for Europe: Principles, Actions and Tools* (Brussels: COM, 2008), 359 final, June 17, 2008, 2.

32. Merkel zur Flüchtlingspolitik, *Europäische Lösung nützt Deutschland*, February 29, 2016, bundesregierung.de.

33. Merkel zur Flüchtlingspolitik.

34. Hyde Flippo, *When in Germany, Do as the Germans Do* (New York: McGraw Hill Professional, 2002).

35. Unabhängige Kommission "Zuwanderung," 11, 12, 23.

36. Gesetz zur Steuerung und Begrenzung der Zuwanderung und zur Regelung des Aufenthalts und der Integration von Unionsbürgern und Ausländern, August 5, 2004, bmi.bund.de.

37. Klaus Stüwe, "Das Zuwanderungsgesetz von 2005 und die neue Migrationspolitik der Bundesrepublik Deutschland," in *Migration und Integration als transnationale Herausforderung: Perspektiven aus Deutschland und*

Korea, ed. Klaus Stüwe und Eveline Hermannseder (Wiesbaden: Springer VS, 2016), 25–48, 30–31.

38. Stüwe, 40.

39. Since the research focusing on partisan programs on immigration is relatively limited; the following overview mainly presents the findings of Klaudia Tietze, who conducted a comprehensive analysis of partisan political objectives on immigration. Klaudia Tietze, *Einwanderung und die deutschen Parteien: Akzeptanz und Abwehr von Migranten im Widerstreit in der Programmatik von SPD, FDP, den Grünen und CDU/CSU*, vol. 19 (Münster: LIT Verlag, 2007).

40. Tietze, 13.

41. Tietze, 89.

42. Ludwig Greven, "Einwanderung und Flüchtlinge: Koalition der Unbarmherzigkeit," *Zeit Online*, November 13, 2013.

43. "Merkel drückt bei Einwanderungsgesetz auf die Bremse," *Handelsblatt*, March 3, 2015. "CDU gibt Widerstand gegen Einwanderungsgesetz auf," *Zeit Online*, July 24, 2015. Note that a contingent for legal immigration would open up an alternative to asylum seekers of the Western Balkan states who have almost no chance of receiving asylum in Germany.

44. Thilo Sarrazin, *Deutschland schafft sich ab: Wie wir unser Land aufs Spiel setzen* (Hamburg: dva, 2010).

45. Sarrazin, 156.

46. Jess Smee, "The World from Berlin: Merkel's Rhetoric in Integration Debate Is 'Inexcusable,'" *Spiegel International*, October 18, 2010; Kate Connolly, "Angela Merkel Declares Death of German Multiculturalism," *The Guardian*, October 17, 2010.

47. Connolly. "Merkel zur Flüchtlingskrise: 'Multikulti bleibt eine Lebenslüge,'" *Der Spiegel*, December 14, 2015.

48. Sommerpressekonferenz von Bundeskanzlerin Merkel, "Aktuelle Themen der Innen-und Aussennpolitik," *Bundesregierung*, August 31, 2015.

49. Antrag der Länder Rheinland-Pfalz, Niedersachsen, Nordrhein-Westfalen, Schleswig-Holstein, "Entschließung des Bundesrates, Zusammenhalt stärken: Flüchtlinge aufnehmen und integrieren—eine gesamtstaatliche Aufgabe in gemeinsamer Verantwortung," *Bundesrat*,

February 19, 2016.

50. Anthony Failoa, "A Nation Rolls Out Its 'Willkommen,'" *The Guardian*, September 11, 2015.

51. Kate Connolly, "Stollen Tops Terror at German Markets," *The Guardian*, December 4, 2015.

52. Sommerpressekonferenz von Bundeskanzlerin Merkel (translation by the authors).

53. Constanze Letsch, Ian Black, and Philip Oltermann, "Merkel 'Horrified' by Syria Suffering," *The Guardian*, February 12, 2016.

54. Ian Traynor, "Germany Announces Curbs on Refugees," *The Guardian*, November 13, 2015.

55. Kate Connolly, "Bavaria threatens refugee challenge," *The Guardian*, October 16, 2015.

56. "Germany and Refugees: Is the Welcome Culture Legal?," *The Economist*, February 13, 2016.

57. "Germany's Refugee Crisis: Merkel at Her Limit," *The Economist*, October 10, 2015.

58. "Germany's Refugee Crisis."

59. "Germany's Refugee Crisis."

60. Florian Gathmann, "Gabriel über Rassisten in Heidenau 'Das ist Pack,'" *Der Spiegel*, August 24, 2015.

61. Stefan Berg, "Das 'Pack-Problem,'" *Der Spiegel*, August 27, 2015.

62. "Berufe bei Merkel-Besuch in Heidenau: 'Wir sind das 'Pack,'" *Der Spiegel*, August 26, 2015.

63. Philipp Wittrock, "Kanzlerin in Heidenau: Merkel und der Mob," *Der Spiegel*, August 26, 2015.

64. "Merkel in Heidenau: 'Danke an jene, die vor Ort Hass ertragen,'" *Der Spiegel*, August 26, 2015.

65. Bundespräsident Gauck bei Flüchtlingen, "Es gibt ein helles Deutschland," *Der Spiegel*, August 26, 2015.

66. "Germany's Refugee Crisis."

67. Melanie Amann, Matthias Bartsch, Jan Friedmann, Nils Minkmar, Michael Sauga, and Steffan Winter, "The Hate Preachers: Inside Germany's Dangerous New Populist Party," *Spiegel International*, February

10, 2016.

68. Amann et al.

69. Philip Oltermann, "Merkel Refuses to Ditch Refugee Policy," *The Guardian*, March 18, 2016.

70. "Germany United: The Trouble with Saxony," *The Economist*, October 3, 2015.

71. Kate Connolly, "Europe's Migrant Fears Ferment," *The Guardian*, January 9, 2016.

72. "Sexual Assaults in Cologne: New Year, New Fear," *The Economist*, January 9, 2016.

73. "Refugees in Germany: Cologne's Aftershocks," *The Economist*, January 16, 2016.

74. Amann et al.

75. "German Immigration: All Down the line," *The Economist*, December 19, 2015.

76. Talk show: The Greens, AfD, CSU, and right-wing extremism expert.

77. Talk show.

78. "Bundesrat Approves Second Asylum Package: Swifter Procedures, Fewer Families to Follow Asylum Seekers," *Der Bundesrat*, February 26, 2016.

79. "Bundesrat Approves Second Asylum Package."

80. "Bundesrat Approves Second Asylum Package."

81. "Germany's Refugee Crisis."

82. "Refugee Crisis: Europe Starts Putting Up Walls," *The Economist*, September 19, 2015.

83. Ian Traynor, "EU Fears Humanitarian Crisis in Greece," *The Guardian*, March 4, 2016.

84. "Hilfe für Griechenland—Merkel will 'Politik des Durchwinkens' beenden," *Focus Online*, March 1, 2016.

85. "Merkel fordert freundliche Aufnahme syrischer Flüchtlinge," *Zeit Online*, August 29, 2013.

86. "De Mazière: Viele 'sichere Gebiete' in Afghanistan," *ZDF heute*, February 2, 2016, bundesregierung.de.

87. "Flüchtlingspolitik 'nicht über den Tag hinaus weitergedacht,'"

Deutschlandfunk, April 19, 2016.

88. "Geschlecht und Asyl: Frauen und Kinder zuletzt," *Spiegel Online*, September 9, 2015.

89. "Tatsächlich sind sehr, sehr viele Frauen und Kinder unterwegs," *Sueddeutsche*, February 4, 2016.

90. "Merkel an Flüchtlinge: 'Erwarten, dass sie wieder in ihre Heimat zurückkehren,'" *Focus Online*, January 31, 2016.

91. Cf. Hellmann, Gunther, Daniel Jacobi, and Ursula Stark Urrestarazu, eds., "'Früher, entschiedener und substantieller?' Die neue Debatte über Deutschlands Außenpolitik," *Zeitschrift für Außen- und Sicherheitspolitik*, Sonderheft 6, 2015.

92. "Schwarz-rot-goldener Boom: Flaggenparade der WM-Patrioten," *Spiegel Online*, June 12, 2006.

93. "Atomausstieg nach Fukushima-Katastrophe: Röttgen sieht bei Deutschland Vorbildfunktion," *Focus Online*, March 11, 2012.

94. "Girl, Not Abducted," *The Economist*, February 6, 2015.

95. "The Hybrid War: Russia's Propaganda Campaign against Germany," *Spiegel International*, February 5, 2016.

96. Kevin Lamarque, "Obama Says Merkel 'Is on the Right Side of History,'" Reuters, October 25, 2016.

97. "Der seltene Gefühlsausbruch der Kanzlerin," *Süddeutsche*, September 17, 2015.

The United Kingdom's Rhetoric of Immigration Management

THE SYRIAN IMMIGRATION CRISIS AND BREXIT

———•◆•———

Clarke Rountree, Kathleen Kirkland, and Ashlyn Edde

On June 23, 2016, voters in the United Kingdom narrowly supported a referendum to leave the European Union (EU). This "Brexit" vote was significantly influenced by immigration issues—including those surrounding the Syrian crisis—which had given rise to anti-immigrant rhetoric from politicians stoking the anti-EU fires. A surprised Prime Minister (PM) David Cameron stepped down and was replaced by his Conservative Party colleague, Home Secretary Theresa May. In explaining the Brexit vote and how her government viewed the goals for a post-EU United Kingdom, May stressed her country's tolerance for and interest in attracting skilled immigrants, but asserted that "the message from the public before and during the referendum campaign was clear: Brexit must mean control of the number of people who come to Britain from Europe."[1]

The United Kingdom's discourse about the Syrian immigration crisis is shaped by British cultural values concerning national independence, experience with EU policies that led to significant migrations from the EU to the UK, and challenges wrought by the Syrian Civil War. The chapter will analyze the discourse of UK leaders and other politicians surrounding the Syrian immigration crisis, as well as the Brexit vote that it influenced.

The chapter will argue that the discourse of the UK's leaders can usefully be understood by figuratively placing what we call the "bureaucratic rhetoric" of Prime Minister Theresa May—with its plain style and absence of affective appeals concerning the Syrian refugees—at the center of the UK's political discourse, and more affective discourse to the left and right of May, where advocates express greater sympathy or antipathy, respectively, for the refugees. May offers a style of rhetoric in the mold of Jessy J. Ohl's "boring rhetoric," which stymies "the forces, energies, and intensities that pass through and between bodies . . . to create the conditions for attitude and action."[2] Ohl was interested in how visual rhetorics of drone warfare used boring images to make the "light war" of US drone strikes into "a bland form of transparency—a boring style of adorning war such that it becomes undeserving of time and attention."[3] We contend that May's bland descriptions of the Syrian immigration crisis and its victims mute the significance of the problem, while not denying it, and make it easier for her to subordinate humanitarian values to national prerogatives respecting border control.

Politicians evincing greater and lesser support for refugees were much more likely to use traditional rhetorical appeals to "galvaniz[e] . . . the senses" and "ignit[e] . . . the minds and bodies of listeners through exposure to well-crafted symbols,"[4] as a prelude to urging support for opening the doors to more Syrian refugees or shutting the border to such "Others." Specifically, as we show, they use emotional appeals, narratives, examples, vivid language, figures, analogies, and identification or disidentification to move their audiences to support opening or closing borders to refugees, while May's "bureaucratic" rhetoric generally avoids these rhetorical strategies. May's "neutrality" in her appeals, we argue, allowed her to avoid uncomfortable associations with racist and intolerant voices on the far right, while effectively backing their policy of closing the door to additional refugees. Her "neutral" rhetoric acknowledged the immigration crisis, as her counterparts on the left (and even her Conservative predecessor David Cameron) had done, without rousing concerns so much that she could not insist on restricting the UK's borders on other grounds.

We will frame our discussion of May's bureaucratic discourse, and the more affective discourses to her left and right, with an initial consideration of the structure of the UK government and its history of immigration policies, before turning to an analysis of the UK's leading national political voices in the Syrian immigration crisis.

The United Kingdom Government

The United Kingdom is a constitutional monarchy. Queen Elizabeth II is the symbolic head of state and the head of the Church of England, carrying on a tradition that began in the 1530s with King Henry VIII. Primary political power lies with Parliament, a bicameral body consisting of an elected and representative lower house, the 650-member House of Commons (HC), and the almost 800-member upper House of Lords, which includes hereditary peers and those appointed by the queen with the advice of the prime minister or a select committee (Lords Temporal), as well as bishops of the Church of England (Lords Spiritual).[5] Legislation is passed by the HC; the House of Lords may review and amend bills, but cannot stop them from passing into law. Laws passed by Parliament are the supreme law in the United Kingdom and cannot be overruled by courts.[6]

The leader who has the support of the HC (typically, the majority party's leader) is appointed prime minister, while the leader of the second largest party becomes the leader of the opposition. Most of the executive cabinet officials come from the House of Commons, typically the majority party. There are twelve parties recognized by Parliament, but two dominate—the Conservative and the Labour Parties. Members of the HC are elected at least once every five years, though two-thirds of the body may call for early elections (usually at the behest of the prime minister).

In 1973, the United Kingdom joined the European Economic Community, later known as the European Union (EU), which has grown into a twenty-eight-member economic partnership that generally supports the free movement of its member citizens among all countries. The United Kingdom was one of a handful of countries that chose not to give up its national currency, the pound, for the widely used euro. As we have noted, in 2016 UK voters in a national referendum narrowly decided to leave the EU,[7] and Theresa May began negotiations with the EU for this "Brexit" from the organization. The decision to leave the EU was influenced to a large extent by immigration issues that this chapter will address,[8] beginning with a review of British immigration law in the next section.

History of Immigration to the United Kingdom

The United Kingdom passed its first significant immigration act, the 1905 Aliens Act, to keep out undesirables, including "previous deportees, fugitive offenders, the mad and destitute, and other 'continental agitators.'"[9] But immigration only recently has become a significant concern for this largest imperial power in world history, which historically has been more a country of emigration than of immigration, providing outlets for its growing population to fan out to colonies on six continents. Those colonists did not flow back to the mother country in significant numbers, so there was little need for limits on immigration. However, after World War II, immigration from the "New Commonwealth" (mostly nonwhite former colonial) countries began to rise, and more stringent immigration policies were created by the Conservative government and acquiesced in by later Labour governments.[10] Chief among these was the 1962 Commonwealth Immigrants Act, which established a system of work vouchers to control the flow of Commonwealth workers into the UK.[11] Subsequent revisions of the act progressively brought the entry of Commonwealth citizens under the same controls that applied to foreign citizens, which critics view as partly a response to a "Keep Britain White" campaign.[12]

British laws on refugees were developed to align with the 1951 Convention Relating to the Status of Refugees, which sought to prevent atrocities such as those during World War II. Notably, Article 33 created the *nonrefoulement* obligation through which states committed to not return refugees who reasonably feared serious harm through a return to their state of nationality or residence. That commitment was limited geographically to Europe, but the United Nations 1967 Protocol Relating to the Status of Refugees extended the obligation to all other countries.[13] And although the United Kingdom joined the EU, it did not join the Schengen Area of free movement for immigrants who reach this area.

Until very recently, the United Kingdom continued its history of negative net immigration. For example, from 1964 until 1983, save for a tiny bump in 1979, net immigration was less than emigration. From 1983 to 1997, positive immigration numbers gradually increased, driven by a number of new developments and policies. These include the 1988 Immigration Act, which ensured that those with permission to move freely within the European Economic Community did not need permission to enter or remain in the UK; the 1989 fall of the Berlin Wall and a new work permit system allowing employers to bring more workers into the UK; the 1993 establishment of the EU allowing nonworkers to enter and remain in member states; and the handover of British Hong Kong to China, which led to an influx of colonial immigrants concerned about living under Communist rule.[14]

Since 1998, there has been a stronger upward trend in immigration to the United Kingdom. That year net immigration surpassed one hundred thousand; in 2004 it surpassed two hundred thousand; and in 2014 it surpassed three hundred thousand.[15] Competing legislative policies made immigration more or less appealing and open. Part of this increase was an effort by the Labour government beginning in 1997 to boost the economy by attracting highly skilled workers to the United Kingdom.[16] Yet, while pursuing this new economic policy, lawmakers were faced with an increase in the number of asylum seekers from wars in Eastern Europe, Somalia, and the Middle East. This made the government worry that its attractive welfare benefits would become a magnet for refugees. The 2002 Nationality, Immigration and Asylum Act included provisions to deter such immigrants—section 54 specifically sought "to ensure that [specified] individuals could not move to the UK for the sole or main purpose of accessing residential accommodation and other services in preference to similar services in the EEA country of origin."[17]

In 2004 immigration pressure came from an expansion of the EU to include poorer eastern European countries: Czech Republic, Estonia, Hungary, Latvia, Lithuania, Poland, Slovakia, and Slovenia (known as EU8 countries), as well as Malta and Cyprus. A large number of workers took advantage of the free-movement provisions of EU membership to relocate to the United Kingdom and other wealthy EU countries. When Bulgaria and Romania joined the EU in 2007, the United Kingdom placed initial restrictions on immigration of workers from those countries that lasted until 2014. The 2008 global financial crisis led the United Kingdom to pass measures to constrain non-EU workers from immigrating.[18]

As public opinion turned against immigration in the late 2000s, Conservative politicians used it as a wedge issue, hanging responsibility on the Labour Party for championing economic migration. That issue contributed to the Conservative Party winning back the House from Labour in 2010 and to David Cameron's ascension as prime minister. But Cameron faced new pressures on immigration almost immediately. In 2011, the Arab Spring led to uprisings across the Middle East and Northern Africa, and a crackdown from Syria's leader initiated a bloody civil war that would send millions of refugees streaming toward Europe. In 2013, Croatia became the twenty-eighth member of the EU, adding another source of economic refugees to the continuing wave. With pressure from the EU to take in Syrians and other immigrants, as well as a continuing flow of economic migrants, politicians to the right of Cameron began fanning the flames of anti-immigration and anti-EU sentiment.[19] The Immigration Act of 2014, championed by then-home secretary Theresa May, sought to limit access of illegal immigrants to banking, health care, housing, and other services, and was followed the next year by legislation clamping down on work by illegal immigrants.[20] Such efforts were not sufficient to appease the Far Right, which soon succeeded in getting the fateful Brexit vote. The next section will begin an analysis of how leading politicians talked about immigrants and immigration, which shaped actions and attitudes toward immigration and inevitably carried implications for the UK's vision of itself as a nation, as a member of the EU, and as a world leader. We will begin with PM David Cameron, who led the United Kingdom from the beginning of the Syrian immigration crisis until 2016.

Immigration Rhetoric in David Cameron's United Kingdom

David Cameron, the United States, and other Western countries consistently condemned the Syrian government's crackdown on protesters and its subsequent war against Syrians. In addressing the ensuing refugee crisis, Cameron deployed a number of rhetorical strategies to raise concerns about the crisis and garner sympathy for the refugees. For example, in 2013 Cameron joined the United States and ten other members at the G20 Summit in St. Petersburg in calling for a UN investigation into Syria's alleged use of chemical weapons against its own citizens, though he stopped short of supporting military action by the United Kingdom to check the Syrian government. He noted that the violence of the civil war was creating "the refugee crisis of our time" as "[a] Syrian becomes a refugee every 15 seconds."[21] By putting the crisis into historical perspective (the "crisis of our time") and calculating the frequency of refugees appearing (in a brief and quantitative frame to which individuals could relate), he conveys the gravity of the situation.

A week later at a Holocaust remembrance he repeated the "crisis of our time" characterization and insisted that "Britain is not the sort of country that wants to stand by [in this crisis]," though he admitted that the Syrian conflict was a complex problem.[22] By characterizing the situation as demanding action by those we are urged to view as noble countries, Cameron puts moral pressure on his audience. To connect the crisis to the United Kingdom, he offered a comparison his audience of constituents in York could easily understand:

> If you look at how many refugees have left Syria and gone to Lebanon, for the scale of Lebanon's population, it would be like 15 million people coming to live in the UK. That's the scale of the movement of people, and the pressure that the neighbouring countries are under.[23]

Such comparisons helped identify those in the United Kingdom with the beleaguered Syrian border countries and to highlight the scale of the problem. He touted the UK's humanitarian assistance to Syrians as second only to that of the United States, again using the actions of noble countries to highlight the seriousness of the problem.

As the Syrian crisis was heating up, so was British concern over immigration from the EU. Cameron had promised in 2011 to reduce net immigration to tens of thousands; but by 2014 those numbers were over a quarter of a million and growing. With elections coming in 2015, he needed to assure voters he was working on what was perceived as a mounting problem.[24] Because the Syrian crisis involved immigration policy, Cameron's address carried implications for that problem as well as for the growth of economic migration. Thus, in a major address in November 2014, Cameron's affective appeals regarding the Syrian problem were tempered somewhat by his insistence that immigration required a strategic national policy with more head than heart. His central theme came early: "Immigration benefits Britain, but it needs to be controlled."[25]

The entire speech alternated between problems and benefits of immigration. In a fundamental identification with immigrants, Cameron called the United Kingdom a "multi-racial democracy," "an open nation," and a "sanctuary" for those fleeing war and persecution, concluding: "We are Great Britain because of immigration, not in spite of it." But he quickly turned to the problems of recent mass migrations to the United Kingdom, including crowded schools, inadequate housing, and communities changing too rapidly for many. He tied together EU immigration with other migration, insisting that it is reasonable that "people want Government to have control over the numbers of people coming here and the circumstances in which they come, both from around the world and from within the European Union." He balanced concerns over "foreign criminals" potentially sneaking in to do harm and immigrants seeking welfare, against the benefits of more "companies, jobs, and investment." This balancing act led him to warn against "those who sell the snake oil of simple solutions."

If the complexity of his discussion left him without an affective appeal pushing his audience toward a particular end—one can envision his audience pondering concerns on "the one hand" and "the other"—he did offer an appeal on who was to blame for the problem: the previous Labour government, whose "lax approach to immigration" lay in its failure "to impose transitional controls on the eight new countries [EU8] which entered the EU in 2004." Cameron promised that he would not make the same mistake, but would mandate "that when new countries are admitted to the EU in the future, free movement will not apply to those new members until their economies have converged much more closely with existing Member States." Cameron subsequently succeeded in his reelection campaign, but tied his own hands somewhat in dealing with the Syrian immigration crisis insofar as he acknowledged problems with immigration and pledged to clamp down on it.

Cameron's second term began during the height of the Syrian immigration exodus to Europe in 2015, and he spoke five days after the saddest and most disturbing visual representation of the crisis emerged: the viral photo of a dead three-year-old Syrian refugee, Aylan Kurdi, whose body washed up on the shore of a Turkish resort. Cameron gave a major address on the crisis that joined it with economic and counterterrorism concerns.[26] While he admitted the crisis was huge, he drew a distinction between refugees and economic immigrants, noting:

> More than 300,000 people have crossed the Mediterranean to Europe
> so far this year. These people came from different countries under

different circumstances. Some are economic migrants in search of a better life in Europe. Many are refugees fleeing conflict. And it is vital to distinguish between the two.

Joining the Syrian crisis with economic migration diluted his affective appeal on behalf of these various groups, as did his general language and dry numbers. He was more vivid and startling in noting that many Syrians were "fleeing the terror of Assad and ISIL [Islamic State of Iraq and the Levant], which has seen more than 11 million people driven from their homes." Again, he invoked a noble tradition in calling it the United Kingdom's "moral responsibility to help those refugees just as we have done so proudly throughout our history." But, instead of throwing open its doors, he insisted that the United Kingdom "must use our head and our heart by pursuing a comprehensive approach that tackles the causes of the problem as well as the consequences."

Like many of his fellow Western leaders, Cameron sought to keep refugees close to home, when possible, by

> helping to stabilise countries where the refugees are coming from; seeking a solution to the crisis in Syria; pushing for the formation of a new unity government in Libya; busting the criminal gangs who are profiting from this human tragedy and playing our part in saving lives in the Mediterranean.

While this brief list of issues contributing to the crisis undoubtedly indicated crucial steps for solving it, and Cameron's morally laden language judged those involved (with words like "criminal gangs" and "human tragedy"), he was not ready to put the United Kingdom in charge of addressing them, especially the ongoing Syrian Civil War. He did prepare the United Kingdom to continue its generous aid and accept his new pledge to take in twenty thousand Syrians (up from the five thousand the United Kingdom had accepted already). By comparison, Germany, which is a quarter larger than the United Kingdom by population, had accepted hundreds of thousands of Syrian refugees by this point.[27] But

Cameron did not pretend to compete with Germany's generosity; more modestly he wanted Britain to "play its part alongside our other European partners." With the dead Syrian refugee child's photo going viral, he assured his audience that "vulnerable children, including orphans, will be a priority." Thus, he built upon the most potent symbol of the crisis, though not without implicitly dividing child refugees from adult refugees.

He turned from the refugee crisis to the issue of terrorism, particularly the continuing concern with ISIL, which was exacerbating turmoil in the Middle East. Covering the refugees in the same speech with terrorism linked them through their religion so that victims required distinction from those perpetrating "Islamist extremist violence." While this juxtaposition could not help but create concern over refugees as potential terrorists, he did not raise that possibility, though he did note that he was employing "new powers to stop suspects travelling."

All things considered, Cameron's warnings about the threat of terrorism were relatively calming, coming months after the attack against the French satirical magazine *Charlie Hebdo* on January 7, 2015.[28] The specter of terrorism would continue to haunt his discussions of immigration for the rest of his tenure as PM. Two months after his address, there were attacks on a concert hall, a stadium, and bars and restaurants in Paris, as well as an attack against a health care center in San Bernardino, California, the following month.[29] The following year three coordinated attacks were made against the Brussels Airport and the Brussels metro.[30] Despite connections that others made between immigration and terrorism, Cameron did not highlight these attacks in major speeches on immigration. Strategic silence can be a powerful rhetoric.[31]

In October Cameron addressed his Conservative Conference and briefly mentioned the Syrian immigration crisis.[32] He admitted that, "like most people, I found it impossible to get the image of that poor Syrian boy Aylan Kurdi out of my mind," implicitly telling his audience that they, too, should be haunted by this case. But he quickly turned to pragmatic arguments that his conservative political audience could back, admitting that with twelve million left homeless in the Syrian conflict, "if we opened the door to every refugee, our country would be overwhelmed." With this hypothetical example and warning, he pushed compassion in a different direction: not "encourag[ing] more to make that dangerous journey [across the Mediterranean]." He reiterated his preference for "helping countries like Syria become places where people actually want to live." But he offered no plan for transforming Syria or even stopping the bloody civil war.

Like many other Western leaders, Cameron implicitly pushes a bodily rhetoric of dissociation, as those immigrating are urged to stay elsewhere (and not come here with "us"). Syrians become those with whom Cameron would have his audience identify with at such a distance that they become a different kind of "others"—humanized, but pitiable victims who are not one with those in the United Kingdom.

In early 2016, the United Kingdom cohosted a conference on the Syrian immigration crisis in London with Germany, Norway, Kuwait, and the United Nations. Cameron welcomed the attendees and set the theme by calling the Syrian immigration crisis "one of the worst humanitarian crises of our time."[33] He acknowledged "a critical shortfall in life-saving aid that is fatally holding back the humanitarian effort." He characterized the refugee crisis as "a desperate movement of humanity, as hundreds of thousands of Syrians fear they have no alternative than to put their lives in the hands of evil people-smugglers in the search for a future." He noted that "Syria's neighbours are struggling under the strain of hosting huge numbers of refugees, and trying to maintain services, and create jobs for their own people." Finally, he insisted that "the long-term solution to the crisis in Syria can only be reached with a political transition to a new government that meets the needs of all its people." He asked for pledges of aid. With vivid characterization ("worst humanitarian crises"; "critical shortfall"), useful metaphors ("desperate movement of humanity"; "search for a future"), and effective figures ("struggling under the strain"), Cameron creates an affective appeal on behalf of the refugees, though he would not use those appeals to open the United Kingdom to additional refugees.

Cameron's rhetoric of immigration constructs the British people as humanitarian, but balances that attitude with a pragmatism and caution that keeps the United Kingdom's role in the crisis mostly monetary. To his credit, he does not embrace anti-immigrant constructions of immigrants as dangerous (as other Western politicians did), but simply as pathetic. He admitted the Syrian immigration crisis was huge and devastating for its victims, using a variety of affective appeals to drive that point home.

On the other hand, Cameron did not shrink from appealing to the British public's growing concerns over the recent rise of immigrants of all kinds and the challenges that followed that growth. He implicated Syrian refugees in these challenges to the extent that he noted the difficulty of distinguishing economic refugees from war refugees.

The anti-immigrant, anti-EU forces, with their appeals to fear and anger, succeeded in getting the Brexit referendum on the ballot in June 2016. Cameron addressed the nation to plead for a no vote.[34] While for the Brexit camp the EU was identified very closely with the immigration problem, Cameron sought to keep them separated. He barely mentioned immigration, other than noting that "we negotiated and enhanced our special status [in the EU]," keeping the United Kingdom "out of the Euro" and allowing us to "[keep] our borders." His biggest appeal for remaining in the EU was economic, particularly the advantages of having "500 million customers on our doorstep." He also touted the national security advantages of working closely with EU states to thwart terrorism. Finally, he warned that with a yes vote "there's no going back."

When United Kingdom voters narrowly supported leaving the EU, Cameron concluded that the people had spoken and announced that he would step down. He noted that "the British people have made a very clear decision to take a different path [than that I advocated], and as such I think the country requires fresh leadership to take it in this direction." He insisted: "I will do everything I can as prime minister to steady the ship over the coming weeks and months, but I do not think it would be right for me to try to be the captain that steers our country to its next destination." That set the stage for his successor, Home Secretary

Theresa May, to take the reins of government. Her discourse on the Syrian refugee crisis, and on immigration more generally, would differ in important respects from those of her Conservative predecessor as well as those to the left of Cameron and the right of the Conservative Party. We turn to these latter voices before returning to May at the "center."

Immigration Rhetoric from Other Political Leaders

One might expect significant differences between Cameron's discourse from his right-of-center Conservative Party, and those of Labour leaders on the left. However, those leaders sometimes sounded like their Conservative counterparts. When Ed Miliband was head of the Labour Party and ran for prime minister in 2015, he was sensitive to public concerns over growing numbers of immigrants and admitted that it was wrong of the previous Labour government not to have "maximum transitional controls" when the EU8 countries joined the EU in 2004.[35] While he promised to "uphold our international obligations to offer a refuge to people fleeing persecution," he also promised to increase the border patrol by one thousand agents, deport immigrant criminals, withhold social support for immigrants until they have worked for two years, and require all immigrants to learn English.

Miliband's mea culpa and tough policies were insufficient to win over frustrated voters, and Cameron won reelection. Miliband resigned from the party's leadership and was briefly replaced by an acting leader before Jeremy Corbyn took over the opposition leadership. With no election on the horizon, Corbyn freely blasted Cameron's government for its lack of humanity as the Syrian immigration crisis reached its apex. At a rally on refugees on the day he was elected Labour leader, he called on the Conservative government to

> recognise your obligations to help people which you're requested to do by law. . . . But above all, open your hearts and open your minds and open your attitude towards supporting people who are desperate, who

need somewhere safe to live, want to contribute to our society, and are human beings just like all of us.[36]

Corbyn's second-person appeal sought to engage the conscience of leaders, to characterize the refugees' situation (as "desperate"), and to identify them with his audience in the most basic of terms (as "human beings"). His repetition of "open" cut through Cameron's "heart and head" binary to suggest that opening (even "minds") would lead to a more humanitarian outlook.

To the right of the Conservative Party, the UK Independence Party (UKIP) was working for an exit from the EU. Its leader, Nigel Farage, told the EU Parliament on September 9, 2015, that the EU's policies toward refugees were opening the floodgates to all sorts of refugees and causing a crisis "of biblical proportions."[37] Such comparisons colorfully highlighted the massive size of the problem, though he quickly moved to qualify the nature of this "exodus." Unlike the Israelites fleeing Egypt, these were economic migrants, he charged, who were "throw[ing] their passports in the Mediterranean," then claiming to be Syrian refugees to gain admission to the EU. If such deceptions were not bad enough, Farage added a security threat to this immigration flow, claiming there was evidence of ISIL using this means "to put their jihadists on European soil." This unsubtle appeal to anger (at being deceived) and fear (from terrorist attacks) made all immigrants suspect, including innocent Syrian refugees.

If Farage was on the fringe of UK politics, he would soon find an ally in PM Cameron's own party. Boris Johnson, the mayor of London and a Conservative MP, addressed the Conservative Party Conference in 2015 and initiated themes that eventually would divide him from the party's leadership as the crisis continued.[38] He complained that membership in the EU wrested control of national borders from the United Kingdom, urging:

It should be up to this parliament and this country—not to Jean-Claude Juncker [president of the European Commission]—to decide if too many people are coming here. Because it is not that we object to im-migration in itself—I speak as the proud great grandson of a Turk who fled his country in fear of his life. . . . It is about who decides; it is about who is ultimately responsible; it is about control. And you will loosen the bonds that should unite society if people feel that their elected poli-ticians have abdicated their ability to control those things that ought frankly to be within their power.

Initially, this statement shifts concern from who the immigrants are to how their entry into the United Kingdom was determined. His personal appeal suggests identification with the immigrants. However, his de-scription of the "bonds that should unite" made immigration by "Oth-ers" problematic, because he noted that those bonds require "shared language, shared cultural assumptions, shared confidence in our politi-cal institutions . . . [as] the ties that unite our society." They also are, by implication, the bonds that divide those in the UK from outsiders, as identification's ironic counterpart, division, provides grounds for a dif-ference in kind and in treatment.

Boris Johnson also created a political division within the Conser-vative Party. While PM Cameron had encouraged Johnson to run for mayor of London in 2008 and applauded his speech to their party in 2015, the next year he found himself at odds with a man he had known since they were both students at Eton, as Johnson supported the "Leave" side while Cameron backed the "Remain" camp in the Brexit vote. Some claimed that Johnson's defection to the "Leave" side was a political ploy to stake out his own path to the leadership of the country, as he became "the chief architect" of Brexit, carrying the banner for what had been UKIP's central policy objective.[39] Speaking before the referendum, Johnson took a swipe at Cameron:

It is deeply corrosive of popular trust in democracy that every year UK politicians tell the public that they can cut immigration to the tens of thousands [as Cameron had claimed]—and then find that they miss their targets by hundreds of thousands, so that we add a population the size of Newcastle every year, with all the extra and unfunded pressure that puts on the NHS [National Health Service] and other public services.[40]

Just as Cameron had illustrated the size of the refugee crisis in Lebanon with an analogy to the United Kingdom, Johnson offered his "Newcastle" analogy to drive home the size of a growth he would stem.

Foreshadowing arguments by future PM Theresa May, he complained of the "opportunity costs" of allowing so many immigrants:

> In our desperation to meet our hopeless so-called targets [issued by the EU], we push away brilliant students from Commonwealth countries, who want to pay to come to our universities; we find ourselves hard pressed to recruit people who might work in our NHS, as opposed to make use of its services—because we have absolutely no power to control the numbers who are coming with no job offers and no qualifications from the 28 EU countries. I am in favour of immigration; but I am also in favour of control, and of politicians taking responsibility for what is happening; and I think it bewilders people to be told that this most basic power of a state—to decide who has the right to live and work in your country—has been taken away and now resides in Brussels.

The contrast between recruiting new doctors and overusing existing doctors offered a stark choice between benefits and costs that disfavors immigrants fleeing persecution and favors those with useful skills. His logical argument that controlling who enters a country is a "basic power of a state" implicates a *narrative* of "original" power that he completes in suggesting that it "has been taken away" by a European power. Thus, he turns a principle of political power into an affective narrative of an unjustifiable "loss" that should anger UK citizens.[41] Reclaiming lost power provides "control," a god-term for Johnson (and later for May).

Unlike May, and contrary to those who interpreted Johnson's "Leave" position as a political ploy, the former London mayor pulled himself out of the running for PM following Cameron's resignation. This does not, however, mean Boris Johnson did not have a considerable impact on the debate. When May won the post, she not only adopted Johnson's "control" theme, but took on the colorful Tory as her foreign secretary.

Immigration Rhetoric in Theresa May's United Kingdom

Theresa May was appointed prime minister on July 16, 2016, rising from the home secretary position following David Cameron's resignation in the wake of the Brexit vote. Although she had supported Cameron's position to stay in the EU, she took her lead from the national referendum and announced, "Brexit means Brexit—and we're going to make a success of it."[42] On the other hand, her ambivalence over Brexit led her to undertake some rhetorical damage control.

After assuming office, May quickly made trips to EU partners to reassure them that the United Kingdom would continue to be an economic and political partner despite Brexit. In some cases, the issue of immigration arose. For example, a few days after becoming PM she met with President Hollande of France. She was asked by a reporter, in light of the Brexit decision, about the Touquet agreement whereby France would prevent immigrants coming to Calais from boarding ships to the United Kingdom.[43] Hollande noted that the United Kingdom was never part of the Schengen Agreement for the free movement of people in this area of Europe, so this separate agreement was necessary. He explained:

> [It] ensures that we can say to migrants that they cannot come to Calais, that there's no point coming to Calais because they won't be able to cross [the English Channel], because the UK will not accept them, and the border security must be watertight so that there's no crossing, at the risk of their lives.

A week later May traveled to Poland to meet with its PM. A reporter asked a question that cut to the heart of the Brexit problem regarding economic immigration:

Prime Minister May, Poland has clearly benefited hugely from the fact that Polish people have been able to work and live in Britain. Given the fact that you've indicated that you want to restrict the number of Polish people coming to Britain in the future, how will you convince your counterparts here in Poland that that will not incur a significant economic cost for Britain? And if I may, there was a lot of debate over immigration during the Brexit campaign. Do you believe that Polish people have made a positive contribution to our country?[44]

May was diplomatic, but marked the change that Brexit was bringing. She insisted that "we value the contribution that has been made to the United Kingdom from Polish citizens who have come to live and work in the UK," promising no changes "while we are members of the EU"; but, she also pointed to "a very clear message that has come from the vote of the British people, that they don't want free movement to continue in the way that it has been in the past, that they do want some control in relation to free movement." She repeated the same sentiment at the G20 Summit in China in September, where she insisted that the Brexit vote was for more control of immigration than under the EU.[45] May's language is plain and unadorned, with scarcely an adjective, a figure, or an emotional appeal (other than her assurance that Polish workers are "value[d]").

May addressed the UN General Assembly a few weeks later and discussed the Syrian refugee crisis, though she tied that issue to the need for a new approach to economic migration.[46] Like Cameron, she sought to help refugees stay in "neighbouring countries [near Syria] . . . through [supports for] education and opportunities to work." Unlike Cameron, she did not emphasize the *strain* immigration had put on those countries; nor did she follow Farage in stressing the biblical proportions of the refugee crisis. Speaking like an economist, she recommended a market-based solution to the problem that included "loans from international financial institutions and access to European markets," as well as a "mobilis[ation of] the private sector to create new jobs in the region for everyone." She does not characterize the potential recipients of these

jobs as *desperate* or *deserving*, but uses the most general language of offering jobs to "everyone."

Her segue from this point connected the Syrians to other migrants,
when she noted: "But in addition to refugees and displaced people fleeing conflict and persecution, we are also seeing an unprecedented movement of people in search of greater economic opportunities through the
same unmanaged channels." The most vivid word she offers is "fleeing,"
not even adding adjectives to characterize the immigrants beyond their
status as "displaced." She sticks to bureaucratic words like "unmanaged
channels" rather than, say, "chaotic processes," to describe what she
deems a problem requiring a solution.

She does not follow Cameron's construction of the United Kingdom
as a multicultural nation with a noble tradition of helping refugees and
working with partners to make the world a better place. Rather, she
admits, "We need to do better. Better for the countries people leave,
for the countries they move through, for the countries they try to get
to—and most of all, better for the migrants and refugees themselves."
While she offers a workable anaphora, the leading term *better* is vague
and generic. Lumping refugees and economic migrants together, she
points to the most visual sign of harm to migrants, warning: "Despite
the huge increase in international efforts, more migrants have died attempting hazardous journeys across borders this year than any other."
She calls for "an honest global debate to address this global challenge."
This is May at her most colorful—weak tea as it is—highlighting deaths
and hazards in a terse narrative; but she lacks even the punch of Cameron's "desperate movement of humanity" and his local analogies to the
international problem, or the constructions of immigrant motives that
inspire anger and fear in Farage's rhetoric.

In her most bureaucratic flourish, May touted the benefits of "controlled, legal, safe, economic migration," while reiterating her most
frequent claim that "countries have to be able to exercise control over
their borders." She played economic migrants against war refugees in
urging that uncontrolled migration "damages economies and reduces
the resources for those who genuinely need protection and whose rights

under the Refugee Convention should always be fulfilled." To her credit, this boring rhetoric does not incite anger against immigrants by playing up harms to innocent Britons. Her most evocative language came in her appeal to push the solution to this problem off on others:

> We must help ensure that refugees claim asylum in the first safe country they reach. The current trend of onward movements, where refugees reach a safe country but then press on with their journey, can only benefit criminal gangs and expose refugees to grave danger.

The warning about "criminal gangs" and "grave danger" suggested her concern for immigrants' welfare and underwrote her willingness to work with other countries to

> do more to support countries where the refugees first arrive, to provide the necessary protection and assistance for refugees safely and swiftly, and to help countries adapt to the huge economic impact that refugees can have—including on their existing population.

She cited Jordon, Lebanon, and Turkey as "success" stories in this regard, and insisted in a terse logical argument that stopping at the first safe country "is also good for the refugees and the countries they come from—because the closer they stay to home, the easier it will be for them to return and rebuild after the conflict."

Without suggesting deception on the part of refugees, as Farage had done, May nonetheless insisted that "we need to improve the ways we distinguish between refugees fleeing persecution and economic migrants," urging that clearer distinctions will help truly needy refugees. She concluded this section by reiterating her constant theme, "that all countries have the right to control their borders," adding gratuitously, for the United Kingdom, "that we must all commit to accepting the return of our own nationals when they have no right to remain elsewhere."

At a follow-on summit hosted by President Obama on the refugee crisis, May sounded a bit more sympathetic to the plight of refugees.[47]

She called the immigration crisis "an urgent matter" and characterized it as involving "more people . . . displaced that at any point in modern history." She did not highlight the United Kingdom's particular role, but instead suggested "it's a matter for which we all have a responsibility, both to provide life-saving assistance and enable people to return home one day."

In January 2017, May laid out her objectives in negotiating the United Kingdom's exit from the EU.[48] Chief among those was controlling European immigration to the United Kingdom. While she wanted "to attract the brightest and the best to work or study in Britain," she insisted "that process must be managed properly so that our immigration system serves the national interest." That interest was not being served by the present system through which record levels of immigration to the United Kingdom had put pressure on the country's schools, housing, and the health system, as well as "a downward pressure on wages for working class people." She avoids agitating the working class over its losses here, sticking to the mild economic metaphor of "downward pressure."

"National interest" is an identification with the state and its citizens at the expense of multinational identification. If she was unwilling to invoke Cameron's "multicultural" description of the United Kingdom, she at least urged that it was not anti-immigrant, but "an open and tolerant country" that was particularly interested in high-skilled immigration. Her marching orders from the Brexit voters compelled her to support the acceptable bureaucratic approach of "control"—"control of the number of people who come to Britain from Europe." She pledged: "And that is what we will deliver."

May's bureaucratic rhetoric is boring in its lack of vivid language, examples, narratives, analogies, identification with refugees, and emotional appeals. Hers is not a rhetoric to move people to act on the crisis, though the arm's-length monetary support she offered was justified if not demanded by her account of the situation. On the other hand, she did not impugn the motives of refugees, even if the economic migrants needed distinguishing from the war refugees. She did not scapegoat refugees, but neither did she offer a passionate case for taking them in. As Perelman and Olbrechts-Tyteca might say, she did not create *presence* for the refugees and their plight that would have brought them more sympathy.[49]

May had an advantage over Cameron in justifying the United Kingdom's approach to the immigration crisis by pointing to the national referendum in the Brexit vote, which gave the prime minister her marching orders. So *she* was not taking the country in this direction, the *voters* were; her democratic accountability required her to "control the borders." She did not represent those voters as either coldhearted nationalists or bleeding-heart humanists; they were reasonable people who wanted control of their borders (as evidenced by the Brexit vote). They understood the facts regarding the Syrian refugee crisis and judged it best for refugees to stay near home, with support from the United Kingdom and others.

May found a toehold of humanitarian concern in pushing for refugees to remain in countries close to their homeland, given the dangers of travel across the seas. Of course, that begged the question of why EU countries did not step in and provide safe transport across the Mediterranean and the English Channel. And she had the logical argument that staying close to home would make it easier for them to return home to rebuild their country, though she offered no clear path for concluding the endless Syrian war.

Conclusions

The Syrian immigration crisis could not have come at a worse time in UK politics. A country unaccustomed to any net immigration at all had been getting pressure from former colonies (especially New Commonwealth countries), eastern European and Middle Eastern wars, an expanding EU (notably the EU8), and non-EU immigration for two decades. Although annual immigration of less than one-half of 1 percent of a nation's population would not faze high-immigration countries, it troubled residents of this island nation. The UK's foreign-born population has more than tripled since 1993; London's population is approaching 40 percent foreign-born residents.[50]

PM Theresa May offered a "boring" and bureaucratic rhetoric that served to *not* move her British audience toward either hatred of immigrants or a strong sympathy that might underwrite a more welcoming policy toward these desperate immigrants. That allowed her to appeal to the Far Right and their Conservative Party champion, Boris Johnson, and appease the majority of "Leave" voters, whom she consistently assured the nation she had heard and would heed. On the other hand, she did not rabble-rouse (as UKIP and Donald Trump did) against these victims of civil war. To the extent that she remained rhetorically neutral, she could acknowledge the problem without acting on it. She could stand up to the EU more easily than her predecessor because the die had been cast through Brexit.

Ironically, the mild May was building upon the rabble-rousing of the Far Right. Farage and others had created anger against and fear of immigrants, scapegoating them for the UK's problems in housing, health, jobs, and a dehomogenizing culture. Boris Johnson mainstreamed concerns over immigrants, though he avoided the dark side of that appeal by sticking to issues of proper national power, making his argument more anti-EU than anti-immigrant. PM May kept both UKIP and Johnson happy by reclaiming national control over the borders and closing the doors to more refugees, while maintaining her rhetorical neutrality.

PM Cameron's more sympathetic rhetoric perhaps reflects his interest in addressing the crisis that arose on his watch, particularly given the UK's responsibilities as a member of the EU. More than UKIP and the post-Brexit May, he had to worry about what the Europeans thought about the UK's efforts in this historic crisis. Domestically he could escape some criticism of the rising numbers of immigrants on his watch by blaming the former Labour government—which was easy to do when their leader and his competitor for PM was engaged in a mea culpa in any case. Following his victory, he had to deal with voices like Jeremy Corbyn, who had the advantage of speaking his mind since the next election likely would not come for five years.

This analysis applies Jessy Ohl's concept of boring rhetoric to verbal, rather than visual, rhetoric. It demonstrates the benefits that can accrue to politicians who avoid affective appeals and speak less movingly. If that means that PM May will not go down in history as another Churchill, she may at least manage the awkward rhetorical task of keeping the majority "Leave" voters happy and not poking EU leaders, whom she wants to maintain good ties with for economic and other reasons.

Notes

1. "Theresa May's Brexit Speech in Full," *The Independent*, January 17, 2017.
2. Jessy J. Ohl, "Nothing to See or Fear: Light War and the Boring Visual Rhetoric of U.S. Drone Imagery," *Quarterly Journal of Speech* 101, no. 4 (2015): 612–632, esp. 615.
3. Ohl, 625.
4. This is Ohl's description of the traditional approach of rhetoric to move audiences (615).
5. "How Members Are Appointed," UK Parliament, https://www.parliament.uk/.
6. "Parliamentary Sovereignty," UK Parliament, https://www.parliament.uk/.
7. A. H. Wheeler, "Brexit: All You Need to Know about the UK Leaving the EU," *BBC News*, December 5, 2017.
8. J. Lowe, "How Did Feelings about Immigration Influence British People's Brexit Votes?," *Newsweek*, June 22, 2017.
9. Kristin Couper and Ulysses Santamaria, "An Elusive Concept: The Changing Definition of Illegal Immigrant in the Practice of Immigration Control in the United Kingdom," *International Migration Review* 18, no. 3 (1984): 437.
10. David Coleman and Robert Rowthorn, "The Economic Effects of Immigration into the United Kingdom," *Population and Development Review* 30, no. 4 (Dec. 2004): 579–624.
11. Couper and Santamaria.

12. Coleman and Rowthorn; Couper and Santamaria.

13. Andrew I. Schoenholtz, "The New Refugees and the Old Treaty: Persecutors and Persecuted in the Twenty-First Century," *Chicago Journal of International Law* 16 (2015): 81–125.

14. Office for National Statistics (UK), *Explore 50 Years of International Migration to and from the UK*, December 1, 2017, visual.ons.gov.uk.

15. Office for National Statistics.

16. Timothy J. Hatton, "Explaining Trends in UK Immigration," *Journal of Population Economics* 18, no. 4 (2005): 719–740; Coleman and Rowthorn.

17. Qtd. in Dallal Stevens, "The Nationality, Immigration and Asylum Act 2002: Secure Borders, Safe Haven?," *Modern Law Review* 67, no. 4 (July 2004): 619.

18. Office for National Statistics.

19. Coleman and Rowthorn.

20. Alan Travis, "Immigration Bill: Theresa May Defends Plans to Create 'Hostile Environment,'" *The Guardian*, October 10, 2013; Caroline Robinson, "The UK's New Immigration Bill Creates Perfect Conditions for Slavery to Thrive," *The Guardian*, August 28, 2015.

21. David Cameron, "G20 Summit: Prime Minister Statement to the House of Commons," September 9, 2013, https://gov.uk.

22. David Cameron, "25th Anniversary of the Holocaust Educational Trust: Prime Minister's Speech," September 16, 2013, https://gov.uk.

23. David Cameron, "PM Direct in York," October 13, 2013, https://gov.uk.

24. "The Observer View on David Cameron's Immigration Speech," *The Guardian*, November 29, 2014.

25. "David Cameron's EU Speech: Full Text," *BBC News*, November 28, 2014.

26. David Cameron, "Syria: Refugees and Counter-terrorism—Prime Minister's Statement," September 7, 2015, https://gov.uk.

27. As of late 2017, Germany had accepted eight hundred thousand Syrian refugees. Valentina Romei, Billy Ehrenberg-Shannon, Haluka Maier-Borst, and Guy Chazan, "How Well Have Germany's Refugees Integrated?," *Financial Times*, September 19, 2017.

28. "Charlie Hebdo Attack: Three Days of Terror," *BBC News*, January 14, 2015.

29. "Paris Attacks: What Happened on the Night," *BBC News*, December 9, 2015. Steve Almasy, Kyung Lah, and Alberto Moya, "At Least 14 People Killed in Shooting in San Bernardino," *CNN*, December 3, 2015.

30. Jon Henley and Kareem Shaheen, "Suicide Bombers in Brussels Had Known Links to Paris Attacks," *The Guardian*, April 1, 2016.

31. See Cheryl Glenn, *Unspoken: A Rhetoric of Silence* (Carbondale: Southern Illinois University Press, 2004).

32. Mikey Smith, "David Cameron's Full Speech to Conservative Party Conference," *The Mirror*, October 7, 2015.

33. David Cameron, "PM's Opening Remarks at Supporting Syria Conference," February 4, 2016, https://gov.uk.

34. David Cameron, "EU Referendum," *The Independent*, June 21, 2016.

35. Ed Miliband, "Ed Miliband's Speech on Immigration," *Labour Press*, April 18, 2015, press.labour.org.uk.

36. Sam Webb, "Jeremy Corbyn Gets Hero's Welcome at Refugee Rally on Day He Becomes Labour Leader," *The Mirror*, September 12, 2015.

37. "Migrant Crisis: Farage Says EU 'Mad' to Accept So Many," *BBC News*, September 9, 2015.

38. "Full Text: Boris Johnson 2015 Conservative Conference Speech," *The Spectator*, October 6, 2015.

39. "EU Referendum: Boris v Dave—a Rivalry with History," *BBC Newsnight*, June 23, 2016. Katrin Bennhold, "To Understand 'Brexit,' Look to Britain's Tabloids," *New York Times* (International Edition), May 2, 2017.

40. "Boris Johnson's Speech on the EU Referendum," *European Union News*, May 10, 2016.

41. Kenneth Burke has noted how easily rhetors shift between temporal and logical orders. See, for example, *A Grammar of Motives* (1950; Berkeley: University of California Press, 1969), 64, 73, 88, 118.

42. "Tributes for David Cameron at His Final Cabinet as UK PM," *BBC News*, July 12, 2016.

43. "PM Statement in Paris: 21 July 2016," https://gov.uk.

44. "PM and Polish Prime Minister Szydło Statements in Warsaw: 28 July 2016," https://gov.uk.

45. "G20 Summit, China: Prime Minister's Press Conference—5 September

2016," https://gov.uk.

46. "Theresa May's Speech to the UN General Assembly," September 20, 2016, https://gov.uk.

47. "PM's Speech at Leaders Summit on Refugees: 20 Sept. 2016," September 20, 2016, https://gov.uk.

48. "Theresa May's Brexit Speech in Full: Prime Minister Outlines Her 12 Objectives for Negotiations," *The Independent*, January 17, 2017.

49. Chaim Perelman and Lucie Olbrechts-Tyteca, *The New Rhetoric: A Treatise on Argumentation*, trans. John Wilkerson and Purcell Weaver (Notre Dame, IN: University of Notre Dame Press, 1969), 115–120.

50. Migration Observatory of the Centre on Migration, Policy and Society (COMPAS) at the University of Oxford, "Migrants in the UK: An Overview," migrationobservatory.ox.ac.uk.

Finnish Discourses on Immigration, 2015–2016

DESCENDANTS OF ISHMAEL, WELFARE SURFERS, AND ECONOMIC ASSETS

———•◆•———

Jouni Tilli

"Immigrants are a positive possibility for Finland's globalizing economy," "Uncontrolled migration of peoples cannot be sustained much longer," "When did Finns and Europeans become such sheep?"[1] These are some of the comments made by Finnish political leaders during the recent refugee crisis. In 2015 a total of nearly 32,500 refugees came to Finland, a number that in itself is not dramatic in a wealthy country with a population of 5.5 million, but given that there was nearly a tenfold increase from 2014, it is not surprising that a heated debate ensued. The situation was exacerbated by the fact that in the fall of 2015 the newly elected right-wing government began to implement its new economic policies, designed to lower wages and cut welfare costs.[2]

In this chapter I will examine the rhetoric of Finnish political leaders on the subject of the recent refugee crisis. The material consists of speeches, statements, interviews, and blog entries from summer 2015 to spring 2016. My approach is based on two assumptions. To begin with, political reality is understood as a symbolic construction, created with the intention of convincing our audience(s) to identify with and lend support to particular rationalizations.[3] For example, immigration is about human beings moving from one location to another. Rhetorically, however, numerous kinds of motives can be imputed to those people, and the phenomenon can be described as a blessing or a curse—and a myriad of other things that fit the frame of meanings within which the situation is being assessed.[4]

Second, human behavior and its symbolic framing constitute a discourse. Discourse holds sway through the production of categories of knowledge, and in so doing it (re)produces both power and knowledge. In this process, discourse defines subjects and positions them in relation to its truth(s) by revealing the limits of what is possible, normal, beneficial, desirable, and even "sayable."[5] Drawing on these premises, my analytical focus is on how immigrants have been constructed in recent Finnish political discourse(s). In other words, I will not examine immigration per se but how and in what kind of discursive contexts immigrants and the crisis are being talked *about*.

First, I will give an outline of Finland's historical position between East and West, then move on to discuss Finland's present migration policies. Then I will analyze the construction of immigrants in recent Finnish political rhetoric. The argument is that although there are three distinctive discourses, economic, threat-related, and humanist, which include different, even contradictory, arguments, they all have in common the fact that they place a heavy emphasis on economic and political concerns and see immigrants predominantly as instruments. Rhetorically, as the chapter purports to show, this is achieved by focusing on the potentiality of immigrants.

Finland, between East and West

In this section I will present an overview of the political history of Finland, focusing particularly on Finland's geopolitical position between

East and West. From the beginning of the Northern Crusades in the late 1100s until 1809, the Finnish Peninsula was a part of the kingdom of Sweden.[6] The Napoleonic wars determined Finland's place in Europe. In exchange for peace with France, Russia joined Napoleon's blockade of Great Britain, agreeing also to bring Sweden into the blockade. In February 1808, unable to persuade Sweden to join, the czar ordered an invasion of Finland. Sweden refrained from sending reinforcements to Finland for fear of a French attack, and Russian forces quickly spread across the area. On September 17, 1809, Sweden signed a peace treaty with Russia, ceding Finland to Russia.[7]

Although Finland enjoyed the status of an autonomous grand duchy, after 1890 Finland suffered increasingly from political oppression at the hands of the Russian authorities. How to respond to Russia's tightening grip provoked a bitter struggle among the Finns at a time when the country was also faced with serious social and economic inequality. Together, this explosive compound resulted, first, in 1917, in the aftermath of the Bolshevik revolution, in independence, and then, as a result of the country's sociopolitical divide, in a four-month-long civil war: socialists and conservatives fought for control until the Whites finally triumphed over the Reds. Independent Finland, then, was part of the new, turbulent Europe that arose from the collapse of the Russian and Austro-Hungarian empires at the end of World War I.[8]

During the years 1939–1945, Finland's place between East and West was never more visible—or more dangerous. Finland, a German ally, was embroiled in the struggle for hegemony in Eastern Europe. Finland stood between the Western democracies and their wartime ally, the Soviet Union. Against the odds, Finland survived years of conflict that resulted in many other small countries losing their independence. After World War II the line between East and West was redrawn again, with Finland falling within the Soviet sphere of influence.[9]

The relationship between Finland and the Soviet Union was, however, rather complicated, as can be illustrated by two conflicting accounts. According to the first account, Finland presented itself to the West as a Nordic parliamentary democracy that simply chose to be neutral, but the reality was that the country was heavily influenced by the Soviet Union: behind the scenes, the Soviets exerted control over the Finnish government, and the Finns, in order to survive, had no alternative but docile compliance (known as "Finlandization"). The second account holds that Finland was a heroic small nation that, by prolonged struggle with its huge neighbor, asserted the right to remain a neutral democracy and maintained its position by its skill and statesmanlike wisdom even in the face of occasional outbursts of Soviet bullying and pressure.[10] Wherever the truth lies, Finland retained its market economy and democratic institutions, creating for itself a secure and prosperous place in the Cold War divide and enjoying amicable relations with both East and West.

The end of the Cold War forced Finland, like other western European neutrals, to reconsider its place in Europe. Sweden's decision to seek EU membership, along with the continuing disintegration of the USSR, threatened to marginalize Finland in the new Europe. In January 1992, just days after the collapse of the USSR, Finland decided to open accession talks with the EU. On January 1, 1995, Finland, along with Sweden and Austria, joined the EU. In 1999, Finland joined ten other EU countries in adopting the single European currency, the euro.[11]

My admittedly simplified overview seeks to highlight that Finland's political culture cannot be understood without acknowledging the country's liminal position. As a small country that has always had to get along with one external authority or another (Sweden, Russia, the EU), it has been beneficial to be internally united—or at least to pose as such. A drawback has been that "rocking the boat" has often been considered inappropriate and even dangerous, and political issues are depoliticized by appealing to "external necessities." On the other hand, the politics of consensus was a key factor in the creation of the Finnish welfare state after World War II. Finland was a latecomer to social welfare compared, for example, to Sweden, and its comprehensive social reforms would not have been possible without extensive cooperation across the political spectrum.[12]

Finnish Immigration Politics and Policies

Although Finland's geopolitical position means that there have always been foreigners living in the country, their number has been rather small and they have originated mainly in the neighboring countries. Finland's population has indeed been homogenous. For example, in 2011 90 percent of the population spoke Finnish as their mother tongue, and in 2015 73 percent of Finns belonged to the Lutheran Church (in 1950 it was a staggering 95 percent). Traditionally Finland has been a country of emigration, not immigration: during the last 150 years, more than 1.3 million Finns have moved abroad (the population today is 5.3 million). In the nineteenth century the emigrants' destination was North America; after World War II it was typically Sweden, in both cases mostly in search of work.[13]

The history of refugeedom in Finland is rather short. The Bolshevik revolution had a significant effect on immigration to Finland. When Finland established its independence, there were about six thousand Russians in the country. However, in the aftermath of World War I and the revolution, the number of refugees from Russia and Eastern Europe arose steadily, the high point being 1922, during which over thirty-three thousand people came to Finland. They were mainly people living in St Petersburg and having ethnic ties to Finland, Ingrians, East Karelians, and members of the elite of the czarist era. From World War II up to the early 1970s the number of foreign citizens coming to Finland was insignificant, and they tended to stay for a short period only. The major reasons for immigration were studying, temporary work projects, and marriage.[14]

The arrival of refugees in Finland from remote countries dates back to 1973, when the country accepted the first 100 refugees from Chile, escaping oppression by the dictator Augusto Pinochet. Between 1973 and 1977 a total of 182 refugees came to Finland from Latin America, the majority of whom returned home after the end of the Pinochet era. During the same decade, in 1979, Finland accepted the first Vietnamese "boat people," fleeing the Vietnam War by boat. The next group of

Vietnamese refugees arrived in 1983.[15] In the early 1990s the first group of Somali refugees came to Finland, and later in the 1990s refugees from the former Yugoslavia arrived to the country.

Until the 1980s Finnish immigration policy had been carried out mainly on an ad hoc basis by various official bodies. As noted previously, during the 1980s the number of immigrants and the diversity of their countries of origin had begun to increase, and a new approach was needed. The first Aliens Act was passed in 1983, legitimated mainly by the alleged threat posed to Finland by international crime. Refugee quotas were introduced in 1985. The quickly outdated Aliens Act was replaced by a new act in 1991, the key motive now being fear of mass immigration from the recently collapsed Soviet Union. The many amendments that subsequently had to be made to this act, too, made it confusing, and a new one was passed in 2004.[16]

It was only in 1997, two years after joining the EU, that Finland put together a coordinated strategy for immigration and refugees. The emphasis was on control, efficiency, and economic considerations. In the strategy text that followed that one (in 2006), benefits and advantages to Finland are emphasized even more: diversity and multiculturalism are now also harnessed to serve Finland's economic development. Thus, in a reflection of the country's geopolitical position and history, Finnish immigration policy has oscillated between fear and control: on the one hand, immigrants, "illegal" ones in particular, have been seen as a threat, but on the other hand, controlled immigration has been seen as an economic asset.[17]

Finland's Migration Strategy, released in 2013, lays down guidelines for migration policy in the long term. The key message is that people who move to Finland must be included in the process of building Finland's "shared future." In addition, immigrants "must be treated as active subjects and participants rather than objects of services and measures."[18]

The strategy sees migration first of all as an opportunity to create "international networks" and "new ways of doing things." In addition, more pragmatically, migration will help to answer Finland's problem with its dependency ratio, but at the same time, competition for workers between countries will increase and so Finland must be able to effectively attract skilled workers. In parallel with promoting openness, the "strategy draws attention to the importance of managing migration and ensuring safety."

Second, migration policy seeks to ensure that new arrivals in Finland are able to make use of their skills and participate in the development of Finnish society. From this it follows that the provision of Finnish and/or Swedish language teaching as well as of other education and training organized as part of labor policy must be increased. Third, the principles of the inviolability of human dignity, the freedom and rights of the individual, and the promotion of justice in society, as set out in the constitution of Finland, serve as a foundation for the acceptance of diversity. Any discrimination occurring in the different areas of life, such as employment, must be systematically monitored.

The most important domestic legislation related to implementation of the strategy is the aforementioned Aliens Act. Its key premise is that people residing in Finland always require a visa or residence permit. However, in the provisions of the Aliens Act, EU citizens are treated separately from third-country nationals. In practice this means that EU citizens and their family members have the right to move freely within the Union: they do not need residence permits, but they need to register their right of residence.

As regards asylum seekers, Finland adheres to the right to asylum as stated in Article 18 of the Charter of Fundamental Rights of the European Union.[19] The Finnish Immigration Service determines whether an asylum seeker is a refugee when it makes a decision on his or her application. Refugee status is granted to those who are given asylum or accepted by Finland under the refugee quota. Asylum seekers stay mainly in reception centers located throughout Finland while waiting for their application to be processed.

Since 2000, Finland has received 1,500 to 6,000 asylum seekers annually. In 2014, the number was 3,651. In 2015 there was a sharp increase in the number, to 32,476, more than 20,000 of whom were from Iraq, 5,200 from Afghanistan, and 2,000 from Somalia. Under its refugee quota,

Finland admits persons recognized as refugees by the United Nations High Commissioner for Refugees and other foreign nationals in need of international protection. For the past few years, the refugee quota has been between 750 and 1,000. By the end of 2015, approximately 7,400 decisions on asylum applications were made, of these 1,879 were positive. Significantly, 3,186 applications were cancelled or withdrawn.[20]

Taking into consideration the significant increase in the number of asylum seekers in the fall of 2015, it is not surprising that public debate on immigration rapidly intensified.[21] In addition to the increase, an important catalyst in the discussion was the fact that at the same time Prime Minister Juha Sipilä's new center/right-wing government (appointed May 29, 2015) was beginning to implement its program, which included several economic reforms aimed at reviving Finland's faltering economy. The crux of these austerity measures was—and is—to lower wages and reduce public spending in order to conform to the EU Stability and Growth Pact.[22]

Rhetorically, in assessing the situation the government has often conflated the economic decline and the refugee crisis. For example, in Sipilä's speech on national television in September 2015, he referred to "the millions on the move" and "the billions of euros moving in human smuggling" in between lamenting the lack of growth of the Finnish economy and the rising unemployment rate and proclaiming that because the national debt had been increasing at the rate of "a million euros per hour for almost seven years," Finland was running out of money.[23] It is no wonder, then, that economic aspects have dominated in recent Finnish political rhetoric related to immigration.

The Economic Discourse

In what I have labeled simply 'the economic discourse,' one of the most pervasive arguments is that migration gives a much needed stimulus to the Finnish economy. The government's program states that "work-related migration that enhances employment in Finland, boosts public finances, improves the dependency ratio, and contributes to the internationalization of the economy" will be promoted. Furthermore, in a country with an aging population, "immigrants enhance our innovation capacity and increase our know-how by bringing their cultural strengths to Finnish society." For this reason, immigration, particularly outside the EU, "should be well managed."[24]

This pragmatic-economic approach was repeated by many politicians, particularly by members of the parties in government. Minister of Finance Alexander Stubb stressed that closing the borders is not a solution, but "we must consider immigration from humane and economic perspectives. It really benefits us."[25] Stubb also used Finland's western neighbor as a positive example and pointed out that one reason why funding of the welfare society in Sweden is on a stronger basis than in Finland is its successful immigration policy.[26] Similarly, Minister of the Interior Petteri Orpo has declared that immigrants are a hugely positive opportunity for Finland, a country with an aging population and one whose economy depends on exports.[27]

To further this aim, Orpo has proclaimed numerous times that he is willing to approve "exceptional measures," even to propose changes in legislation, in order to "get immigrants into work as quickly as possible." No stone will be left unturned in this task, nothing can be ruled out, not even the possibility that wages will have to be "flexible downward."[28] Not surprisingly, the minister was immediately criticized for attempting to create a cheap labor market at the expense of immigrants. Significantly, not only was this criticism voiced by the opposition, but also by Timo Soini, chair of the (right-wing populist) Finns Party, which was also in the government until June 2017.[29]

In addition, the economic discourse includes a more negative stance. In such rhetoric, the key claim is that immigrants, especially refugees and asylum seekers, are a burden on the economy: it is claimed that their integration is extremely expensive and it takes a very long time for them to be able to provide for themselves, independent of the Finnish welfare system. This argument has been used, for example, by a member of the European Parliament (for the Finns Party) and chair of the Finns Party from June 2017 onward, Jussi Halla-aho, a highly controversial and very popular politician who was convicted of incitement to racial hatred in 2012. He stated in a demonstration against mass immigration in October 2015 that more than half of the people coming across the Mediterranean were not Syrian refugees but Iraqis and Somalians fleeing from unemployment and corruption. According to Halla-aho, although their flight was understandable, it constituted an immense problem because there simply was not enough work in Finland:

> We are being told that these people [immigrants] will put right our population pyramid and improve our dependency ratio. However, it is mentioned only in passing that this will happen only *if* they become employed. We have twenty-five years of difficult experience of humanitarian immigration from precisely these countries. If the unemployment rate among people from these countries has been 70 percent year after year and decade after decade, does anyone seriously think that in the middle of an economic slump Finland will be able to integrate into its workforce such a vast increase in the number of newcomers? We do not believe this.[30]

Halla-aho continued on to say that the fact that many immigrants, including refugees, have been integrated into Finnish society does not alter the big picture, and this is what must be kept in mind when drawing up a "sustainable immigration policy." Over fifty thousand people, he predicted bleakly, were expected to come to Finland in that year (2015), and the cost during the asylum process alone would exceed five hundred million euros; nor do the costs end there, because many immigrants will have to rely entirely on social security for years to come. Similar rhetoric has been used by others, for example by the MP and vice-chair of the National Coalition Party, Janne Sankelo, who estimated in November 2015 that if the same pace of immigration continued, "The limit of Finland's [economic] capacity would be reached within a year."[31]

MP Wille Rydman (National Coalition) contributed another aspect to the economic rhetoric, suggesting that immigration was not spontaneous but was a business conducted by human smugglers. He claimed that travel agencies "sell asylum package trips to their clients, including consultation about what to say and where and to which countries to continue." The result was that "these people, advised by smugglers, moving in Europe illegally and without proper identification" will not give their fingerprints until they reach the country where they want their asylum application to be processed—and people would rather jump into the Mediterranean than register anywhere else than Finland.[32] Here, then, refugees are constructed as gullible customers who benefit smugglers at Finland's expense.

Granting refugees a slightly more active role, the secretary of the Finns Party, Riikka Slunga-Poutsalo, was even more provocative in her rhetoric. She demanded that "living standard surfers" must be deported immediately. According to her, only about 20 percent of refugees arriving in Finland were really in need of help; the rest were men aged between eighteen and fifty who should be defending their fatherland, and for this reason "it seems that they cannot be counted as refugees." Similarly, Petteri Orpo estimated that two-thirds of asylum seekers were not in grave danger and therefore entitled to protection, but were merely after better living conditions.[33] In other words, most of the immigrants and refugees are social cheats exploiting the welfare system.[34]

Slunga-Poutsalo emphasized further that Finland was too attractive because of its social security system; the solution to the crisis was to reduce benefits. "At a time when the government is forced to cut back what is available to all Finns, resources cannot be allocated to people who are entering the country without any justification—let alone used to support the smuggling business, which is more profitable than drug trafficking," she declared.[35] The argument used here, that is, the negative impact of immigration on employment opportunities and wages together with the socioeconomic burden that immigration puts on the welfare system and education, has been one of the most persistent elements of the discourse on European immigration since the 1990s.[36]

In the first line of argumentation it is stressed that immigrants will benefit the Finnish economy while in the second, more pessimistic view, immigrants and refugees are depicted as either ruinous of the economy or the pawns of smugglers, either way a burden to the country. In the first discourse, immigrants are used to further the government's economic policies. In the second one, the economic argument is turned upside down with the claim that naïveté or ideologically based wishful thinking prevent proponents of the first argument from seeing the real results of their policies and the sinister motives of the cheaters or smugglers.[37]

In this economic discourse, immigrants are being rhetorically constructed as economic instruments or abusers. For either purpose, they are more often than not treated as one homogenous group: asylum seekers, quota refugees, and other immigrants are all seen in terms of their potential for Finland's prosperity. The implication is that if immigrants do not bring any economic advantage to Finland in the shortest possible time, their presence is pointless and should be prevented.[38] The overall result is that the discourse is a pragmatic and dehumanizing one: the phenomenon, that is, the movement of people, is to be brought under control immediately, and people on the move are merely objects being used in the pursuit of allegedly nobler (or baser) economic purposes.[39]

The Discourse of Threat

In addition to economic considerations, a discourse based on the construction of threats has been very evident in the rhetoric of Finnish political leaders. The historical term "migration of peoples" (*kansainvaellus* in Finnish) has been used to illustrate the problem that immigrants pose to European identity and European values.[40] As the most prominent example, President Sauli Niinistö declared in his speech at the opening of parliament in February 2016 that "the stream of immigration" to Europe, as to Finland, was largely a "migration of peoples," that is, was based on something other than imminent danger at home.[41]

According to the president, this growing stream of people challenged "Europe, Finland, Western thinking, and the Western value system" as

well as "the whole Western ability to help." By this Niinistö meant that
international agreements, EU directives, and national laws based on the
idea that everyone will be helped have made it possible for "anyone who
is able to utter the word 'asylum' to enter Europe and Finland," although
there might be no real basis for the claim. As a result, European values
were facing a dangerous dilemma:

> Europe cannot sustain uncontrolled migration of peoples much longer.
> Our values will give way if our capacity to cope is overstretched. It so
> happens that good intentions are creating a bad situation for everyone.
> It is alleged that most, if not almost all, of the measures that might be
> taken to control the process are in breach of international rights and
> agreements. The result is that we cannot do what many people consider
> necessary.[42]

Niinistö then pointed out that any international agreements that
were devised now would definitely be stricter but still be able to protect
human rights. According to the president, there were no good options:
"We must consider carefully whether to protect European values and
people as well as those in actual danger or to uphold international obligations without considering other consequences." He then suggested
that first the "European system of values and order must be secured" and
that those in actual danger must be helped, but at this point those seeking only better living conditions for themselves could not be assisted.[43]

The president's overt argument was, paradoxically, that the *number*
of people coming to Europe threatened the system based on *universal*
rights of movement and asylum seeking. However, the covert message
seems to be that the values of those on the move are inconsistent with
European values. President Niinistö supported his arguments with a
dramatic analogy with the migration of peoples: Europe, and Finland as
a part of it, are facing an assault comparable to that which led to the fall
of the Roman Empire. Immigrants are thus subsumed into a monolithic
whole, a horde of barbarians who are threatening Europe's identity and
security.[44]

Another example of the discourse of threat comes from an MP from the Finns Party, Teuvo Hakkarainen, who combined identitarian and securitarian concerns with a biopolitical approach.[45] Referring to a recent study according to which the population in many small towns in Finland is "skewed" because there are more single men than single women, Hakkarainen said in the Finnish parliament:

> Taking into consideration our population structure, how are we sup-
> posed to integrate this Islamic group into our country? We have 155
> towns with too many young men and an unbalanced gender distribu-
> tion, like in China. Well, now they have started to put among us these
> men, descendants of Ishmael, who have always waged war against each
> other. There will never be peace. It is an impossible equation—the fu-
> ture will be dark if this continues. I say, as I have said before, that we
> should close our borders, and the best protection against Islamization
> is barbed wire.[46]

Drawing on a strand of thought the Nazis developed to its ex-
treme, Hakkarainen claimed that the natural and immutable character of immigrants, whom he takes to be all young Muslim men, is derived "biologically" from their alleged ancestor Ishmael.[47] The biblical allusion to Ishmael further suggests that his "descendants" will resemble "wild donkeys" constantly on the warpath even against their own brothers.[48] Hakkarainen said that because these people are bellicose by nature, neither integration nor peace is possible. The immigrants also constitute a biopolitical threat to the demographic equilibrium of the country: they will steal Finnish women and upset the natural composition of the popu-
lation.[49] Thus, in this process defined as "Islamization," immigrants are constructed in terms of racialist essentialization.

Finally, in this discourse refugees were also constructed as a potential threat in a more complicated way. For example, drawing on traditional securitarian concerns, MP and chair of the Left Alliance Paavo Arhinmäki warned that the crisis was being used by terrorists to undermine Western societies. Using the terrorist strikes in November 2015 in Paris

as an example, he stressed that terrorists were trying to turn different groups of people against each other by "sowing hatred, fear, and chaos." Arhinmäki declared that "in Europe Daesh is attempting to turn the original population against refugees—against those who are fleeing to Europe from the cruelty of Daesh."[50] Hence the leftist leader constructed refugees as potential "weapons" cunningly used by ISIS (Islamic State in Iraq and Syria) to undermine the internal security and unity of Europe.[51]

In what has been perhaps the most common type of threat rhetoric among Finnish political leaders, immigrants' values are seen as incompatible with Finnish values, which in turn are identified with European values. Immigrants are seen as representing an immutable, homogenous, and potentially dangerous Islam. They are also constructed as a biopolitical threat to the "original Finnish population." Immigrants are depicted as belligerent, animalistic, and horny. Finally, it is implied that refugees might bring warlike conditions to Finland as well, one way or another.

What is highlighted in this discourse too is not individuals, but mass behavior: immigrants are depicted either as a horde guided by their primitive instincts or as merely involuntary vessels and the tools of a suspicious religious ideology, in contrast to rational Europeans and their allegedly superior order.[52] As a result, immigrants are an identitarian, biopolitical, and securitarian threat, and immigration is presented as a matter of national security; the implication is that in such circumstances even exceptional measures can be taken against those who pose this threat.[53]

The Humanist Discourse

In the humanist discourse the focus is on the predicament of refugees and asylum seekers and their rights and freedoms, but here too there are economic considerations. Representatives of this discourse have been mainly, but not exclusively, from opposition parties in parliament. Criticizing the government's proposal that permission for people already resident in Finland to bring in family members would require a net income of twenty-six hundred euros a month (for a spouse and two children), MP and chair of the Green Party Ville Niinistö declared that the worldview on which the proposal was based was incomprehensible.[54] He continued with a powerful rebuke:

> Have we not hoped precisely this, that the young men who have come to Finland should not stay here without their families? Have we not hoped precisely that they could get an education and be employed in Finland? Tightening the conditions for family members' residence permits would mean that it would be impossible for an immigrant working as a nurse, for example, to have any hope of getting her loved ones to Finland. It is not the right message to be giving if we say that even if you do your best for this country, we will not allow you to be with your nearest and dearest.[55]

According to Niinistö, the proposal was an example of "desperate fumbling" by the government, which was overreacting to the immigration crisis in a way that meant everyone would lose. Most importantly, it was also the beginning of the slippery slope toward curtailing individual freedom, the result of "imprudent hillbilly populism," which Finland could not afford.

The chair of the Swedish People's Party, Carl Haglund, similarly used a humanist approach with an economic twist. He criticized the government's plans to conduct an investigation into the costs of immigration: "The purpose of this is unclear. The government has apparently not noticed that the Institute for Economic Research and the Research Institute of the Finnish Economy have already pointed out that Finland needs more people in order to save our welfare system because our nation is ageing."[56] Haglund went on to say that it remained a mystery how Finland would be able to attract immigrants while "Sipilä and his friends are standing at the border putting price tags on people's heads."

He then declared that the Swedish People's Party distanced itself from policies that ignore the poorest and those in most need of help. "In the light of all this, one cannot but regret the attitude of PM Sipilä's govern-ment toward international solidarity," Haglund declared. He concluded that the government's policy was a result of the "simplified populism of the Finns Party," which was now winning out over its cabinet allies, the National Coalition Party and the Center Party. The Green Party chair and his Swedish People's Party colleague thus both used tragic irony to suggest that the government's attempts to control immigration would backfire in terms of both humanitarianism and economics.

Taking the humanist emphasis a step further, Paavo Arhinmäki was one of the very rare politicians who questioned the very idea of framing the situation as a crisis. He pointed out that despite the increasing num-ber of immigrants, Finland was far from facing a refugee crisis; the actual crisis was in Syria, Iraq, Turkey, and Lebanon. Criticizing the use of terms such as "welfare surfers" and "illegal asylum seekers," Arhinmäki then observed that it was very unlikely that Finland's social benefits were a reason for becoming a refugee, and that failure to have a personal ID did not deprive anyone of the right to seek asylum: Jews fleeing from Nazi persecution, for example, and Soviet dissidents, were not turned away just because they did not have passports.

The Left Alliance leader also bewailed the fact that human smugglers were taking advantage of the plight of people fleeing from war as well as of those seeking better living conditions. "Unseaworthy vessels, often with barely enough fuel to enter international waters, are overloaded with people," he stated, adding gloomily that "either those drifting on the Mediterranean are rescued or they drown. The Mediterranean has become a sea of death."[57] Arhinmäki concluded by condemning the gov-ernment's cut (by over 40 percent) to development aid that, he claimed, would do nothing to prevent people having to leave their homes in the first place. In this way refugees were compared emotionally with the victims of the Holocaust and the Soviet purges, and legitimate and "il-legitimate" refugees were all victimized by focusing on their suffering at the hands of smugglers.

MP Erkki Tuomioja, a member of the Social Democratic Party, also stood out from other commentators by underlining the diversity rather than homogeneity among immigrants. He said that the many different reasons behind people's movement should not be forgotten: it was obvious that such a great number of people included "criminals, fortune hunters, impostors, and maybe even some terrorists with evil intentions," but the overwhelming majority of refugees were in need of and were entitled to protection. Most of them, too, were hoping to return to their homes and rebuild their country as soon as it was safe to do so, he claimed.[58] Here, more than in most of the other accounts, immigrants are constructed as active agents; interestingly, however, they are expected to contribute to the development of their countries of origin, not of Finland.

It is important to note that the boundaries of the humanist discourse do not run along the government-opposition divide. For example, using less dramatic imagery than MPs of the opposition, Minister of Finance Alexander Stubb stressed that despite the difficulties posed by the crisis, refugees and asylum seekers must be treated in a way that respects their dignity as human beings.[59] Using similar rhetoric, Prime Minister Juha Sipilä stressed that although the refugee crisis was an unforeseen challenge and the economic situation serious, Finns must be able to respond with humanity.[60] In addition, occasionally humane considerations functioned as a bridge over the government opposition divide. Referring explicitly to the statements by some MPs of the Finns Party, Minister of Education and Culture Sanni Grahn-Laasonen (National Coalition) stated that people are essentially the same despite the part of the world they have been born in and that "fear, prejudice, and heartlessness are a far greater threat to Finland than anything from outside could be."[61] Thus, the minister posited herself rhetorically to the same discourse with MPs of the opposition, with right-wing populism as their common target.

A fascinating contribution to the debate was made by a bishop, Jari Jolkkonen, who preached at the opening ceremony of parliament in February 2016. The opening and closing services of the parliament, held in Helsinki Cathedral, are among the most visible and significant ties between the Lutheran Church and the Finnish state. Broadcast live on television and the internet, the occasion is a rare opportunity for a bishop to preach to the political leadership. Quite often the sermons have been an interesting nexus of political and theological discourses; indeed, the bishop delivering the parliamentary sermon can be seen as a politician him- or herself.[62]

Jari Jolkkonen applied the Lutheran doctrine of original sin to the crisis.[63] According to him, the principal reason for the predicament in Iraq and Syria could be traced to man's essential nature as a sinner: the situation in the Near East showed what happened when the "selfishness and evil in human nature" were allowed free rein once the institutions of society had collapsed. The bishop declared that such institutions serve peace and justice and cannot be taken for granted, but must be worked for. Jolkkonen argued that weakening them was not automatically a blessing:

> There are an unforeseen number of refugees knocking at our gates. They come from countries in which traditional institutions such as the state, the judiciary, and a free press have all collapsed. This has not resulted in a happy civil society but in chaos and everyone's war against everyone. Everyone, particularly the weakest members of society, is suffering.[64]

The bishop was here combining criticism of the government's attempts to dismantle the structures of the welfare state with a theological assessment of the origins of the refugee crisis. He constructs refugees as the victims of poor policies. They are human beings like Finns: tainted by original sin and in need of a stable society. He is saying, in other words, that the universal potential for evil has been let loose as a result of the destruction of societal institutions and structures. Also, an obvious implication of the biblical allusion is that the gates should be opened to those who knock.[65]

This can be seen as a critique of a common feature of Western immigration rhetoric, namely, the conceptualization of a country with its infrastructure and institutions as a "container"—in the Finnish case underlined with the image of having a concrete gate that could be

knocked—that is about to collapse under external pressure.[66] As noted
by Jonathan Charteris-Black, the container metaphor is persuasive in
political rhetoric because it merges time with space. In Finland's case we
have seen that controlling immigration through maintaining the security
of borders has been used to claim control over the pace of both economic and cultural change. Importantly, thus also suspicion associated
with the "penetrators" of the container is heightened.[67]

Not altogether unexpectedly, similar criticism has been made by
the Christian Democrats. According to Päivi Räsänen, MP, and those
responsible for the party's immigration policy, immigration must be
"both humane and controlled": while those in need must be helped,
Finland must be able to decide who is permitted to enter.[68] At the same
time Räsänen demanded that "hundreds of millions" of euros should be
allocated to promote immigrants' integration into society because the
risk of social exclusion and poverty is six times higher among immigrants than among those born in Finland, and is especially high among
people without any education at all. At its worst, marginalization can
lead to radicalization, she warned.[69] Thus religious leaders introduced a
Lutheran approach to the debate, arguing that state structures are God's
way of ruling the secular world and that they therefore need to be re-
spected and used humanely.

The humanist discourse is rather ambivalent as regards to how immigrants are constructed rhetorically.[70] On the one hand, refugees are
seen as the victims of civil war and flawed politics and are attempting
to rebuild their lives. On the other hand, they are very often used as
political leverage. As for example Trudy Govier has pointed out, the
status of victim is often associated with passivity: victims are easily seen
as innocent, needy, and helpless, meekly anticipating sympathy and
assistance—without doubt a morally powerful position to be exploited
politically.[71] As seen in the humanist discourse, this makes it possible to
construct human beings rhetorically as agents and at the same time to
treat them as instruments.

Conclusion

In Finnish political rhetoric on the recent refugee crisis, immigrants have been constructed within the framework of three discourses. The economic discourse is based on the alleged benefit or harm of immigrants to the Finnish economy, with the unifying theme of constructing immigrants as economic instruments. The discourse of threat, in turn, depicts immigrants as an identitarian, biopolitical, or securitarian threat. Finally, the humanist discourse constructs immigrants mainly as human beings, but ones whose agency is diminished by their victimhood. In the rare cases when immigrants are treated as active agents within the frame of these discourses, their agency is almost without exception cast in a rather dubious light. This is at least partly due to Finland's political history and culture: immigrants are easily seen as people who rock the boat—or penetrate the container.

The construction of immigrants is highly politicized. What I mean by this is that in all the discourses, immigrants and refugees are quite enthusiastically utilized as a means to either criticize the government or—by the government—to promote its own policies; and, in the bishop's case, to reproach all politicians. On the other hand, occasionally immigrants' suffering united politicians from both the government and the opposition against the populists. Thus, immigrants are used for political ends, regardless of the way they are constructed rhetorically. In this sense, the results of my analysis testify to the aptness of Kenneth Burke's claim that once means are brought to the fore, they begin to dominate the given rhetorical landscape.[72]

It is also worth underlining that the crisis as a phenomenon is given significantly less attention than immigrants or refugees. In other words, reasons behind the situation were discussed far less than motives and identities of the immigrants. A telling example of a typical way to "assess" the complexity of the situation is President Sauli Niinistö's enigmatic rhetorical question in his New Year's speech of 2016: "Is it not the case that the source of these evils and misfortunes lies further back in the past and the dam is now breaking under its pressure?"[73]

The discourses also coexist and overlap in many ways. It is not uncommon for two—occasionally even three—of them to be present in any one speech given by a political leader. There also seems to be considerable variance *within* the political parties. That said, the economic discourse has been mainly employed by politicians from the government parties, while arguments derived from the other two discourses have been used by politicians from the government and the opposition alike. In addition to the fact that the government is responsible for the state's economy, one likely reason for this is the government's decision to link the economic crisis with the immigration issue in its public rhetoric.

It is important to note that economic concerns are conspicuously present in all three discourses. Even when immigrants are seen in a positive light, this is very often tinted with shades of economic pragmatism. This is not surprising, bearing in mind the European financial crisis and the triumph in the last twenty years of neoliberal political rhetoric with its emphasis on economic calculability and competitiveness. For example, Maurizio Lazzarato has pointed out that contemporary (Western) economies are occupied with production of the "possibles" and mobilizing individual and collective attention toward what will happen—anticipation, in a word.[74]

Consequently, it is not surprising that in all of the discourses presented here, what is most salient is a preoccupation with the "potentiality" of immigrants—and not only in relation to the economy. In the three discourses the way the "essence" of immigrants is constructed is heavily affected by hopes (and fears) regarding how their potentiality will be actualized.[75] However, as Kenneth Burke has noted, since a mere tendency or potentiality is just as likely *not* to be actualized, it is probable that attempts will be made to bring the given phenomenon under control and make it predictable. On the other hand, potentiality can be taken as foreordained, which can result in a deterministic and racist conception of those who are seen to possess the potentialities.[76] Both these rhetorical aspects are forcefully present in the Finnish immigration discourses. When the future of the nation depends on immigration, the present plight of those in need is easily ignored, and human beings are assessed mainly in terms of the positive and negative contribution they might make to the national good in the future.

In this way the Finnish immigration discourses also illuminate an aspect of contemporary Western welfare societies. As famously pointed out by Ulrich Beck, these kinds of societies are conspicuously future-oriented because they are occupied with preventing or minimizing risks and maximizing potentialities, not production and distribution of goods, at least not the way they were earlier. The risks (and potentialities) faced are particularly problematic because delimiting them spatially, temporally, or socially is extremely difficult. Consequently, their global scale is what constitutes an immense challenge to political leaders. On the other hand, their magnitude and contingency render such phenomena a fruitful basis for manufacturing uncertainty, which, in turn, is a versatile political argument. As a result, those who can produce or concoct the symbols that capture tangibly enough the negative or positive potential of a given phenomenon and use it in their rationalizations have the upper hand.[77]

As, for example, Michel Foucault and research inspired by his work have stressed, present-day risks and potentialities, more often than not, pertain to the features of human beings, as individual subjects and groups, and their contribution to the vitality and security of a given population.[78] However, while in existing research literature the focus is on themes such as fertility, biotechnology, and social care, it is important to understand also how immigration is being assessed in terms of a similar framework. Indeed, as we have seen in the course of this chapter, global mass immigration an example par excellence of contemporary politics occupying itself with bringing the ambiguous potentiality human life on the move under calculation, guidance, and control. Importantly, my analysis also illustrates the manifold rhetorical constructions that accompany such endeavors.

Notes

1. Petteri Orpo, "Maahanmuuttajat ovat Mahdollisuus Kansainvälistyvälle Taloudelle," *Mandaatti 2016*, May 6, 2016, presser.fi. Sauli Niinistö, Speech by President of the Republic Sauli Niinistö at the Opening of Parliament on February 3, 2016, presidentti.fi. Jussi Halla-aho, Facebook update, *Facebook*, November 20, 2015.

2. Finland is a democratic republic with a multiparty parliamentary representative system. The president is the head of state, is responsible for foreign policy, and is commander in chief of the defense forces. The prime minister is the head of government; executive power is exercised by the government. Until June 2017, the government consisted of three parties, the Centre Party, the National Coalition Party, and the Finns Party. In the opposition were the Social Democrats, the Left Alliance, the Green Party, the Swedish People's Party, and the Christian Democrats. In June 2017, Jussi Halla-aho was elected chair of the Finns Party, which resulted in a split into parties, the Blue Reform Party and the Finns Party. The former inherited position in the government, while the latter moved to the opposition.

3. Kenneth Burke, *Language as Symbolic Action* (Berkeley: University of California Press, 1966), 5; Murray Edelman, *Politics as Symbolic Action: Mass Arousal and Quiescence* (New York: Academic Press, 1971), 31.

4. Kenneth Burke, *Attitudes toward History* (Berkeley: University of California Press, 1984), 5.

5. Michel Foucault, *Archaeology of Knowledge* (London: Routledge, 2002, 130–131; Foucault, "Politics and the Study of Discourse," in *The Foucault Effect: Studies in Governmentality*, ed. Graham Burchell et al. (Chicago: University of Chicago Press, 1991), 58–60.

6. Jason Lavery, *The History of Finland* (Westport: Greenwood Press, 2006), 31–32.

7. Lavery, 51–52; also Risto Alapuro, "The Intelligentsia, the State, and the Nation," in *Finland: People, Nation, State*, ed. Max Engman and David Kirby (London: Hurst, 1989), 147–165.

8. Lavery, 88, 91; Edward Dutton, "Finland's Cold War Legacy,"

Contemporary Review 1690 (2008), 307.

9. Lavery, 112, 133.

10. Dutton, 306–311; Christopher S. Browning, *Constructivism, Narrative and Foreign Policy Analysis: a Case Study of Finland* (Bern: Peter Lang, 2008), 200–214; Anthony James, "A Northern Paradox: How Finland Survived the Cold War," *Contemporary Review* 1538 (1994): 113–122.

11. Lavery, 156.

12. See Pauli Kettunen, "Nordic Welfare State in Finland," *Scandinavian Journal of History* 26 (2001): 225–247.

13. Tuomas Martikainen et al., *Muuttajat: Kansainvälinen muuttoliike ja suomalainen yhteiskunta* (Helsinki: Gaudeamus, 2013), 26–27.

14. Jouni Korkiasaari and Ismo Söderling, *Finnish Emigration and Immigration after World War II* (Turku: Siirtolaisuusinstituutti, 2003), 6–7.

15. Korkiasaari and Söderling, 8.

16. Antti Kanniainen, *Kansanedustajien Mielipiteitä Maahanmuutosta Uhkana ja Mahdollisuutena* (Turku: Finnish Institute of Migration, 2010), 44–45; Antero Leitzinger, *Ulkomaalaispolitiikka Suomessa 1812–1972* (Helsinki: East-West Books, 2008).

17. Kanniainen, 46.

18. "Government Resolution on the Future of Migration 2020 Strategy," Ministry of the Interior, June 13, 2013, eapmigrationpanel.org.

19. "The right to asylum shall be granted with due respect for the rules of the Geneva Convention of July 28, 1951 and the Protocol of January 31, 1967 relating to the status of refugees and in accordance with the Treaty on European Union and the Treaty on the Functioning of the European Union."

20. "Rapid Increase in the Number of Asylum Seekers," Ministry of the Interior, 2017, reliefweb.int.

21. In fall 2015 and early 2016 there were numerous occasions on which Molotov cocktails were thrown at reception centers for asylum seekers.

22. See Stability and Growth Pact, European Commission, 2013, ec.europa.eu.

23. Juha Sipilä, Prime Minister Juha Sipilä's Speech on the Finnish Broadcasting Company YLE on September 16, 2015, *Valtioneuvoston*

Kanslia, vnk.fi.

24. "Finland, a Land of Solutions," Strategic Programme of Prime Minister Juha Sipilä's Government May 29, 2015, December 2015, valtioneuvosto. fi.

25. "Kokoomus Puolustaa Maahanmuuttoa: 'Siitä on Oikeasti Meille Hyötyä,'" *Helsingin Sanomat*, August 18, 2015, hs.fi.

26. Alexander Stubb, "Vierailu Vastaanottokeskukseen" (blog entry), August 30, 2015, alexstubb.com.

27. Orpo.

28. "Ministeri Orpo Lupaa, että Maahanmuuttajat Saadaan Töihin: Tarvittaessa Palkoissa Joustetaan Alaspäin," *Helsingin Sanomat*, January 16, 2016, hs.fi.

29. "STTK:n Palola Torjui Ykkösaamussa Orpon Esityksen Maahanmuuttajien Palkkajoustoista: 'Halpatyömarkkinat Eivät Ole Kenenkään Etu,'" *Helsingin Sanomat*, January 16, 2016, hs.fi.

30. Jussi Halla-aho, Speech at "Jotain rajaa" Demonstration on October 10, 2015, youtube.com.

31. "Janne Sankelo: 'Suomen Kestokyvyn Raja Tulee Vastaan Vuodessa,'" *Kokoomus*, November 30, 2015, kokoomus.fi.

32. Wille Rydman, "Turvapaikka Hölmölästä" (blog entry), September 14, 2015, willerydman.fi.

33. "Sisäministeri Orpo: Suomi Myöntää Turvapaikan Vain Joka Kolmannelle Hakijalle," *Yle*, November 11, 2015, yle.fi.

34. See Christopher Hart, *Critical Discourse Analysis and Cognitive Science: New Perspectives on Immigration Discourse* (New York: Palgrave, 2010), 75–77.

35. "Slunga-Poutsalo: Elintasosurffarit Käännytettävä Pikaisesti—Eriarvoistavat Tuet Poistettava," *Suomen uutiset*, August 21, 2015, suomenuutiset.fi.

36. Ayse Ceyhan and Anastassia Tsoukala, "The Securitization of Migration in Western Societies: Ambivalent Discourses and Policies," *Alternatives* 27 (2002): 21–39; Hart.

37. Jussi Halla-aho, "Vielä ö-Luokan Ehdokkaista" (blog entry), March 3, 2015, halla-aho.com; Jussi Halla-aho, "Työperäinen Maahanmuutto" (blog entry), September 23, 2007, halla-aho.com.

38. Hart, 73. The government program also reflects the aforementioned economic tension between benefits and problems. In addition to stressing the positive economic effect immigration has on the economy, it states that "an independent study of the costs of migration and its impact on Finnish society will be conducted to enable fact-based discussion, better integration policies, and better decision-making."

39. Kenneth Burke, *A Grammar of Motives* (Berkeley: University of California Press, 1969), 283–288.

40. "Migration of peoples" refers to the mass migration that affected the Roman world from approximately the end of the fourth century to the beginning of the ninth century and largely brought about the fall of the Roman Empire.

41. Also, Rydman.

42. Sauli Niinistö, Speech by President of the Republic Sauli Niinistö at the Opening of Parliament on February 3, 2016.

43. This is a continuation of a theme the president began in August 2015 in a speech to the Ambassadors' Seminar in which he stated that "among those heading for Europe there are some who have mischief in mind." Sauli Niinistö, Speech by President of the Republic Sauli Niinistö at the Ambassadors' Seminar, August 25, 2015, preseidentti.fi.

44. See Clarke Rountree, "Instantiating 'The Law' and Its Dissents in *Korematsu v. United States*: A Dramatistic Analysis of Judicial Discourse," *Quarterly Journal of Speech* 87 (2001): 21.

45. According to Michel Foucault, in biopolitics "the basic biological features of the human species" are "the object of political strategy." Michel Foucault, *Security, Territory, Population: Lectures at the Collège de France, 1977–1978* (New York: Palgrave, 2007), 1.

46. Teuvo Hakkarainen, Speech at a Plenary Session of the Finnish Parliament, May 24, 2016, eduskunta.fi.

47. Burke, *A Grammar of Motives*, 26–29.

48. According to Genesis 16:12 Ishmael "will be a wild donkey of a man; his hand will be against everyone and everyone's hand against him, and he will live in hostility toward all his brothers."

49. This is a neater version of the rhetoric, particularly popular in social

media, in which refugees are constructed as (potential) rapists. See Hart, 19–24.

50. Paavo Arhinmäki, "Puhe Puoluevaltuustossa" (blog entry), November 21, 2015, paavoarhinmaki.fi.

51. See Ceyhan and Tsoukala, 24–26.

52. This is a common topos of Western political thought and rhetoric: the East, often embodied by Russia or Islam, is represented as the negative counterpart to the West. See Attila Melegh, *On the East-West Slope: Globalization, Nationalism, Racism and Discourses on Central Europe* (Budapest: Central European University Press, 2006). For example, Karina Horsti has pointed out that both work-based immigrants and asylum seekers were also constructed in terms of masses, streams, and floods in the Finnish media in the early 2000s. Karina Horsti, *Vierauden Rajat: Monikulttuurisuus ja Turvapaikanhakijat Journalismissa* (Tampere: Tampere University Press, 2005).

53. See Barry Buzan et al., *Security: A New Framework for Analysis* (Boulder, CO: Lynne Rienner Publishers, 1998).

54. The proposal was approved by the Finnish parliament on June 22, 2016.

55. Ville Niinistö, Speech at the Green Party Delegation Meeting, February 13, 2016, *Ville Niinistö*, villeniinisto.fi.

56. Carl Haglund, Speech at the Swedish People's Party Congress, *SFP/ RKP*, June 6, 2015, sfp.fi.

57. Paavo Arhinmäki, "Suomi ei Voi Sulkea Silmiään Maailman Hädältä" (blog entry), August 26, 2015, paavoarhinmaki.fi.

58. Erkki Tuomioja, "Pakolaiskriisi, Suomi ja Globaali Vastuu," *Tuomioja.org*, September 17, 2015, toumioja.org.

59. Alexander Stubb, Speech at the National Coalition Meeting on Europe, February 29, 2016, alexstubb.com.

60. Juha Sipilä, Prime Minister Juha Sipilä's Speech on the Finnish Broadcasting Company YLE, September 16, 2015.

61. Sanni Grahn-Laasonen, "Me Ihmiset Emme Ole Niin Kovin Erilaisia" (blog entry—also published in newspapers), August 30, 2015, sannigrahnlaasonen.fi.

62. Pasi Ihalainen, "The Lutheran National Community in 18th Century

Sweden and 21st Century Finland," *Redescriptions* 2005 (9): 80–112.

63. The Augsburg Confession (article II) states that due to the fall of Adam "all men begotten in the natural way are born with sin, that is, without the fear of God, without trust in God, and with concupiscence."

64. Jari Jolkkonen, Sermon at the Opening Ceremony of the Parliament of Finland February 3, 2016, evl.fi.

65. See Luke 11:10.

66. See Hart, 134–144.

67. Jonathan Charteris-Black, "Britain as a Container: Immigration Metaphors in the 2005 Election Campaign," *Discourse & Society* 17 (2006): 563–581; see also Eric M. Blanchard, "Constituting China: The Role of Metaphor in the Discourses of Early Sino-American Relations," *Journal of International Relations and Development* 16 (2013): 177–205.

68. Päivi Räsänen, "Tolkullinen Maahanmuuttopolitiikka Korostaa Inhimillisyyttä ja Hallittavuutta," *Kristillisdemokraatit*, February 2, 2016, kd.fi.

69. Päivi Räsänen, "Hälytyskellojen Tulisi Soida Maahanmuuttajanuorten Syrjäytymisriskin Vuoksi," *Kristillisdemokraatit*, November 28, 2015, kd.fi.

70. For a similar observation see Michalinos Zembylas, "Agamben's Theory of Biopower and Immigrants/Refugees/Asylum Seekers: Discourses of Citizenship and the Implications for Curriculum Theorizing," *Journal of Curriculum Theorizing* 26 (2010): 31–45.

71. Trudy Govier, *Victims and Victimhood* (Peterborough: Broadview Press 2015), 11–16, 29–30.

72. Burke, *A Grammar of Motives*, 287–288.

73. Sauli Niinistö, New Year Speech by President of the Republic Sauli Niinistö on January 1, 2016, tpk.fi.

74. Maurizio Lazzarato, "From Capital-Labour to Capital-Life," *Ephemera* 4 (2004): 192–193.

75. See Aristotle, *Rhetoric*, Book I, Chapter 3, 1358b.

76. See Burke, *A Grammar of Motives*, 43, 252–261.

77. Ulrich Beck, *World Risk Society* (Malden. MA: Blackwell, 1999); Robert Danisch, "Political Rhetoric in a World Risk Society," *Rhetoric Society Quarterly* 40 (2010): 172–192.

78. Michel Foucault, *Power: Essential Works of Michel Foucault, 1954–1982* (New York: Free Press, 2000); also, for example, Luis Lobo-Guerrero, "Bio-Politics of Specialized Risk: An Analysis of Kidnap and Ransom Insurance," *Security & Dialogue* 38 (2007): 315–334.

Japan's Prime Minister Abe on the Syrian Refugee Crisis

A DISCOURSE OF SENDING BUT NOT ACCEPTING

——·◆·——

Kaori Miyawaki

The rapid rise of violence by the Islamic State in Iraq and Syria (ISIS), particularly in the mid-2010s, exacerbated the flow of refugees from Syria and its neighbors, creating a global crisis. More than 4.3 million Syrians had left their home country by the end of 2015 and needed humanitarian assistance.[1] While European countries grappled with a flood of Syrian refugees using land and sea routes, the United States and other economically developed countries distant from the conflict were asked to take in refugees and do their part in this crisis. Japan is one such country. This chapter focuses particularly on Japanese prime minister Shinzo Abe's rhetoric responding to the Syrian refugee crisis.

Japan has approximately 127 million people and the third largest GDP in the world.[2] Japan's budget contribution to the United Nations is the second largest after the United States, at 12.53 percent of the total budget in 2010.[3] However, although Japan's donations to aid those suffering has been larger than most of other countries, it has accepted very few refugees. Japan accepted only eleven refugees in 2014.[4] In 2015, 7,586 people filed for refugee status, but the Japanese government recognized only twenty-seven refugees.[5] In contrast, a total of 229,000 persons were granted refugee status in the EU28 in 2015 in the first instance, with 56,000 more given subsidiary protection status, and 22,000 more granted permission to stay for humanitarian reasons.[6] Germany had almost 175,000 applicants, followed by 22,300 in Italy, 18,000 in France, 13,900 in Austria, and 10,100 in the United Kingdom.[7]

Japan is an economically developed country that embraces non-Western culture and traditions. Its cultural differences help to explain its closed-door response to the Syrian refugee crisis, even as it adapts a rhetoric of responsiveness and concern. In this chapter, I first argue that Abe's rhetoric puts a strong emphasis on Japan's contribution to education, public health, and economic support for war refugees while downplaying its low acceptance of refugees. Second, I argue that Abe's rhetoric fails to draw a clear distinction between immigrants and refugees, and uses the logic of economic growth when discussing both immigrants and refugees. Abe rhetorically constructed "immigrants" and "refugees" as economic resources. Obviously, such framing downplays humanitarian concerns. In what follows, I explain the political and cultural background of Japan, review the history of Japanese immigration and refugee policy, and analyze Abe's speeches and comments regarding the Syrian refugee crisis.

Japanese Politics and Culture

The current Japanese political system was established after Japan's defeat in World War II. Japan is now a democratic country and its constitution, in the drafting of which the United States played a huge role, became effective on May 3, 1947. The constitution declares the sovereignty of the people. The constitution defines the emperor as the symbol of Japan and of the unity of the people, but he holds no power in the government. The

Japanese government employs a parliamentary cabinet system. Executive power is vested in the cabinet, and the prime minister is designated by the Diet.

Shinzo Abe has served as the prime minister of Japan since December 2012. Abe is a member of Jiminto (the Liberal Democratic Party), which holds the largest block in both the House of Representatives (the lower house) and the House of Councilors (the upper house). Abe is known as a patriotic leader. His book *Utsukushi Kunie* (*For a Beautiful Nation*), published in 2006, discusses his political vision of creating a "beautiful Japan, which is full of energy, chances, and kindness; respects spirits of autonomy; and opens to the world."[8] His noted visit to the Yasukuni Shrine reflects his patriotic attitude. Yasukuni enshrines and memorializes "souls of men who made ultimate sacrifice for their nation since 1853 during national crisis such as the Boshin War, the Seinan War, the Sino-Japanese and Russo-Japanese wars, World War I, the Manchurian Incident, the China Incident and the Greater East Asian War [World War II]."[9] Abe visited Yasukuni in December 2013 while serving as prime minister. Given that Yasukuni is dedicated to Hideki Tojo and other military leaders of World War II, his visit fueled criticisms from China and South Korea. He has stopped visiting since then.

Except for a few years, Jiminto has been a major party in postwar Japan. In 2009, Minshuto (the Democratic Party of Japan) became the major party. However, Minshuto's cabinet quickly lost popularity after its poor management of the 2011 Tohoku earthquake and tsunami. Its policies on social welfare and the economy also were criticized, leading to a loss in national elections. Jiminto won the election in 2012 and has been the major party since then, with Abe serving as prime minister. Jiminto also won the election in July 2016 and is expected to remain the leading party.

The Japanese government welcomes foreign visitors for tourism, but has few permanent foreign residents. Foreign visitors to Japan reached 19.74 million in 2015.[10] However, Japan is still an ethnically homogeneous country. According to *Statistics Japan*, Japan had approximately 1,724,000 registered foreign residents in 2015, which is only 1.3 percent of the total

Japanese population.[11] *Statistics Japan*'s 2013 data indicate that 58.5 percent
of the foreign residents are from East Asia (Korea, China, and Taiwan).[12]
Japan welcomes foreign tourists, but restricts immigration.

The Japanese word *gaijin* (alien) reflects Japanese society's attitude
toward other cultures. Intercultural communication scholars have noted
that the word *gaijin* reinforces the boundary between us (Japanese) and
them (outsiders).[13] Because of such criticisms, Japanese media carefully
avoid using this word; but Japanese citizens still use it colloquially,
probably without any conscious intent of discriminating against "*gaijin*."
Japanese people, especially elderly people, often call foreigners *gaijin-san*,
which means "Mr. or Ms. Alien." Although Japanese people are generally nice to *gaijin-san*, foreigners are forever outsiders in Japanese society,
regardless of their level of cultural assimilation. Such attitudes persist,
even when foreigners have lived in Japan for a long time and adapt the
Japanese language and culture.[14] Even individuals born and raised in
Japan by parents who are *gaijin* are often regarded as *gaijin* due to their
non-Japanese features.

Such low acceptance of different cultures comes from Japanese history of homogeneity. Japan is an island nation. Due to its geographic
location, traveling to countries beyond China was unrealistic for most
Japanese people until the postwar era. Such limited interactions with
other cultures led Japan to adapt foreign, mainly Chinese, cultural traditions (e.g., Buddhism, Confucianism, Chinese characters, laws, and arts)
and reconstruct them in a distinctly Japanese way.[15] Such isolation was
reinforced during the Edo era (1603–1868) by government restrictions on
international trade. Until US commodore Matthew Perry forced Japan
to open its doors to international trade in 1853, the Japanese government
allowed trading only with China and the Netherlands. The long-lasting
Edo era worked to distinguish Japanese culture from that of the Chinese
mainland. For example, ukiyo-e (in art) and haiku (in poetry) were developed during this era.

Confucianism and Buddhism also influenced Japanese homogeneity
and cultural continuity. Although a majority of current Japanese citizens
do not practice a specific religion, Japanese people's values and mentality

are still based on Confucianism and Buddhism. For example, when they pass away, a majority of Japanese people are buried in the graveyard of a Buddhist temple. Each tombstone is for *ie* (family), not for individuals. Such practices confirm the continuity of their family and culture, and this can reproduce the sense of "us" as those who have Japanese ancestry.

Japanese blood is a determiner of who is Japanese. In current Japanese *kokuseki hou* (citizenship laws), Japanese citizenship is given only when one or both parents are Japanese.[16] Foreigners can obtain Japanese citizenship if they pass the requirements, but they have to give up their citizenship in their home countries.[17] The legal system further confirms Japanese society's attachment to continuity as well as its inflexibility toward people who do not fit into traditional Japanese roles and culture. Such attitudes undoubtedly influenced the Japanese government's decisions about accepting Syrian refugees. In the next section, I briefly review Japanese immigration policy and refugee policy as a backdrop for understanding the immigration rhetoric of Prime Minister Abe.

Japanese Immigration Policy

The Immigration Control Law, originally enacted in 1952, provides the basic framework for immigration policy in postwar Japan. The law was not designed to encourage migrants to settle in Japan; rather, the law served to monitor and control foreigners.[18] In 1989, the Japanese government reformed the Immigration Control Law, which reorganized visa categories to accept more professional and skilled personnel while excluding unskilled foreign laborers.[19] Acceptance was limited to skilled laborers who could support Japanese economic growth.

The Japanese government also has discussed accepting more immigrants as a way to tackle its rapidly aging population and low birthrate. In February 2014, the Cabinet Office announced that "Japan will likely only be able to maintain a population of more than 100 million if it accepts 200,000 immigrants annually from 2015" while bringing fertility rates back to 2.07 by 2030.[20] In 2014, the Cabinet Office announced that

Japan would accept more immigrants in the future. Working through a group sponsored by Prime Minister Abe, Sentaku suru Mirai Iinkai (Committee for Future Selection), Kazumasa Iwata, the head of the Japan Center for Economic Research, proposed that Japan should increase its acceptance of migrants gradually and accept two hundred thousand foreign migrants annually after 2050.[21] This plan would increase Japan's foreign residents from current 1.8 percent to 6 percent in 2015, and 13 percent in 2100.[22]

Although the Cabinet Office seeks ways to accept more immigrants, it does not intend to increase the number of permanent foreign residents. Prime Minister Abe insisted that Japan should give more foreigners three- to five-year visas rather than let a massive number of immigrants permanently settle in Japan.[23] Abe noted: "What are immigrants? The U.S. is a country of immigrants who came from all around the world and formed the [United States]. Many people have come to the country and become part of it. We won't adopt a policy like that."[24]

According to Abe, his proposal is "not an immigration policy" but allows temporary migrants to work in Japan and "raise incomes for a limited period of time and then return home."[25] In Abe's rhetoric of immigration, immigrants are appreciated only for sustaining the Japanese economy, not for multiculturalism or globalization. Immigrants Abe intends to accept are temporary workers, and his rhetoric seems to reduce migrant workers to a labor force, rather than individual human beings with different and valuable cultural backgrounds.

Despite the government's proposal for increasing temporary migrants, Japanese citizens do not seem interested in accepting more foreign-born migrants. For example, a national poll conducted by the *Yomiuri Shimbun* in 2015 shows that 39 percent agree or somewhat agree with accepting immigrants to maintain the Japanese population, while 61 percent disagree or somewhat disagree.[26] In the same poll, 33 percent indicate that Japan should accept more foreign labors, while 64 percent answered no.

Furthermore, there are media reports of antiforeigner sentiment, especially against Koreans. For example, the *Japan Times* reported a group of ten to fifty people planned to march on public roads in Kanagawa prefecture in a rally aimed at "purifying Japan,"[27] although the district court ruled their actions were ethnic discrimination or hate speech. The closed nature of Japanese culture may temper Abe's rhetoric of immigration and refugees, even for economic purposes. Letting foreign-born individuals become citizens would be an unpopular political decision in Japan.

Japanese Refugee Policy

Most of the current foreign residents in Japan are permanent and temporary immigrants, not refugees. Postwar Japan's refugee policy began in 1975, when the Vietnam War ended. Japan accepted more than eleven thousand refugees from Vietnam, Laos, and Cambodia who escaped from their countries by boat.[28] Japan signed the United Nations Refugee Convention in 1981 and started to accept asylum applications.[29] However, although the door was open, it was barely cracked. In 1983, Japan established its own criteria that asked refugees to prove they were being persecuted.[30] Given that the criteria are difficult to meet for most refugees, who are not trained to make such arguments, the Japanese government has approved very few refugee visas. In 2014, approximately 5,000 people applied for refugee visas in Japan, a 53 percent increase from the previous year, and only eleven were approved.[31] The Justice Ministry of Japan reported 429 Syrians were staying in Japan as of June 2015.[32] However, while 63 Syrians requested refugee status, Japan has accepted only 3 of them by the start of 2016.[33] Without refugee status, they are not eligible for Japanese language lessons, job training, and other various programs that help their settlement.[34] It is also difficult to invite family members to Japan without refugee status.[35] The Japan Association for Refugees notes that the Japanese government deals with refugees as targets of "control" rather than as victims "being rescued," complaining that the policy deviates from global standards.[36] António Guterres, the UN High Commissioner for Refugees, also claimed that Japan's asylum system is rigid and restrictive.[37]

Although Japan's low approval rate of asylum applicants has been criticized, the majority of Japanese citizens support the policy. The majority of Japanese citizens are not open to accepting refugees. A national poll conducted in December 2015 by the *Mainichi Shimbun* indicated that 37 percent said Japan should accept more refugees, while 44 percent said Japan should not.[38] *Asahi Shimbun*, another major newspaper in Japan, conducted a survey in January 2016 and found that 24 percent said Japan should accept refugees proactively while 58 percent answered they do not think so.[39] The results are similar to the survey on refugee and immigrants conducted back in 1996 by *Asahi*. In 1996, only 22 percent answered Japan should accept more refugees and migrant workers, while 65 percent answered Japan should keep the present rate.[40]

Global criticism of Japan's refugee policy was a rhetorical challenge for Abe when he spoke to the global community about the Syrian refugee crisis, given the need to respond to the crisis while also managing the antirefugee sentiment of Japanese citizens. Accepting more refugees is an unpopular policy in Japan, and he could lose his popularity if he promises the global community to do so. The next section discusses how Abe resolved or failed to resolve those rhetorical challenges and considers the implications of his rhetoric.

Abe's Rhetoric on the Syrian Refugee Crisis

Abe has delivered speeches annually to United Nation General Assembly as prime minister of Japan since 2013. This section analyzes speeches delivered in 2013, 2014, and 2015 as Abe's rhetoric addressed both the global community and his own citizens. Japan was elected to one of the five nonpermanent seats on the UN Security Council on October 15, 2015, and it was Japan's eleventh time serving.[41] Japan has been appealing to the global community to be given a permanent seat on the Security Council. Therefore, speeches delivered by the prime minister to the UN General Assembly, where all members are present, are significant opportunities for Japan to demonstrate its global leadership to other nations. But with Abe's hands tied by domestic politics on the refugee crisis, it was hard for him to show leadership in this crisis. Generally, Abe's rhetoric avoided mentioning Japan's low acceptance of refugees, waffled on his definition of refugees and immigration, and situated the Syrian refugee crisis in the frame of Japanese domestic economy, not global humanitarian issues. In short, he played to his domestic audience while trying to put the best face on Japan's policy for the international audience.

Amid the rise in violence in Syria, Abe delivered a speech at the Sixty-Eighth Session of the UN General Assembly on September 26, 2013. At the beginning of his speech, he touched on the situation in Syria, where the use of chemical weapons had led to international condemnation. He acknowledged that the number of refugees was drastically increasing and declared that "Japan will provide thorough support and the greatest possible cooperation towards the international community's efforts to dispose of Syria's chemical weapons."[42] Although he mentioned that "the number of refugees is soaring" and called it an issue of "urgency,"[43] his speech did not include any possibility of Japan accepting Syrian refugees. Silence has rhetorical power to direct people's perception. Like the zero in mathematics, silence is an absence with a function, and a rhetorical one at that.[44] Abe could have explained why Japan would be able to (or not be able to) accept Syrian refugees to the global community. However, he chose not to mention it at all. Potential meanings for silence include the person lacks sufficient information to talk on the topic, the person feels no sense of urgency about talking, or the person is avoiding discussion of a controversial or sensitive issue out of fear.[45] Abe's speech seemed to avoid discussing Japan's acceptance of refugees due to global criticism. Abe could please the global audience if he promised Japan would accept more refugees; but such a policy would hurt his popularity in Japan. Abe also could clarify why Japan would not accept more Syrian refugees, but this rhetoric could make Japan look irresponsible to the global community.

Instead of promising to accept Syrian refugees, Abe emphasized Japan's contribution of human and monetary resources. Abe noted: "In order to extend help to refugees, Japan's Non-Government Organizations and volunteer organizations are working across national borders."[46] He also mentioned his government is working to "undertake the training of staff working at medical centers" and to "deliver portable X-ray devices and other medical equipment to those areas."[47] However, he did not explain how such an increase of resources would help with the displacement of Syrian refugees.

At the end of his speech about the Syrian situation, Abe noted Japan's additional monetary contributions. He declared: "I would like to announce that the Government of Japan will newly provide additional humanitarian assistance to Syria and surrounding countries of approximately 60 million US dollars and implement it right away."[48]

Unlike his rhetoric on Japan's acceptance of refugees, this announcement was very specific, offering a concrete amount of monetary aid the Japanese government would offer. This tells the global audience that Japan's contribution to the Syrian situation was money, not accepting refugees. Such emphasis on Japan's economic power was found elsewhere in this speech as well. Abe situated Japan's economic growth as his primary agenda: "My obligation first of all is to rebuild the Japanese economy to be vibrant, and then to make Japan a dependable 'force' that works for good in the world."[49] He added that "the Government of Japan will implement ODA [official development assistance] in excess of 3 billion US dollars over the next three years."[50] In this speech, Abe described Japan's primary role for the refugee crisis as monetary support, and any possibility that Japan would accept Syrian refugees was avoided.

A year later, the number of refugees from Syria was still increasing. Abe made an address at the Sixty-Ninth Session of the General Assembly on September 25, 2014. Although the Syrian situation was urgent, Abe used most of his speech to justify why Japan should have a permanent seat on the Security Council, discussing Japan's efforts regarding increasing gender equality, official development assistance, and UN peacekeeping operations. Responding to global criticism on gender equality, his speech discussed how Japan was encouraging women to participate in the workplace and insisted that Japan could become a global leader for gender equality. His choice of topics in this speech suggests that the Japanese government did not see acceptance of Syrian refugees as a critical issue to gain global support for its permanent seat. Abe did not mention Syria in this speech at all.

Abe briefly noted that "the Middle East is in a state of unrest" and that Japan regarded the activities of ISIS as "a serious threat to international order."[51] Abe's rhetoric in this year still avoided referring to any Japanese acceptance of Syrian refugees and again put an emphasis on Japan's monetary contributions. He declared that "Japan will implement 50 million dollars of emergency assistance right away" to support the region.[52] Abe's rhetoric implicitly leaves the problem of providing Syrians a refuge to other countries.

On September 29, 2015, Abe delivered a speech at the Seventieth Session of the General Assembly. In this speech, Abe mentioned the refugee crisis as a challenge to the UN. Noting the importance of the issue again, he reiterated Japan's human resources and monetary contributions, again avoiding any mention of accepting refugees. For example, at the beginning of the speech, Abe declared that Japan would support Syria and Iraq with US$810 million, triple what Japan provided the previous year.[53] Instead of accepting refugees, Abe emphasized how Japan would help other countries that were harboring refugees, noting that Japan would give US$2 million to Lebanon and US$2.5 million for countries close to the EU, such as the Republic of Serbia and the former Yugoslav Republic of Macedonia.[54] He acknowledged that this money was for "countries neighboring the EU that are grappling with the acceptance of refugees and migrants."[55] Thus, Japan would continue to hold refugees at arm's length, though it would fund those countries that embraced refugees.

Almost as if he were blending the refugee crisis with his previous year's speech on gender equality, Abe emphasized Japan's role in the refugee crisis as providing resources overseas, particularly to women. He introduced a story of a female refugee at a Palestinian refugee camp in the south of Damascus. The woman was carrying the *Maternal and Child Health Handbook*, which Japan distributed at a refugee camp in Syria.[56]

Through such stories, Abe particularized the aid, which his earlier cita-
tion of abstract dollar figures had not. He was not so particular about
explaining why Japan would not accept refugees itself. Even as the
numbers of refugees accepted by the EU, and Germany in particular,
mounted, Abe remained silent about his own country's reluctance to
open its doors.

The three speeches present Japan as concerned about the crisis, as
generous, as supportive of other countries that harbored Syrian refugees,
but, ultimately, as silent on its own failure to accept even a trickle of
refugees. Others noticed the absence of any mention of a refugee policy.
After the 2015 speech, a journalist asked Abe if Japan would accept Syrian refugees. Abe was finally trapped and could not simply use silence as
an answer. He first explained his new economic policy and responded to
the question by framing the crisis as global:

> This refugee issue is a problem that the global society must work on
> together. In speaking of the [Japanese] population problem, Japan
> has many contributions to make before accepting immigrants: we need
> to support working women, working elderly citizens, and raise [our]
> birth rate. Japan is going to fulfill its responsibility on the refugee issue.
> Japan wants to make contributions to changing the soil that creates
> refugees.[57]

Abe seemed to talk about Japanese immigration policy as a response to
the question about refugee policy, and this is problematic. His answer
was in Japanese, and the statement as quoted was offered in a translation
that did not capture important distinctions. Abe clarified that he was
responding to the issue of *nanmin* (refugees) at the beginning. He framed
the refugee issue as a global issue. However, when he moved to discuss
the Japanese stance toward the issue, he used the term *imin* (immigrants)
and argued Japan has many things to do before accepting immigrants.
He strategically switched from the term *refugee* here. In this answer, distinctions between the two different concepts (refugee and immigrant)
were not explained, and this made it difficult for audiences to follow

his argument. Definitions are "rhetorically induced," directing and deflecting people's understanding of the world.[58] Abe could have provided his definition of *nanmin* (refugees) and *imin* (immigrants) if he needed to reference the two different concepts. Although the use of such definitions could raise the possibility of several distinct definitions,[59] having no shared definition obviously could lead to confusion, misunderstanding, or frustration on the part of an audience. Thus, Abe's answer was interpreted as Japan's reluctance to accept refugees (and immigrants) and criticized globally.

Although Abe did not define the two concepts in his answer, it is possible to grasp them by examining the rhetoric of his government. Immigrants are defined by the government as skilled but temporary labor workers in the context of aging society. Due to the decline of birth rates, the Japanese government is concerned about how Japan will be able to sustain its economy and social welfare systems. Abe's cabinet proposed to accept more temporary, skilled immigrants to boost the Japanese economy.[60] Although immigrants could bring benefits other than economic growth (e.g., resources for cultural enrichment), such goals are not noted in policies by Abe's cabinet.

Refugees, on the other hand, are not discussed in the context of Japan's economic development. While the Japanese government did not put negative labels on refugees, such as calling them "security risks," this does not mean Japan sees refugees positively. While refugees could stay, work, and pay taxes in Japan, the Japanese government does not encourage such possibilities. As the history of Japanese immigration policy and Abe's answer at the press conference suggest, Japan would not accept unskilled immigrants. Refusing to accept more refugees is justified by the Japanese government's assumption that refugees are unskilled and permanent immigrants, which Japan would not welcome. As national surveys reveal,[61] the Japanese do not welcome immigrants or refugees because they wish to remain ethnically homogeneous.

Abe's rhetoric got a mixed reception in Japanese society. His attitude not to accept refugees pleased many users of the Nichannel (Channel 2), the best-known anonymous web-based board.[62] However,

Katsuya Okada, then the leader of the opposition party Minshinto (formerly Minshuto) criticized Abe's comment at the UN. "His comment at the UN was probably very confusing for foreigners, but it tells us his attitude toward this [refugee] problem. . . . He regards refugees as a workforce. This comment can nullify Japan's monetary contribution."[63] Shogo Watanabe, who represents the Japan Lawyers Network for Refugees, also argued: "What is needed here is the willingness to take in Syrian asylum seekers across the board. That may require lots of willpower and commitment, but that's how other countries are coping with the situation."[64] Sadako Ogata, who served as United Nations High Commissioner for Refugees from 1991 to 2001, also criticized Abe's statement and Japan's refugee policy. In an interview by *Asahi*, she stated that Japan's acceptance of a handful of refugees was "not enough at all" and pointed out that the Japanese government failed to discuss what sacrifices Japan could or could not make for international peace.[65] Ogata insisted that Japanese society was still in the process of forming its opinion about the refugee crisis. She acknowledged that Japan's "island mentality" had not completely changed, while insisting the Syrian refugee crisis provided Japanese society an opportunity to discuss the issue of accepting refugees.[66]

Abe's rhetoric and policies between 2013 and 2015 explicitly described Japan's role as a country that donates money and resources, while implicitly acknowledging that it does not accept refugees. More recently, there was a tiny change in this position. On May 20, 2016, Abe announced that Japan would accept 150 Syrians as exchange students, not as refugees, over five years.[67] This new policy was announced before the Group of Seven leaders gathered for a summit in Mie prefecture, Japan. This could have served as a response to global criticism of Japan's low acceptance of refugees, before Abe saw the G7 leaders.[68] However, although Abe decided to accept more people from Syria (the number is miniscule compared to those accepted by Germany, Turkey, and other European countries), he avoided labeling them refugees. This suggests that Japan still is not ready to accept refugees. The frame Abe used in this exchange program is similar to the one for immigrants in the context of aging society and economic growth. Japan accepts temporary immigrants from Syria, but the door is open exclusively for people who can contribute to future economic growth and education.

This student exchange program explains the reason behind Abe's lack of definitions in the press conference. Practical benefits, such as economic growth, are always central in Japanese immigration policies. Providing a safe space for refugees is not a strong reason for Japan to open its doors, regardless of the refugees' devastating conditions; only people who can bring practical benefits are allowed to enter and stay. When Abe's argument was based on this logic, he could use the term *immigrants* and *refugees* interchangeably because both immigrants and refugees are temporary foreign visitors who are supposed to bring economic benefits in the future.

Although the student exchange program clarified Abe's stance toward refugees—accepting only those who will bring benefits to Japan—Abe used this program to suggest to the international community that Japan is making a considerable contribution to the Syrian refugee crisis, though money again was the primary contribution. On September 20, 2016, Abe made a statement at the Leader's Summit on Refugees United Nations Trusteeship Council Chamber, led by US president Barack Obama, in New York. At this summit focusing on refugee issues, Abe proposed three actions Japan would take: providing monetary support, offering resource development, and accepting up to 150 refugees. Unlike previous speeches at the UN, Abe promised the international community that Japan would accept refugees.

The first action Abe proposed was providing US$2.8 billion to refugee-hosting countries between 2016 and 2018 and US$100 million to the World Bank's Global Crisis Response Platform, which launched on the day of the summit.[69] Although the amount of money Abe proposed was higher than the previous year's US$810 million, the strategy Abe took was the same: presenting Japan as a country that provides monetary support.

The second proposed action also sounded similar to ones in last year's UN speech. Abe stated that Japan would provide resources and support Syrian refugee children,[70] continuing the same approach to monetary support to Syria and other countries.

The third action was somewhat new in Abe's rhetoric delivered to international audiences. Abe declared that "Japan will accept refugees."[71] That general statement was quickly qualified in that this is simply the student exchange program he proposed in May 2016. In the statement, Abe noted that Japan will accept up to 150 Syrian students in the coming five years and if those students wish to bring their families, Japan will welcome them within Japan's institutional framework.[72] Up to 150 students in five years is not a huge contribution when the world is discussing a mass exodus of refugees, and the selective nature of the exchange student program is problematic; but Abe's declaration of Japan accepting refugees represented progress and a new effort to tackle the crisis. It shows Abe's sensitivity to international criticism. By accepting a very small number of selected student refugees, Abe could show his flexibility in responding to the crisis. The small number of refugees Japan will accept also allowed Abe to keep his domestic audience happy. Although Japan's stance toward refugee acceptance has changed only slightly, Abe touted this tiny refugee program for its benefits to Japan as well.

Conclusion

Japan's contributions to the UN have led it to be chosen as a nonpermanent member at the Security Council eleven times. However, on the issue of Syrian refugee crisis, Prime Minister Abe has limited Japan's role. Abe introduced Japan as a nation contributing to world peace with its funds and resources, as well as a modest acceptance of student refugees. Although the Japanese government has attempted to increase temporary immigrants for Japan's economic growth, the door for refugees is practically closed; and this fact was silenced in Abe's rhetoric. My analysis of Abe's rhetoric and Japanese immigration policies reveals that Abe maintained the logic of economic growth when discussing immigrants;

only immigrants who will bring benefits are allowed to stay. Japan will accept Syrians as "international students" but not as "refugees," because in the logic of economic growth, refugees do not bring benefits to Japan and are not worth accepting.

Increasing acceptance of either immigrants or refugees is unpopular among the Japanese public and undoubtedly influenced Abe's rhetorical and political choices. In the democratic political system of Japan, remaining popular to the public is crucial for all politicians to stay in office. Abe's answer at the press conference has been criticized by global media, but his comments would be appealing to conservative Japanese citizens who are welcoming to foreign visitors but not to permanent residents from foreign countries, whether immigrants and refugees. The devastating conditions ISIS has created are reported every day, but Abe's rhetorical and political choices put its threatening fire on the opposite shore for Japanese citizens.

Unlike many other leaders faced with the pressure to address the Syrian immigration crisis, Prime Minister Abe did little to construct the immigrants themselves, with the exception of the maternal health book provided to a refugee—which hardly addresses a devastating need. Dwelling on the victims of the Syrian Civil War might have put more pressure on him to address what he would do about such desperate people, particularly providing them with a safe refuge.

Likewise, his descriptions of the crisis are spare, though they support a humanitarian construction of the troubled situation. And the increasingly generous monetary contributions he offers from Japan imply that he believes this is a crisis requiring significant help.

While the verbal context of his speeches downplays the suffering he might otherwise be pressed to address, the larger international context could not but make his failure to offer refugees safe haven appear as an intentional omission. Thus, the *unsaid* here can serve as the *loudly said*. Unlike, say, President Donald Trump, who implies that he might take in refugees if they did not represent a security risk,[73] Prime Minister Abe refuses to say or give reasons for not offering asylum. For Westerners, this may fit stereotypes of Oriental inscrutability; for Easterners, it may embody a fitting rhetorical practice that emphasizes harmony by leaving aside those things that might increase tensions.[74]

Finally, the generous monetary support Abe touts as Japan's contribution may serve, economically and rhetorically, as compensatory to Japan's failure to take in refugees. While it risks creating a distinction between wealthy countries that would rather not get their hands dirty taking in refugees and poorer countries that could provide that service, it does appear to use significant generosity to offset this failure.

Notes

1. Sayuri Daimon, "Helping Refugees Requires More Than Financial Help," *Japan Times*, January 1, 2016.

2. "July 2016 Report," *Statistics Japan*, July 2016, stat.go.jp; "GDP Nominal Ranking 2016," *Statistics Times*, April 14, 2016, statisticstimes.com.

3. Marjorie Ann Browne and Luisa Blanchfield, "United Nations Regular Budget Contributions: Members Compared, 1990–2010," Congressional Research Service, January 15, 2013, fas.org.

4. Shunshuke Murai, "Japan Recognizes Only 27 Refugees, Despite Rising Numbers of Applications," *Japan Times*, January 23, 2016.

5. Murai.

6. "Asylum Statistics," *Eurostat*, April 20, 2016, ec.europa.eu.

7. "Asylum Statistics."

8. Shinzo Abe, *Utsukushi Kunihe* [For a Beautiful Nation] (Tokyo: Bungei Shunjyu, 2006).

9. "About Yasukuni Shrine," *Yasukuni Shrine*, yasukuni.or.jp.

10. "Japan Tourism Hits New Record; Government to Let Hotels Expand Floor Space," *Japan Times*, June 15, 2016.

11. "Jinkou Suikei (July 2015, Kakuteichi) [Total population in July 2015, finalized]," *Statistics Japan*, July 2015, stat.go.jp.

12. "Kokusekibetsu Seiki Nyukoku Gaikokujin Su [The foreign resident population by home countries]," *Statistics Japan*, 2013, stat.go.jp.

13. Masamichi Okazaki, "Ryugakusei kyoiku no haikei ni aru nihonbunka

no tokusei to nihonsyakai no heisasei [Characteristics of Japanese Culture and Closeness of Japanese Society behind Education for International Students]," *Arts Liberalities* 51 (1992): 14.

14. Okazaki, 14.

15. Okazaki, 15.

16. [Japanese] Ministry of Justice, "Kokuseki hou [Citizenship laws]," 1950, moj.go.jp.

17. [Japanese] Ministry of Justice.

18. Chikako Kashiwazaki and Tsuneo Akaha, "Japanese Immigration Policy: Responding to Conflicting Pressures," *Migration Policy Institute*, November 1, 2006, migrationpolicy.org.

19. Kashiwazaki and Akaha.

20. Murai.

21. "Imin de Nihon no Jinko Ichiokunin wo Ijidekiruka Seifu no Giron ga Honkakuka [Can Immigration Keep the Japanese Population of One Hundred Million? The Government's Discussions Are Developing]," *Huffington Post* (Japan), February 25, 2014, huffingtonpost.jp.

22. "Imin de Nihon no Jinko Ichiokunin wo Ijidekiruka Seifu no Giron ga Honkakuka."

23. Reiji Yoshida, "Success of 'Abenomics' Hinges on Immigration Policy," *Japan Times*, May 18, 2014.

24. Yoshida.

25. Yoshida.

26. "2015 7–8 Gatsu Yuusou Zenkoku Seron Chosa [National poll by snail mail, June–August, 2015]," *Yomiuri Shimbun*, http://www.yomiuri.co.jp/feature/opinion/koumoku/20150826-OYT8T50064.html?from=yartcl_popin.

27. "Anti-Korean Group Calls Off Hate-Speech Rally in Kawasaki amid Protests," *Japan Times*, June 5, 2016.

28. Akiko Horiyama, "Syria Nanmin Mondai Kanedake Shien Nyukoku ha NO Sakoku Hippon ni Kibishii Mesen [Syrian Refugee Crisis, Support only through Money and No to Entry, Criticisms toward Closed Japan]." *Mainichi Shimbun*, October 6, 2015, http://mainichi.jp/articles/20151006/dde/012/010/007000c.

29. "No Entry: As the World's Refugee Problem Grows, Japan Pulls Up the Drawbridge," *The Economist*, March 14, 2015, http://www.economist.com/news/asia/21646255-worlds-refugee-problem-grows-japan-pulls-up-drawbridge-no-entry.

30. Horiyama.

31. Daimon.

32. Daimon.

33. Daimon.

34. Daimon.

35. Daimon.

36. "No Entry."

37. "No Entry."

38. "Mainichi Shimbun Seron Chosa [A national survey by *Mainichi*]," *Mainichi Shimbun*, December 7, 2015, http://mainichi.jp/articles/20151207/ddm/002/010/140000c.

39. "Data wo Yomu Seron Chosa kara: Nanmin no Ukeire Kawaranai Syokyoku Shisei [From data in national survey: Unchanged passive attitude toward refugee acceptance]," *Asahi Shimbun*, January 30, 2016, http://digital.asahi.com/articles/DA3S12184937.html?rm=150.

40. "Data wo Yomu Seron Chosa kara."

41. "Japan Elected for Record 11th Time to U.N. Security Council Nonpermanent Seat," *Japan Times*, October 16, 2015.

42. "Address by Prime Minister Shinzo Abe, at the Sixty-Eighth Session of the General Assembly of the United Nations," September 26, 2013, *Prime Minister of Japan and His Cabinet*, http://japan.kantei.go.jp/96_abe/statement/201309/26generaldebate_e.html.

43. "Address by Prime Minister Shinzo Abe."

44. Cheryl Glenn, *Unspoken: A Rhetoric of Silence* (Carbondale: Southern Illinois University Press, 2004), 4.

45. Richard L. Johannesen, "The Function of Silence: A Plea for Communication Research," *Western Speech* 38 (1974): 25–45.

46. "Address by Prime Minister Shinzo Abe."

47. "Address by Prime Minister Shinzo Abe."

48. "Address by Prime Minister Shinzo Abe."

49. "Address by Prime Minister Shinzo Abe."

50. "Address by Prime Minister Shinzo Abe."

51. "Address by H.E. Mr. Shinzo Abe, Prime Minister of Japan at the Sixty-Ninth Session of the General Assembly of the United Nations," Ministry of Foreign Affairs, September 25, 2014, http://www.mofa.go.jp/fp/unp_a/page24e_000057.html.

52. "Address by H.E. Mr. Shinzo Abe."

53. "Address by Prime Minister Shinzo Abe at the Seventieth Session of the General Assembly of the United Nations," Ministry of Foreign Affairs, September 30, 2015, http://www.mofa.go.jp/fp/unp_a/page4e_000321.html.

54. "Address by Prime Minister Shinzo Abe at the Seventieth Session."

55. "Address by Prime Minister Shinzo Abe at the Seventieth Session."

56. "Address by Prime Minister Shinzo Abe at the Seventieth Session."

57. Yoshino Taichiro, "Abe Syusho Nanmin Ukeire Toha? To Toware Jyosei no Katsuyaku Koureisya no Katsuyaku ga Saki [Prime Minister Abe answered 'women's and elderly's participation should come first' as a response to the question on refugee acceptance]," *Huffington Post* (Japan), September 30, 2015, http://www.huffingtonpost.jp/2015/09/30/abe-refugee_n_8219324.html.

58. Edward Schiappa, *Defining Reality: Definitions and the Politics of Meaning* (Carbondale: Southern Illinois University Press, 2003).

59. Chaim Perelman and Lucie Olbrechts-Tyteca, *The New Rhetoric: A Treatise on Argumentation*, trans. J. Wilkinson and P. Weaver (Notre Dame, IN: University of Notre Dame Press, 1969), 214.

60. Murai; Yoshida.

61. "2015 7–8 Gatsu"; *Mainichi Shimbun*; *Asahi Shimbun*.

62. "Asahi Shinbun 'Syria Nanmin wo Kokuren ga Ukeirero ttute Itsuteru yo' [The UN says Japan should accept Syrian refugees]," *Mera Red*, September 6, 2015, http://mera.red.

63. Katsuya Okada, "Teirei Kisya Kaiken [Press conference]," October 9, 2015, http://www.katsuya.net/topics/article-5627.html.

64. Osaki Tomohiro, "Several Groups Urge Abe to Pledge to Accept Syrian Refugees," *Japan Times*, September 29, 2015.

65. Takashi Ohsima and Yuri Imamura, "Sadako Ogata: Accepting Refugee Is a Part of Active Pacifism," *Asahi Shimbun*, September 24, 2015, http:// digital.asahi.com/articles/ASH9P2VWLH9PUHBI00H.html?_ requesturl=articles/ASH9P2VWLH9PUHBI00H.html.

66. Ohsima and Imamura.

67. Ayako Mie, "Japan to Take in 150 Syrians as Exchange Students after Criticism of Harsh Refugee Policy," *Japan Times*, May 20, 2016.

68. Ayako Mie, "Leaders Expected to Focus on Economy, Refugee Crisis," *Japan Times*, May 25, 2016.

69. "Statement by His Excellency, Mr. Shinzo Abe Prime Minister of Japan at the United Nations Summit for Refugees and Migrants United Nations Trusteeship Council Chamber in New York Monday, 20 September 2016," http://www.mofa.go.jp.

70. "Statement by His Excellency."

71. "Statement by His Excellency."

72. "Statement by His Excellency."

73. See the chapter on the United States in this volume.

74. See, for example, Roichi Okabe, "The Concept of Rhetorical Competence and Sensitivity Revisited: From Western and Eastern Perspectives," *China Media Research* 3, no. 4 (2007): 74–81.

The United States' Immigration Rhetoric amid the Syrian Refugee Crisis

PRESIDENTS, PRECEDENTS, AND PORTENTS

————•◆•————

Ellen Gorsevski, Clarke Rountree, and Andrée E. Reeves

It's a big problem! We don't know anything about them. We don't know where they come from, who they are. There's no documentation. We have our incompetent government people letting 'em in by the thousands, and who knows, who knows, maybe it's ISIS.

—Donald Trump, April 25, 2016

There are no easy answers to Syria. . . . But so many families need help right now; they don't have time. And that's why the United States is increasing the number of refugees who we welcome within our borders. That's why we will continue to be the largest donor of assistance to support those refugees. And today we are launching new efforts . . . because in the faces of suffering families, our nation of immigrants sees ourselves.

—President Barack Obama, September 28, 2015

T he United States is a nation of paradoxes when it comes to immigration. Over time, Americans have both welcomed and shunned immigrants, touting and warning of the economic, social, and security consequences of opening the door to the "huddled masses" who come to the United States seeking refuge from wars and other disasters, or simply for a better life. The 2016 election of Donald Trump in the midst of the worst refugee crisis since World War II represents a turn toward a less welcoming, more hostile rhetoric of immigration.[1]

Trump won the 2016 US presidential race as the most recent voice in the country's intermittent anti-immigrant history. However, his scapegoating strategically built upon four significant developments that made his anti-immigrant message particularly potent. The first development is the massive illegal immigration from Latin America (particularly Mexico) over the past thirty years that has resulted in almost eleven million undocumented people now residing in the United States (3–4 percent of the population).

The second development, roughly coinciding with the first, is the economic decline of the middle class, primarily because of automation, globalization, US tax policy, the weakening of unions, and exploding health care costs.[2] Trump prominently pushed another cause, linking the influx of illegal immigrants to middle-class decline. For example, in July 2015 the presidential candidate claimed of illegal immigrants: "They're taking our jobs. They're taking our manufacturing jobs. They're taking our money. They're killing us."[3]

Trump's closing economic metaphor, "They're killing us," was used more literally with respect to other outsiders, in a third development involving the security of the United States. Since the attacks of September 11, 2001, and although many more Americans die at the hands of fellow US citizens,[4] Americans have been fearful of terrorist attacks, particularly from Islamic groups such as al-Qaeda and ISIS (Islamic State in Iraq and Syria). Despite attempts by President George W. Bush and President Obama to assure Americans that, unlike members of these militant groups, mainstream Muslims are peaceful, it has proven easy for fearmongers to raise suspicions of all Muslims. Candidate and later president Trump, for example, connected Islam to terrorism by repeatedly using the term "radical Islamic terrorism," insisting that "political correctness" had kept the two former presidents from so linking Islam with terrorism.[5]

Trump's strategy of blaming "Others" for economic and security problems plaguing the United States was supported by many in his conservative coalition worried about a fourth significant development: the "browning" of America in light of the growth of minority populations over the past several decades. While population growth has slowed among whites, minority groups have made large gains. In 2016, nonwhites were the majority among United States kindergartners, by 2020 they are expected to be a majority of all children, and by 2044 no one racial group will be the majority.[6] The Trump administration has pursued proposals that will slow this trend, such as eliminating the "diversity lottery," which more equitably opens the doors to immigrants from non-European countries.[7]

At least since Richard Nixon's "Southern Strategy," Republicans have made appeals based upon "dog whistle" statements that implicate race, successfully pulling voters in southern states to their party through their resistance to the civil rights agenda that President Johnson initiated with the Civil Rights Act of 1964.[8] GOP dog whistles turned into unsubtle jabs at minorities by Trump as candidate and president, such as when Candidate Trump accused Gonzalo Curiel, a US-born federal judge of Mexican heritage, of being biased against him in a case over Trump University because "He's a Mexican"—a comment that even GOP Speaker of the House Paul Ryan called "the textbook definition of a racist comment."[9]

Postelection analyses have shown that racial bias was a key motivating factor for many Trump voters. Thomas Wood's examination of the 2016 American National Election Study compares 2016 to previous election years and concludes:

> Since 1988, we've never seen such a clear correspondence between vote choice and racial perceptions. The biggest movement was among those

who voted for the Democrat, who were far less likely [than Trump voters] to agree with attitudes coded as more racially biased.[10]

The racial bias of many in Trump's base made them particularly susceptible to appeals that scapegoated nonwhite others for economic, security, and cultural threats. Or, from another perspective, Trump was able to *build* his coalition by turning white angst into fear of nonwhite others and anger at the ways in which they purportedly undermined American greatness. The wide black brush with which Trump painted brought minority American citizens, including Curiel, Black Lives Matter protestors, black sports figures, and others into his scapegoated "Other" category. And notably for the purposes of this chapter, it drew Syrian refugees into this scapegoating strategy, making them emblematic of the threat coming from the Middle East.

This chapter analyzes the discourse of government and political leaders concerning the Syrian immigration crisis, especially that of Donald Trump as a candidate and now as president. We focus on Trump particularly given his prominence in the immigration debate since his candidacy, the frequency and vehemence with which he has addressed immigration issues, and the unique way he has wedded economic, security, and cultural concerns to build fear and hatred for "outsiders" for political purposes. Specifically, he used the scapegoating of those he viewed as "outsiders" to build and secure a political coalition to elect him and support him through the turmoil that has followed his assumption of the presidency.[11] In line with earlier chapters, this chapter provides the political and historical context for recent immigration rhetoric, including a description of the basic structure of the US government,[12] which determines immigration policy, the history of immigration in the United States, and recent discourse by Trump and other leaders and political figures, notably candidates in the 2016 presidential race, which coincided with the height of the Syrian immigration crisis.

The United States' Political System and Immigration History

The United States is a constitutional democracy comprising fifty states and sixteen territories, including American Samoa, Guam, Puerto Rico, and the United States Virgin Islands. The federal government has three branches of government: legislative (the House of Representatives and the Senate), executive (the president and dozens of executive agencies), and judicial (the Supreme Court and other federal courts). This government of tripartite authority and checks and balances is responsible for developing, writing, passing, implementing, defending, and interpreting laws affecting immigration. Governance and policy are complicated by the fact that the United States has a federal system that distributes powers to both the national government and the state governments. Thus, for example, although the federal government oversees immigration, some states have made forays into immigration policy by enacting laws affecting migrants. Regional interests and state and local politics complicate the context and application of immigration discourses and laws.

The US president is elected through a process "that is both democratic and federal," through a "complex" staging system of votes from the Electoral College.[13] While presidential elections occur every four years, members of the House of Representatives face election every two years, and senators every six years—with one-third of Senate seats up for election every two years to ensure constant representation of the states. Because House members are elected so frequently, elections and electioneering are never far from public life. Presidents have a maximum of two terms or ten years (if serving part of another president's term). Once elected, members of Congress have no term limits, and federal judges are appointed for life.

The United States has been significantly defined by the history of immigration. Early American colonists included refugees from religious persecution as well as colonists seeking economic opportunities in the American wilderness.[14] Continual immigration of new working bodies was a political and economic necessity for labor-intensive production of crops like tobacco and cotton in the southern states.[15] By the late eighteenth and into the nineteenth centuries, a class-based system of indentured servitude gave way to a rigidly race-based, highly profitable system of slavery.[16]

Apart from the regulation of the importation of slaves (who were considered property, rather than immigrants in any case), there were no immigration laws at all for much of the history of the United States. When laws were passed, they tended to reflect racial divisions. Thus, Chinese workers welcomed to the West in the early nineteenth century to help build railroads were shut out by the 1882 Chinese Exclusion Act, which stopped their migration and marginalized Chinese immigrants already in the United States until the 1940s.[17] But the door was still wide open to Europeans, more than twenty million of whom immigrated between 1880 and 1924. The Immigration Act of 1924 sought to stem the flow of "inferior races" in favor of northern European migrants. The basic purpose of this act was "to preserve the ideal of United States homogeneity."[18] Accordingly, in addition to stanching the flow of Italians, southern and eastern Europeans, and Jews, the 1924 law also barred most immigrants coming from Asia. This system largely shaped US immigration until 1965, when President Johnson, during his reform of civil rights laws in the United States, pushed through a revision. The 1965 Immigration and Nationality Act "committed the United States, for the first time, to accepting immigrants of all nationalities on a roughly equal basis."[19]

In dealing with refugees in particular, the United States has a mixed record. The United States infamously turned away more than nine hundred German Jews escaping the Nazi regime on the ocean liner *St. Louis*'s "Voyage of the Damned" in 1939. Closer to home and more recently, the United States opened its doors to Cubans fleeing the Communist Castro regime, but largely closed those doors to Haitians fleeing economic hardship and repressive regimes from the 1970s to 2000s.[20] The United States also took in some refugees in the Western Hemisphere fleeing natural disasters, though in 2018 President Trump called for two hundred thousand Salvadorans and forty-five thousand Haitians who fled earthquakes to return to their nations.[21]

The largest immigration in the past fifty years has come from Mexico, whose shared border with the United States makes it easy for workers to move back and forth between the countries, particularly for seasonal agricultural work. But differences in the economic plights of the two countries led millions of these immigrants to stay illegally in the United States, providing employers with cheap and plentiful labor until anti-immigrant politicians forced action on the issue. President Ronald Reagan, who as governor of California had thumbed his nose at migrant workers seeking better pay and working conditions in the 1960s,[22] nevertheless pushed through the Immigration Reform and Control Act of 1986, which gave amnesty to three million illegal immigrants living in the United States while tightening controls on the hiring of illegal aliens. By 1996, facing increasing hostility to Mexican immigration, President Clinton signed a batch of laws rolling back immigrant access to federally funded programs, such as food stamps.[23]

Hostility to immigrants took a new direction after the attacks of September 11, 2001, shortly into George W. Bush's presidency. Immigration systems were placed under the Department of Homeland Security in 2003. The Immigration and Naturalization Service (INS), whose very name includes the path toward citizenship, was replaced by the Immigration and Customs Enforcement Agency (ICE), which clearly emphasized the police work of immigration control.[24] As post-9/11 additions listed in the appendix demonstrate, new millennium immigration has been securitized and criminalized.

With regard to immigration from the south, President George W. Bush, who is fluent in Spanish and often showed sympathy for illegal Mexican immigrants, unsuccessfully pushed a temporary guest worker program to bring undocumented workers out of the shadows and into businesses that needed them. He also agreed to partial fencing of the southern border to prevent unauthorized crossing.[25] President Obama appeared to want to prove his toughness on immigration and earned the unofficial title of "Deporter in Chief" for sending away 2.5 million illegal immigrants.[26] Despite Obama's strong enforcement, by the 2016 elections Republicans were accusing him (and Reagan before him) of coddling illegal immigrants.[27]

Donald Trump was elected president after the most hostile anti-immigrant campaign in recent memory, promising to build a huge wall across the southern border and make Mexico pay for it. In his first week in office he signed an executive order banning all people from six predominantly Muslim countries from entering the United States, the third iteration of which the US Supreme Court narrowly upheld.[28] He also revoked President Obama's executive order protecting "Dreamers"—children brought without documentation to the United States by their parents—from deportation. While he asked Congress to address the issue through legislation, it has taken no action as of this writing.

In the next section we turn to the discourse of Trump and others concerning the Syrian immigration crisis. In particular, we look at the 2016 presidential candidates campaigning during the height of the Syrian immigration crisis, as well as select members of Congress.

Characterizations and Constructions

Descriptions of immigrants during the Syrian refugee crisis mirrored US history in ranging from positive to negative. Progressive leaders, such as erstwhile presidential candidate Senator Bernie Sanders, humanized immigrants, often characterizing them as "victims." Conservative political leaders, such as Republican candidate and future president Donald Trump, recently have portrayed immigrants as security threats and cultural "Others."

President Obama and Democratic presidential candidate Hillary Clinton both suggested that sensitive matters of diplomacy and foreign policy needed to acknowledge the humanity of Muslim immigrants to the United States. Both urged modest support for refugees caught up in the Syrian refugee crisis.

OBAMA'S DISCOURSE ON THE SYRIAN IMMIGRATION CRISIS

In this post-9/11 context, the Syrian refugee crisis, with its millions of civilians fleeing a brutal civil war, has been problematic even for those sympathetic to civilians caught up in this humanitarian crisis. President Obama had to tread lightly when cracking the door only slightly to Syrian refugees, admitting:

> There are no easy answers to Syria. . . . But so many families need help right now; they don't have time. And that's why the United States is increasing the number of refugees who we welcome within our borders. That's why we will continue to be the largest donor of assistance to support those refugees. And today we are launching new efforts . . . because in the faces of suffering families, our nation of immigrants sees ourselves.[29]

In this speech to the United Nations from fall 2015 he announced that the United States would accept ten thousand Syrian refugees—a drop in the bucket compared, for example, to the hundreds of thousands who immigrated to Germany, a nation with a population one-quarter that of the United States.[30] By 2016, the United States had taken in fewer than five thousand Syrian refugees.[31] Although these efforts were modest, Obama's rhetoric did paint Syrian refugees in sympathetic terms, as "families" who are "suffering," and the issue as urgent since refugees "need help right now."

Obama also identified Syrians with people of every other nation, insisting:

> Today, our concern for them [Syrian refugees] is driven not just by conscience, but should also be driven by self-interest. For helping people who have been pushed to the margins of our world is not mere charity, it is a matter of collective security.[32]

Such humanitarian appeals were typically accompanied by such talk of security and of the need to address the source of the refugee crisis in the brutal regime of Bashar al-Assad in Syria, a "dictator who slaughters tens of thousands of his own people."[33] But despite Obama's boast that "as President of the United States. . . . I lead the strongest military that the world has ever known," he was unwilling to deploy the full force of that military and involve the United States in yet another Middle Eastern conflict, though the United States stood ready "to protect my country or our allies, unilaterally and by force where necessary."[34]

He repeated this sentiment in his final State of the Union Address in 2016, where he insisted that his approach was the smart one, whereby

> America will always act, alone if necessary, to protect our people and our allies; but on issues of global concern, we will mobilize the world to work with us—and make sure other countries pull their own weight. That's our approach to conflicts like Syria, where we're partnering with local forces and leading international efforts to help that broken society pursue a lasting peace.[35]

Overall, President Obama presented Syrian refugees as innocent victims of a brutal dictator for whom he was willing to provide significant financial aid while accepting a relatively small number into the United States. He presented himself and the United States as humanitarian but unwilling to address the crisis and its causes more directly.

When Obama addressed the Islamic Society of Baltimore in February 2016, he expressed concern over internal threats to innocent American Muslims following terrorist attacks by ISIS-inspired Muslims in Europe and in San Bernardino, California, but he did not mention Syrian refugees at all.[36] His voice was already being diminished by the lengthy 2016 race for president that would feature his former secretary of state, a progressive independent senator and a real estate developer turned reality television star. Before addressing the Republican candidates, we will turn to Democrats.

DEMOCRATIC CANDIDATES FOR PRESIDENT
ADDRESS THE SYRIAN IMMIGRATION CRISIS

As a presidential hopeful, in Clinton's favor was her repackaging of Teddy Roosevelt's proven warrior rhetorical style in both discursive and visual arguments. Back in 1988, a helmeted Democratic presidential nominee Michael Dukakis was lampooned for riding in a tank since he had proposed to cut military funding. In rhetorical terms, via undercutting militarism, he was painted as being weak. One of Hillary Clinton's strongest attributes in her rhetorical arsenal was her crowning suasory image as a leader in the War on Terror. Clinton famously was photographed in the "Situation Room" with President Obama, Vice President Biden, and high-level military personnel watching the raid that would kill archenemy Osama bin Laden, mastermind of the 9/11 attacks. Unlike Dukakis, Clinton's discursive and symbolic appeals to voters as a war hawk helped bolster her case for being "fit" to serve as commander in chief. Indeed, given patriarchal constructions of women as emotional and weak, she may have been overcompensating.

Regarding Syrian refugees, in fall of 2015 Clinton mixed proimmigrant discourse with acknowledgments of security concerns in the war on terror. For example, Clinton first stated, "We [the United States] have always welcomed immigrants and refugees. We have made people feel that if they did their part, they sent their kids to school, they worked hard, there would be a place for them in America."[37] This proimmigrant discourse was matched in the same stump speech with assurance that she would harness the full might of "our defense and intelligence professionals" to run meticulous background checks on all prospective refugees to ensure national security.[38] This humanitarian/security combination is also featured in her statement:

> We're facing the worst refugee crisis since the end of World War II and I think the United States has to do more. I would like to see us move from what is a good start with 10,000 to 65,000 and begin immediately to put into place the mechanisms for vetting the people that we would take in.[39]

Clinton's "balanced" approach offers a wide-ranging "guesstimate" of how many refugees she would accept, perhaps to avoid being pinned to specific large numbers by opponents of immigration. Her construction of the historic magnitude of the crisis is used to justify the larger numbers of refugees she would support.

Clinton's main primary challenger, Vermont senator Bernie Sanders, seemed different enough from Clinton to have been far more appealing to the demographic of progressive and younger voters. But on the issue of Syrian refugees, he sounded a lot like Clinton. When asked how many refugees the United States ought to take in as compared to the sixty-five thousand suggested by the United Nations High Commissioner on Refugees, Sanders responded:

> I think it's impossible to give a proper number until we understand the dimensions of the problem. What I do believe is that Europe, the United States, and countries like Saudi Arabia and the United Arab Emirates [both US allies receiving military aid] must address this humanitarian crisis. People are leaving Iraq, they are leaving Syria, with just the clothes on their backs. People have got to respond, and the United States should be part of that response.[40]

Like Clinton, Sanders here appeals to the "humanitarian" aspects of the crisis. Sanders conveys American progressive ideals of welcoming immigrants. Nonetheless, Sanders is purposefully vague and seemingly intentionally clueless in suggesting that we do not sufficiently understand "the dimensions of the problem." His suggestion that allies could be pressed to take in refugees allows him to largely dodge the security concerns raised by others.

In the same interview, Sanders goes on to distinguish his voting record of being against the post- 9/11 war in Iraq, for which his opponent Hillary Clinton had voted. Sanders then affirms this Bush-instigated war "destabilized the Middle East," which, suggests Sanders, contributed to the present Syrian war and the crisis of refugees. Here Sanders is able to use Clinton's hawkish stance and past prowar vote to connect her to the "mistakes" of President George W. Bush's administration and to show further that he, Sanders, would be more perspicacious and a better leader than either Bush or Clinton. Sanders illustrates this by suggesting, "If you look at the transcript [of my 'Nay' vote on the Iraq War's Authorization for Use of Military Force], that much of what I [said then that I] feared has happened."[41]

Overall, the Democratic presidential candidates appeared sympathetic, but guarded. They spoke to terrorism fears broadly circulated by the Republican side of the presidential race, giving them a mixed progressive-conservative message on Syrian immigrants. They also constructed the United States and its people as welcoming of immigrants and refugees, crafting a story of American identity to support their modest humanitarian efforts.

DONALD TRUMP AND THE REPUBLICAN RESPONSE
TO THE SYRIAN IMMIGRATION CRISIS

Donald Trump was an unlikely presidential contender. A brash New York real estate developer who starred in the popular reality television show, *The Apprentice*, and who had been a Democrat, he emerged in conservative politics following the rise of the right-wing Tea Party movement that opposed President Obama's health care law. Trump fueled racist, anti-immigrant, anti-Obama sentiment by backing the "birther" movement that disputed Obama's nationality. For example, starting in 2011, Trump asked: "Why doesn't he [Obama] show his birth certificate?" on ABC's *The View*; "I want to see his birth certificate," to Fox News' *On the Record*; and "I'm starting to think that he was not born here" on NBC's *Today Show*.[42] Birthers claimed that since Obama's birth father was from Kenya and Obama claimed he was born in Hawaii, he must have a fake birth certificate, making him ineligible for the office he held.

Donald Trump's anti-immigration rhetoric was central to his presidential campaign's appeal: His campaign slogan, "Make American Great Again," as Kenneth Burke might note, implied both disorder and a fall from the "order" that was America in its earlier "greatness."[43] Immigrants are Trump's primary scapegoat in this alleged decline, and his symbolic (and literal) eviction of them is his primary path back to American greatness. This "Othering" of immigrants also implies that they are not part of the "American" family, appealing to those concerned about the browning of the United States population, and providing a solid foundation for building his narrow (but winning) coalition.[44]

During Trump's run for the presidency, urging that the country was in "disorder" seemed like a stretch. Obama had spared the country from the most significant threats of the Great Recession that began at the end of George W. Bush's second term, though the economic recovery had been slow. He brought unemployment from the recession high of 10 percent to 4.7 percent, creating 15 million jobs.[45] The stock market boomed. Inflation remained low. Obama got the United States out of the war in Iraq and began to scale back significantly troop numbers in Afghanistan, which had become site of the longest and most expensive war in United States history. Post-Bush respect from the international community garnered Obama a controversial Nobel Peace Prize. Although the Middle East was in turmoil following the Arab Spring and the increasingly deadly civil war in Syria, Obama appears to have followed public sentiment in keeping significant commitments of US troops out of conflicts in that region. Domestically, violent crime continued a twenty-year decline to one-quarter of the 1993 rate.[46] Although there had been terrorist attacks during Obama's presidency from domestic plotters, there were no 9/11-scale attacks.

Despite this positive legacy, Trump argued that the economy was terrible, that violent crime was rampant, and that we were in imminent danger of attack by foreign terrorists.[47] All of these he said were the result of feckless political leaders and evil outsiders. He claimed that positive economic statistics from the government were fake. He insisted that trade deals such as the North American Free Trade Agreement and the pending Trans-Pacific Partnership trade pact were lousy deals for the United States, reversing decades of Republican support for such agreements. He claimed that such trade deals had led US companies to ship jobs overseas. He said that NATO countries were freeloading on the United

States, spending too little on their own defense, and he suggested that a lack of toughness was responsible for the rise of ISIS, promising that he would "bomb the shit out of [ISIS]" and that he would wipe them out very quickly.[48]

Trump's scapegoating during the campaign began with his announcement of his candidacy for president, where he raised fear of Mexican immigrants. He claimed: "When Mexico sends its people, they're not sending their best. . . . They're sending people that have lots of problems, and they're bringing those problems to us. They're bringing drugs. They're bringing crimes. They're rapists."[49] He pledged to build a gigantic wall across the southern border of the United States and make Mexico pay for it. In addition to negatively characterizing Mexicans, he also implied a policy on the part of the Mexican government—as if they had arranged to "send" these immigrants across the border.[50]

Trump used the same xenophobic rhetorical strategy to attempt to discredit one of his Republican rivals, Texas senator Ted Cruz. In February 2016, Trump lumped Cruz in with refugees, threatening on Twitter, "If @TedCruz doesn't clean up his act, stop cheating, & doing negative ads, I . . . [will] sue him for not being a natural born citizen."[51] Trump's accusations further cemented the mythology of immigrants as criminals by linking Cruz's father to President Kennedy's assassination.[52] For his part, Cruz tried to outdo Trump in xenophobic response to the Syrian refugee crisis, stating, "What Barack Obama and Hillary Clinton are proposing is that we bring to this country tens of thousands of Syrian Muslim refugees. I have to say, particularly in light of what happened in Paris [where terrorists staged deadly attacks], that's nothing short of lunacy."[53]

Trump's campaign and presidential rhetoric involving Mexicans and other immigrants was part of a larger strategy that included Muslims, such as Syrian refugees. Trump called for a "Muslim ban" to prevent terrorist attacks.[54] The day after a domestic terrorist brutally attacked an Orlando, Florida, nightclub in June 2016, Trump said that the nation was at risk from "a better, bigger version of the legendary Trojan horse" brought by Syrian immigrants. He called the modest numbers of Syrian immigrants in the United States a "tremendous flow," and despite elaborate vetting (taking eighteen months or more for each immigrant), he insisted: "We don't know who they are, they have no documentation, and we don't know what they're planning."[55] He warned a crowd in Rhode Island in April 2016 to "lock your doors, folks" because "a lot of them" were settling nearby.[56] Despite characterizing Syrians as potential threats, he insisted, "We all have hearts." His heart, however, was not large enough even to help the refugees financially, as he insisted "the Gulf states [can] put up the money."[57]

Trump often used examples to vivify the threat from immigrants. In his speech to the Republican National Convention accepting the party's nomination for president, he emphasized the threat from Mexicans, noting that record numbers of "illegal" immigrants were being released by the Obama administration, leading to mayhem, such as

> a border-crosser [who] was released and made his way to Nebraska. There, he ended the life of an innocent young girl named Sarah Root. She was 21 years-old, and was killed the day after graduating from college with a 4.0 Grade Point Average. Number one in her class. Her killer was then released a second time, and he is now a fugitive from the law. I've met Sarah's beautiful family. But to this Administration, their amazing daughter was just one more American life that wasn't worth protecting. No more.[58]

Trump's synecdochal strategy used horrendous exceptions to stand in for all immigrants, tarring them all with a threatening brush.[59] He omitted details that would diminish the "killer" designation given to the immigrant in this example, notably that the death was the result of drunk driving rather than intentional murder.

Although Trump lost the popular vote by three million, he won enough votes to carry the Electoral College, particularly with close wins in Michigan, Wisconsin, and Pennsylvania. He attracted those who did not trust Hillary Clinton, antiabortion voters, diehard conservatives who support less taxation and regulation, and a key group that was particularly swayed by Trump's message scapegoating outsiders: white working-class men who had watched jobs with livable wages dry up, particularly in manufacturing and mining. A 2014 Pew Research study found that 2014 wages were about 10 percent lower than those in 1973 when adjusted for inflation, despite productivity having nearly doubled over the same period.[60] The wealthy, on the other hand, garnered 96 percent of income gains between 1981 and 2011, thanks to tax restructuring that began with Ronald Reagan.[61]

Instead of blaming tax-cutting and union-busting politicians, automation, globalization, or capitalism generally, Trump assured this economically anxious group of voters that their problems were caused by immigrants and other outsiders. He painted these outsiders as stealing American jobs and threatening the homeland. He used the most vicious of terms, creating a tragic rhetoric that pitted working Americans against others who were different from them in ethnicity, dress, religion, and values. His economic and foreign policy messages appealed to fear of others and scapegoated them. He disparaged American politicians who failed to curtail immigrants and allowed our country to reach this allegedly sorry state.

Five days after Trump's surprising win, he vowed to begin deporting Mexicans, telling CBS's *60 Minutes* on November 13, 2016:

> What we are going to do is get the people that are criminal and have criminal records, gang members, drug dealers, where a lot of these people, probably 2 million, it could be even 3 million, we are getting them out of our country or we are going to incarcerate. . . . But we're getting them out of our country, they're here illegally.[62]

Although studies have shown that immigrants actually commit fewer crimes, on average, than those born in the United States, Trump's repeated claims about their criminality and his vivid examples of rare crimes helped make Mexicans and other immigrants suitable scapegoats to explain the loss of "greatness" in America.

He also claimed that immigrants were stealing American jobs. In April 2017 he used an executive order to limit the HB-1 visa, the type tech companies had used to hire foreign workers when US workers were not available. Trump claimed that "widespread abuse in our immigration system is allowing American workers of all backgrounds to be replaced by workers brought in from other countries to fill the same job for sometimes less pay," and insisted, "This will stop."[63]

Trump's anti-immigrant rhetoric joins resentment over Mexican immigrants with fear of Muslim terrorism to build an overall "Other" that is opposed to a nostalgic politics of white, Christian, European-American identity. Innocent Syrian refugees thereby were caught up in presidential politics and a radically regressive Trump administration.

In the face of persistent and largely unprecedented turmoil in the Trump administration, Trump has held on to the bedrock base of his political coalition by doubling down on a divisive strategy that deploys immigrants as prime scapegoats in the "fall" of the United States.[64]

OTHER AMERICAN POLITICIANS

Members of Congress weighed in on the Syrian crisis on many occasions, mostly in response to actions taken by President Obama and President Trump on immigration and during the 2016 presidential race after Trump made immigration a key issue in his own campaign. After President Obama announced that he was increasing the number of Syrian refugees the United States would accept, Senator Jeanne Shaheen (D-NH) introduced a resolution endorsing his actions. The Senate resolution detailed the enormous numbers of refugees, noted that Europe was "facing its worst refugee crisis since World War II," and insisted that all countries had a "moral responsibility" to help these refugees. The resolution included a note on the need for security as a continuation of current practices, which it recognized as "robust and thorough screening."[65] The resolution, more reasoned than emotional, clearly demonstrated the magnitude of the crisis, stressed the great numbers of refugees taken in by Syria's neighbors and European allies (and, by contrast, the miniscule numbers taken in by the United States), and suggested that security was not a problem in meeting the moral responsibility of the crisis. The resolution failed to make it out of the Republican-controlled Senate.

The House did take action two months later. Following the terrorist attacks in Paris on November 13, 2015, it passed a bill to ban Iraqi and Syrian refugees from entering the United States until the government could certify that the refugees did not pose a security risk.[66] Representative (later senator) Marsha Blackburn (R-TN) spoke in support of the bill.[67] She linked asylum seekers with terrorists in her opening, announcing: "I rise today to discuss the issue of the Syrian refugees and the Islamic State terrorists who are coming across our southern border." She dovetailed concerns over terrorists and asylum seekers by warning, "There is simply no method that will allow us to determine with 100 percent accuracy whether Syrians or illegal aliens that we resettle into the United States are really ISIS jihadists." Ignoring lengthy screening processes for Syrians, she asked and answered: "Do we know who these people are? No. Are they properly vetted? No." Hers is typical of the fear-based appeals of many Republicans that eclipsed (indeed, ignored) all moral and humanitarian concerns.

One of two Muslim members of Congress, Representative Keith Ellison (D-MN), countered such emotional appeals with arguments from history and reason, noting: "We've had 750,000 refugees come into this country since the year 2001. None of them—not one—has been engaged in terrorism." He urged the House not to "revamp our whole refugee resettlement program . . . simply because of intimidation by [ISIS]."[68] So Ellison turns the fear evinced by Blackburn and others into a form of weakness on the part of elected officials that should be resisted.

Senator Harry Reid (D-NV), the former Senate majority leader, was among the most expansive and eloquent in challenging the efforts of Republicans to end asylum for Syrian refugees over security concerns, invoking history and American ideals, characterizing Syrian refugees in sympathetic terms, and warning against ill-conceived policies and bigotry.[69] Alluding to Emma Lazarus's poem from the Statue of Liberty, he insisted that desperate Syrians are the "huddled masses" spread "all across Europe and the Middle East" today. That identification with immigrants we have welcomed was bolstered by sympathetically characterizing the fleeing Syrians as "mothers cradling infants and fathers carrying children in their arms" while "in search of safety and a better life." He noted his father-in-law, Israel Goldfarb, was such an immigrant, associating the Syrians with family. He noted he was "disappointed by Republican fear-mongering and bigotry," and warned against "repeat[ing] the dark days of the 1930s when many Americans resolved to turn away helpless refugees fleeing Nazi Germany." He invoked Kenneth Burke's identification by division, making his audience consubstantial with the refugees on the basis of a shared hatred, since these refugees "hate Assad . . . [and] [t]hey hate ISIS"—"the same evil rulers we are fighting." In turning against innocent Muslims, he warned, "we are playing into [ISIS's] hands." Reid provided a detailed overview of the screening process, which "takes an average of 18 to 24 months," to assure his audience that adequate precautions against terrorist infiltrators were in place. Finally, he defined Americans as those who "come to the defense of the defenseless," insisting: "That is who we are. We are America."

Over the next three years, a number of Democrats would use similar strategies to urge a more welcoming policy toward the Syrian refugees, particularly after candidate Trump called for a Muslim ban and then, as president, implemented a ban on six predominantly Muslim countries. Democrats highlighted the magnitude of the problem, calling it "one of the greatest humanitarian crises of our time," "the largest refugee crisis in the history of the world."[70] They sympathetically characterized the plight and desperation of the refugees as "some of the most vulnerable people in the world fleeing danger and death" and "escap[ing] chaos," "desperate families fleeing unspeakable violence."[71]

Democrats called the screening process for refugees "rigorous,"[72] involving "20 steps."[73] They decried a ban on Muslims as contrary to our values: "unAmerican,"[74] "morally reprehensible"[75] and "unconscionable,"[76] "discrimination in its purest form"[77] that is "destroying the very principles of compassion, of humanity, of being a refuge."[78] They insisted that it flew in the face of our history as "a haven of refuge for people fleeing political and religious repression around the world"[79] and as "a country that was built by immigrants."[80] They criticized the ban as ill-advised for not including countries where known terrorists have originated,[81] for "fuel[ing] ISIS propaganda,"[82] for offering "an appalling affront to American interests,"[83] and for representing "a false choice" between "security and liberty."[84] Additionally, Trump's ban was called unconstitutional for "instituting a religious test as to who can get into this country,"[85] and running contrary to the beliefs of the Framers of the Constitution.[86] Democrats quoted from Trump's campaign statements about banning all Muslim to demonstrate his intent to apply an illegal religious test to immigrants.[87]

Overall, then, the Democrats urged that considering the size of the crisis, the desperation of the refugees, and the adequacy of safeguards for screening them, Trump's policies were immoral, illegal, and ill-advised. He was trampling American values and traditions. While Trump would divide Americans from Syrian immigrants as "others," Democrats would identify with them as consubstantial with the United States as a nation of immigrants.

The security argument of Democrats was challenged each time terrorist attacks demonstrated the threat from radicalized Muslims. After a December 2015 domestic terror attack in San Bernardino, California by first- and second-generation Pakistani Muslim immigrants and a March 2016 coordinated international attack on Brussels by Muslim terrorists, Senator Tom Cotton (R-AR) offered a proactive military strategy to solve the problem by reversing Obama's retreat from the Middle East and

> turn[ing] this moment of anguish into a galvanizing event, one that steels the resolve of the United States and our allies to do what it takes to defeat radical Islamic Jihadism . . . [and] execut[ing] a real strategy that brings the war to ISIS in Syria and Iraq, that puts America in the lead, and that destroys this civilizational cancer at its source.[88]

Oklahoma Republican senator Jim Inhofe concurred, insisting that taking down ISIS would increase American security; thus, he tweeted:

"It is time for a White House that will rebuild our military, protect our borders & execute a clearly-stated strategy w/ allies against ISIL [ISIS]."[89] Senator Marco Rubio (R-FL) then directly tied the Syrian refugee problem to ISIS in insisting that the terrorist organization was "recruiting people to enter this country as engineers, posing as doctors, posing as refugees. We know this for a fact."[90]

As this review of congressional discourse on immigration demonstrates, a yawning divide developed between the humanitarian discourse of Democrats and the security-driven discourse of the Republicans. In part this chasm can be explained as discourse that follows the party leaders—the humanitarian discourse of President Obama versus the security/othering discourse of candidate/President Trump. It also fits the current image and membership of each party—Democrats emphasizing diversity and multiculturalism versus and Republicans emphasizing "traditional" values that support their largely white Christian base.

The Devolution of American Political Rhetoric on Immigrants

Across America's convoluted historical relationship with immigration, we find supportive and rejectionist rhetoric, politics, and policies. The United States largely earned the appreciative inscription on the Statue of Liberty in opening its doors to tens of millions of European immigrants from the late nineteenth to the early twentieth centuries, even as it closed the door to Chinese immigrants. The Immigration Act of 1924 drew distinctions among Europeans as well. In more recent times, post-9/11 discourses tied security concerns to immigration and made the United States wary of Muslim immigrants.

Trump's discourses effectively meld concerns over illegal immigration from Latin America (especially Mexico) with concerns over Muslim terrorists to paint all immigrants as threatening American lives, American jobs, and American culture. He uses vivid (and extremely rare) examples of violent crimes by immigrants to substantiate fears of immigrants. He attacks US laws and policies to suggest that they are inadequate to stop or screen dangerous immigrants from entering the country. He never mentions contributions of immigrants to the US economy but suggests they sponge off of our social systems and take jobs from "true" Americans. And this message has resonated with and coalesced a white conservative base feeling angst about the US economy, terrorism, and the growing ethnic diversity of the United States, leading Republicans in Congress to follow suit, while Democrats have opposed Republican claims and policies regarding immigration generally and Syrian immigration particularly. On the other hand, concerns over security—partly from terrorist attacks and partly from the anti-immigrant drumbeat of Trump and his party—have forced Democrats to defend immigrant screening measures and announce their concern for Americans' safety. Rhetorically, though, Democrats would have us identify with Syrian immigrants, while Republicans would have us disidentify with them and scapegoat them for our problems.

The Syrian immigration crisis coincided with the developments that made Trump's supporters concerned about America's loss of "greatness." Long-brewing social, economic, and security problems made Syrian and other immigrants handy scapegoats for problems that could be connected to them by unscrupulous rhetors who loaded them with all manner of "sins" that Trump sought to purge from the American homeland.

Appendix. A Summary of Pro-, Neutral-, and Anti-immigrant US Legislation

Pro-immigrant Legislation	Neutral to Immigrants	Anti-immigrant Legislation
Naturalization Acts of 1790, 1795, and 1798 were designed to create "uniform naturalization" standards for all immigrants to the United States.	The 1819 Steerage Act determined and regulated what foreigners were coming into the United States on ships.	Alien Friends Act of 1798 enabled president to identify persons deemed spies or treasonous, to be barred from entering the United States or from obtaining citizenship.
The 1864 Immigration Act set up immigration commission heads and processes, and protected immigrants from compulsory military service.	The 1847 and 1855 Passenger Laws were set up to identify foreigners coming into the United States via merchant ships and steamships.	Alien Enemies Act of 1798 enabled deportation or imprisonment of male immigrants from nations considered enemies of the United States.
The 1943 Magnuson Act repealed the 1882 Chinese Exclusion Act, enabling Chinese immigrants to enter the United States per quotas set up in 1924 Immigration Act.	The 1885 Contract Labor Law prevented foreigners from coming into United States as indentured servants.	The 1862 Anti-Coolie Law was passed to stop Chinese immigrants, derogatively referred to as "coolies," from coming into the United States on American ships.
The 1943 Bracero Appropriations made it possible for farm laborers, especially from Mexico, to immigrate into the United States as agricultural laborers.	The 1918 Wartime Measure made it illegal for foreigners to enter the United States with fake documents and required US citizens to use valid passports for travel out of and returning to the United States.	The 1875 Page Law prohibited immigration from China, Japan, and "coolies" and women prostitutes from Asian countries.

The 1945 War Brides Act enabled the spouses and children of US military servicemen to immigrate to the United States.	The 1940 Nationality Act codified more clearly who could become a US citizen by birth, by being a resident in a US Territory, and exempted religious and other immigrants from military service.	The 1882 Chinese Exclusion Act, the 1892 Geary Act, and 1902 Scott Act made it illegal for Chinese to immigrate to the United States or its territories, and established punishments for Americans who tried to bring them to the United States.
The 1946 Alien Fiancée and Fiancées Act and the 1946 Chinese War Brides Act allowed betrothed and married spouses of US servicemen to immigrate on a nonquota basis.	The 1941 Wartime Measure let officials determine who could be barred from immigrating based on possibility of endangering the United States.	The 1882 Immigration Act taxed all immigrants upon arrival in US ports, and prevented persons deemed "idiots, convicts" or incapable of self-care to be turned away at borders (not permitted to immigrate).
The 1948 Displaced Persons Act enabled mainly white European persons (with dependents) fearing political, racial, religious, or related persecution to immigrate to the United States.	The 1990 Immigration and Nationality Act set up the Diversity Visa Lottery Program, through which high school–educated and work-trained foreigners may apply to immigrate to the United States from world areas determined by the attorney general and secretary of state based on criteria such as total numbers of persons who immigrated into the United States from the nation in past five years proportionate to that nation's total population.	The 1892 Immigration Act prevented all "idiots, criminals, paupers" and persons with communicable diseases from entering the United States; ships would need to return the rejected persons to their points of origin.

The 1917 Immigration Act reiterated prior acts preventing Chinese persons and persons deemed socially undesirable ("idiots, prostitutes," etc.) from entering the United States. It also taxed and gave literacy tests to immigrants upon entry to the United States and fined vessels bringing in persons deemed unfit.	
The 1921 Emergency Quota Law placed quotas on numbers of immigrants by country, and reiterated previous anti-Asian "coolie" acts.	The 1951 Public Law 78 Extension of the Bracero Program continued the legal immigration mainly from Mexico of agricultural laborers and their families.

The 1965 Immigration and Nationality Act revoked quota system that was set up in 1924, favoring instead skills-based and needs-based immigrant criteria.	The 1924 Immigration Act reinscribed quotas that were generous to Western European nations such as Germany but which severely restricted the annual numbers of immigrants from Eastern European, Russian, African, Middle Eastern, and other areas deemed to be less desirable. The act also made it possible for wives, children, religious, or scholarly professionals to immigrate with approved foreigners per quota criteria.
The 1968 Armed Forces Naturalization Act enabled persons who had served in the US armed forces during Vietnam or other conflicts to immigrate to the United States.	The 1952 Immigration and Nationality Act greatly limited immigration from certain countries based on Cold War fears of spreading communism. President Truman initially vetoed it, deeming it discriminatory, but eventually Congress passed it.
The 1975 Indochina Migration and Refugee Assistance Act enabled refugees from Vietnam and other Southeast Asian nations to immigrate based political refugee status.	The 1996 Personal Responsibility and Work Opportunity Reconciliation Act was set up to disincentivize immigration based on newly and highly curbed welfare and other public assistance programs access for undocumented and documented immigrants.

	The 1996 Illegal Immigration Reform & Immigrant Responsibility Act clarified disincentives to immigrants seeking public assistance and to US employers seeking to hire undocumented laborers and to step up border patrol enforcement and penalties for smugglers of immigrants.
	The 2004 Intelligence Reform and Terrorism Prevention Act / National Intelligence Reform Act reorganized government divisions involved in immigration, securitizing, and militarizing them in the post-9/11 global war on terror.
The 1982 Amerasian Immigration Act enabled some dual- or multiethnic, multicultural children of American GIs to immigrate to the United States when they met key criteria.	
The 1986 Immigration Reform and Control Act amended the Immigration and Nationality Act so that undocumented resident aliens could apply for and gain legal resident or other documented US immigrant statuses.	

The 1991 Armed Forces Immigration Act enabled aliens who served honorably in the US military for at least 12 years to apply for United States naturalization.	The 2005 Real ID Act institutionalized the 9/11 Commission suggestions to increase defense funding for antiterrorism, standardize forms of immigrant documentation, and limit immigration based on war-on-terror criteria.
The 2000 Hmong Veterans Naturalization Act enabled those who served in support of US military in 1961–1978 in Vietnam, Laos, or Thailand, and their spouses or children, to immigrate to United States.	The 2006 Secure Fence Act was passed as part of the war on terror to increase physical border barriers of maritime and land, and to enhance technology for surveilling and controlling ingress/egress along US borders.
The 2000 Bring Them Home Alive Act enabled foreigners who assist in returning Korean War or Vietnam War POWs and others to apply for naturalization.	
The 2000 Child Citizenship Act enabled foreign minor children being legally adopted by US citizens to gain citizenship upon legally documented entry to US soil, provided intricate international adoption processes are legally followed and completed.	

Source: Information adapted from Sarah Starkweather, "US Immigration Legislation Online," University of Washington–Bothell, 2007, library.uwb.edu.

Notes

1. President Trump is reported to have asked members of Congress why the United States has to open its immigration to people from "shithole countries" like Haiti and the African continent. See Eli Watkins and Abby Phillip, "Trump Decries Immigrants from 'Shithole Countries' Coming to United States," *CNN*, January 12, 2018.

2. This decline has been widely documented. Katherine Whittemore, for example, reviewed six books in 2013 alone on the decline of the middle class. "Six Books Examine the Decline of the Middle Class," *Boston Globe*, January 19, 2013.

3. Quoted in Brennan Oban, "Do Immigrants 'Steal' Jobs from American Workers?," Brookings Institution, August 24, 2017, brookings.edu. Brennan notes that illegal immigrants often work in jobs that Americans don't want.

4. Eve Bower, "American Deaths in Terrorism vs. Gun Violence in One Graph," *CNN*, October 3, 2016. A 2017 Chapman University poll found 61 percent of Americans are afraid, with unafraid or being afraid based along party lines. "Fear of Extremism and the Threat to National Security: Chapman University Survey of American Fears 2017," Wilkinson College of Arts, Humanities, and Social Sciences, Chapman University, October 11, 2017, https://blogs.chapman.edu/wilkinson/2017/10/11/fear-of-extremism-and-the-threat-to-national-security/.

5. Nahal Toosi, "Breaking with Bush and Obama, Trump Talks about 'Radical Islamic Terrorism,'" *Politico.com*, February 28, 2017.

6. Domenico Montenaro, "How the Browning of America Is Upending Both Political Parties," NPR, October 12, 2016.

7. "Trump Immigration Plan Could Keep Whites in United States Majority for up to Five More Years." *Washington Post*, February 6, 2018, General OneFile, gogalegroup.com. Watkins and Phillip.

8. Clarke Rountree, "Introduction," *Venomous Speech: Problems with American Political Discourse on the Right and Left*, ed. Clarke Rountree (Santa Barbara, CA: Praeger, 2013), I: xxv–xxvii.

9. Lydia O'Connor and Daniel Marans, "Here Are 13 Examples of Donald Trump Being Racist," *Huffington Post*, February 29, 2016.

10. Thomas Wood, "Racism Motivated Trump Voters More than Authoritarianism," *Washington Post*, April 17, 2017.

11. Mary Stuckey has argued that presidential rhetoric serves the important function of coalition maintenance, and that defining who is an American is a key concern of that discourse. *Defining Americans: The Presidency and National Identity* (Lawrence: University Press of Kansas, 2004).

12. Readers from the United States will forgive our review of basic facts about the US government, which are provided for international readers who may be less familiar with the workings of our democratic republic.

13. Judith A. Best, "Presidential Selection: Complex Problems and Simple Solutions," *Political Science Quarterly* 119 (2004): 40.

14. Library of Congress, "America as a Religious Refuge: The Seventeenth Century, Part 1," from *Religion and the Founding of the American Republic*, loc. gov.

15. Abigail Swingen, "Labor: Employment, Servitude and Slavery in the 17th Century Atlantic," in *Mercantilism Reimagined: Political Economy in Early Modern Britain and Its Empire*, ed. Phillip J. Stern and Carl Wennerlind (New York: Oxford University Press, 2014), 50–51.

16. Swingen, 50–51.

17. *The Chinese Exclusion Act*, documentary film, Ric Burns and Li-Shen Yu, directors. *American Experience*, PBS.org, May 29, 2018.

18. Department of State, Office of the Historian, the Immigration Act of 1924, history.state.gov.

19. Tom Gjelten, "The Immigration Act that Inadvertently Changed America," *The Atlantic*, October 2, 2015.

20. Denise M. Bostdorff, "Rhetorical Ambivalence: Bush and Clinton Address the Crisis of Haitian Refugees," in *Who Belongs in America? Presidents, Rhetoric, and Immigration*, ed. Vanessa B. Beasley (College Station: Texas A&M University Press, 2006), 207–235.

21. Miriam Jordan, "Trump Administration Says That Nearly 200,000 Salvadorans Must Leave," *New York Times*, January 8, 2018.

22. Nathan Heller, "Hunger Artist: How Cesar Chavez Disserved His

Dream," *New Yorker*, April 14, 2014.

23. Tanya Broder, Avideh Moussavian, and Jonathan Blazer, "Overview of Immigrant Eligibility for Federal Programs," December 2015, National Immigration Law Center, nilc.org.

24. ICE, as pungent political rhetoric, has CIA connotations going back to late Cold War era programs such as Project ICER.

25. Clarke Rountree, *George W. Bush: A Biography* (Westport, CT: Greenwood Press, 2010), 158–159.

26. Serena Marshall, "Obama Has Deported More People than Any Other President," *ABC News*, August 29, 2016.

27. "GOP Front-Runners on Immigration: 1980 and Today Trump's Immigration Plan: Deport the Undocumented, 'Legal Status' for Some," *CNN*, January 19, 2016. The Republican presidential primary particularly highlighted the use of immigration as a wedge issue, with front-runner Donald Trump making the most radical claim, that he would deport all eleven million illegal immigrants and build a wall across the entire southern border with Mexico. See, for example, "GOP Front Runners on Immigration."

28. Adam Liptak and Michael D. Shear, "Trump's Travel Ban Is Upheld by Supreme Court," *New York Times*, June 26, 2018.

29. Barack H. Obama, "Remarks by President Obama before the United Nations General Assembly," September 28, 2015, obamawhitehouse. archives.gov.

30. Obama.

31. Noah Bierman and Kurtis Lee, "How Donald Trump's Speech Attacking Hillary Clinton Compares with the Facts," June 23, 2016, *Los Angeles Times*.

32. Obama.

33. Obama.

34. Obama.

35. Barack Obama, "State of the Union Address," January 12, 2016, Washington, DC, americanrhetoric.com.

36. Barack Obama, "Address to the Islamic Society of Baltimore," February 3, 2016, Baltimore, americanrhetoric.com.

37. As quoted in Hannah Fraser-Chanpong, "In Dallas Clinton Weighs in on

Syrian Refugee Crisis," *CBS News*, November 17, 2015.

38. Fraser-Chanpong.

39. As quoted in Rebecca Kaplan, "Hillary Clinton: United States Should Take 65,000 Syrian refugees," *Face the Nation*, CBS News, September 20, 2015.

40. As quoted in Bernie Sanders's interview with Chuck Todd, *Meet the Press*, NBC, September 13, 2015.

41. As quoted in Sanders's interview with Chuck Todd.

42. Ashley Parker and Steve Eder, "Inside the Six Weeks Donald Trump Was a Nonstop Birther," *New York Times*, July 2, 2016.

43. The order/disorder framework is developed most thoroughly by Burke in *The Rhetoric of Religion* (Berkeley: University of California Press, 1961).

44. A study of voter survey data from early in 2016 by John Sides, Lynn Vavreck, and Michael Tesler concludes that "Trump performs best among Americans who express more resentment toward African Americans and immigrants and who tend to evaluate whites more favorably than minority groups." Reported in Michael Tesler, "A Newly Released Poll Shows the Populist Power of Donald Trump," *Washington Post*, January 27, 2016.

45. Kristin Doerer, "4 Economists Evaluate Obama's Economic Legacy," *PBS Newshour*, January 12, 2017.

46. Pew Research Center, "5 Facts about Crime in the United States," February 21, 2017, pewresearch.org.

47. These sentiments are reflected in a number of speeches and statements, including the following: Donald Trump, "Announcement of Candidacy for Republican Presidential Nomination, July 15, 2016"; in Jonathon Gatehouse, "The Rise of Donald Trump: The 10 Moments That Shaped the Most Ridiculous, Unexpected and Divisive Political Campaign in United States History," *Maclean's*, November 21, 2016, 21; Donald Trump, "Speech Accepting the GOP Nomination for President," July 21, 2016, NPR; Donald Trump, "Campaign Speech in Pensacola, FL [annotated]," September 9, 2016, NPR; Donald Trump, "Campaign Speech in Phoenix, AZ," August 31, 2017, *Los Angeles Times*.

48. Pamela Engel, "Donald Trump: 'I Would Bomb the S—out of ISIS,'"

Business Insider, November 13, 2015.

49. Gatehouse.

50. Trump implies a strategy that actually was a part of the 1980 Mariel boatlift, whereby Cuban president Fidel Castro allowed a group of Cubans to emigrate to the United States along with large contingent of convicted criminals and mental patients.

51. Quoted in Eugene Scott, "Trump Threatens to Sue Cruz for 'Not Being a Natural Born Citizen,'" *CNN*, February 12, 2016.

52. Nolan D. McCaskill, "Trump Accuses Cruz's Father of Helping JFK's Assassin," *Politico.com*, May 3, 2016.

53. As quoted in Fraser-Chanpong.

54. Mallory Shelbourne, "Trump Call for Muslim Ban Deleted from Site after Reporter's Question," *The Hill*, May 8, 2017.

55. David Miliban, "The Best Ways to Deal with the Refugee Crisis," *New York Review of Books*, October 13, 2016.

56. As quoted in Engel, "Trump on Syrian Refugees."

57. As quoted in Engel, "Trump on Syrian Refugees."

58. Donald Trump mentions Sarah Root during the immigration section of his speech. KETV Channel 7 News, Omaha, Nebraska, July 21, 2016, www.ketv.com.

59. The synecdochal strategy takes a part to stand for the whole; in this case, a singular negative example stands in for all immigrants, tainting them with the same black brush. On this function, see Kenneth Burke, *A Grammar of Motives* (Berkeley: University of California Press, 1969), 507–509.

60. Pew Research Center, "For Most Workers, Real Wages Have Barely Budged for Decades," October 9, 2014, pewresearch.org. Economic Policy Institute, "Productivity-Pay Gap," August 2016, epi.org.

61. Henry Blodget, "Amazing Charts Show How 90% of the Country Has Gotten Shafted over the Past 30 Years," *Business Insider*, October 15, 2011.

62. "President-Elect Trump Says How Many Immigrants He'll Deport," November 13, 2016, *60 Minutes*, CBS News.

63. Josh Siegel, "Trump Restricts Immigration Program that Took this American's Job," *Daily Signal*, April 21, 2017.

64. The turmoil of Trump's presidency is so well documented that we will not elaborate it here, other than to note that there are credible charges of his frequent lying in public statements, ongoing scandals involving alleged sexual relationships, possible corruption, and possible collusion with the Russians to win the election; unprecedented turnover in personnel in his administration, and his impulsive use of Twitter to make controversial statements about his own Justice Department and its employees, Black Lives Matter sympathizers, and a white nationalist rally in Charlottesville, Virginia, among other things. For a review of some of these problems, see Stephen Collinson, "The Exhausting First Year of Donald Trump's Presidency," *CNN*, January 15, 2018.

To take another example, Trump addressed a campaign rally in Michigan on April 28, 2018, and claimed, "We [the United States] don't have borders," "[The Democrats] don't care about our borders or crime," "If we don't get border security, we'll have no choice. We'll close down the country," and "Our laws are so corrupt and so stupid—I call them the dumbest immigration laws anywhere on Earth." Quoted in Chris Cillizza, "The 57 Most Outlandish, Outrageous and Offensive Lines from Trump's Michigan Rally," *CNN*, April 30, 2018.

65. "Senate Resolution 268—Expressing the Sense of the Senate Regarding the Syrian Refugee Crisis," *Congressional Record*, September 24, 2015, S6941.

66. "Paris Attacks: What Happened on the Night," *BBC News*, December 9, 2015. Demirijian Karoun, "Senate Likely to Reject Bill Barring Syrian and Iraqi Refugees from Entering the United States," *Washington Post*, January 19, 2016, A11.

67. "Syrian Refugees," *Congressional Record*, November 18, 2015, H8285–H8286.

68. As quoted in Amy Goodman, "First Muslim Member of United States Congress: Restrictions on Syrian Refugees Driven by Fear, Xenophobia," *Democracy Now*, November 25, 2015, democracynow.org.

69. "Syrian Refugees," *Congressional Record*, November 19, 2015, S8114–S8115.

70. Representative Marc Veasey (D-TX), "President Trump's Immigration Ban," *Congressional Record*, January 30, 2017, H722. Senator Dick Durbin

(D-IL), "Disapproving a Rule Submitted by the Department of the Interior," *Congressional Record*, March 6, 2017, S1602.

71. Representative Barbara Lee (D-CA), "The American Philosophy," *Congressional Record*, February 2, 2017, H924. Representative Donald Payne Jr. (D-NJ), "President Trump's Immigration Ban," *Congressional Record*, January 30, 2017, H722. Representative Mark Takano (D-CA), "The American Philosophy," *Congressional Record*, February 2, 2017, H927.

72. Payne.

73. Representative Pramila Jayapal (D-WA), "The American Philosophy," *Congressional Record*, February 2, 2017, H924.

74. Payne; Representative Terri A. Sewell (D-AL), "President Trump's Disgraceful Executive Order," *Congressional Record*, January 31, 2017, E110; Lee, H924; Representative Yvette Clarke (D-NY), "The American Philosophy," *Congressional Record*, February 2, 2017, H925.

75. Lee, H924.

76. Clarke, H925.

77. Jayapal, H923.

78. Jayapal, H923.

79. Representative Jamie Raskin (D-MD), "The American Philosophy," *Congressional Record*, February 2, 2017, H922.

80. Jayapal, H923.

81. Raskin, H922.

82. Lee, H924.

83. Clarke, H925.

84. Jayapal, H923.

85. Jayapal, H924.

86. Clarke, H925.

87. Durbin, S1602.

88. As quoted in Amber Phillips, "Congress's Reaction to Brussels Is Full of Sound and Fury, Signifying Almost Nothing," *Washington Post*, March 22, 2016.

89. As quoted in Phillips.

90. Demirijian.

Conclusion

———◆·———

The phenomenon to which national political leaders covered here have given meanings and explanations is rather simple at its core: human beings changing their location from one place to another. However, as we have seen in the course of the book, there exists a wide array of explanations ascribed to the phenomenon and even a wider selection of motives rhetorically imputed to the people who are on the move.

The situation has been defined as a humanitarian or refugee crisis, a period analogous to the barbarian invasions of Rome; a flood, a flow, an unarmed invasion, smuggling, or simply immigration. The people, in turn, have been constructed as refugees, victims, immigrants, Muslims, a threat, an economic burden (or asset), welfare surfers, or guests, just to name a few examples. In this regard the rhetoric analyzed here draws substantively on traditional commonplaces and stereotypes about immigration and refugees.

What is striking are the manifold political aims affecting the rhetorics of immigration. This can be understood only in relation to a complex web of political purposes and audiences, domestic and international. To begin with assumed roles and geographical proximity to Syria, whether a given country serves as a gateway or transit country, destination country, or a tertiary country has a strong impact on its rhetoric. The immigration discourse of all countries is shaped also by domestic political considerations, such as divisions between the government and opposition parties, whether there is an election in progress, and the general political climate. A given country's history with war and immigration also shapes these views. And the economic needs of countries play a role as well.

This chapter concludes the volume first by examining the ways rhetoric related to immigrants and refugees has been politicized in the analyzed countries, with a particular focus on the geographical position of a given country in the crisis. After this we will discuss the most prominent transnational themes that emerge from the rhetoric of national political leaders.

Germany, the most significant European destination country in the recent crisis, has received well over a million refugees. In a country with a past that continues to engender "moral guilt toward the world," refugee rhetoric may be seen as compensatory, reflecting attempts to improve the image of the country. Simultaneously, the different audiences at home have had to be taken into consideration. Consequently, Chancellor Angela Merkel's rhetoric is an illustrative example of the attempt to balance between promoting a German "culture of welcome" and countering accusations of being naive.

Angela Merkel has both emphasized the need to show "Germany's friendly face" and called for "fair distribution of burdens" among the EU countries. She has also declared that "German multiculturalism is dead," stressing the need for active integration measures instead of treating immigrants as "guest workers" who would eventually return to their home countries. Therefore, as Julia Khrebtan-Hörhager and Elisa Hörhager point out, in her attempts to address different audiences at home and abroad the chancellor has been at the same time applauded for her humanitarian aspirations and ambitions for inclusion, and criticized for not being able to bring "the asylum chaos" under control.

The United Kingdom is another destination country at the western rim of Europe. The refugee crisis had an immediate and profound political effect: the "Brexit" vote in summer 2016 was decisively influenced by immigration, as anti-immigrant and anti-EU politicians capitalized on the notable growth in immigration in recent years in a country that for centuries had experienced net emigration. The result, the UK leaving the EU, also caused a change in the political leadership as PM David Cameron stepped down and his Conservative Party colleague Theresa May took the reins.

Rhetorically the United Kingdom is a fascinating case. Trying to balance between different audiences, David Cameron "ping-ponged" between humanitarian concern and political complaint over immigrants, attracting criticism from both left and right. While Cameron's approach sought to balance heart and head in his public discourse, this changed with the Brexit vote. Cameron's successor, Theresa May, offered a style that was so pragmatic and unemotional as to warrant the description "bureaucratic." While she did not characterize immigration as a threat, neither did her "boring" rhetoric stir her audiences to humanitarian action. Indeed, it seemed calculated to fall flat in that respect, as there was no new action (beyond ongoing financial support) she was seeking. She appeased the more rightwing populists in the UKIP Party by emphasizing the need for border control and urging immigrants to stay close to home (and, by implication, out of the UK). She also promoted one of their heroes, London Mayor and Conservative MP Boris Johnson, to Foreign Secretary, sending a message that was unmistakable concerning the future of refugee policy in the UK.

In Finland, a Northern destination country with very little immigration before the recent crisis, economic rhetoric has framed the discussion. Compared to Germany, for example, the number of refugees who came to Finland in 2015 was not dramatic for such a wealthy country. At the same time when the crisis reached Finland in fall 2015, the newly-elected right-wing government began to implement austerity policies claiming that Finland was on the brink of economic collapse.

In addition to the fact that in a small country with a traditionally homogenous population immigrants are often seen as people who dangerously "rock the boat," the government's rhetorical strategy has depicted refugees in terms of their potential (or the lack of it) for improving Finland's prosperity. This contrasts with traditional discourses that constructed refugees as security threat or victims of war, the crisis as a humanitarian tragedy, or Islam as incompatible with Finnish culture and values. In competing versions of the economic constructions that prevailed, immigrants either rescue the economy as much-needed labor force or they ruin it by straining the welfare state. Peculiarly, in Finland the rhetorical frontier does not coincide with the government-opposition divide. Liberals in the cabinet have often aligned themselves with the opposition against their populist colleagues in the government, who, in turn, have accused both groups of being gullible. Deriving from Finland's political history on the border between East and West, and its continuous efforts to construct itself as an organic part of the west, political leaders from all parties heavily emphasize Finland's embrace of European or Western values.

The so-called gateway or transit countries reveal a realm of political rhetoric of a different kind. For the main gateway to Europe, Greece, the situation has been a "crisis within a crisis," as Yiannis Karayiannis and Anthoula Malkopoulou state in their chapter. Greek politicians have had to grapple with a severe economic crisis simultaneously with the refugee crisis. In Greece the rhetorical border is between the main opposition party, the conservative New Democracy, and the key player of the government, the leftist SYRIZA.

Stressing the phenomenon as "smuggled immigration" threatening the already strained economy, New Democracy has claimed that "broken Greece" is exactly what SYRIZA wants in order to promote its own political aims. And most importantly, this position will allegedly deepen the friction with the EU that counts on Greece to "curb the flow" to Europe. SYRIZA, in turn, shifts the focus and constructs the situation as a major humanitarian problem that has tragically revealed that the EU is dominated by an ideology alien to its values. Protecting refugees is a "historical legacy of European civilization," for which a common European solution is needed. Interestingly, these two main political forces accuse each other of enabling far-right extremism.

Serbia, another gateway country that suffered greatly in the 1990s' Yugoslav wars and a severe economic crisis, shows an even more palpable tension between domestic and international audiences. The political leaders have balanced between their domestic audiences pushing toward nationalism and anti-immigrant sentiment on the one hand, and acting "European" in order to further Serbia's accession negotiations with the European Union on the other hand, as Ivana Cvetković Miller illustrates in her chapter.

This is accomplished by telling Serbians that these immigrants are merely "passing through" to more prosperous countries. By assigning migrants agency to decide what is best for them, Serbian political leaders in fact claim that their country is not attractive enough to immigrants. In this way it has been possible to calm domestic audiences and respond to criticism by political opponents. However, at the same time the Serbian prime minister has stated that Serbia is acting more "European," that is, more humanely and responsible than some other member states, particularly in its application of the refugee quota system. This rhetorical strategy is affected by the country's history: Serbia is often still represented as a primitive, violent, racially and culturally inferior Balkan territory somewhere between the Orient and Europe. In any case, the tightrope results in an odd mixture of negative self-image and an insistence on its Europeanness as a positive feature of the country.

Poland, often seen as an eastern gateway to the European Union, is a country in which the debate over the last two years has focused on distinguishing between "refugees" and "immigrants." As Jarosław Jańczak shows, the issue is a highly political and moral one: because hosting refugees is seen as a legal and moral obligation, by defining them as "economic immigrants" whom the country cannot afford, the obligation no longer holds. People coming from the eastern neighbor with strong ethnic ties to Poland, Ukraine, have been defined as proper "refugees," in contrast with Syrians or Iraqis, while in reality the situation is often the exact opposite.

The analysis of Polish political leaders illustrates particularly well how immigration rhetoric has been connected to identity politics. In the Polish conservative discourse immigration symbolizes the troubling processes that are taking place in the Western EU, cast as the erosion of the nation state, the disintegration of cultural unity based on Christianity, and the loss of public order. Here Germany in particular is constructed as the main culprit because it has "opened its borders" and is now trying to get the other member states to pay for its mistakes. To counter this collapse of values and its inappropriate policies, true "Polishness" is represented as the alternative—and Poland the last bastion of "Westernness." The paradoxical argument is that the West must be protected from itself lest "westernization" lead to downfall of the western values.

In Hungary, another border country, the central political figure is Prime Minister Viktor Orbán, a national-conservative strongman who has been criticized by the European Union for his centralization of power and curtailing freedom of speech. In Orbán's rhetoric the refugee crisis has been politicized against the EU. According to the Hungarian leader, Europe is based on Christianity and the sovereignty of "free and independent nations," values which the EU now is attempting to tear down. By constructing immigrants as "host animals," the prime minister has accused the European Union of spreading "internationalism" and "cosmopolitanism"—an argument that has proven very successful for a domestic audience in a country with a difficult past under Soviet-led socialism.

Although in Viktor Orbán's rhetoric at home *Brussels* is a metonymy of failure, toward international audiences his tone has been different. Unlike, for example, some British politicians, he has never suggested leaving the EU, and he has even urged EU audiences not to pay attention to his rhetoric at home. All in all, the Hungarian case shows, first, how accusations of politicization are an effective way to further one's own policy in front of different audiences. Second, Hungary and

Poland reveal a significant strand of conservative rhetoric: critique of the European Union for turning away from "European values" without a campaign to actually leave the union.

In Turkish rhetoric immigration has been an extremely intense matter. Since 2011 three million Syrians have arrived in Turkey, most of them without refugee status recognized by Turkish law (which grants such status only to people coming from European countries). Consequently, the authoritarian President Erdogan has defined them as "guests" based on religious brotherhood, and Turkey as the "host"—literally "the ones who help." However, the seemingly humanitarian rhetoric has enabled a highly pragmatic political approach to the situation. It has left the refugees subject to the authority and good will of the host, and implied that they would be returning to their home country in an undefined future.

As İnan Özdemir-Taştan and Hatice Çoban-Keneş point out, the prolonged guest status has *de facto* left the Syrians without a status recognized by international law, making it possible for the government to use them as the political situation at home and abroad requires. First, the Turkish leadership has announced plans to confer citizenship on Syrian refugees in an effort many see as an attempt to build a neo-Ottoman empire to control Eurasia. Second, to support the previous effort, it has been insisted that Turkey has to act quickly lest the western countries steal the most skilled workers among the refugees. Third, the refugees have been used by the political leadership to speed up accession negotiations with the European Union. The opposition, seeing political machinations in these moves, has criticized the government for betraying both Turkey and human rights.

The two tertiary countries examined, Japan and the United States, add yet another aspect to the politicization of the crisis. Finding refuge in these countries was not a matter of taking additional trains to reach a safe haven (even the UK could be reached via the Channel Tunnel); they were half a world away and could easily stop refugees from flying into their airports. To begin with Japan, Prime Minister Shinzo Abe has constructed the phenomenon first and foremost in economic terms. The key factor in his discourse is how immigrants contribute to the country's economic prosperity, as well as how the best economic immigrants can be identified. At the same time, Abe has emphasized that the crisis is something that has to be tackled by helping people in need, notably by keeping them close to their countries of origin and away from Japan. His humanitarianism is completely financial.

As Kaori Miyawaki shows, Abe's approach addresses a domestic audience worried about economic burdens or cultural erosion, as well as the international community's calls for solidarity. Interestingly, the political opposition has met Abe on his own economic grounds, insisting that immigration is precisely what the aging country needs for improving its economy and challenging its problematic "island mentality." The Japanese construction of immigrants in terms of economic value resembles the rhetoric of many Finnish political leaders, perhaps because both are wealthy countries with very few immigrants and a homogenous and aging population.

The United States is an example of pro- and anti-immigrant rhetoric, featuring bipolar swings between the lofty ideals inscribed on the Statue of Liberty and Donald Trump's "Trojan Horse" trope of Islamic terrorists hidden among the refugees. As Ellen Gorsevski, Clarke Rountree, and Andrée Reeves note in their chapter, in the 2016 presidential elections immigration was one of the central issues. The Democratic candidate, Hillary Clinton, exemplified the need to balance humanitarianism and security. She stressed the need to accept more refugees while acknowledging the importance of more effective ways to vet refugees. In this sense Clinton continued the rhetorical path of Barack Obama, although the latter put more emphasis on welcoming immigrants as a collective responsibility than the former, particularly when appealing to the Democratic base in the primaries.

Donald Trump, eventually elected president, harnessed xenophobia and racism to boost his campaign. Trump has used scapegoating rhetoric against Muslim refugees and domestic political opponents alike, likening being a Muslim to being a terrorist. Such scapegoating of "Others" was even applied to political opponents, as Trump suggested that both President Obama (through his Birther rhetoric) and Republican presidential rival Ted Cruz were born outside the United States and thus not eligible for the high office. This rhetoric contributed significantly to the atmosphere of rampant suspicion: it supported Trump's notoriously successful message that the elite is so utterly corrupt that his conspiracy theories might be true. This stance led him to conclude that restrictive immigration policies and a strong military response is required for what most of the world has deemed a humanitarian crisis.

In addition to rhetoric related to the geographical position of a country discussed earlier, four transnationally important themes emerge. First, the crisis functions as a scene for political performance, with refugees and immigrants as instruments for burnishing a given country's image abroad as a responsible member of the international community, often at the expense of a neighboring country. The message has been clear: because our neighbors are not taking care of their border control sufficiently, "we" have been put into a difficult situation. This argument culminates in Turkey's Erdogan's rhetoric in which the whole of Europe is in debt of gratitude to Turkey for taking care of the issue.

Second, as regards European countries, the European Union and European (or western) values constitute a rhetorical touchstone. Effectively, the crisis is viewed as a *kairotic* event that defines the nature of what being "European" means and determines the continent's future. The irony is that the necessity of confirming a given country's Western identity by acting "European" has been important in all cases, but some have carried this out by stressing openness and integration, while others have emphasized the need to close the borders against allegedly destructive influences. Also interestingly, in the latter strand of rhetoric, authentic Europeanness can be found near the eastern border of the EU, not from Brussels or from Berlin.

For example, in the new EU-member states at the border of the union, Hungary and Poland, and in an aspiring member country, Serbia, those in power have stressed that their way of tackling the immigration issue is in line with European values. Ironically, Hungary and Poland, in particular, have been criticized by their liberal opponents at home and abroad for acting against the ideals and traditions of Europe. The

EU, almost as a retort, has been scolded for betraying the values it was originally built on and thus being the one to blame for the situation. Internally, governments such as the conservative one in Finland, have been criticized by the leftist opposition who tout a more lenient immigration policy for being "anti-European," and also by rightist populists pressing for a stricter policy. In other words, what constitutes "European" differs dramatically from country to country, and even within the same country, based on one's stance on immigration!

Criticism toward the European Union is based on what Albert O. Hirschman has defined as the perversity argument. According to its proponents, the action proposed or undertaken will not only involve unacceptable costs but will also produce, via a chain of unintended consequences, the exact contrary of the objective being proclaimed and pursued.[1] In this case, the ways the EU has been taking care of immigration will cause significant damage or even destroy Europe as we know it, making the EU a scapegoat for European problems. At the same time the EU has pleaded for solidarity to bring the crisis under control in the name of a common European future.

Third, very often refugees and immigrants are used to implicitly construct what, for example, proper "Polishness" or "Finnishness" *is not.* Attempts to use immigration as a way to define the national essence via negation have been particularly noticeable in countries which have been (and to a great extent still are) ethnically and culturally homogenous, with right-wing populist parties as major political forces. As Ernesto Laclau (among others) has stressed, a strategy characteristic of populist rhetoric based on negation tends to lead to "emptiness" of the identity in question; it is only *difference* that matters, not the actual content. Thus, in anti-Islam rhetoric, *Christianity* often is used as a term that determines "us"; the nitty gritty details of doctrinal substance are less important. Thus, Christianity is defined as culture in such a general way that renders the concept actually quite "empty" or abstract—and as malleable suitable for political purposes.

In this strand of populist political thought a society reaches a sense of its own cohesion by an excluded—and very often demonized—other.

Hence, the other is an internal *sine que non* for a differential identity. In Laclau's words, "totality has to be present in each individual act of signification," rendering all other differences "equivalent in their common rejection of the excluded identity."[2] Consequently, an "immigrant" or a "refugee" is a synecdoche of differences; that is, while being a singular human being, she or he at the same time represents all that separates "the people" from its significant negative "other." This metapolitical transformation, precipitated by populism, results in polarization of a whole political culture; it sets the framework for understanding politics and discussing societal matters.[3] That is to say, the result is that politics *as usual* is being conducted in terms of this fundamental dichotomy.

Fourth, it is interesting to note how homogenous the overall "catalog" of immigration rhetoric has been in the countries examined in the volume. Rhetoric pertaining to immigration is strikingly similar in spite of, for example, the actual number of immigrants or refugees in a given country. Lamentations about the destruction of the economy or depictions of immigrants as various kind of threats can be found mutatis mutandis in virtually every analyzed country, in spite of differences in its economic situation or changes in its crime rates. Rhetoric indeed travels faster than people do. Versatility, on the other hand, renders immigration rhetoric a powerful lever for furthering one's domestic policies. Many national leaders across the political spectrum have accused each other of treating immigration as a potential way to gain more voters for themselves or advancing their political agenda. Also, those in power have assured that the situation is under control, while their critics have underlined the lack of it.

As regards the politicization of immigration rhetoric, it must be borne in mind that there is a significant difference in public reaction to the phenomenon depending on whether the people entering a country are defined as impostors, soldiers, or victims fleeing a civil war. Because the crisis touches upon some of the most profound issues of communal life such as citizenship, national economy, collective safety, and national identity, intensity is high and the gap between villains and heroes easily develops into a chasm. However, since it is very difficult to pinpoint those who are "true refugees" and who "impostors," all those entering a country are potential suspects.

The "immigrant" emerges as an ambivalent political symbol. Saturated with contradictory meanings, it is difficult to pinpoint what or who the "immigrant" actually is. In addition to the concrete physical displacement related to the phenomenon, the meanings of "immigrant" are constantly on the move. More often than not, this takes place between the extremes, from the victim to the agent of terror and violence, from the vital worker to "bogus, or undeserving, asylum seeker," from women and children in need to gang rapists. On a more general level, "immigrant" symbolizes moral and cultural collapse of the West as well as the realization of mercy and the requirement to help those in need.

As a result, the rhetorical figure that haunts us, the "immigrant," symbolizes simultaneously danger, loss, hope, and humanity. At the same time "we" are continuously asked to identify or dissociate ourselves with (or from) the "immigrant." It is precisely this kind of circulation of a formative symbol without a fixed referent that continues to evoke intense feelings, from love and compassion to fear and hate; and the more this kind of symbol circulates, the more powerful it becomes.[4] The chapters of this volume testify to the complexity and political usefulness of such rhetoric.

Notes

1. Albert O. Hirschman, *The Rhetoric of Reaction: Perversity, Futility, Jeopardy* (Cambridge, MA: Harvard University Press, 1991), 11, 81.
2. Ernesto Laclau, *On Populist Reason* (London: Verso, 2005), 68–72.
3. See Alain Badiou, *Metapolitics* (London: Verso, 2005).
4. Sara Ahmed, *The Cultural Politics of Emotion* (Edinburgh: Edinburgh University Press, 2004), 44, 47, 73–74.

Contributors

—•◦•—

Ashlyn Edde earned an MA in professional communication at the University of Alabama in Huntsville pursuing a master of arts in professional communications. Edde's specialty is in rhetoric, specifically in Burkeian theories and various forms of rhetorical criticism.

Elisa I. Hörhager is currently working for the German Federal Foreign Service. From 2014 to 2016 she was a research fellow in the interdisciplinary project Protecting the Weak: Processes of Framing, Mobilisation, and Institutionalisation in East Asia at the Goethe University, Frankfurt am Main. She holds an MA in political science from Albert-Ludwigs-University, Freiburg and the Institut d'Études Politiques, Sciences Po Aix-en-Provence, as well as a postgraduate MA in EU international relations and diplomacy from the College of Europe in Bruges. Her studies and research have been supported by the Franco-German University, the Federal Ministry of Education, and the Volkswagen Foundation. Her publications include papers and articles on the politicization of disasters, cosmopolitan justice, China-ASEAN relations, and China-EU relations.

Ellen Gorsevski, PhD, Pennsylvania State University, is associate professor and communication program coordinator in the School of Media and Communication at Bowling Green State University. Gorsevski's research focuses on contemporary rhetoric of peace, social justice, and environmental justice movements. Research interests include environmental rhetoric and critical animal studies, international/intercultural rhetoric, political rhetoric, social movement rhetoric, media criticism, and nonviolent conflict communication. Her books include *Dangerous Women: The Rhetoric of the Women Nobel Peace Laureates* (2014) and *Peaceful Persuasion: The Geopolitics of Nonviolent Rhetoric* (2004). Her articles are in such journals as *Quarterly Journal of Speech, Western Journal of Communication*, and *Environmental Communication*.

Jarosław Jańczak, PhD, is associate professor, political scientist, Europeanist, and researcher of borders at the Faculty of Political Science and Journalism, Adam Mickiewicz University, in Poznan, Poland, and at the Department of European Studies, European University Viadrina in Frankfurt am Oder, Germany. He is the author of over one hundred academic articles, a participant in a similar number of academic conferences, and has been a guest lecturer at several universities in North America, Europe, and Asia.

Yiannis Karayiannis is assistant professor in the Department of Political Science, University of Crete. His research interests and publications focus on political discourse analysis and rhetoric, the analysis of contemporary forms of power and government, and Greek politics. He is one of the founding members of the research network for the analysis of political discourse of the Hellenic Political Science Association.

Hatice Çoban Keneş, PhD, is assistant professor at Munzur University, Turkey. Her main areas of study are discriminatory discourses, media studies, and migration. In addition to several book chapters and articles on discriminatory discourses about disadvantaged groups in Turkey, she is the author of the book *Yeni Irkçılığın Kirli Ötekileri: Kürtler, Aleviler, Ermeniler* (Dirty others of new racism: Kurds, Alawites, Armenians).

Julia Khrebtan-Hörhager is assistant professor of communication at Colorado State University and director/leader of Summer Education Abroad programs in Europe. She is a former lecturer on German and Italian studies at the University of Denver, global scholar/codirector of global studies for Semester at Sea/Institute for Shipboard Education, and a holder of 2016 and 2012 International Communication Association Top Paper Awards for her work on German–Italian multicultural relations. Her research, teaching, and consulting interests are in intercultural and international communication, European studies, global conflict, international cinematography, politics of memory, and critical media studies.

Kathleen Kirkland earned an MA in professional communication at the University of Alabama in Huntsville. Kirkland's specialty is in public relations, with a specific interest in media relations.

Anthoula Malkopoulou is a researcher and docent in political science at the Department of Government, Uppsala University. She publishes mostly in democratic theory, often with the use of historical and rhetorical sources, including the anthology *Rhetoric, Politics and Conceptual Change* (with Kari Palonen, 2011) and the monograph *The History of Compulsory Voting* (2015). She is also coeditor of the journal *Redescriptions*.

Ivana Cvetković Miller is assistant professor of journalism at California State Polytechnic University, Pomona, and a doctoral candidate in the Department of Communication and Journalism at the University of New

Mexico, with research and teaching interests in journalism, technology, and culture. She primarily focuses on discursive and rhetorical practices in news and the institutional sphere in relation to migration and mobility in Europe, particularly in Serbia. Her work has been published in several internationally recognized journals, including *Journal of Communication Inquiry, Newspaper Research Journal*, and *Journal of Media Communication and Film*.

Kaori Miyawaki, PhD in communication, University of Wisconsin—Milwaukee, is an instructor at Ritsumeikan University, Japan. She specializes in rhetorical criticism, and her dissertation investigates the citizenship of Japanese Americans during World War II. She also studies intercultural communication, focusing on Japanese politics and cultures.

Heino Nyyssönen is a senior political scientist who teaches European political science, world politics, and contemporary history at the University of Turku, Finland. His most recent book and articles deal with the backlash against democracy in Hungary and beyond.

Andrée E. Reeves is associate professor of political science at the University of Alabama in Huntsville. Her research and teaching interests include U.S. government and politics, particularly Congress, the presidency, American political parties and interest groups, public policy, intergovernmental relations, and state and local government. A product of a mixed marriage—a Republican mother and a Democratic father—she grew up in Kentucky and Washington, DC.

Clarke Rountree is professor of communication arts at the University of Alabama in Huntsville. He has published dozens of essays and five books on political and legal rhetoric, including *Judging the Supreme Court: Constructions of Motives in* Bush v. Gore (2007), which won the Kohrs-Campbell Prize in Rhetorical Criticism, and *Venomous Speech: Problems with American Political Discourse on the Right and Left* (2013).

İnan Özdemir Taştan, PhD, is a peace academic dismissed from her post at Ankara University Department of Public Relations with a statutory decree issued under the state of emergency in Turkey. Her main areas of study are political rhetoric, elections, and media studies. In addition to several book chapters and articles, she is one of the authors of *Seçimlik Demokrasi* (Elective Democracy), a book about the discourse of democracy in election speeches of Turkish political leaders. She is also the editor of academic journal *Kültür ve İletişim* (Culture & Communication).

Jouni Tilli is a research fellow at the Helsinki Collegium for Advanced Studies, University of Helsinki. His ambition is rhetorical criticism and theory, particularly in relation to politics and religion. He is also interested in the relationship between religion and nationalism and the political uses of the past. His dissertation on clerical war rhetoric won the Best Dissertation Award from the University of Jyväskylä in 2012, and his monograph *Suomen pyhä sota* (Finland's holy war) won the 2014 Christian Book of the Year Award (Finland). In 2017, he was given the Emerging Scholar Award by the Kenneth Burke Society.

Index

———•·•———